Two Sides of One River

European Anthropology in Translation
Published in Association with the Society for the Anthropology of
Europe (AAA)
General Editor: **Sharon R. Roseman,** Memorial University of
Newfoundland

This new series introduces English-language versions of significant works
on the Anthropology of Europe that were originally published in other
languages. These include books produced recently by a new generation
of scholars as well as older works that have not previously appeared in
English.

Volume 1
*Disenchantment with Market Economics: East Germans and Western
Capitalism*
Birgit Müller

Volume 2
Strangers Either Way: The Lives of Croatian Refugees in their New Home
J. Čapo Žmegač

Volume 3
*Developing Skill, Developing Vision: Practices of Locality at the Foot of the
Alps*
Cristina Grasseni

Volume 4
*The Colours of Empire: Racialized Representations during Portuguese
Colonialism*
Patrícia Ferraz de Matos

Volume 5
*Two Sides of One River: Nationalism and Ethnography in Galicia and
Portugal*
António Medeiros

Two Sides of One River

Nationalism and Ethnography in Galicia and Portugal

António Medeiros

Translated by

Martin Earl

Berghahn Books
New York • Oxford

Published by
Berghahn Books
www.berghahnbooks.com

English-language edition
©2013 Berghahn Books

Portuguese-language edition
©2006 António Medeiros
Dois lados de um rio: nacionalismos e etnografias em Portugal e na Galiza
Imprensa de Ciências Sociais, Instituto de Ciências Sociais
da Universidade de Lisboa

Library of Congress Cataloging in Publication Data

Medeiros, António, 1963–
  [Dois lados de um rio. English]
  Two sides of one river: nationalism and ethnography in Galicia and Portugal /
António Medeiros; translated by Martin Earl.
     p. cm. — (European anthropology in translation; v. 5)
  Translation of: Dois lados de um rio.
  Includes bibliographical references and index.
  ISBN 978-0-85745-724-0 (hardback: alk. paper)
   1. Nationalism—Spain—Galicia (Region) 2. Ethnology—Spain—Galicia
(Region) 3. Nationalism—Portugal. 4. Ethnology—Portugal. I. Title.
  DP302.G2M4313 2012
  320.540946'1—dc23

                                                                    2012012577

British Library Cataloguing-in-Publication Data

A catalogue record for this book is available from the British Library

Printed in the United States on acid-free paper

ISBN 978-0-85745-724-0 (hardback)

For Rosa, Chica, Zezinha, and Ana my dear daughters

Quero quero chorar desconsoladamente o meu cabelo castaño escuro
(I want I want to cry unconsolably over my dark brown hair)
Álvaro Cunqueiro

Contents

Figures

Acknowledgments

The years that have passed, the quantity of places and adventures that came my way during the completion of this book, make any evocation of accumulated debt an impossible task of memory. I am already troubled by the omissions, which I cannot imagine will not be exposed.

My first stays in Galicia were made possible by a grant I received from the Spanish Ministry of Foreign Affairs. Later, it was under the auspices of a project funded by the Fundação para a Ciência e a Tecnologia [The Foundation for Science and Technology] that allowed me to continue with my fieldwork in the Minho and in Galicia, as well as documentary research which took me to a variety of places.

Over the years, Brian Juan O'Neill supported my work with interest and a refined critical acumen. He was the crucial figure behind the process of bringing this book to term, originally a doctoral dissertation; I thank him for all of the customary support, but also for much more that is imponderable, that only comes of friendship. As well, there are several colleagues which I would like to thank in the Anthropology Department at ISCTE, where I have the privilege to work: Paulo Valverde, a great friend, whose tragic death affected me profoundly; Manuel João Ramos; Filipe Verde; Jorge Freitas Branco; João Leal; and Raul Iturra. Their friendship and light-hearted irony—also that of Catarina Mira—gave me strength at critical moments. I would like to thank my students, from a range of subjects over time. I owe them for the interest and kindness with which they listened to the still-unformed digressions that anticipated this book. Fernando Catroga provided pointed criticism of the original dissertation, a valuable contribution that I cannot forget.

At the University of Santiago I am indebted to several teachers. These would include Xaquín Rodríguez Campos, Marcial Gondar, Nieves Herrero, Xusto Beramendi, and Miguel Cabo. I met with James Fernandez in a variety of places—even in Santiago de Compostela—and I am very thankful for the interest that he always demonstrated for my work. I would like to thank Michael Herzfeld from Harvard University, for agreeing to be the adviser on the project that gave birth to this book and for allowing me to participate in a brilliant seminar whose discussions so inspired me. In Madrid, friends of mine, renowned academics, such as María Cátedra and Enrique Luque, cannot be forgotten; not to mention the efforts of Emílio Rodríguez Lara and Laura Llera, the editor and translator, respectively, of the Spanish version of this book published by CIS/Siglo XXI of Spain. I would also like to thank Jesus Azcona (University of Basque Country) and Frances M. Slaney (University of Regina, Canada) for advice, favors, and innumerable acts of kindness.

I remember being received warmly at the Padre Sarmiento Institute for Galician Studies by Xosé M. González Reboredo and the solicitude and encouragement of Isabel Romani, Mila, Concha, Mercedes, and Isidro. At the Museu do Pobo Galego, where I spend a great deal of time, thanks are due to Maria Jose Cerviño, Rosa Mendez, Isabel Mendez, and Carlos Martinéz. In the Penzol Foundation (Vigo) I could always count on the solicitude of Miriam López and Manolo, and at the CGAI (A Coruña), that of Alexandre Villodas. I was also inspired by the fresh ideas of Alfonso Mato, whom I met at the Galician Institute of Information. I would also like to praise the well-known Galicianists whom I had the honor to come to know. I was invited to the home of Pilar Vásquez Cuesta and was received by Isaac Diáz Pardo in his home. I had the privilege to meet often with an extraordinary individual, Baldomero Cores, at the "Padre Sarmiento." I met and admired D. Antonio Fraguas, at that time the dean of Galician ethnographers. I spent many unforgettable days with the best of my new Galician friends during the end of the 1990s. I am speaking of Xerardo Pereiro, Manuel Outeiriño, and Antonio Presado—important young academics, all of them passionate about the land, in spite of their holding different political positions. My heartfelt thanks go out to them now, and also to their families, who always invited me warmly into their homes. I cannot forget to thank other friends from various places in Galicia for all they did for me: Lalo, Tareixa, Douglas, Suso and María, Rafael, Pilar, Rut, Luísa, María, Guillerme, Miguel, Kelly, and Mari Té.

In the Minho, as well as during all of the interviews over the years, personal relationships formed through my fieldwork: I recall José Silva in Chafé, Jorge Lage and Antónion Domingues in Soajo, António Gonçalves and D. Blandina in Castelo do Neiva, and my great friend Mr. Manuel Azevedo in São Paio de Antas and his large family. There are other friends in the Minho to which this book owes a debt of gratitude: Benjamim Pereira, João Alpuim, Fátima Coutinho, Carlos Viana, André Sousa, Eugénia Queiroz, and Abílio Lima de Carvalho. Inês and Joana Areal, and so too Rosinha, often kept me company on trips to the

"the classical land of our traditions and ancient customs." In Lisbon, I would like to mention my friendship with Ana and Manuel, of Jorge and Maria Manuel, with Clarinha, Brian, Paula, and with Manel, and that of Odile who spent time here. Also I would like to dedicate a word of appreciation to Pedro Lains and Clara Cabral for placing the original manuscript in the Imprensa de Ciências Sociais of the ICS.

I dedicate this book to the memory of my paternal grandmother and of my father, but also to my mother, my aunt, and my brother. Sofia and my daughters will know that everything is theirs.

Foreword

"The Peopling of the Imagination"

In the last quarter century, anthropology and related social sciences have come to a much more developed understanding of the famous maxim attributed to the early twentieth-century sociologist W. I. Thomas. To paraphrase it slightly in a way pertinent to the impressive investigation the reader has before him here: "If men imagine situations as real, they are real in their consequences." Thomas used the word "define" rather than "imagine," but in more recent decades the power of the imagination, and the cultural imaginary as it is called, in framing and shaping human apprehension and activity is seen, day in and day out, as more often influential than the logical, definitional capacity, or at the least as antecedent to its "precisions."

In Antonio Medeiros's grand and, one must say, imaginative work on the "nationalization of provincial culture" in the northwest corner of Spain and Portugal, the case is quite persuasively made for the presence and role of the imagination in giving birth over the last century and a half to a sense of Galician and Portuguese national being and becoming. The impressive compilation of relevant texts that the Portuguese anthropologist sets before the reader, themselves so often complex works of the imagination, has demanded of the author imaginative resonance and resource in their understanding, and ethnographic persistence in ferreting out their resonance in the vox populi.

A revelatory analytic term of recurrent use in this book is *palimpsest*. It is quite apt. The many texts he treats, many of them laid one upon another over nearly a century and a half, constitute a thickly layered palimpsest built up on both sides of the Galician and Portuguese border. For so scholarly and percipient an author, as he himself points to, "the total sum of available resources for describing a country's overall characteristics and the distinction between different parts, reads like a palimpsest of literary, iconographic, and academic representations that are inextricably superimposed." Finally "inextricable" they may be, but the reader will yet marvel and appreciate the "extrication" that is achieved here. Behind this extrication there is no simpleminded notion of what a national culture at any level will be. Medeiros maintains an acute awareness that the discovery of national being is always a "multiauthored" achievement, a figurative production, a "continuous composition of metaphors," as he reiterates, which are not often susceptible to easy interpretation. Withal the reader will find here remarkable and informing sensitivity to the varying strategies of representation of these two related peoples, strategies of claiming national being, of claiming to have found the essence of one's locality and one's person writ large. Take the revelatory exploration of one metaphor especially, "individuated being," a metaphor first introduced by the American anthropologist Richard Handler to describe the way that a nation, a collectivity or plurality really, can come to understand itself as a person, a singularity, writ large, clearly bounded, continuous in identity, and susceptible, like its source referent, to the mortal risks of the life cycle.

When speaking of the Galicians and the Portuguese, one says "related peoples" because underlying the political tensions produced over centuries by the nation building of the two states, Spain and Portugal, fraternal feelings persist. This is particularly the case in Galicia where an easily discoverable lusophilia rests upon a primordial sense of common origins and common language. This probably dates back to or even before the Roman province of Gallaecia which included present day Galicia and the north of Portugal. A Portuguese anthropologist, like Medeiros, will have always, as the reader will find out, that sympathetic if undercurrent bridge of sensed common nature—a "latent and continuous solidarity," he calls it—to bolster and encourage him in his travels and studies to the north of his homeland. The consequence is a particularly anthropological combination in the author of thoughtful investigative contemplation combined with emotive identification, or otherwise put, a combination of a positive emotional interest in "the other" controlled, filtered, and refined by carefulness and balance of critical thought.

Galicians' thinking about their local being in relation to their everyday being as a part of the Spanish state in Madrid, or as a part of the west European Atlantic periphery, is in itself hardly easy to interpret. Moreover Galicians are famous in Spain for the complex vectoring of their thought. This is a stereotype summed up perhaps best in the proverbial pleasantry that if you meet a Gallego on the stairs it will be difficult to learn from him whether he is going up or going down. In fact this bit of mischievous jocularity is not an irrelevant trope for some of the vectors of Galician thought Medeiros here reveals. He is fertile in pointing to the vectored tensions in the cultural nationalism under investigation. A good example arises in his discussion of the influence of the massive emigration of Gallegos since the nineteenth century to the New World, largely Cuba and Argentina. The celebration of Galician culture being developed back home, abetted by the nostalgia and homesickness they felt for it living abroad, could be uplifting to these far-off emigrants. But at the same time they were discovering how down putting were the (usually called Anglo-Saxon) attitudes of northern Europeans and North Americans towards things Spanish and Portuguese. Meanwhile, at home in Galicia the steady if uncertain advance of a multithreaded Galician national culture was almost always confounded if not impeded by a sense of the advantages of identification with the national Castilian state and its language, abetted by the strong contribution that Galicians could and were quite evidently making to it in literature and politics, from Emilia Pardo Bazán, Ramón de Valle Inclán, and Manuel Rivas to Francisco Franco, Manuel Fraga, and the newly elected president of Spain, Mariano Rajoy. ...

And as far as the Portuguese-Galician relationship, there are complex and contrary vectors there as well, The solidarity, the *filolusismo* or lusophilia in Galicia has not prevented Gallego mockery of the backwardness of the Portuguese or other awkward denigrations of their close relatives. In counterpart the Portuguese don't hesitate to point out the pretensions of the Galicians. For example, they readily remark how Castilian modern Galician sounds to their ears, surely a disheartening observation to Galician language nationalists and their desire to escape the overbearing presence of the language of the Spanish state, Castilian, the language of Cervantes!

Because this devoted and extensive investigation is taking place in what for many readers in the English-speaking world may well be a peripheral and provincial part of the Iberian Peninsula, the topic itself risks being disqualified out of hand by the uncertain significance of its referent. In fact the phenomenon and problematic of nationalism in the modern world, and the imperialism into which it so easily devolves, has become one of the great topics of inquiry for any thinking person and very surely for a percipient and critical investigative mind like that of Medeiros. Since the eighteenth-century decline and collapse of the ancien régimes and their feudal justifications for recurrent aggrandizing warfare, their replacements, the emerging national state entities of the nineteenth and twentieth centuries, have justified their pyrrhic aggressiveness by claims of threats to their freedom to be dominant in the world or to the well-being of their imagined national communities. The widely influential work of Benedict Anderson on precisely this issue of "imagined community," a keying influence for Medeiros, demonstrates how important a challenge nationalism has become to our modern understanding. Hecatomb after hecatomb of succeeding international wars over these last two hundred years urges the topic upon us. The focus in this book may seem minor and small of scale, but the insight offered to the reader concerning the slippery slope from the desire for identity to the desire for dominance and the resultant creep towards heroics in the name of hierarchy is major.

Though this book is written by an anthropologist and is rich with anthropological insights from both a widely consulted literature and persistent ethnographic presence, this does not mean that anthropology or anthropologists themselves in their research have or could escape the framing of the world order of the last several centuries in nationalistic terms. Indeed the historian of anthropology George Stocking has long argued that anthropology itself has done most of its work inevitably framed and influenced by succeeding configurations of nationalism. These have been the evolving interests of and in *the national:* the historical progress from nation building, to empire building and the most recent dedication to the development of a, so often self-interested, *international* order. This evolutionary scheme of understanding is also recurrently present in Medeiros's ponderings of the nation as configured in the local subjects of his inquiry. As a convincing study of very large ambitions realized in the small, it will have an important effect upon any thoughtful and attentive reader, discovering in him or her the unsuspected presence and even naturalized place of the national framework of understanding.

Given that anthropological understanding is always concerned with alterity, always comparative, a distinct value here is the comparison of the two distinct nation buildings that have gone on adjacently, across the brotherly border. For Portugal has had its own particular journey from nineteenth-century "peasant romanticism" to the late-twentieth-century identity politics in a world of tourism and its potential riches. What emerges as a difference, though a difference never flogged by Medeiros, is the constant preoccupation in Galicia with the oppressive presence of the central cultural and political power, Madrid, the Spanish state, and its Castilian culture and language. In Portugal we see a central—and more worldly, we might say—preoccupation, with the outside world and with how the images of local culture involved in building a national being might contribute to or argue against the world's stereotypic images about the "dark portugee." But here also, even to offer that simple contrast, is to subvert a much more subtle and revelatory examination of the many equally subtle and richly revelatory texts produced in Portugal seeking to define and imagine its own place and its own local being beyond and below the surface of the superficial comparisons upon which the commerce of nations is so often based!

When one speaks here of a greater world awareness in Portugal than in Galicia or Spain, one refers not only to the enforced isolation of the Franco state during the four decades of that regime in Spain but also to the fact that Portugal preserved its colonial empire much longer than Spain. The responsibilities real or imagined to this larger colonial community had an inevitable impact on a sense of national being. During those authoritarian years in Spain and Portugal, more or less coincident from the late 1920s to the 1970s, Portuguese centralist authorities could evoke these colonial responsibilities to the effect of the obligation to national loyalty. In Spain, to which only remained their miniscule possessions in Equatorial Africa, the Western Sahara, and the walled enclaves of the Western Mediterranean coast, touting the colonial obligations of the central state could only have a minimal effect. Just here, in this persuasive Portuguese use made of imperial responsibility, the author finds an important difference between Galician and Portuguese nationalism. In various multiethnic manifestations, according to province, in world's fairs and expositions and multiprovincial parades the succeeding Portuguese regimes could to some effect bind together the twenty-one provinces, Iberian and overseas, into one overarching identity, an imperial whole. It could argue through the images presented and paraded the *e pluribus unum* of a worldwide Portugal and the nationwide loyalty that was its effect and due. In Spain such superordinate loyalty to empire could only be mildly, perhaps only derisorily, argued to counter the stronger feelings in the peripheralized provinces like Galicia or Catalonia that it was they who were being colonized by the central Castilian state, and not the ones living at the center of a great colonizing power, such as the Portuguese-speaking and Portuguese-enacting empire.

Here as well Medeiros enters into the thick palimpsest of documents to reveal the stereotypes that were part and parcel of these imperial/colonial manifestations and expositions. For those imperial or world's fairs and parades were hardly accurately ethnographic in exhibiting, as they were urged or inspired to do, the ethnic and cultural differences present in the great imperial whole. Most often they dealt in simplified iconic representations, caricatures of provincehood whether of the Minho of northern Portugal or the Mozambique of East Africa. Moreover, latent in these provincial representations lay a certain competitive identification of provincials one with another and an effort, hence, to give as much exotic content to the local culture of the Minhotans as to that of the Mozambiqueans. It was an unnatural pressure on self-representation distinctly stereotyping and much different than the Castilian pressure on Galician identity. In any event, in Portugal in contrast to Galicia, and in the other historic regions of the Spanish periphery, there were no well-defined regional demands or regional independence arguments inspiring by senses of the colonial oppression of the center.

I have worried above that the English-speaking and English-reading reader of this fine translation of the original Portuguese might find this detailed investigation into the search for national being and becoming going on in northwest Iberia peripheral and provincial. But of course there is a much larger being and becoming, a much more widespread cultural nationalism to which Galician and Portuguese cultural nationalisms have more recently come to relate—that of the revival of the Celtic nations, the Celtic revival, generally. For a century and a half at least the Galician culture imaginary has embraced—*imagined* would be a better word—the Celtic past as a place of possible ethno-genealogical anchorage. With the disappearance of Franco authoritarianism and the writing of the 1978 democratic constitution, aptly called an "ethno-genetic" constitution for its dividing of Spain into autonomous regions, each challenged to more adequately define the distinct culture that justified its autonomy, there has been an increased emphasis on Celtic roots and an increased identification and participation with the Seven Nations of the Celtic Fringe of Western Europe.

Of course there had long been a feeling in Galicia, as in its neighboring seaside provinces Asturias and the Basque country, that they were Atlantic peoples living *in* a Mediterranean country but not fully *of* it. The revival of the Celtic fringe countries, all of the Atlantic periphery, combined with some archaeological and prehistoric evidence of the prehistoric *Celtoi* invasion and settling of northwest Iberia, reminded them that they too were fringe peoples who might claim Celtic identity. Moreover the Statute of Autonomy of the new constitution gave, ironically, full stimulus for further discovery and celebration of these Celtic roots and of its essential Atlanticism. In any event in the last quarter century both Galicia and its adjacent northwest province Asturias have fully participated as two of the Seven Celtic nations in the week-long Interceltique Festival in Lorient Brittany. Portugal too has been tempted by this identity claim.

In Portugal there had long been a debate as to whether the Portuguese were an Atlantic or Mediterranean people. But because, as the author demonstrates, there never were in Portugal any well-defined regionalist demands, nor especially remarked oppressed feelings in the provinces, and most important, no constitutionally defined Statute of Autonomy obliging a cultural search for a distinct identity, the Celtic Revival in

Portugal has only been a very recent presence. In terms of the rooting of present identities in the prehistoric past, the Lusitanians of the pre-Roman world have usually been the preferred ancestral anchorage. But recently, perhaps in response to the tourist advantages of such a marketable identity as the Celtic one, the Celtic Revival has come to Northern Portugal. There is in fact some archaeological evidence of a prehistoric Celtic presence and perhaps somewhat more than for Galicia despite all its proclaimed Celtic hill forts, or *castros*. Medeiros's last chapter is devoted to various manifestations of the coming of the Celtic revival to northwestern Iberia and its uncertain mix into the amalgam of Galician and Portuguese national identities that he has so perspicuously detailed in the proceeding chapters. It makes for an interesting envoi.

At one place in this compleat study Medeiros refers to "the unequaled efficacy of poetic and aesthetic metaphors in the establishment of knowledge about nations." Indeed "the peopling of the imagination" with a sense of national being so often rests on the skillful appeal to the figurative imagination. The author is skillful in detecting these in the many, many texts and living persons he has consulted in his accompanying ethnography. He is perceptive in teasing apart their implications and intertwinings one with another. This perhaps is the very heart of the "meaningful method" that he has employed in illuminating just how the national imagination does obtain to a feeling of the "individuated being" of an entire population. It is no mean feat of inquiry and interpretative argument.

This book is such a tour de force in its way that it can not be easily read in one sitting or even a dozen, and it is of a subtlety of understanding difficult if not impossible to parse satisfactorily in any set of simple summaries. For the anthropologist and professional culture historian this book will be a continuously important resource and reference. But for the general reader, could one suggest, it might best serve as a night table book, lying nearby ever ready and available for progressive short ponderings, as the reader proceeds progressively along after the author in his extensive exploration of "the peopling of the 'national' imagination" among these two peoples of northwestern Iberia. The reader might each night in his or her half hour, before the mind descends into the realm where the imagination holds riotous sway, take several instructive steps more into the omnipresent national question, in these previously unknown localities where he or she might not otherwise have ventured. It may seem mischievous to leave the prospective reader of this thick and extraordinarily aware and conscious book supine before it in the last hour of his or her day. But in some way this book is so conscious of its challenges and so capable and replete with inspired phrasings and balanced understandings of the ironies involved in nation building, yet, in the end, treats of a subject matter rising from a more deeply motivated and less conscious realm of human beingness, it corresponds to the deeper realm where the individual wrestles with the collective identity and the realm to which the nocturnal reader will shortly return. Just there where the reader is on the point of losing mastery of his imagination, there on that so-often-mysterious frontier of individual and communal beingness, what better companion than Medeiros and his work of illuminating access to those deeper intuitions of who and how we are, or may be, as a people!

James W. Fernandez
University of Chicago

Chapter 1

States in the Northwest

"Crossing over into Spain" was a challenge for the boys during family excursions to the mountains in the beginning of the 1970s. After passing Lindoso, the last village, an iron chain marked the border of Portugal at a little bridge; from there on the road, deserted and covered with pine needles, continued on into Spain. There were no border guards in sight, but the mothers would fret when their sons set even just a single foot on the other side of that vertical border—that "magical" boundary between nation-states (Taussig 1997). In 1993, I was present at a repeat performance of one of those youthful transgressions of old in the same mountainous spot where the two peninsular states are joined. This happened on a walk in which I participated as the guest of a group of ramblers. The group was made up of an old couple, small farmers who were hosting me during the fieldwork I was then engaged in, their children, and respective spouses and grandchildren, all of them residents of a coastal parish of the Minho province of Portugal. After the picnic in the hills the men and the boys went off together on a ramble to the border, with the idea of *crossing over into Spain,* as we told ourselves with a certain excitement. The border controls had already been abolished between countries of the European Union, and the iron chain that had marked the limit between the two states in that remote place was gone. We crossed the small bridge and walked a few more meters. Upon return we guaranteed the others that we had put a foot *outside the country, in Spain*—which provoked a lot of teasing and joking for the rest of the afternoon and for some days after.

The day we took the hike nobody made any reference to Galicia, the contiguous region on the other side of the border, these days known officially as the Autonomous Community of Galicia and recognized as one of the historical nationalities that make up the Spanish state as de-

scribed by the new political-administrative framework legitimized by the
Constitución Democrática of 1978. We never chanced upon any of the
graffiti that has in the last few decades begun to appear on Portuguese
roads close to the northwest border. *Galiza nom é Espanha,* or *Galiza
Ceibe*—i.e., "Galicia is not Spain" or "Free Galicia"—are the most common inscriptions, appearing on the walls of bus stops or on traffic signs
in fairly deserted areas.

I imagine, however, that those furtive fragments of Galician nationalist discourse would have been lost on my travel companions, or would
have taken them quite by surprise. Indeed, *Spain* and *Spanish* were the
generic denominations used when speaking about trips to Vigo (an occasional shopping destination), or of the long trips by automobile to
France that passed over the roads of the present-day Autonomous Community of Galicia, or of any casual contacts with people that came from
there. In the final analysis, for my erstwhile hosts, "Galicia" or "Galicians" were strange terms that did not lead to the use of commonplace
references of identification, contrary to the case of terms such as "Spain"
and "Spanish." The adjective "Galician," however, is frequently used in
the area where they live and in the whole of the area that surrounds the
municipalities of Esposende and Viana do Castelo, areas of the province
of the Minho, which I know well for biographical reasons.

But these usages do not presuppose direct references to Galicia or to
its inhabitants; for example, there is a kind of flax called *galego* that is no
longer cultivated in the area and is only alluded to today when "traditions" that have disappeared are referred to. *Galegas* are also the most
common form of cabbage plant and also a kind of cow of great girth and
a yellow hide, rare today, but very common when animal traction was
indispensable to agricultural work. On the other hand the adjective *galego* can also be used, as it is in the rest of Portugal, to refer to a variety of
products of mediocre quality, arduous work habits, or to a crass lack of
urbanity (Morais Silva 1999). But the use of these terms in the Minho
is, in fact, rare, in contrast to their common employment in Lisbon and
in the farmlands of the south of the country.[1]

The difficulty that my old hosts had in identifying *Galiza* and the
galegos was suggestively paralleled in the difficulty they also felt in recognizing themselves as *minhotos,* or even in distinguishing the province
of the Minho as an area differentiated from Portugal. This difficulty was
shared by many of their fellow *minhotos,* as I verified when I did my
fieldwork in two rural parishes of the province at the beginning of the
1990s. For this reason, I decided to alter the initial plans of my project
and to focus my research on an analysis of the tradition of ethnographic
and topographical descriptions of the Minho and on the way in which

it had spread. This was a determinant in the process of the "nationalization of culture" (Löfgren 1989) of the middle classes in Portugal in the
closing years of the nineteenth century and the first three decades of the
twentieth.

Since then, the elites of the principal urban centers of the Minho
have become familiar with these descriptions, appropriating them and
manipulating them to represent local identities at the municipal level.
However, the greater part of the inhabitants of this province—especially
those who are less educated and whose relationship with working the
land is still a direct one—do not know, for the most part, about this
collection of topics, of which, notwithstanding, descriptions of the rural
population are an essential part. Their unfamiliarity could be thought of
crudely as bringing into play the sense of Karl Marx's famous observation of peasants that "they cannot represent themselves, they must be
represented" (1984: 127).

Starting in 1997, I decided to pursue a comparative study of topo-
graphic and ethnographic descriptions that had been produced with
respect to Galicia during the nineteenth and twentieth centuries. My
purpose was to understand how the integration in a different state and
the existence of a specific nationalist discourse had marked differences
in the ways that two bordering regions in the northwest of the Iberian
Peninsula have been represented, each belonging to a different state but
whose similarities are frequently alluded to. Thus, in 1997 and 1998 I
did bibliographic research and fieldwork in Santiago de Compostela, a
place that had been famous for centuries as a pilgrimage destination and
as a university city. In more recent decades, Santiago has become the seat
of the government of the Autonomous Community of Galicia as well
as a center for demonstrations by the Galician nationalist movement.
It is here where the construction of and the schooling in a nationalist
Galician culture have been very active processes—benefited by the recent creation of an autonomous government and by the vivacity of the
nationalistic militancy—which have had an extremely varied influence
on the daily lives of my informants.

In spite of the fact that rhetorical references to the affinities with
Portugal play an important role in the articulation of the Galicianist
discourse that was consolidated at the end of the nineteenth century, I
began to understand in Santiago that they were of a very stable and of
generalized character (see chapter 6). For example there were no references to the regional diversity of the neighboring country, or to the
peculiarities that are typically ascribed to the Minho and the Trás-os-
Montes. These are the Portuguese provinces adjacent to Galicia, knowledge of which would lead one to believe that finding reason in those

claims of affinity was justified. My interest in understanding how the different nationalist discourses had molded specific ethnographic and topographical knowledge and the contemporary possibilities for their use was underlined by these facts.

In 1997 and 1998 I lived in Santiago de Compostela for eleven months. If we credit what the newspapers said at the time, this was the rainiest winter of the twentieth century, a rather significant bit of data in the northwest of the Iberian Peninsula, especially in a city that is known as the "bacio da Galiza."[2] Contrary to this, the inhabitants of Braga—another city of the same geographical area that also has a notable ecclesiastical history—would say that their city is the "penico do céu."[3] We might, with a certain degree of irony, discover the pertinence of certain influential arguments maintained by Benedict Anderson (1991) in the difference between these two coarse designations. I do not intend to spend too much time on the weather in this book, but these anecdotal references do justice to some of the initial concerns of this work—despite the general similarity of pluviometric conditions in both contexts, the established formulas used to describe the Minho and Galicia are uniquely different. In summary form: the Minho is habitually described as a sunny Arcadia, while the descriptions of Galicia— equally bucolic—emphasize the often recurrent rain. If we look closely at the origins of these commonplace descriptions, we will recognize that the sunny image of the Minho originated outside of the province itself, while the most characteristic descriptions of Galicia, in which the rain is a subject of praise, were produced by natives of the region. I believe that this can serve as a pertinent illustration of the ideological differences between the ways of referring to "province" and "nation," which is an important theme for the arguments that I intend to make in this book, as I will gradually detail throughout its development.

"Forgotten" Galicia

At the end of 1997 and in 1998, during sporadic visits I had begun to make from Santiago de Compostela, I was able to give an account to my erstwhile hosts about the innumerable similarities that I recognized between Galicia and the area where they lived—in the topography, in the ways the fields were worked, and in the climate. Many of the words that I knew were used by my older informants from the parish—"provincialisms" that their children and grandchildren no longer knew, or avoided—were now being used in Galicia in texts and talks given by university professors, politicians, and personalities on television. To any attentive observer, the lexical similarities to the Portuguese—marked by the presence of archaisms (Cintra 1983; Vasconcelos n.d.)—spoken in the fields of the Minho were evident in these recent appropriations into Galician. They arose in an urban context and among prestigious circles where even up until quite recently their employment would have been improbable.[4]

It was with great surprise that my old hosts from the Minho greeted this news of affinities with Galicia. They suggested to them that there were similarities in a part "of Spain" that, suddenly emerged as differentiated from the more ample whole, which had become more familiar. Those evenings spent in front of the fireplace might be easily imagined as a maieutical exercise. Conversations with older peasants—usually thought to be preservers of ethnic essences (Williams 1993)—might now be portrayed as moments of remembrance of the existence of an earlier community between Galicia and the Minho, before the divergence imposed by the contingencies of political history over the last nine centuries.

"Presuppositions of non-coevalness" (Fabian 1983) related in ideological terms to those that I am now setting into motion with this example mark a great part of the ethnographic texts—both older and more recent—cited in the bibliography of this book. However, the meanings behind the way they are set to work are greatly varied, justified, as they are, by contextual uses. One of Jorge Dias (1907–1973) and E. Veiga de Oliveira's (1910–1990) proposals (and these are the two most relevant Portuguese ethnologists of the latter half of the twentieth century) provides us with a highly suggestive illustration of these presuppositions: "The Peninsular Northwest ... was the cradle and origin of Galician and Portuguese culture and, still today, certainly forms the psychological substratum of the modal personality of these two peoples" (1962: 4). This is the judgment that the authors make following a citation of James Frazer in which he suggests, "The great intellectual and moral forces which have revolutionized the educated world have scarcely affected the peasant" (Dias and Oliveira 1962: 3).

But, speaking categorically, references to Galicia by my peasant interlocutors from the Minho were nearly nonexistent. On the contrary, they frequently made general references to Spain and to the Spanish, with the intention of indicating differences in national character. In 1910, another famous Portuguese ethnologist, Adolfo Coelho (1847–1919)—reflecting on the iconographic register of a remote skirmish on the banks of the Minho river and of the respective legend that identifies the attackers coming from the other side of the river as "Spaniards"—suggested that "the idea of the country is formed on opposition" (1993: 261).

Apparently, this was the general mechanism of identification that my hosts brought into play (Barth 1998; Lévi-Strauss et al. 1977). They used "Spain" as a reference for the neighboring country as a whole, and stressed "oppositions" without apprising themselves of the affinities that could easily be recognized in the adjacent region located to the north of the Minho River. Their references to the neighboring country and its inhabitants were extremely stereotypical, and were made with "Andalusia in mind," even if only vaguely; they are also unsupported by erudite references that would allow for enlarging upon these metonymic senses characteristic of the mention of Spain and the Spanish, as James Fernandez argued (1988).[5]

None of the members of the family had traveled to Santiago de Compostela and they knew surprisingly little about the city. However, the distance between the two places is small, and, moreover, these days they are linked by motorway for most of the journey. As with Galicia, Santiago de Compostela was simply a name, which my friends from the Minho recognized with difficulty, without registering clear identifying references to a city famous for so many reasons. (see, for example, Turner and Turner 1978 and Otero Pedrayo 1991). On one of my 1997 visits I promised the head of the family, a very religious older man, that we had to take a trip together to Santiago de Compostela—a promise which I have, sadly, yet to fulfill! But initially my old host's expectations about taking the promised trip were low, even though he had been much moved to learn for the first time that the tomb of one of the apostles was to be found so close to home. Sameiro, Fátima, Rome, Bethlehem, and Jerusalem comprised the most significant points in his topology of the Christian world, a theme that had come up in our past conversations. None of the most renowned sanctuaries of Spain were part of his cosmography, which, at the time, surprised me, especially the fact that he knew nothing about the religious importance of Compostela.

Nevertheless, one of my friend and host's earliest and most influential memories from childhood had to do with Galicia. It dated back to the summer of 1936, when that region was rapidly taken over by the revolting soldiers under Franco's control (Tusell 1999; Carr 1982). During the summer in question, a fugitive—a *deserter from the Spanish War,* as he said—was found hidden in a hayloft in the area surrounding his house. His presence was reported by one of the neighbors to the Republican National Guard. He was then captured in order to be conducted back to the border and handed into the custody of the rebel soldiers—a common practice of Portuguese authorities of the day. As my host assured me, all those who witnessed the capture knew what the prisoner's most probable destiny would be because explicit news about the frequency of summary executions in zones controlled by the revolting soldiers was rife in the village.[6] The denouncement and the circumstances surrounding the capture of this deserter from the Spanish War had terribly upset my informant, who, on many occasions, evoked that tragic moment in 1936. These recollections always reached a conclusion with the habitual comment—which he also used in all those circumstances in which he detected cruelty or a lack of piety—that *we are all Catholics* or *we are all children of God.* Thus would he recognize a shared human condition and the universality of ethical obligations in terms that we can consider characteristic of the Minhotan peasants' vision of the world. This cosmology is profoundly influenced by the values of Catholicism, an ample and suggestive theme that has already been taken up in relevant inquiries (Pina-Cabral 1989).

In a text whose influence has been far reaching in recent years, Benedict Anderson has argued that from the end of the eighteenth century another way of "apprehending the world" has grown out of the decline of "religious communities" and of the "spheres of dynastic influence" as frameworks for belonging. This is tied to the presence of a new type of "imagined political communities": nations. The oldest antecedents for this new way of apprehending the world could be recognized in the Europe of the sixteenth century and were intimately connected to the development of the press and to the spreading of its respective products. Decisive transformations in individuals' subjective perceptions of belonging were given emphasis through these means (Anderson 1991).[7]

According to Anderson, by the time of the First World War, this new form of imagining political communities would have generally spread to the European masses. For example, the forms of patriotic mobilization observed during the Great War—or later, the ways in which the memory of the war were commemorated—would be proof of the effectiveness with which the propagation of definitions of national belonging had been pursued in previous decades in the context of the particular states involved in the conflict. Thus, the Great War stands out as the hinge moment, one which unveiled not only the nationalizing action of the states but the proselytizing of a variety of nationalist movements at the substate level. Many of these demands were responded to at the end of the war with the creation of new states, or gathered strength in the years following, those years that constituted the "apogee of nationalism" in Europe and the rest of the world (Hobsbawm 1992; Mazower 1998). During this same period, in the Iberian Peninsula various national movements at the substate level were consolidated in Spain—as happened in Galicia, which I will detail below—even as the nationalizing activities of the two states intensified (Ramos 1994; Fusi 2000).

For my Minhotan informant, and for many of his compatriots of the same age and living in similar circumstances, not knowing about a famous place in the religious topology of Catholic Europe went hand in hand with the difficulty they had in identifying Galicia or the Minho. On the contrary, the readiness with which the older inhabitants in that rural context would mention Portugal and Spain as a way of identifying themselves, to differentiate themselves from the inhabitants of the neighboring state, was notable. At the same time, various topological and ideological references of a religious origin seemed to mark out their vision of the world in a very relevant way. If we take B. Anderson's arguments into account, this vision would seem part of a range of discrepant and anachronistic representations. But the author is completely clear about how the new forms of imagining political communities were securely under the control of the political classes and the more rarefied intellectuals and that literacy and access to technologies and habits of consumption—which had not yet reached many parts of the world—were indispensable resources for the spreading of these new conceptions (see also Gellner 1983; Revel 1989; Smith 1991).

The processes of the diffusion of the new forms of imagining political communities must be taken into consideration if we want to explain both why so many inhabitants of the Minho have difficulties in identifying themselves as Minhotans and, as well, the nature of the obstructions that the popularization of a Galicianist discourse underwent in Galicia over time. However, it will be important to first give an account of certain more general delimitations and how they affected the possibilities of imagining nations—or regions—and creating discourses about them in the Iberian Peninsula at the end of the nineteenth century and throughout the first half of the twentieth.

Auctoritas

Just as in the rest of Europe and in America, throughout the nineteenth century, nationalist discourses in the context of the two Iberian states, two monarchies with old and well-defined metropolitan borders, managed to thrive (Fusi 2000; Álvarez Junco 2001; Mattoso 1985; Sobral 1999). The effects of their diffusion allowed for an increasing number of inhabitants to represent themselves, whether Spanish or Portuguese, as conscious participants in political communities that were now imagined as nations. For examples of the relative efficacy that these processes of nationalization enjoyed, we can take the emotional patriotic reactions that two moments of crisis at the end of the century provoked in each of these states. I speak, respectively, of the British ultimatum given to Portugal in 1891 and of Spain's loss of its most important colonies in 1898 (Catroga 1993a and 1993b; Cachu Viu 1997; Fusi 2000). Nevertheless, the weakness of both states in promoting an effective "nationalization of the masses" during the nineteenth century and even in the first decades of the twentieth was obvious (Mosse 1975), particularly in rural contexts. To be exact, these processes were only exercised in a systematic and effective way under the vigilance of authoritarian regimes, once the twentieth century was really underway.

In Portugal, for example, the implementations of mass programs of nationalization under the Constitutional Monarchy and the First Republic and until the 1930s were recognizably feeble; this, in spite of the acute conviction, starting in the late nineteenth century, on the part of the political and intellectual elites that such programs were necessary (Ramos 1994). Likewise, with respect to Spain, various authors have recognized a similar range of deficiencies in the actions of the state during the same period, which were only obviated later by Franco's authoritarian government (see, for example, Álvarez Junco 1996; Romero Salvadó 1996; Fusi 2000). In both cases, the debilities of programs designed to nationalize the masses revealed the difficulties that were encountered in standardizing official primary education, which took a long time to consolidate—a problem that has been emphasized by the comparative literature (see, for example, Gellner 1983—who is especially emphatic; but also Weber 1983; Mosse 1975; Hobsbawm 1992).[8]

The decisive difference between the two Iberian states in terms of the imagination of national communities should be clearly delineated. The intellectual elites of Spain debated a variety of possible nations during the end of the nineteenth century, a discussion that continued into the twentieth century. Contrary to this, during the same period in Portugal the discourse was over just one nation and it coincided with the preexistent state—a representation that up until this day has not been brought into question in any significant way (Sobral 1999).

In more recent decades—once new democratic regimes had been established in both countries—a plurality of "peripheral" nationalist demands reemerged in Spain, along with centrifugal programs for the nationalization of the masses that, casuistically, had already found more or less relevant expression in the period before the Spanish Civil War. In Portugal, as has been said, the concomitance of the state and nation from the nineteenth century onwards was consolidated and remained unchallenged, in spite of all of the contingencies resulting from the changes in the forms of governance in 1910, 1926, and 1974. As I have suggested, this representation was intentionally emphasized and

vigorously popularized through the means of nationalizing policies put
in place by the authoritarian regime in power between 1926 and 1974
(Rosas 1994; Paulo 1994; Andrade 2001).

Taking into account the examples given above, we should underscore the importance that the state had as the most eminent delimiting
reference for the possibilities of imagining political communities in the
Peninsula. Firstly, these were the spaces that were overridingly discussed
as nations at the outset of the nineteenth century. Since that time, it
has been in these state-level contexts that the Portuguese and the Spanish were "produced" (Gellner 1983) in an intentional and continuous
fashion, even if these processes were subjected to relative weaknesses
and delays. On the other hand, it is obvious that there were intrastate
borders—initially defined by political-administrative authorities and
through discourses proffered about the state—which more effectively
defined the possibilities of imagining other communities such as provinces, regions, or nations in their respective contexts.

With respect to Spain, which is the more complex case, we can see
that the most substantial expression of peripheral nationalisms and the
different regionalisms was, as a rule, determined by the exterior limits of
the state and also by the respective internal divisions, which, over time,
were articulated with growing clarity.[9] As such, during the nineteenth
century there were "provincialist" and "regionalist" claims that preceded,
respectively, the declaration of self-named "nationalistic" movements
arising at the end of the nineteenth century in Catalonia and the Basque
Country and later in Galicia. New studies of the territory of the state
that erudite elites undertook in the eighteenth century had fixed the
knowledge of the differences of the various provinces and the use of the
concept itself. For a long time, these notions remained unrefined, but
were finally quite fecund as a resource for emerging classifications.

In this fashion, generally, each of these peripheral nationalist discourses emerges "provincialized"—having been previously defined by
the territorialization of competencies, powers, and privileges contrived
at the state level along with notions of knowledge that were elaborated
at this same broader level. On the other hand the narrow demarcation
of contact in intrastate zones had already become, on the political and
cognitive planes, extremely relevant in the nineteenth century.[10] Fron-
tiers were imposed—*borders,* Giddens (1985)—that very effectively delimited the expression of peripheral nationalisms occurring later, in spite
of the more or less daring irredentist formulas that we can detect in
each of the cases.[11] In this way, with respect to Galicia, it was against
"the body" (Assayag 1997) provided by the administrative divisions that
the Spanish state had recognized that the particularist claims of nation-

alistic Galicians were consistently made. In Portugal, on the contrary, regionalist discourses were hardly prominent. It can be proven that their emergence, very rare and always weak, was above all fomented by the distribution of political competencies by the state—or following its wishes—and also by references to proposals of knowledge previously produced at this more ample level (see chapter 7).

In the terms suggested by Pierre Bourdieu, we confront a question of who, in general, has the authority to define limits. We can say that in the long term the *auctoritas* of the states was imposed as a decisive instance of the delimitation of potential regionalist and nationalist claims (Bourdieu 1989: 114). It should be noted that the relevance of symbolic acts of "authorization" to which Bourdieu refers have anachronic validity, to the extent that his argument is founded upon the Indo-European etymology of the words that denote acts of power. However, starting in the nineteenth century, the evocation of political-administrative divisions that are more or less remote in time and that had delineated powers and privileges in the Peninsula—old kingdoms, earldoms, or specific charters that relatively enduring balances of powers had configured—gained rhetorical importance as a framework for new community discourses. The legal arguments that had been the most important references of political legitimization, equal to the force of arms (see a magnificent Iberian example in Schaub 2001; see also Giddens 1985) ceded to contemporary proposals articulated by artists, men of letters, and scientists who practiced new disciplines. In the nineteenth century, these were the people who gained the authority to gauge the legitimacy of "national" or "regional" demands and even to intervene as protagonists in their political defense. One example, which has to do with Galicia, will allow us to illustrate these terms of discursive novelty, in the end characteristic of nationalistic statements.

Imaginations

In the nineteenth century historians, poets, at least one geographer—generally polymath men of letters—proposed the new terms for expressing "Galicia": in time, in space, and in the specifics of its various inhabitants. In this way Galicia was increasingly referred to as "province," "region," "nationality," and "nation," creating a group of founding monuments of nationalist discourse that are still being manipulated today. (cf. developments in chapter 3). In the majority of cases, these producers of new forms of referring to Galicia wrote in Spanish and, eventually, went on to look for their fortunes, more or less successfully,

as men of letters in the state's capital.[12] This description would hold
for Manuel Murguía (1833–1923), historian and polymath, author of
vivid and pioneering definitions of Galician nationality, and, as well, a
particularly active *regionalist* politician (see chapter 3). Some of these
definitions appear in his 1888 book entitled *Galicia,* which is most re-
vealingly characterized in a prologue I came across in the recently published edition of this book. It is worth citing this introductory piece
written by one of our contemporary historians:

> The reader has in his hands the reedition of a book that first appeared
> a century ago, in 1888. It was a beautiful tome of nearly one thousand
> and two hundred pages, its corners illuminated and covered in red cloth
> with rich geometrical decorations, stamped in relief in four colors above
> which the great coat of arms of Galicia was embossed. It belonged to
> the collection *España. Sus monumentos y artes. Su naturaleza e historia,*
> which the Barcelonan publisher, Daniel Cortezo, published during these
> years using the latest advances of the epoch in the art of printing, as, for
> example, the photographs spread through the book, whether on normal
> pages, or on heavier stock, which were included so that the buyer could
> frame them according to the instructions of the curious "*Plantilla para la
> colocación de las laminas*" at the end of the book.
>
> In accordance with the spirit of the collection, the goal of this work was
> to make Galicia known to the rest of the Spanish. And it would be dif-
> ficult to find a more enthusiastic and authoritative singer of its virtues
> and beauty than Murguía. However, it is not only because of this that
> one might believe that we have here an out of date tourist guide, volu-
> minous and auspicious. If this were the case, its republication would not
> be as justified. "It is not for the pleasure of proclaiming the beauty of our
> countryside […] nor to exalt the country that one loves, that we describe
> it so: it is, yes, so that we know our country, know better its history, its art,
> the interior life of the people on which it is based," he himself tells us.
>
> And because of this design and the text's construction, the result proba-
> bly seems somewhat unusual for one who doesn't know about his manner
> of thinking and his fundamental trajectory. In effect, it is not very com-
> mon that in an informative book not less than two hundred and twenty
> pages are dedicated to prehistory, mythology and folklore, nor that, in
> the chapters reserved for the principal cities, Murguía's most important
> contributions to the study of the history of Galicia appear to be summa-
> rized and carved up and his concept of the country's *being* and *should be*
> are left implicit. This is enough to indicate that this is an unusual text of
> its genre. (Beramendi, in Murguía 1998: i–ii)

This page is very suggestive for those of us who are familiar with much
of the recent literature dedicated to the study of nationalism, princi-

pally that work which is more directly inspired by the ideas of Benedict Anderson. We have, in the first instance, the reference to a publishing project that proposed a knowledge of "art," of "nature," and of "Spanish heritage," which sought to provide the wealthy classes, throughout the state territory, with references of nationalization. It was, it should be emphasized, a private publishing project in the city that was the most industrialized in Spain and a bastion of the new bourgeois strata that were then gaining political ground all across the state.[13] The initiative emulated similar ones recurring in the whole of Europe—with significant manifestations in Portugal as well—which explains the vital role that "print capitalism" (Anderson 1991) had at the time as a vehicle for nationalizing the wealthier classes.[14]

It was the proposal to create a vision of the whole of the Spanish nation—profusely illustrated—which justified the publication of *España. Sus Monumentos y Artes. Su naturaleza e história* [*Spain. Its Monuments and Arts. Its Nature and History*]. It should, however, be remarked upon that the book was elaborated using a "modular" approach (Anderson 1991), that is, according to the monographic survey that each one of the more clearly distinguished parts of the territory of the state received in the context of the collection. In *Galicia*—one of the monographs that the ample project, in its original form, included—Murguía established the possibility of recognizing a Galician "nature," and the manifestations of "art" and of Galician "heritage," which are made known to the readers in this quality. There are also, as is emphasized in the preface to the reedition, contributions that describe a specifically Galician prehistory, history, folklore, etc.

The terms that Murguía employs to close his "Introducción" of Galicia are especially curious, as much for their ambiguity as for the biblically inspired vocabulary: "Would it be, as *soon as* Galicia intends it, a guiding province. *Galicia already* has *its* Golgotha *but will have its Tabor* as well, since *it* will *appear* transfigured before the eyes of those *who have ignored, or deny it*" (Murguía 1988: 15, italics mine). A remark made by Raymond Williams provides an effective comment on this sentence. Williams said that in the uses of the term *region* "there is an evident tension within the word, as between a distinct area and a definite part," stressing, however, that the second sense is more prominent, that it ends up being related to the term *province*. He even notes that these connotations—and the possibilities for an implicit tension—were emphasized by the recent development of nation-states and the forms of knowledge brought about by these processes. (Williams 1988: 264–66).

Murguía's work presents us with a good example of the type of conflicts that Williams discusses: it is a provincial discourse—that is, the discourse of a "definitive part"—that which, in the first place, justifies this specific contribution; it is in this quality, finally, that it finds its place within the context of the original edition. Notwithstanding, *Galicia* also ends by clarifying vital differences—contained in terms whose legitimizing force was new: a history, folklore, etc., of its own—and as a definitive register of an entity. In the end, as Murguía would suggest, this was a corrective to those that "do not know her [Galicia] or deny her." At the time *Galicia* was published, its author was also formulating the first "regionalist" claims, of which he was, in subsequent decades, the most consequential ideologue and principal interpreter, as activist and politician. (Beramendi and Nuñez Seixas 1995; Máiz 1984, 1997).

This work's "concept of the country's *being* and *should be*" would be "implicit," as the author of the recent prologue would have it. This is a formula that, at the end of day, merely modulates the meaning of the very suggestive biblical terms that Murguía had already proposed in 1888. Any one of these formulations seems significant in terms of gauging the pertinence of Pierre Bourdieu's observation that elucidates the "performative" dimensions implied in the concept of region (1989: 107 and ff.). On the other hand, if we entertain Richard Handler's suggestion, who says that a region "is a nation writ small" (1988: 117), and if we also recognize that the path which Murguía took in *Galicia* is a very systematic manipulation of the items that Orvar Löfgren called the "do-it-yourself-kit" for nationalisms (Löfgren 1989; see also Thiesse 2000), we will then easily recognize that Murguía was employing the most powerful metaphors that exist for nationalist discourses. As Richard Handler says:

> The content of national being is national "character," "personality," "culture" and "history." Yet in nationalist ideology, these are subordinated to individuated being, which is the primary reality. In other words, the existence of a national entity is a primary assumption, rarely questioned, but the content of national being is the subject of continual negotiation and dispute. (1988: 51)

The example we have been discussing up until now suggests we should consider not only the old action of the state, but as well, and above all, the most recent nationalist discourse occurring at the state level as a requisite ideological reference for the possibilities for enunciating nationalistic formulations on a more restricted scale. In Spain peripheral nationalisms arose formulated in the wake of new forms of speaking as a nation about the space of the state whose first pioneering expressions date to the eighteenth century, but were above all consolidated in the nineteenth century (Fusi 2000 and Álvarez Junco 2001, who provide precise evidence of these precedents). Peripheral nationalisms emulated arguments of the same character, appropriating them in a segmentary form (Evans-Pritchard 1940). If we follow Handler's above-cited terms, this would create the possibility of speaking about the existence of other "national entities" and of initiating, as a consequence, "disputes" over the respective "history," "character," and "culture," etc.—disputes that continue to this day and that decisively mark contemporary Spanish political life.

Throughout the nineteenth century, the possibility also grew in Portugal for certain strata of the population to reflect as a nation upon the larger political community into which they were integrated. Also fundamental in this process were, unsurprisingly, the ideas about this knowledge created by artists, men of letters, and scientists who, in more or less imaginative forms, appropriated models of efficacy then being tested "in the context of intense international permutations," as A. M. Thiesse says (2000: 16). In earlier works (Medeiros 1994, 1995) I wanted to show how through descriptions of the Minho some of the items legitimized to represent national cultures were proposed at the end of the nineteenth century in Portugal. These descriptions emerged as a representation of the countryside by antonomasia and were an example emulated later when the possibilities of referencing the national territory divided into various "provinces" was popularized, each of which was recognized to have specific and mutually distinct ethnographic and topographical characteristics. This was a slow process of predication, consolidated only at the beginning of the twentieth century and which was relatively popularized through the state's initiative starting in the 1930s, even though, as I have suggested, the knowledge did not become universalized, remaining inaccessible to the illiterate strata of the rural population (*vide* chapters 7 and 8).

Taking the metaphors identified by Richard Handler as a reference, what remains absent from the descriptions of the Minho—and, generally, from the other Portuguese provinces—are the attributes of complete individuation, the identification of the "being" that the nationalist discourses of the periphery ended up proposing in Spain from the end of the nineteenth century onward. As a rule, in Portugal those attributes were only proposed for the all-embracing entity, the "Portuguese nation," and then superposed upon the territorial body of the state. For example, if arboreal and anthropomorphic metaphors were frequently used in relation to the Minho, it is in relation to its condition as a part that is normally underscored as being the "root," "trunk," or "heart" of the Portuguese nationality, to cite some of the frequent images in the stereotypical descriptions of this province.

In Portugal we do not find performative claims for regional identity like those that Manuel Murguía used in order to talk about Galiza. To explain such important qualitative differences we can take to heart what Llobera called "the materiality of the ideational" (1998: 331; see also a Galician illustration of this search in González Reboredo 2001). But with Hobsbawm, we can see that this is an inglorious and ironic task and that the objective criteria of nationality "are themselves fuzzy, shifting and ambiguous, as useless for purposes of the traveler's orientation as cloud-shapes are compared to landmarks" (1992: 6).

The Path of Traditions

Eric Hobsbawm classified the forms of production of new traditions in Europe—which were very intense in the period of 1870 to 1914—by distinguishing between official and unofficial proposals. He referred to the first initiatives as "political" and the second as "social." As the historian says, they are imprecise terms, but useful as references to the immense variety of these processes and our ability to distinguish between them; I believe that we can also use them here to our advantage. The intensity of this creation of outmoded traditions is justified in the following way: "Quite new, or old but dramatically transformed, social groups, environments and social contexts called for new devices to ensure or express social cohesion and identity and to structure social relations" (1985: 263). Crucial here is the fact that these processes of the nationalization of the masses on the state level (and Hobsbawm suggests that they are extremely varied) characterize the particular period that he points to, in which, in his words, "state, nation and society converged" (265).

If we keep in mind the differing speeds at which this convergence occurred, and which came late in both cases, as I have already noted, the sentence just cited above is pertinent to what happened in Portugal and Spain. On the other hand, the appearance of peripheral nationalist or regionalist movements in the context of the Spanish state obliges us to categorically question their appropriation directly following the transition from the nineteenth century into the twentieth. We have to necessarily recognize coexistent projects of nationalization in this case, ones that are parallel and competing; i.e., projects that did not arise under the protection of the power of the state for the good part of their historical course, until the recent establishment of the *Estado de las autonomías*.

The diffusion of new knowledge about the Minho and Galicia was carried off efficiently among the more literate and wealthier social strata of these states' respective populations. They were very restricted groups who had access to books, magazines, or a variety of forms of consumption, through which the socialization to these references of supralocal identification most frequently occurred. Following Hobsbawm, we can say that the knowledge of the Minho or of Galicia was propagated in a "social" way. In fact, in each case, "political" initiatives—that is, those promoted by the state or by organized political movements (Hobsbawm 1985)—were not prominent, or they proved themselves to be inefficient for large periods of the nineteenth and twentieth centuries if we use the extent to which they reached the masses as a measure of success.

In the Minho, those general characteristics still pertain to this day. State initiatives to promote representations of this province—and, generally of a variety of provinces—were always sporadic and rare. Regional movements of consequence that chose to propagate the recognition of the provinces as political communities rarely appeared in Portugal. It was above all through offers that emerged in the context of a market of images, of dress, of leisure practices and tourism, that the middle classes throughout the whole country were able to disseminate and absorb knowledge about rural Portugal and its diversity. As has been said above, this was one type of knowledge that references to the Minho epitomized in pioneering terms. That market found its most vigorous expression in the major cities and remained inaccessible to the greater part of the inhabitants of the province itself (see chapters 7, 8, and 9). But it would be erroneous to suggest that there was a definitive dichotomization between rural and urban contexts of the possibilities for knowing the nation and its internal diversity. These were related mainly to whether one belonged to the upper classes and to having a formal education, as happened in Spain or in any other European state.[15]

For most of the nineteenth and the twentieth centuries, the Spanish state did little in the way of expanding the teaching of regional diversity to the masses. On the contrary, the involvement of the state in this area was dominated during a long period (1939–1975) by a decided repression of all proposals geared toward the recognition of peripheral nationalities, exercises that had been relatively free until 1936. During the last two decades, in contrast, the intervention of the Spanish state following the promulgation of the constitution of 1978 has become decisive in these pedagogic processes. Compared to the Minho, the case of Galicia is certainly more complex. Nevertheless, from the moment that Galicianist claims began to emerge at the end of the nineteenth century, the capacities of the various regionalist or nationalist political associations for generalizing the recognition of Galicia as a region or a nation among the majority of its inhabitants were feeble. But after 1981, the *Estatuto*

de Autonomía de Galicia entrusted the government itself with competencies and specific resources for divulging the knowledge of Galicia as a
community among all of its inhabitants, at the same time that the organized activity of various nationalist parties and associations grew.

We can now get closer to the reasons why so many inhabitants of the
Minho have difficulties, even today, in seeing themselves as Minhotans,
and better understand the obstacles faced throughout the period in the
popularization of the regionalist and nationalist discourses about Galicia. I believe that this should be undertaken by looking at some of the
more unpredictable ways through which the masses became nationalized in Portugal and Spain, ways that predated ineffective interventions
on the part of the respective states.

Visions and Pilgrimages

In the rural context of the Minho where the intensity of religious practices
is notorious, the surprising lack of references to Santiago de Compostela
as a religious destination can be explained if we take into account that
pilgrimages to the tomb of the Apostle have varied in frequency through
the centuries. Roughly, we can say that compared with the cosmopolitan splendor of the Lower Middle Ages, when pilgrims from the whole
of Christendom were coming to Compostela (Otero Pedrayo 1991), a
process of decline had set in, which has been uninterrupted for centuries
and has continued until recently.

Taking the broader view, I now consider that the perception of decline that involves the history of the pilgrimages to the tomb of the
Apostle is stressed in the *Galeguista* or Galicianist discourse as a metaphor for the decline that the nation of Galicia had suffered. This could
be the touchstone for referring to the uses of the language or of past
expressions of the political entity of Galicia—allowing for the identification of a lost "golden age," ruined by the centralizing policies promoted
by the Catholic monarchs at the end of the fifteenth century and persist-
ing through subsequent centuries (Barros 1994).

In fact, the references to the medieval splendor of Galicia form a very
prominent rhetorical motif, in which we can see clearly how the "myth
of regeneration" was appropriated, that which Anthony Smith considers
to be the "central principle of nationalism" and an especially powerful
reference for these forms of collective mobilization (Smith 1999: 67 and
ff.). We should emphasize that during this centuries-long period the role
of the state in the cult of the Apostle St. James was effectively strengthened and that this strengthening had its origin in the seventeenth cen-

tury, a hinge-period in the process of the construction of modern states (Giddens 1985; Fusi 2000). These state appropriations were even more marked in the first decades of control by Franco's autocratic regime, when the "St. James' [or Santiago] Day" was declared Spain's National Day, a holiday whose commemoration would now be celebrated by the whole of the Spanish territory.

On the contrary, in more recent years the popularization of the pilgrimage to Santiago has spread once again beyond the borders of Spain due to the efforts made at promotion, which have brought the Compostelan chapter together with the new autonomous government of Galicia. These days there is a massive flow of pilgrims and tourists arriving from many different places to the city. Likewise, the historical city center has been recognized by UNESCO. These initiatives taken to promote Compostela as the center where tourists and pilgrims can visit the tomb of the Apostle Santiago can be considered to be a facet in a current process of "European construction" (or Europeanization) (Borneman and Fowler 1997; also Herzfeld 1992a). Funds provided by the European Union have played a great importance in financing these initiatives, and the revitalization of the traditional routes to Santiago and the cult of the Apostle are very much marked by the recent invention (Hobsbawm 1985) of various traditions. To these traditions Galician meanings are most frequently attributed, but they double as European and cosmopolitan meanings as well (while mention of militaristic and state connotations emphasized throughout the last centuries are implicitly censored).

Sponsored by the local intelligentsia and community funding, in various places around the Minho the medieval pilgrimage routes to Compostela have recently been mapped. In more recent years pilgrimages there on foot have become more frequent, even if these are still minority initiatives organized in the most important cities and whose participants are still, in a certain fashion, drawn from the elites. During my fieldwork it was with the Portuguese participants on the new pilgrimages to Santiago that I recognized greater readiness to identify Galicia as distinct from the rest of Spain and witnessed the articulation of positive descriptions of the idiosyncrasies of the Galicians. These differences could occasionally be described as a singular "culture," valuable in the European context, whose affinities to the culture of the "North of Portugal"—or to "Portugal"—were frequently suggested.

Borneman and Fowler tell us that "Europeanization is fundamentally reorganizing territoriality and peoplehood, the two principles of group identification that have shaped the modern European order" (1997: 487). This is a process that brings together complex forms with the consolidation of the autonomies and peripheral nationalistic discourses in Spain and also with the recent appearance of proposals for regionalization in Portugal. For Galician nationalists, a "Europe of Nations" is seen as the future, in which Galicia would justifiably fit; for defenders of regionalization in Portugal, it is a "Europe of regions" that is most frequently alluded to. In the majority of these proposals, the presence of state borders shapes the limits of the proposals made; however, it is also possible to recognize the appearance of increasingly imaginative formulations that diminish that presence and take on the more ample European political context as a principal reference (cf., generally, Goddard et al. 1994). However, in the rural parishes of the Minho where I did my fieldwork, Santiago de Compostela was still a pilgrimage destination ignored by many of the inhabitants. And in the Minho, by contrast, trips to the Sanctuary of Fátima are frequent and draw many recruits, as had already happened in earlier decades with another Marian sanctuary, Sameiro, on the outskirts of Braga. These were phenomena that from the first decades of the twentieth century were locally consolidated, a fact that allowed me to gather memories of their intensification from local inhabitants.

The final period of the nineteenth century and the beginning of the twentieth were fertile times for apparitions throughout Catholic Europe and for the appearance of new forms of religious pilgrimage. These were generalized phenomena directly related to wider ideological confrontations around the continent; but the period has also been described as the "age of nationalisms" and of their apogee (Hobsbawm 1992). This temporal coincidence is suggestive if we take into account the meanings of national character that many of these religious apparitions—mostly Marian—were given.

Also in Portugal the frequent occurrence of supposed apparitions, pilgrimages to new sanctuaries, and the "missions of re-Christianization" were expressions of an intensification of the religious militancy that gained growing visibility towards the end of the nineteenth century, but which, above all, intensified during the years 1910–1940.[16] In the Minho, these manifestations of religiosity left expressive marks in rural contexts, for example, punctuating the countryside with new large stone crosses and churches and altering the religious practices of its inhabitants, thus shaping traditions of religious practice that still thrive today. In one of the parishes where I did my fieldwork I was told about the occurrence of apparitions during the 1930s. According to the accounts, the revelations of the local visionary—a *miraculada* ["the miracled one"]—were very similar to those of the famous shepherds of Fátima, containing as well messages on the destiny of Portugal and the world. The comments made in this paragraph could also be applied to Galicia, where stone crosses and chapels, dated inscriptions, new images on old altars, etc., suggest that the campaigns of re-Christianization during those first decades of the twentieth century were just as intense. At this time as well, in both regional contexts a great quantity of periodicals taking up the position of the Catholic Church also flourished at levels that, as a matter of fact, were much more abundant and vigorous, in the second case, than that of the contemporary Galician nationalist press (see chapter 3).

In the Minho, a number of my informants could remember the stories they had been told about the frequency of the "missions" during the first years of the twentieth century, or of the enthusiastic organization of the first pilgrimages to the Senhora do Sameiro Sanctuary and soon afterwards to Fátima. The oldest among them were aware of the fact that these initiatives were part of acts of revenge and confrontation with the *masons*—a term still used, but which the young parodied—on a national level. We have, thus, in these memories, direct, local echoes of ideological confrontations that reach a peak in Portugal during the years of the First Republic. A citation taken from Pierre Sanchis will sufficiently suggest the intimacy maintained between religious phenomena and the expressions of nationalism during a key year in Portuguese history of the twentieth century.

> "Nationalism will arrive soon to Portugal," we read in the *Distrito de Portalegre* in 1923. In fact, there was an attempt in 1925 that failed. But in 1926 a military revolt organized in Braga, during the National Mariano Congress itself, brought it to power. And there it continued until 1973. The Catholics had bound themselves to the coup d'état in various ways, preferably by indirect means, but above all, in the ideological impregnation that permitted the success of the coup. The episcopacy maintained its distance to avoid a scandal. But the Catholic social base enthusiastically joined on from the first moment. "Miracle of our Lady of Sameiro," they called it (Sanchis 1983: 201).

So, with "nationalism" now entrenched in Portugal and distinct expressions of it having already begun as early as the beginning of the nineteenth century, it soon came to inform the positions of all political quadrants. On the other hand, as I have suggested, 1926 can effectively be considered a hinge year, since it initiated a period of decisive nationalizing initiatives of an autocratic nature imposed by the state. These would become especially vigorous by the time we reach 1933 and 1934, when processions and exhibitions increased (see an example in chapter 8), but also interventions in the countryside, in urbanism and in the erection of monuments. However, in spite of these pointed efforts—and

other than the very emblematic school buildings—the ostensive marks
of these nationalizing interventions of the state, which were above all
brought to bear in the towns and cities, are very sparse in the country's
villages. Yet, the forms of religious mobilization, which date back to the
first decades of the twentieth century, were a relevant vehicle for the
nationalization of the less favored and sparsely educated rural stratum
of society. These people maintained a certain distance from the forms of
civic and political mobilization, of lay rituals, of the practice of sports
and the habits of reading, all means through which the nationalization
of culture of the middle classes had proceeded since the previous century. Many of my older informants who had participated in the Marian pilgrimages to Sameiro and Fátima since childhood recognized, for
example, the national meaning of the apparitions at Fátima. These were
the meanings contained in the sermons and hymns, which many knew
by heart, that underlined how Portugal played a redeeming role in the
concert of nations. It would seem that the greater part of the nationalization of the older inhabitants of the two Minhotan parishes where I
did my research was accomplished through religious rites.

My intention is not to present a detailed survey of the deficits of national references in those people connected to working the land, people
of little formal education—or potentially illiterate—whom I met in the
"field." But I would like to emphasize that with these Minhotan examples—for which we could find very close parallels in Galicia—such lacu-
nae were noticeable among older generations and could be attributed to
the scarcity of interventions on the part of the state. To paraphrase Eugen Weber's[17] most famous title, it could be said that in a certain way the
possibility of recognizing "peasants" in the Minho—or in Galicia—was
related to the debility of the actions of the states in the molding of the
Portuguese and the Spanish in rural contexts (Redfield 1973).

Nevertheless, what I wanted to suggest above was that the nationalization of the peasants also occurred through less predictable avenues, an
example of which were the very intense forms of religious mobilization
in the beginning of the twentieth century. The minutiae of knowledge
about the diversity of the provinces were absent in this case—namely,
those that were based in ethnographic characterizations—that had
originated with the nonreligious forms of nationalization of knowledge
among the bourgeoisie. In truth, those characterizations frequently accentuated the persistence of superstitions and supposedly immemorial
practices, that were seen as being like vestiges of "paganism" among
the peasantry. On many occasions—with a greater or lesser degree of
vehemence, according to the political positioning of whomever was
opining—the religious mobilizations were described as forms of dena-

tionalizing the rural strata, which was, it was supposed, more preserving of "national" essences, or *pátrias* as they were called at the time. The "fanatic" missionary as the corruptor of the innocently "pagan" beliefs of the rustics is a stock figure in much of the Portuguese and Spanish literature of the end of the nineteenth century.

In noting the surprisingly important role that religious rites had in Portugal and Galicia as sui generis vehicles of the nationalization of the masses, I would like to remark on certain influential proposals in which we can see the suggestion that a metamorphosis, or a linear succession between ancient religious rites and modern nonreligious nationalizing rites, has occurred, the latter merely appropriating the recognized efficacy of the former (Mosse 1975; Gellner 1983; Anderson 1991; Llobera 1998). It was George Mosse who brought to our attention most incisively the fact that the characteristics in nationalisms of a new secular religion had been turned into a "cult of the people," based on a recent concept of popular sovereignty and marked by the presence of new myths and symbols. In his opinion, these would be efficaciously propagated through "liturgical" forms, or rites and celebrations—the transmission of "national mysticisms," new senses of belonging whose establishment would account for the efficacy found in the processes of nationalization of the European masses during the nineteenth and twentieth centuries (Mosse 1975: 1–2). Mosse illustrates his thesis by taking as his principal reference the analysis of the German case in which the nonreligious characteristics of these rites—occasionally referred to as "neo-pagan"—were taken to the extreme. However, many of the rites that took place in Germany and also in other European countries (see for example, Nora 1992; Hobsbawm 1985; Wilson 1976) were expressed feebly, inconstantly, and late in Iberian contexts, where, contrastingly, religious rites seemed to have been prominent vehicles of nationalization.

Beyond an explanation—certainly very demanding—of those casuistical differences between European states, I believe that it is the general possibility of highlighting the mnemonic and pedagogical power of rituals and of *performances* that is necessary. For this reason, I have mainly taken into account arguments proposed by Victor Turner (1990 and 1967), James Fernandez (1986), and Paul Connerton (1989) in order to emphasize the ritual—or "more or less ritual" (Connerton 1989: 40)—character of some of the more successful forms for the transmission of references of national belonging set in motion in Portugal and Galicia in the past, but in our times as well—an emphasis that will also be applied in chapters 2, 9, and 10. In another important group of chapters—5, 6, and 8—I illustrate the importance that the pursuit of ethnographic interests in Portugal and in Galicia had in the consolidation of nationalist discourses. This is still a question of great current interest in Galicia—and generally in Spanish peripheral nationalities—given the vigor of the process of "nation construction" that has taken place during the last quarter century. These overlappings of ethnographic practice with nationalist discourse are less clear, certainly, in the Portugal of our days. Notwithstanding, I believe that it is worth noting some of the general problems that anthropologists encounter who work in the context of nation-states; to this end, I will take examples from certain recent ethnographies produced in Portugal. It is with an interrogation of the notion of culture—central in the history of anthropology, but also in nationalist discourses and in the action of states—that I will take up the consideration referred to above.

Stories of Anthropology— (Also) a Prodigal Daughter of Nations

The questions raised by conceptualizations of the term *culture* are complex; when this term is employed by anthropologists, the risk of imprecision is a strong. This is due to a myriad of competing definitions and to the excessive breadth claimed by each of them. Gratuitous and uncritical usages of comfortable clichés tend to multiply, even as, recently, incitements to abandon the term have increased, as happened in a vigorous argument put forth by Lila Abu-Lughod as early as the beginning of the 1990s (1991).[18] Richard Shweder notes how ironic these incitements are to abandon the use of the concept when he observes that other disciplines have lately taken up "culture" as a research topic "with increasing frequency" (Borofsky et al. 2001: 437–38). In my opinion, there is a risk of falling into an even more ironic situation than that of consenting to the usurpation that Shweder denounces. We are at risk of abandoning the use of this emblematic notion when its use is being universalized, its appropriations are producing consequences in a great variety of social contexts, and it is imposing itself as a decisive reference in the transformation of contemporary societies (Herzfeld 2001; Thomas 1992; Hannerz 1992).

Recent incitements to abandon the concept of culture reflect disenchantments over the loss of the role played by anthropologists, who were for so long responsible for the plenipotentiary bestowal of "cultures" on exotic populations. Thus the chances are multiplying that today's anthropologists will encounter in remote lands specialized codifications that were created during the twentieth century. These possible encounters should be seen as mementos of demiurgic times in the history of the discipline, but they should also be used as opportunities for further study, going beyond the registers that they habitually inspire. The interest in this positive posture is demonstrated in a rarely cited text by James Clifford—"Identity in Mashpee" (Clifford 1988: 277–346)—in which outdated anthropological codifications create a foundation for a fascinating ethnography of current political disputes.

But there are also a great variety of situations in which culture does not result in an attribution that we can fix in time, one resulting from the solitary work of an anthropologist, a specialist constrained by his or her own "invention" (Wagner 1975)—but rather they derive from an already-extant formulation that has been politically manipulated over time. Ostensively, this is the case of the cultures that nationalist movements composed for their own use, identifying reasons and monuments of national identity under the influx of Romantic ideology (Herzfeld 1986). In fact, as soon as we find the history of anthropology written with greater breadth, or when we confront versions of other specialists, we confirm communities of origins, replicas, overlapping of suggestive routes in all of that which the notion of culture touches upon. Namely, we are put in mind of the fact that culture came to be considered an attribute of a wide diversity of groups studied around the globe, but that it had already been one belonging to European nations—or to nation-states—and that the intellectual origins of the two types of uses were not discrepant.[19] For this reason we can say that when we consider the recent practice of doing anthropology at "home" (Jackson 1985) a circle is closed, and we are dealing with a kind of disturbing reencounter with the old presence of nationalist discourses and their uses of the notion of culture.

In 1992 I chose two contiguous parishes in the Minho as the location of my first fieldwork. I was interested in themes that had grown out of the social anthropology done in Europe during the 1970s and 1980s and that was represented by significant versions in Portugal. For me, the most significant and immediate references were the works of Brian O'Neill (1984) and João de Pina-Cabral (1989), which had been carried out in the north of Portugal, a context that both of these authors valorized even if this valorization was accomplished in a diffuse fashion. For their part, these two authors took the early work—and pioneering work in Portugal—of José Cutileiro (1971a and 1977) as an important reference of interlocution for their own proposals. Indeed, they cite Cutileiro as the most immediate counterpoint that allowed for an emphasis on originality of phenomena that they had at hand and to delineate references to the existence of regional differences in Portugal from a new disciplinary perspective.

I believe that these examples of dialogue between the works of anthropologists operating in the same country suggest the presence of a disturbing coexistence. We recognize in all of the cited titles attention being paid to relevant themes circulating internationally and comparable preoccupations of very ample breadth going shoulder to shoulder with a forceful attention to the framing proposed by the nation-state. In Portugal—if we consider Hobsbawm's observation cited above to be valid (1985)—a gradual "convergence" between state and nation and society had evolved as well resulting in a variety of questions that were problematical in various ways for anthropologists. In the works referred to—all of which can be considered classics of the social anthropology produced in Portugal—we can discern, in addition to the differences among their respective preoccupations, certain common characteristics. Thus, all three involve themselves with the study of rural communities; they relativize in varying degrees the national space as a reference for contexts; they ask to be seen as contributions to projects of anthropological comparison regionalized on an ample scale—and a sufficiently original one!—that turn out to be significant only for specialists well versed in the history of anthropology (see Fardon 1990 as a very perspicacious general reference).

In José Cutileiro's book we find that certain central topics in the tradition of Mediterranean anthropological studies are favored, mainly "patronage," but also "honor and shame" (see also Davis 1977).[20] Cutileiro employs bibliography originating from this tradition for theoretical and comparative uses, though he does so in a very restrained way, and avoids generalizations (Cutileiro 1971a, 1977; Herzfeld 1987; Davis 1977). The representations of honor and shame are important axes of the analysis that is conducted in a parish in the Alentejo, whose ecological characteristics are initially emphasized as being "Mediterranean." However, in the elaboration of this work what is mainly stressed is the attention attributed to political dependencies in relation to the state context. Thus, the author shows himself to be attentive to the local consequences of the hierarchical exercise of administrative powers—the parish, the municipality, the district, and the central government—and also to the "corporate organisms," more recent sources of power instituted through legislation produced by the *Estado Novo* ["New State," 1933–1974].[21] In this argument, the province where the parish is located, the Alentejo, is not, in the end, taken into account as a relevant reference in the sphere of the analysis as conducted.

O'Neill studies a very tiny locality—"a small mountain village"—situated in the northeast of Portugal, and he focuses his analytic energies on a very minute discrimination between the different "social groups" hierarchized in this context, a hierarchy whose existence demonstrates that it is founded on differentiated access to land ownership. References to the provincial context (the Trás-os-Montes) are sparse in O'Neill's work and apparently not, or only slightly, valorized. Indeed, it is an ecological context, "Terra Fria," that receives the greater part of the attention as a context for supralocal framing. At the same time, certain allusions, hardly emphatic, to the town hall permits an accounting of the intervention of the state at the local level. O'Neill discusses the existence of a supposed "egalitarianism" present in "mountain communities" throughout Europe, a thesis maintained by a variety of specialists and one that the author intends to counter with his contribution. But his most effective references of comparison—the more direct targets of his polemical proposal—are the results of the works focused on scattered mountain communities in a vast area in the northern Iberian Peninsula. This is a context in which the author recognizes that the favorite topics within the ambit of the prestigious tradition of "Mediterranean" studies, which were then highly valued as a general reference of Europeanist anthropologists, are absent.

João de Pina-Cabral suggests that we frame our comparative approach in a much different way in relation to anterior examples. In his work we find an argument for characterizing "the peasant worldview" of the residents of two rural parishes located in the Minho, an approach that is justified through references to Robert Redfield's famous theses (1973). As a counterpoint to the worldview maintained by the peasantry, Pina-Cabral identifies the "great tradition," cosmopolitan and culturally hegemonic, maintained by the provincial bourgeoisie residing in the urban areas of the province (1989: 56 and ff.). In his introduction, Pina-Cabral indicates in a footnote that there are more viable possibilities for the comparison of these materials in relation to data originating in Galicia than with that which comes out of the south of Portugal. In his own words: "So many are the differences between the north and the south of Portugal that *A Portuguese Rural Society* (1971), by José Cutileiro, cannot be considered a natural companion to this study. A much closer example is the work of Carmelo Lisón in Galicia" (Pina-Cabral 1989: 30).

Even though the work of Cutileiro could be called atypical in a variety of ways, in the three books mentioned above, the references to what the "peasants" think with respect to death, property, the relationship between men and women, etc., are plentiful. On the other hand, and paraphrasing Michael Herzfeld (1985), none of them pay much attention to what the peasants and primary school teachers, for example, might think in common.[22] Put in another way, the questions posed by the presence of the erudite cultures that nationalisms have produced are by and large ignored (Gellner 1983).

To be exact, however, and again among these works, only that of Pina-Cabral takes the study of "culture" as its goal, suggesting the regional representativeness of the results that he gathers in a circumscribed rural context. In his own words: "The Minho, taken as a whole, manifests a cultural identity that distinguishes it clearly from other Portuguese provinces." A little further on he is even more specific: "When, during this work, I refer to the Minhotan peasants or to Minhotan culture, I have in mind particularly the Upper Minho." Nevertheless, in this more restricted space, Pina-Cabral still accounts for the "different and more picturesque" or atypical character that would characterize some of the province's mountain villages, like Soajo, Lindoso, or Vilarinho da Furna. These are famous villages in the history of ethnographic interests cultivated in Portugal since the nineteenth century; as a matter of fact, it was the very diffuse set of these interests that allowed for the consolidation of the contemporary use of Cabral's adjectives.

As I wanted to suggest above—and want to document in some of the chapters that compose this book—the "clear distinction" of the Minho can be understood mainly as the result of *imagining the nation,* which intellectuals of the nineteenth century exercised. As such, they were part of an erudite culture produced by the nationalist discourse diligently (and with large doses of fantasy) set in motion—what Anne-Marie Thiesse calls "the IKEA system of national identity construction" (2000). That setting into motion in the Portuguese case consists of various items that the production of a knowledge of the Minho indeed furnished, having followed models that were already prestigious in the international arena and subject to updating and adjusting in successive periods.

The Minho was compared to Scotland, Ireland, Flanders, Switzerland, Brittany, and "Arcadia"—but seldom to Galicia—and the prestigious descriptions of these places were emulated. Emulations authored by Portuguese intellectuals as influential as Alexandre Herculano (1810–1877), Oliveira Martins (1845–1894), and Leite de Vasconcelos were often replicated by other less famous writers and became relatively successful and permanent descriptive clichés (see chapter 7). Curiously, very similar allusions occurred in the descriptions of Galicia, even if the meanings of their appropriations were very different. For example, one of the clichés frequent in the popular literature of the end of the nineteenth century was the description of Galicia as the *Suiza española* [Spanish Switzerland], against which nationalist intellectuals inveighed for obvious reasons: they preferred to imagine it as an Ireland, and also "Celtic," as well as "martyred," but with independence similarly promised. (see chapter 3).

The identification of the Upper Minho had the same erudite origins, even if in this case the arguments for *its* definition were always diffuse. The minting of that designation fell to Alexandre Herculano who used it for the first time by referring in a vague way to the most mountainous part of the Minho (Herculano 1934; Vasconcelos 1980b). This author was the first to produce one of those unavoidable references in the definition of a national identity, the first history of Portugal, of 1848 (Thiesse 2000; Torgal et. al. 1998). On the other hand, the Upper Minho is a name that has been used to refer to political claims made by the elites of a variety of urban centers in the district of Viana do Castelo. This occurred mainly from the 1920s and 1930s onwards, having as a rule served localist goals without effective projection across the whole of the district, whose territory would only gradually take on this designation of the "Alto Minho."

Here, once again, we see the constancy of the state: it is the district— that nontraditional "Jacobin" imposition so often denounced—that becomes gradually "naturalized" (Bourdieu 1989). Even today, those localized claims for regional identity are legitimized by the appropriation of the topics that the nationalist discourse had produced about the Minho as a whole. Diffuse ethnographic reasons are appropriated and give rise to the very modestly articulated claims to "traditions" or to the "popular culture" belonging to each of the municipalities. This scale of appropriations reveals difficulties, which until today have not been overcome, of articulating for the Upper Minho—or the Minho—performative "regionalist" demands of a "being" "for itself" (Bourdieu 1989; Handler 1988; Marx 1984). In these localist demands, I reiterate, the old stereotypical descriptions of the "Minho" emerge out of the nineteenth century and are appropriated in bits and pieces and constantly manipulated. By contrast, the meticulous and perspicacious work of João de Pina Cabral—that so categorically gauges the "culture" itself of the Minho—has not been until today appropriated politically in any significant sense. I believe these discrepancies are suggestive because they speak to us of the efficacy of the processes of the production of "iconicity" (Herzfeld 1997a) delineated by nationalist elites and imposed by the state actions. They also illustrate the challenges to the practice of anthropologists in the European context.

Webs of Meanings in the Northwest

I believe that the special difficulties that anthropologists are faced with in analyzing national cultures and their influxes into the small localities where they conduct their studies should be emphasized. These difficulties have been habitually ignored. With respect to this, Claudio Lomnitz-Adler's commentary is suggestive. His reference is to Mexico, but his words can be applied generally:

> Thus the demise of national culture as a scientific topic has not abolished the problem of national culture itself; analytical incompetence in the question of national culture—and, as we shall see, in regional culture generally—has provoked contradictions in the theoretical and methodological frames of social scientists. These contradictions have exiled the subject from social studies and it has found safe harbor in the interpretative essay. Although many of these essays contain important ideas and observations, they have not allowed an accumulation of knowledge because they have been too closely linked to the political needs which give rise to them. They are made to be consumed in a particular conjuncture. After they are consumed, they merely sink into the past and sit on the sediment of reusable stereotypes. (1992: 13)

Two points in this observation seem to stand out: the general similarity noted between regional and national cultures with respect to the difficulties of their respective analyses; and the place of prominence attributed to essays and to their efficacy in crystallizing politically actionable representations of national identity. Up until now I have intended to create a defense of the first of these points in an introductory form: recognizing that the "imagination" of the region—or of the province, and the difference can be recognized only in political arguments and in metaphors put into play—is helped by the same processes that are put into play to imagine nations. In the end, they are products of the same provenance—"modern" and "erudite" cultures that nationalist discourses produce (Gellner 1983). I want to valorize, by contrast, the "sediment of reusable stereotypes," disqualified by Lomnitz, and see Michael Herzfeld's suggestion as the more sensible approach, which maintains that it is in stereotypes—and in their practice—that we find, in large measure, "the object" of research into "ethnic character and nationalism" (1992b: 67). The term "reusable" that Lomnitz uses is appealing in various ways, namely, in that it permits the introduction of necessary clarifications of certain characteristics of this book.

With respect to Galicia, I am proposing a study that is mainly focused on the present (even though the archival work I did there has been significant). For contrast, I start from an approach to descriptions of the Minho that are already historical—chapters 7, 8, and 9—giving an account of the course they took at the end of the nineteenth century and during the first decades of the twentieth, as well as some of the appropriations that they were subject to at the time. The justification for this difference is simple: in the Minho there have not occurred even to this day any regionalist manifestations that took the province as a whole as a reference, nor has the state attributed political status to the province. Thus, its flourishing in this particular period should be seen as a facet of an historical process of the nationalization of culture on the part of the middle classes in Portugal.

Returning to the original considerations with which I opened this chapter, the lack of knowledge of the Minho that the peasants and their descendents in two parishes revealed currently has very few possibilities presently for redemption. Knowledge of the Minho as a province—produced in the nineteenth century and the beginnings of the twentieth—persists as a ruin or "sediment" of stereotypical descriptions whose political activation occurred during a privileged epoch and was justified for reasons to do with the state. Today, the manipulation of those ruralist stereotypes is incumbent upon local elites involved in the production of "cultures" or "identities" merely on the level of the municipality or strictly at the local level, as *bracarenses, maiatos, vianenses, limianos, soajeiros,* etc. As I have already suggested, what has happened in Galicia in recent years is completely different. There, old stereotypes—proposed namely in essays—that also date back to the end of the nineteenth century and the beginnings of the twentieth are today constantly reutilized. They give body to the representations of Galician culture—that serve, obviously, contemporary political intentions—the expressions of which are projected onto the territory of the Comunidade Autónoma with increasing ease, making them familiar to a majority of the population.

Galicia, whose political entity has long been the object of performative assertions—as I have suggested above in citing a nineteenth-century historian—has today, as a consequence of transformations that have taken place since 1978 via the reconfiguration of the Spanish state, an institutionally recognized existence. Ulf Hannerz suggests, "For the four major frameworks which should take us at least a long way toward a comprehensive accounting of present day culture flow, then, I use the terms form of life, market, state and movement" (1992: 47). Although still only partially, and with obvious weaknesses and many conflicts, in recent years the last three of these "frameworks" have been projected over the whole of the autonomous space of Galicia, creating a new form of shared life among Galicians, one which is already articulated by the references to a new national culture.

In this study I have mainly been inspired by a pragmatic suggestion made by Richard Handler, which affirms that we should "see culture as a thing." Following his suggestion, I want to account for some of the principal "lines" and "entities" through which, over time, representations of cultures specific to the Minho and to Galicia were "objectivized" (Handler 1988: 13–16). But another of the anthropological definitions of culture—this one especially famous—can also be appropriated, as soon as we strip it of a certain mystifying adjective. I (re)cite Clifford Geertz: "The concept of culture I espouse … is essentially a semiotic one. Believing with Max Weber that man is an animal suspended in webs of significance he himself has spun, I take culture to be those webs, and the analysis of it to be therefore not an experimental science in search of law but an interpretative one in search of meaning. It is explication I am after, construing social expressions on their surface enigmatical" (1973: 5). The representations of "Galician culture" that the nationalist intellectuals articulate, the contemporary process of their popularization, the legal formulations and the bureaucratic processes with which they are brought up to date or the daily disputes over their interpretation that they provoke, can be the object of an approach guided by Geertz's definition. Likewise, the "culture of the Minho" that the nationalist discourse in Portugal invented can be interpreted in light of these honorable precepts. However, the adjective "enigmatic," used dramatically by Geertz, calls for a coda; I believe this to be found in the famous first pages of *Deep Play: Notes on the Balinese Cockfight* (Geertz 1973: 412 and ff.). Prosaically, in these two cases that I intend to look at, I believe that we can put aside the supposition that there are a priori enigmas to consider. By doing so, we are left with *webs of significance* that we can try to unweave, always keeping in mind "the point of view of the native" as first principle.

Notes

1. In Lisbon—an important destination for emigration since the end of the eighteenth century until the beginning of the 1930s—it was the low status of manual laborers or small retailers coming from Galicia that consolidated the negative references of their identification as an ethnic group (Vásquez Cuesta 1991; Taboada 1955; Marçal 1954). The use of the expressions "arre galego" [giddy-up Galician] or "trabalha como um galego" [work like a Galician] would be familiar mainly for the well read, or those who have lived in Lisbon, where, in the oldest neighborhoods, the proverbial "Galician" might still today be an old tavern keeper from the "country of waiters"—a literary example, among many, of the qualifications of contempt that took place during the emigration en masse of Galicians to the Portuguese capital. The compendium of jokes about the Galicians spread on a national scale through books, newspapers, and magazines towards the end of the nineteenth century, but today would only be familiar to those who are in the habit of reading these dated texts. In addition to disdainful literary references, and for a number of reasons, the

Portuguese elites had greater mechanisms for understanding Galicia as a distant part of Spain, whether because they maintained claims based on remote or noble family origins in the "Old Kingdom of Galicia" or through tourism. On the other hand, references to Galicia as the place where the Portuguese language originated and the first steps toward founding the Portuguese state occured are familiar to all Portuguese who finish high school. In addition to these very limited references, the majority of Portuguese are unaware of the positive terms of description of Galicia and the Galicians created through regionalist and nationalist discourses that intend mainly to counteract the negative stereotypes active in the rest of the Spanish state and that were already assiduous in the literature of the Siglo de Oro [Spanish Golden Age] (see an eminent register of these old uses and of the vehement way in which they are rejected in Castelao 1976).

2. "chamber pot of Galicia"

3. "chamber pot of the sky"

4. It can be said that a great part of Northern Portugal and Galicia share an impressive array of similarities—in climates, geography, linguistics, ethnographies, etc.—as will be suggested by a comparison of the results of a variety of academic disciplines that have studied each of these contexts. These are affinities that have never received sustained attention as a whole because in Portugal and Spain, academic practices are contained by state boundaries, or, in the case of Spain, in the context of a range of nationalistic discourses.

5. As an anecdotal example of more developed Flamencan representations, a Portuguese friend of mine who visited me in Galicia cited Garcia Lorca's famous poem, "Muerte de Antonio 'el Camborio.'" In the poem the Guadalquivir River is alluded to, but we were close to the Umia River, in Caldas de Reis, between Vigo and Santiago de Compostela, and it was raining. So, if another type of semantic association had been put into play, we would have been able to say that the mist, the rain, and all of the circumstances were "Celtic" (Chapman 1982). But my friend had no idea that Galician intellectuals had defined Galicia in opposition to the ostensive *Flamencan* worldview, which orients the representation of Spain for the European and North American public (Fernandez 1988).

6. Curiously, a supposed "cruelty" was one of the clearest traits belonging to my Minhotan informer's stereotypical perception of the *Spaniards* (a characterization, moreover, widespread in Europe, and stemming from an older erudite discourse, the "characterology of nations," which was popularized at the beginning of the eighteenth century) (Crépon 1996).

7. Recently, Anthony Smith has produced an important critique of the limits of Anderson's theses—calling them "postmodernist"—while generally criticizing the "modernist paradigm" in its explanation of nationalism (Smith 1998). In my personal opinion, even though Smith's criticism contains a range of pertinent points—as a matter of fact, many of the ideas in the present work are taken from his extensive and influential oeuvre—the author has not systematized a theoretical alternative to the "modernist" arguments maintained by Ernest Gellner (1983) and Eric Hobsbawm (1992) or the "postmodern" theses of Benedict Anderson (a work that A. Smith takes as a corollary to the anterior ones).

8. In Portugal the intention to universalize primary education was only fulfilled, and slowly, under the new authoritarian regime that followed the military coup of 1926, which brought to a close a series of initiatives begun in 1870 (see the entry for "Primary Education" [*Ensino primário*], in Rosas and Brito 1996; see also Ramos 1994; Andrade 2001). In the rural parishes of the Minho referred to above, the local

establishment of official primary schools was characteristically late in coming and only happened in the 1940s. As such, a great many of the adult inhabitants of this region were illiterate, while the rest of them were educated in private schools run by *mestres* [independent schoolmasters] who served a privileged minority of students, in substandard working conditions. The feebleness of formal education in Galicia until the 1940s reflected the general state of affairs throughout the whole of Spain (see for example Bello 1973, an impressive document that draws together observations made in Galicia in 1929, part of a group of studies conducted under the auspices of the state that describe a dramatic situation). However it was the construction of schools and the hiring of schoolmasters in the rural areas of Galicia that justified many of the association-creating activities of Galician emigrants in South America in the first decades of the twentieth century with the intention of correcting the great lack of state initiatives (Nuñez Seixas 1988).

9. See chapter 2 with respect to Galicia; see, generally, for Spain, Morales Moya 1998, Fusi 2000, and Álvarez Junco 2001; Revel 1989 and Williams 1988: 264–66.

10. See the brilliant study by Peter Sahlins (1989); see also the distinctions proposed between "border" and "frontier" by Giddens (1985) and as well the "nuances" suggested by the detailed considerations of Revel (1989).

11. In fact, these are formulations present in the various peripheral nationalistic discourses. In Galicia this curious topic was approached in a suggestive fashion (López Mira, 1998).

12. The Galicianist discourse was articulated at the end of the nineteenth century and the first decades of the twentieth by educated elites of the middle class, in many cases state civil servants; of relevance here is that the number of teachers of the state educational system was impressive in their numbers (Beramendi and Nuñez Seixas 1995; Villares 1997; see also the data presented by Hroch 2000 with respect to the social constitution of the nationalist movements in a variety of European contexts).

13. Where, by the way, during the 1880s, the Catalanistic discourse was taking shape, the first—and most successful—of the peripheral nationalisms that arose in the Peninsular context (Marfany 1995; Tusell 1998). Fusi (2000) found a direct relationship between the precocious success nationalism in Catalonia had and the vitality of the local press. Today, a wide range of publishing activity in the Catalan language sustains the most ample "community of readers," unequalled among official minority languages in Spain. The vitality of the "print capitalism" based in Barcelona is very well known, in fact; for example, it is there that a range of works that take Galicia as their subject are still published today, for the most part written by authors with nationalist interests.

14. In the Iberian Peninsula these publishing initiatives, which in the decades of the 1880s and 1890s were enhanced through elaborate illustrations, were mostly inspired by French examples. The importance that various methods of reproducing images—newly available and perfected at the time—had in these projects is quite significant, since they allowed for imagining, literally, the particularities attributed to nations, and for the spreading of the capacity to recognize them. The considerations that might grow out of a regard for the ideological fundamentals of projects like *España. Sus Monumentos y Artes. Su naturaleza e história* are endless; but we might also cite the similar and equally lavish *A Arte e a Natureza em Portugal* [*Art and Nature in Portugal*] (1902). For example, terms such as *art, heritage,* and *nature,* whose relationship to the formulation of nationalist discourses was unequivocal, gained new meanings during the nineteenth century. I refer the reader to some of the most relevant comparative literature: for example, Le Goff (1984), Smiles (1994), Sears

(1989), Belgum (1998), Cachin (1997), França (1993), Tobia (1998), Frykman and Löfgren (1996), and Riegl (1999).

15. For example, it is as common in the Minho as it is in Galicia to find complete collections of illustrated magazines that from the late nineteenth to the early twentieth century spread this kind of knowledge in manor houses and in the homes of the rural bourgeoisie. What is more, in these two contexts we find not only subscribers, but also assiduous and relatively famous contributors to said magazines living in the countryside. A famous intellectual of the first half of the twentieth century, the poet António Correia de Oliveira (1878–1960), resided for decades on an estate in one of the parishes where I did field work in the Minho. He can be counted among one of the most notable "*reaportugueseadores*" (Ramos 1994), namely because he was an illustrious singer of rural Minhotan traditions, recognized in his time as a "nationalist poet." The poet's attempt to *reaportuguesar* [to Portugalize once again] his coparishioners was, however, discreet: they did not know his verses and recall him as a distant figure, only rarely glimpsed outside the walls of his property. Correia de Oliveira, according to the stories of his visitors, kept the windows of his manor house that gave to the sea permanently closed. In this way he wanted to symbolize his position on the "vocation" and "destiny" of the "Portuguese nation" (Ramos 1994, for an account of these positions at the end of the nineteenth century and the beginning of the twentieth). Locally, the closed windows of the manor house were recalled only as one of the many eccentricities of the behavior of this poet and husband of the *hidalga*. An example in Galicia can be recognized in the story of the famous writer Emília Pardo Bazán (1851–1921), who lived for long periods in her *pazo* (or small palace) on the outskirts of the city of A Coruña.

16. In this paragraph I follow very closely comparative suggestions proposed in two important works by W. Christian (1992 and 1996; see as well Turner and Turner 1978). Cf., on the other hand, Mosse (1988), who offers a useful résumé of the most significant ideological confrontations that marked Europe during the nineteenth century and the first half of the following century, emphasizing the militant resistances on the part of the Catholic Church to the laicization of society. Jon Juaristi (1999) furnishes many revealing notes—even though they are hurried and hardly systematic—on the appropriations of the Marian cults by Basque nationalism of the twentieth century. By contrast, the works of Christian prove the relevance of the echoes of the state in the most significant apparitions verified in the first decades of the twentieth century and the political uses that they inspired at this level. Such uses would have been common in various countries, patent in the stereotyped contents of the messages transmitted by the seers about the destiny of nations and the world. With respect to Portugal, the work of Pierre Sanchis (1983) is especially curious for the variety of references that he proposes, giving an account of the transformations of the forms of religiosity and of the respective relationships with the political circumstances that thrived at the state level during the twentieth century.

17. A paraphrase of Weber's famous study, *Peasants and Frenchmen: The Modernization of Rural France 1870–1914* (1976).

18. See a recent debate between Borofsky and others (2001), in which Richard Shweder provides a summary critique of the influential definitions of this central notion; see also Kuper's recent reflections (1999), which demonstrate great latitude and perspective.

19. See, for example, Stocking (1968) and also Handler (2000), Kuper (1999), Barnard and Spencer (1996), and Barth (1992). These are perspectives that can be expanded by consulting Williams (1993 and 1988), Eagleton (2000) or even Eliot (1996).

Liss (1996) approached the inheritance of a German education in the work of Franz Boas, in whose valorization of the singularity of cultures Stocking (1968) perceives more an echo of Herder than of Tyler; see even Eksteins (2000) and Geuss (1996) for his use of the notion of *Kultur* and of *Bildung* in Germany in the nineteenth century and at the beginning of the twentieth.

20. Significantly, a text by José Cutileiro himself, published in 1971 in Portugal, analyzes, in a surprisingly unforgiving fashion, the vestiges of colonialist postures in the early practice of British social anthropology in the context of Southern Europe (1971b). A related denunciation is taken up again, even more severely, but by now with greater subtlety in a later text by Pina-Cabral (1991).

21. These worries are mainly justified because "patronage" is a central theme in this work. This had been John Campbell's lesson (Campbell 1964, one of the titles cited by Cutileiro in the brief bibliography of *Ricos e Pobres no Alentejo*). Cutileiro's work, however, stands out in the field for the detailed historical and political contextualization of state affairs (Davis 1977). The author's native status and great knowledge of the political conditions in force at the level of the state explain these peculiar characteristics of his study (see as well Lisón Tolosana 1966, a similar example, even if his preoccupations with political contextualization are less clear).

22. This is an example of interrogations that are today more easily articulated form the point of view of those interests that have been key in recent years (see, as examples, Herzfeld 1986, 1987, 2000; Handler 1988; Thomas 1982; Appadurai 1988; Foster 1991; Fernandez 1986, 1994; Lomnitz-Adler 1992).

Chapter 2

On Galicia Day

Many are the celebrations that take place in Santiago de Compostela on 25 July, each one of them involving multitudes. Santiago is the city's patron saint; this is the *great day* of celebrations promoted by the *concello* [city council] and the streets and the parks fill with people, all of them in a festive mood. Religious celebrations also reach their peak on this day on which the flux of pilgrims is at its highest. Likewise, Santiago is the *patrón de España,* and Compostela—where supposedly the Apostle is entombed[1]—has become the center of highly ceremonial, state-sponsored commemorations. More recently 25 July was given the status of a national Galician holiday; for this reason new ceremonies and more or less ritualized political manifestations have emerged linked to this day (Connerton 1989), a new reason for the increase in the numbers of people who flow into the city from all across Galicia.

Since 1643 the state commemorations of 25 July have been formalized by Spain's act of consecrating its patron. This act is designated as the *ofrenda al Apóstol* and takes place in the cathedral at the end of the morning. From this date onwards, the *ofrenda* could count on the occasional presence of the king—as happened recently, in 1999—or of one of his representatives, the *delegado regio;* it is always a political moment of great solemnity. Under Franco the symbolic importance of this day was given state prominence. Particularly emphasized was the imperial and militaristic dimension of the cult of the Apostle. Throughout the centuries martial associations have lain thick and heavy over the invocation of Santiago and are still a patent fixture in the official ceremonies held each year by the state in Compostela.

But 25 July has also been considered, since 1920, to be the *Dia de Galiza,* a denomination defined by the Irmandades da Fala, the first political association in Galicia to formulate a doctrine and maintain explicit nationalist claims. In 1978—sheltered by the new democratic constitution of that year—the *Día Nacional de Galicia* was brought into law by a decree issued by the Xunta de Galicia (Cores 1985). An institutional act that takes place in the Galician parliament is the main focus of this special day. But it is also formally marked as part of the state celebrations that is referred to in the previous paragraph: for the last two decades, it is the *España de las autonomías* that has been celebrated in the *ofrendas al Apóstol.*

Today, in spite of an official designation that is in force—*Día Nacional de Galicia*—25 July can be referred to in other ways that also carry a national Galician sense. *Día da Patria Galega* is the alternative designation that carries the most ideological weight. This very precise form—emerging in 1973 and employed in writing by the nationalist left[2]—has crystallized into an intentional counterpoint to the official designation that emerged later and is to this day unacceptable to those sectors. *O 25 de Xullo,* however, is the colloquial form most used by the nationalists to refer to this special day; this was how my informants in Santiago ordinarily designated it, even if sometimes they would use *Día da Patria*—a simplified form, also effective in establishing a distinction from the official designation.

On one occasion, an Andalusian informant—invoking the imposed celebrations of the *patrón de España* holiday—told me that "25 July was the day of almost everything" under the Franco regime. In the Galicia of the most recent decades the pertinence of this ironic observation has been forcefully underlined, because the overlapping of holidays and designations that fall under the invocation of this day have grown, a fact that multiplies the possibilities for analyzing the symbolism behind it (see Geertz 1973). In this chapter, based on observations made in Santiago de Compostela on this date for four consecutive years, 1997–2000, as well as on various articles appearing in newspapers, I will describe the typical way in which of some of these commemorative acts are played out. I will concentrate on an account of the forms used by political organizations of the nationalist left in their representation of Galician society and culture on this very important day. On these occasions, however, other rituals and symbols are put into play, whose "operational meaning" (Turner 1967: 51) alludes to other, wider levels of community, which will also be important to take into consideration.

A Day of Almost Everything

For many people in Galicia, 25 July continues to be designated as *Día de Santiago* or *de Apóstolo,* old ways of naming it whose use persists.

In these names we can recognize a more universal meaning than those that were noted in previous paragraphs, even if it is difficult to detach the religious connotations of Santiago from appropriations of his figure by the state, which have been prominent over the years in Spain. I noted in the previous chapter the debilities that marked the process of the "nationalization of the masses" in Spain up until the end of the 1930s. I also gave an account of how this underwent important steps under the dictatorial regime of General Franco, when the state provided ideological and material resources, with an efficiency that was until then unprecedented, in order to inculcate nationalizing references. Militant National Catholicism became intertwined with the propagandistic efforts of the state, creating one of the more emblematic characteristics of the regime in power until 1975 (Carr 1982; Tusell 1998).

Today the recognition of the Apostle Santiago as *patrón de España* would be a reference to the shared culture of the Spaniards who grew up under the Franco regime. The equestrian and bellicose figuration of *Santiago Matamoros* [St. James the Moor Slayer] is familiar to everyone; it was reproduced with special intensity during the dictatorship in a diversity of forms once its uses—already very old—were intensified as a national symbol of Spain. Today, however, an important part of Galician society sees the overlapping of meanings that state appropriations of this icon presume as polemical. These are polemics that emerge within the ambit of the Galician discourse already referenced by other symbolic valuations consolidated over time. The majority of Galicianist authors would emphasize with justified pride how effective the European and universal projection of Santiago and their city is, while suggesting another form of representing the apostle, as "St. James the Pilgrim." From this perspective, the iconic figuration of Santiago as *Matamoros* favored by state appropriations through the centuries and up until 1975 is frequently and justifiably discredited.

Santiago de Compostela has been one of the most well-known destinations of Christian pilgrimage throughout nearly a millennium—the Galician Jerusalem, or the Galician Rome, as is so often heard, even if its projection was more intense during the first centuries of the second millennium, as I have already pointed out in the first chapter. Let me cite two characteristic passages from Ramón Otero Pedrayo (1888–1976), one of the most eminent of Galicianist intellectuals of the twentieth century:[3]

> Because Zebedeu's son, the one who laid the nets into the warn waters of the sea of Galilee, wanted to lay them in the endless, roaring Atlantic; if he was born Jewish he remained Galician by the choosing of his tomb, a voluntary agreement and not dependant upon fate as happens with births. In this way Santiago was Galician and was universal, attracting all

of Christianity, without distinguishing between lineage or languages. Do
you want a better and more exemplary definition of *Patria Galega*? (cit.
in Quintana e Valcárcel 1988: 49)

The insistence on these topics, which Otero glosses in inimitable
fashion, becomes particularly intense in the first period of affirmation of
the Galician nationalist movement between 1918 and 1936 (see chapter
3). In the pages of periodicals, and under a variety of literary and iconographic forms, the intentions to Galicianize the representations of the
apostle become very clear, invested, as they were, with a symbolism that
differentiated Galicia and its presumed "European" vocation. This connection with Europe would be justified by remote ethnic relations and
by the regularity of traffic maintained by the pilgrimages to Compostela.
This interpretation was proclaimed as a counterpoint to a supposed in-
troversion that the rest of Spain suffered from and that the figure of the
Matamoros symbolized.

The persistence of older forms for designating 25 July can be understood as an indication of the weakness of the attempt to nationalize the key identifications of the inhabitants of Galicia. However, in
more recent decades, the process has accelerated. Its most important
protagonists, as we have seen, are the autonomous government of the
Community and the left wing of the nationalist movement. Indeed—
beyond the confusions imposed by the coexistence of various designations—there are many Galicians who still ignore this process, or who
possess few references to the new commemorative meaning of 25 July
as *Día Nacional de Galicia* or *Día da Patria Galega*. For example, each
year televised surveys are conducted on the street in order to understand
how new designations of national meaning are gaining currency. Many
of the responses that the reporters of TVG [Galician Television] obtain
are notably hesitant. In the end, the majority of Galicians grew up under
Francoism, a period of systematic repression of nationalist manifestations, while the commemorative traditions invented by the institutions
of the autonomous government and by the nationalist movement are
still recent.

Curiously, already in 1923 an article from the publication *A Nosa
Terra* would suggest the following in a special edition dedicated to the
Día de Galicia: "For the last three years we, the nationalists, have come
to celebrate the *Día de Galicia* and today it is all Galicians who celebrate
this patriotic festivity, understanding its transcendent symbolism" (*A
Nosa Terra*, no. 189, 1923).[4] This was a very optimistic and militant
description, which we can securely put into perspective. The next number of the same periodical, of 15 August, gave an account of how insignificant and sparse the commemorations had been. It surveyed the few

localities where Galician flags had been raised and the scarcity of festive mobilizations that were verified only in the two major cities, Vigo and A Coruña. Not even in Compostela were initiatives registered, the city where, today, all of the *25 de Xullo* commemorations, as I have already pointed out, are centered. The fact that there were only four hundred copies of the issue distributed on 25 July 1923 (*A Nosa Terra,* no. 190, 1923) is particularly suggestive of the difficulties of mobilization. If we follow the news of these commemorative acts in the press of the day until 1936, our general impression will be of the sparse participation that the celebrations of the *Día de Galicia* inspired, except for perhaps in the literary celebrations that were reported in the few publications sympathetic to the incipient nationalist movement, but which were, at any rate, erudite and appealed only at a quasi-emotional level.

During the dictatorship of Primo de Rivera (1923–1930) mass patriotic demonstrations were hardly given full rein; the years of the Second Republic were few and troubled, and very soon after 1936 all commemorative acts with a Galician character were prohibited. Under the autocratic regime of Franco, only a single mass in memory of the poet Rosalía de Castro (1837–1885) marked this special day. According to photographic documentation, just a few dozen people appeared at the mass—which took place in the Church of Santo Domingo de Bonaval, the Panteón de Galegos Ilustres; nevertheless, this was inevitably the reference given when my Galician informants spoke of the persistence of nationalist ideas during the dictatorship. In 1973, when the regime had already weakened and the militants of the extreme nationalist left had become clandestinely active, the *misa de Rosalía* began to attract more people. There were confrontations with the police, and the day now carried, definitively, the designation *Día da Patria Galega,* which from that point on was appropriated by the sectors mentioned above. But it has only been in the most recent years of the *transición democrática,* starting in 1976, that the nationalist commemorations of 25 July in Santiago de Compostela have gained permanent and multitudinous expressions.[5]

The concentration of nationalist demonstrations in Santiago on 25 July will provide a measure of the strengths and weaknesses of the movement. The symbolic reasons used to justify why Galicianists gather in Santiago are very important, and today many thousands participate in the *Día da Patria* commemorations. But this is also a demonstration of its weaknesses: should these demonstrations spread to the various cities and towns of Galicia, it is hard to imagine that they could be significant. The establishment of the city of Santiago as the center of the commemorations of 25 July in the national sense was propitiated by various factors that converged over time. In the first place, it has to do with the result of the character of the *Día de Galicia* rallies over many decades: discreet and attended by only small minorities. We saw in the religious act of the homage to Rosalía the first effective expression of this focusing of commemorations within the city that, before, were held outside of Compostela. In a more indistinct fashion, Santiago had been, since the nineteenth century, accumulating some of the "sites of memory," a process mainly consolidated in recent years. On the other hand, the centrality granted to Santiago following the institutionalization of *España de las autonomías* in 1978 made the city the most efficacious stage for all the claims of sovereignty and for the *anticentralista* protests supported by the nationalist movement.

As we will see below, some of the most significant texts written for the commemorations of the date—or, more generally, about being Galician—suggest on an emotional level a generalized and simultaneous sharing by all of Galicia of these festive feelings and a sense of belonging. In fact, the history of Galicianism is otherwise, and was contrived out of the efforts of a small number of intellectuals and politicians devoted to the creation of these feelings of communion. Their intentions often fell flat because of the indifference of the masses, as innumerable texts of various periods will also easily suggest.

Many of the people that I met in Santiago de Compostela were well informed of the meaning that is today attributed to 25 July by the nationalist movement; for a good part of my local informants, *O 25 de Xullo* was very strictly identified with the *Día da Patria Galega*. They habitually disdained that which they said were the Spanish connotations of the official celebrations promoted as the *Día Nacional de Galicia,* viewed as a mere extension of the state celebrations of the *patrón de España.* However, *Día da Patria Galega* is, in fact, the least recognized designation. Indeed, more easily recognized are the older and simpler designations that carry a religious connotation, like the Day of the Apostle, or *Día de Santiago.* On the other hand, in terms of that which touches upon the national sense of the commemoration, *Día de Galicia* has become the most cross-cutting and popular of the current designations, because the history of its uses stretches back the furthest, to the 1920s, and also because it overlaps the designation made official in 1978.

In certain circumstances, the use of the more traditional designations can be interpreted as political. I came to understand this well in July of 2001, when a Compostelan friend told me that he would have to stay home if I went to Santiago on the *Día do Apóstolo.* During this telephone conversation, the term that I was using was *aportuguesado* [that is, slanted toward the Portuguese] and quite neutral, "Dia da Galiza." On the other hand, Juan Berenguel clearly knew about my scholarly interests; so the repeated use that he made of that form of designation (*Día do Apostólo*) was transparently emphatic. My informant was an academic, and, in addition to our friendship, he was very conscious of his condition as "informant" and of the uses I would make of his opinions. In this way he emphasized his disdain for the left-wing factions of the Galicianist movement. For a better understanding of the way in which the various commemorative ceremonies that take place in Compostela on 25 July unfold, I believe that the persistence of these equivocal terminologies should be emphasized from the beginning. According to the celebrated title by J. L. Austin, the designations for this day also occurred as words that are used "to do things" (Austin 1970). Namely, they reflect ideological dissensions—brought to the fore by the presence of a specific nationalist discourse—which are very prominent in the context of contemporary Galician society.

The Galician Xunta and the Parliament conduct the official commemorations of the *Día Nacional de Galicia* with specific ceremonies— which the majority of Galicians only get news of through full coverage via TVG. These consist of a ceremonial session that takes place in the Galician Parliament on the afternoon of 25 July, at the end of which *medallas de Galicia* are awarded to institutions and Galician citizens whose actions have been considered relevant. Then the president of the Galician Xunta will lay flowers on the tomb of Alfonso Daniel Rodríguez Castelao (1886–1950), in the Panteón de Galegos Ilustres, an act that is replicated in various ways, as we will see below. Buried alongside Rosalía de Castro and other notable Galicians, Castelao is today the most remembered figure in the history of the Galicianist struggle for recognition. An iconic figure acknowledged generally throughout Galicia, his ideas are, as we shall see below, widely cited in nationalist demonstrations on the *25 de Xullo*. But the appropriations of this historical figure that have occurred in Galicia during the last two decades are many and complex; his biography and the contemporary appropriations of his memory justify a closer look, which will be necessarily brief.

Castelao was a cartoonist and a plastic artist, but also a nationalist politician and an intellectual who worked in a variety of literary forms. He was very active in his *Terra* until 1936, and he died in exile in Buenos Aires in 1950. Among the survivors of Franco's purges of the Galician sphere, he was the most active in contesting the new regime from his various locations of exile. As far back as the beginning of the last century his cartoons and their captions had become famous in Galicia for the bitter humor he employed to denounce the misery and oppression from which the poorest of Galicians, his contemporaries, suffered. Over the years his political engagement was highlighted in his graphic work as it appeared in a variety of newspapers, magazines, and exhibitions. Today these cartoons, captioned with sayings that have become proverbial, are reprinted in a range of formats and frequently inscribed as graffiti, recognizable today by a majority of Galicians.

The nationalist left sanctified the figure and the political opinions of Castelao—above all, those which were contained in his most important work, the book *Sempre en Galiza* (1943)—as emblematic references for their claims. But today Castelao is also an icon that has been officially appropriated by the upper hierarchies of the Galician government, which the PP of G [Partido Popular de Galicia, the Popular Party of Galicia] controls. These intersecting appropriations of his memory have made him into a guardian figure for the national culture that has been produced in Galicia during recent decades. Castelao's mortal remains were transferred from Buenos Aires to the Panteón in 1984, via an initiative of the centrist coalition, which held power in the first years of the autonomous government. This spectacular initiative angered many nationalist sectors, which viewed the political act as an abusive and opportunistic appropriation; but as well, the more firmly *españolista* right wing resented the sanctification, enabled by the conveniences of a new political reality, of a supposed *rojo* [a red, i.e., leftist in a colloquial sense] and secessionist. There were various demonstrations and confrontations provoked by this polemical process of transfer.

There are two tombs in Santiago around which form the focal point for people attending the commemorations of 25 July: that of St. James, which is inside the cathedral, and that of Castelao, located in the Panteón de Galegos Ilustres. This location, eminent in the Galicianist memory, was instituted when, in 1891, the mortal remains of the poet Rosalía de Castro were transferred to the church of the old Bonaval convent near the old part of the city. Over time, the remains of five important figures were buried there in the following order: Alfredo Brañas (1859–1900), politician and theorist of Galician regionalism; the sculptor Francisco Asorey (1889–1961); Ramón Cabanillas (1876–1959), celebrated as the *poeta da raza;* Domingos Fontán (1788–1866), geographer and author of the first modern map of Galicia; and, as mentioned above, A.D.R. Castelao. Today, around the perimeter of the former Dominican convent's walls, we find, in addition to the Panteón, the Museo do Pobo Galego and the Centro Galego de Arte Contemporánea, an institutional triangle that makes this location a dense repository of Galician national memory. But it is principally regarding the cathedral and the tomb of the Apostle that the symbolic disputes about 25 July are the tensest.

Around the Cathedral

It is still morning when the crowds gather in Compostela to participate in a series of impressive commemorative acts: the state ceremonies,
which culminate in the *ofrenda al Apóstol* and the political rally of the
Bloque Nacionalista Galego (BNG). The state-sponsored ceremonies
last through the morning, beginning with a military parade in the Praza
do Obradoiro in front of the cathedral, on the western end; this is followed by a procession comprised of a number of military, ecclesiastical,
and civil authorities; then the *misa del Apóstol* is held, finishing with the
reading of the *ofrenda,* solemnly delivered by the king or by the royal
delegate. Sometime later nearing lunchtime, by 1:30 PM, the BNG's
large rally takes place in the Praza da Quintana—contiguous with the
east façade of the cathedral—after the crowd that attended the *misa del
Apóstol* and the *ofrenda* within the cathedral have dispersed.

The military festivities unfold in front of the representatives of the
state, of the autonomous government, and of the army. In 1999, when
the king of Spain was present, all of the dignitaries gathered upon an
ostentatious platform installed opposite the Rajoy palace (which closes
the square on its western end), in front of the cathedral. This ceremony
attracts many tourists and curiosity seekers, a silent crowd, suspended
in the solemnity of the act, which is punctuated by the commands that
direct the mass of troops present. The spectators are contained in a very
small area of the square—which opens onto Rúa do Franco, where the
largest part of the crowd gathers—so that the review of the troops can
proceed freely, with the highest degree of solemnity, over the stone-
paved Obradoiro. In 1998, from the midst of the spectators, an unexpected voice was raised: *Viva Galiza Ceibe!* [Long live free Galicia!]—the
man who had yelled out was immediately and forcefully removed from
the square by the military police.

Once the troops have dispersed, the hieratic cortege enters the square.
It includes the city's archbishop, other bishops, the chapter of the cathedral, and the brethren of the military orders, carrying a small image
of the pilgrim Santiago in silver on a litter beneath an ornate canopy.
The procession circles outside the cathedral from the Porta de Praterías
on the south façade, in a counterclockwise direction, in order to meet
the dignitaries who leave the platform and follow the religious cortege,
which finally climbs the stairs and enters the church. It is in front of
Santiago's altar that the *ofrenda al Apóstol* occurs, the reading of a text by
the king or by his delegate, to which the Compostelan prelate responds.
The ceremony culminates in a moment that is famous among all visitors

to Compostela, the incensing of the church. The emotion of the people present is palpable when the gigantic censer—the *botafumeiro*—glides over their heads, with each one of its swings from one end of the nave to the other opening mouths in dumbfounded *ohs*!

Also impressive are the commemorations of the *Día do Patria Galega* organized by the BNG. The commemorative program, staged by this "front" of parties and nationalist associations, is very orderly and complex, following a well-scripted plan that remains relatively unaltered year to year. It consists of a large parade that winds its way through the old part of Compostela before flowing into the Praza da Quintana. This is where the demonstration is held, which always ends with a moving rendition of the Galician anthem by the thousands of people present. Later a picnic is held in a chestnut wood on the edge of the city, already described as "traditional" in the news reports of recent years.

In addition to the area around the cathedral, throughout the old city sundry other 25 July commemorations take place. These are sponsored by various and hardly representative political forces. In 1998, for example, a very small group of members of an organization of the extreme right congregated in the Praza Mazarelos, in a demonstration protesting against the separatist connotations that they saw in all of the other commemorations held in the city on that day. They evoked the *patrón de España* and his imperial avatar, a conception that today has been discredited by all of the other political sectors of Spanish society. This particular demonstration was not held in the years following 1998. My informants in Santiago told me that these gatherings had had importance mainly in the years of transition after the death of Franco and that at the time there were frequent and serious physical confrontations with nationalist militants.

On the other hand, an independentist organization of the extreme left, the FPG—Frente Popular Galega—habitually gathers in the small Praza do Toural to commemorate the *Día da Patria Galega*. There are many red flags and perhaps less than 150 supporters present. They are hemmed in by an even larger crowd of the curious, while Xosé Luís Méndez Ferrín speaks from the platform, the writer who some hope will be the first Nobel Prize winner working in the Galician language. Another very loud group of young people, one of the other formations (also independentist) of the extreme left, the AMI—Assembleia da Mocidade Independentista—march rapidly up and down the cities most important streets; I see them passing by on the Preguntoiro, down the Rúa Nova, and Rúa Vilar. They excite the tourists who take many photographs; they run quickly through the streets with the red flags, blue and white Galician flags, effigies of Che Guevara and of Castelao, Palestinian scarves, and even some Portuguese flags, shouting slogans against *globalización, patriarcalismo,* and *españolista* oppression.

These days the Esquerda Galega—a "party of white collar workers"—of the moderate left normally enacts a discreet *ofrenda floral* to Castelao in the Panteón de Galegos Ilustres. A variety of similar offerings, starting the day before and staggered with precision to avoid embarrassing overlaps, are made there. Other political forces extremely important in the political spectrum of the Comunidade Autónoma, like the PP of G or the PS of G (Partido Socialista de Galicia), do not stage notable public demonstrations on 25 July, except for these very characteristic *ofrendas florais* made to the most charismatic of the ideologues of Galician nationalism.

Galicia Rising

In 2000 I traveled early one morning from Ourense to Santiago de Compostela in order to attend the commemorations of the *25 de Xullo*. At dinner the day before, my local informants seemed to me quite unmotivated; they were two university teachers, very dedicated nationalists, but I could not convince them to accompany me the following morning. They told me that the heroic days of participating in the *Día da Patria,* when this had called for a more demanding militant stance at the end of the 1970s and the beginning of the following decade, were already past. At the time there had been far fewer participants and a very plausible risk of confrontations with protesting *españolistas* and with the police. While the nationalist demonstrations were forbidden access to the interior of the old city and to the Praza da Quintana, which would change starting in 1984, participants frequently experienced police charges. Their evocation of excursions organized from Ourense at the end of the 1970s when they were both very young were nostalgic in tone; they described to me how those trips on the *25 de Xullo* to Santiago were like pilgrimages. Today, in their opinion, the spirit of those years of resistance and enthusiasm had somehow been broken. Today, everyone goes in their own car; in Santiago the gathering is well organized and, as a result, less enthusiastic, and the demands of the supporters were framed within narrow and predictable boundaries.

It rained heavily as I made my way to Santiago, still very early in the morning. I didn't see a single one of those famous busses that harked back to the "heroic" times of my Ourense acquaintances. The traffic was slow and already getting denser after Lalín; I saw some Galician flags on the automobiles that passed me. The weather started to clear while the BNG parade began to come together in the Alameda de Santa Susana.

Despite the disengagement of my friends from Ourense, the truth is that in the years in which I went to the commemorations of the *25 de Xullo* the number of participants at the nationalists' big demonstration grew increasingly, making the Praza da Quintana seem increasingly smaller. According to the calculations—always optimistic—which appeared in *A Nosa Terra*, there were 20,000 demonstrators in 2001. From the end of the 1970s onwards, this same publication invariably refers to gatherings above 10,000 people; in 1985 it reports a crowd of 30,000 *25 de Xullo* demonstrators. But these are numbers that the calculations of the police and reporters of the most important daily newspapers published in Galicia always downplay significantly. In any case, no one— not even *Nosa Terra*—denied that the 2001 concentration of people had been the largest ever to be brought together for the commemoration of the *Día da Patria Galega*. There were many people who couldn't get into the Praza da Quintana and who listened to the speeches from the streets leading to it, on the stairs of the Porta de Praterías or by the Acebacheria outside the square.

Various commentators from the media and also many of my informants concur in indicating a move towards the political center—a growing moderation—in the discourse of the BNG in recent years. This moderation is patent in the concrete proposals for good governance, or in defense of the various causes capable of resonating widely among the populace; this seemed to be proved by the huge turnout at the 2001 demonstration. There have been gains in the election results of the BNG, and among its leaders there is the hope of participating in the government of the Comunidade Autónoma sometime in the near future. The most optimistic among them combine these expectations with a hoped-for crumbling of the party in power in the immediate aftermath of the retirement of the charismatic Manuel Fraga, already an octogenarian in noticeably bad health.[6] A piece written on a site of one of the most radical groups of the Galician left—the AMI (Assembleia da Mocidade Independentista) recently described the BNG with contempt and a surprising string of adjectives: *pseudonacionalismo moderado galeguista institucional* (www.galizalivre.org). As such, they were denouncing the *posibilismo* and the tactical acceptance of the limits of the *Estatuto de Autonomía* that has guided the actions of the BNG. However, an outside observer—in spite of my disillusioned Ourensean informants or the adjectives of the Mocidade Independentista—would be surprised by the force of the paradoxes offered up in the speeches of the *25 de Xullo* in the Praza da Quintana, whose general tenor I will describe below.

Each year that I attended the commemorations I was impressed by the unchanging sequence of commemorative acts organized by the BNG. The route of the parade is repeated, parting from the Alameda, the old meeting place of the peasants—*labregos*—coming from the villages to participate in the weekly cattle fair which was held there until 1971. The organization is taken care of ahead of time, with a great hubbub and a lot of enthusiasm, until, finally, with everything in order, the march sets off. The pipers, dressed formally in white and with red sashes at the waist, lead the way, separate from the rest. These are followed by the party leaders and the foreign guests.[7] Finally the crowd brings up the rear. Moving counterclockwise, the march rounds a part of the old city and winds through one of the doors of the old wall and finally arrives at the Praza da Quintana.[8] The march is noisy: there are more pipers scattered through the procession and some are playing the drums, interrupting the chants that rise up from the crowd. These can get drowned out, but are inevitably repeated by those who come behind. I see some of my acquaintances pass by in the parade, some in the front line, near the leaders, others scattered in the crowd, carrying Galician flags or banners printed with slogans. I wave to them. The city is partially surrounded by the immense cortège, in which each year new groups are added, new claims made in an attempt to allegorically represent Galicia as a nation in constant expansion. For example, it was only in 2000 that I noticed the presence of groups of gays and lesbians, with rainbow-colored placards and banners; more common was the presence of workers of well-known firms in crisis and *colectivos* of neighbors, environmentalists, feminists, etc.

The march moved down the street, going around the old walled enclosure, until it penetrated the narrow streets of the center of the city. At last, the participants of the parade gathered in an enormous crowd, filling little by little the whole of the Praza da Quintana. It would not be at all inaccurate to say that in the propaganda of the BNG and the speeches delivered that day, that one could find suggestions that this parade represented the true Galicia, and not the mere rally of a political party. In the report on the *25 de Xullo* of 2001 published in *A Nosa Terra* the procession is described in disconcerting fashion:

> Why is it that they look at us like that? Those of us who are on the way to the Praza da Quintana and curious tourists that contemplate us from a distance observing us disapprovingly, like people from a distant planet. Perhaps they're waiting for one of the three gift-bearing Wise Men to toss them caramels. Now we're thinking: don't stare at us like that, join the march. Some do, discovering that the fact of not being Galician today is not an obstacle to entertainment and learning. To attend the *Día da*

Patria is to learn about our popular culture, our customs and also our gastronomy. The march's political meaning does not preclude the presence of people of other nationalities. (*A Nosa Terra* 27/7/2001)

The lightness of the tone of this recent description contrasts with others that are quite a bit more serious and that can be found in the same newspaper over the years, especially up until 1983, a year of change in all of Spain, when conditions of democratic normality began to be consolidated, and to which a majority of the nationalist parties accommodated themselves (Tusell 1999c). In this description from *A Nosa Terra*, we will recognize certain affinities with the description of a *desfile folclórico* in Asturias by the anthropologist James Fernandez; some of his conclusions about the way in which certain representations of provincial cultures have become, in recent years, reconcilable with those of the state of Spain seem entirely reasonable. Fernandez accounts for the ironic tendencies patent in the first case, which contrast with the rigorous seriousness in the case of the second (Fernandez 1986: 288–92). I believe that the similarity is partial, however, because it is the nation that makes up the Bloque parades, and the nation that informs the speeches given at the demonstration as they articulate declarations of principle that are essential to the Galician nationalist discourse. These speeches are made with a definitive seriousness that goes beyond the festive celebration of the differences between national cultures, which are so well tolerated in the Spain of recent years, and which the passage cited above in some way seems to suggest. The coexistence of different registers of seriousness will account for some of the paradoxes that mark the political life in *España de las autonomías*.

In 1984, as we have seen, being a hinge-year in which the forms of commemoration observed today by the BNG were delineated, *A Nosa Terra* described the beginning of the demonstration in the Praza da Quintana (referred to as the "Praza do Nacionalismo") in the following manner: "The (political) act at Quintana had begun with a reading of passages from *Sempre en Galicia*, recited by Eduardo Gutiérrez, who directed himself to those present underlying the fact that Quintana has come to be the 'the symbol of the liberated *Terra*,' since here the voices of our predecessors had sounded" (*A Nosa Terra* 252, 30/7/84).

In the Quintana dos Mortos

In the speeches delivered at the BNG demonstration on each *Día da Patria*, the Praza da Quintana is always alluded to as the "Quintana dos Mortos." This is because an old cemetery dating back to the High Middle Ages was located there. This is a type of evocation with proven efficacy in nationalist discourses, one of nationalism's most characteristic "myths," as Anthony D. Smith suggests (1999). But, beyond this general verification it is important to underline the very special force that the mention of the dead has in legitimizing feelings of belonging to the community in Galicia. Since the end of the nineteenth century, this has been a theme favored in the ethnography done in Galicia. Today, I believe that it is significant that there are concurrences between the ethnographic recognition of this very specific characteristic, the importance of the evocation of the dead in the history of the nationalist discourse, and the objectification of culture (Handler 1988). I will try to demonstrate this point below (see the excursus annexed to chapter 5). Without further ado, I would like to account for the continuities that can be recognized in the Galician nationalist discourse, considering the allocutions given on the occasion of the *Día da Patria*. In these, the theme of the *Santa Compaña*—an imagined procession of the dead well known by anthropologists that have worked in Galicia—arises as a recurrent motif.

Alba de Groria is a beautiful text by Castelao, written during the 1940s when he was already exiled in Argentina. In reference to an imagined and ideal Galicia Day, we are offered a sequence of powerful metaphors with which to symbolize the fatherland. The first images of this text suspend all awareness of the cruel contingencies of history that followed in the years after 1936 and suggest that the Galician nation warrants the simultaneous participation in a fixed moment in time on 25 July (see Anderson 1991):

> "Today the bells of Compostela announce an ethnic celebration, daughter, perhaps, of a pantheistic religion predating Christianity, whose altar is mother earth. ... And the rhythmic tolling of the bells—of all the bells of Galicia, in a happy cacophony—like the tumult of astral horses arriving out of the celestial spiral pushing Apollo's chariot, which brings light and heat to the world in shadows. Today is the *Día de Galiza*, and this is how it begins.

> This is how the solemnity of this day begins, Galicia's largest celebration, the celebration of all Galicians. (1951: 1)

In the passages that follow, the theme of the *Santa Compaña* is glossed in a surprising way, an appropriation that confirms Castelao to be the most eminent of the mythmakers of Galicianism (Smith 1999). It should be noted that the preoccupation with creating myths was very present in the mind of Castelao, something he shared with some of his

contemporaries—those who were more informed about certain of the
more influential political and philosophical currents of the end of the
nineteenth century and beginning of the twentieth.[9] In this perspective—contrary to the ethnographic descriptions of this "corporación de
mortos," which is always parochial (Lisón Tolosana 1988)—a crucial
transmutation of representativeness occurs in the pages *Alba de Groria*.
Suddenly we have the evocation of the *Santa Compaña* as an allegory
for the history of Galicia: "It is better to evoke something of the unreal,
something purely imaginary, something that with its symbolism lets us
see the past in taking advantage of the future, as a good experience. We
can imagine, for example, a *Santa Compaña* of immortal Galicians in an
unending procession." Castelao then cites figures from Galician history,
a lengthy list covering many centuries, from the heresiarch Priscilano, in
the fourth century, to the figures that illuminated Galicia in the nineteenth century and in the beginning of the twentieth. The list is quite
inclusive, finding room for all of the most notable Galicians, even those
who devotedly served Castilian monarchs or those who wrote in Spanish. The enumeration ends with Ramon del Valle Inclán, who, at the
time, had only recently died, and to whose evocation Castelao attaches a
surprisingly awful note: "and in the end the great Don Ramón not completely fleshless." In this far-reaching evocation of the historical figures
born in Galicia there are many figures capable of being "suborned" who
marked the history of the Spanish state. But this is simply a rhetorical
step that precedes the negation of the contingencies of history so that
the eternity of the nation can be proclaimed:

> Fortunately, Galicia depends, for its eternity, on something more than a
> truncated history, it depends on a Tradition of imponderable value and
> this is what is most important for conquering the future.
>
> When the Santa Compaña of dead Galicians, that passes before our
> imagination, loses itself in the density of a distant forest, with this same
> imagination we will see, rising out of humus of mother earth, of our
> land, saturated with human ash, an infinite multitude of little lights and
> fireflies, who are the unnamed beings that no one remembers, all of them
> together forming the substratum of Galicia that couldn't be bribed. These
> nameless souls are the ones who created the idiom by which you speak,
> our culture, our arts, our ways and customs, after all, that which makes
> Galicia different. … This multitude of little lights and fireflies represent
> what we were, what we are and what we will always be, always, always.
> (1951: 3–4)

Very similar types of images are reiterated in the speech of the leader
of the BNG, Xosé Manuel Beiras,[10] which typically closes the Quintana

demonstration on the *25 de Xullo* with a vibrant performance. In fact, extensive citations of Castelao were a constant in the speeches that I heard from 1997 to 2000. According to the reports that I checked, these were citations that had been reiterated at many previous demonstrations on the *Día da Patria*. One can recognize in Beiras's speeches a framework of motifs already recurrent in the literature dating back to the 1920s and 1930s, when the first outbreak of Galician nationalism was consolidated, and which the book *Sempre en Galiza* would eventually summarize in 1943.

The pedagogy of the decisive themes of Galicianist claims can now be brought up to date with mentions of current political battles, pacts based on circumstances, and the short-term hopes in the random initiatives of the unions or the local political leaders. But it is the eternity of the Galician fatherland, the persistence of its injuries and of its struggles, and the millenary certainty in its future redemption that are always at issue in the closing speech at the Quintana demonstration; the *return to Ithaca,* as X. M. Beiras called it 1999 and 2000, puzzling the less schooled among the crowd. In 2001, the leader of the Bloque cited William Faulkner—the short story "As I Lay Dying." Also that year, in speaking about Manuel Fraga and of his government, Beiras said that they were "a power and a hierarchy that is already in a phase of agony." But he also cited Gabriel García Márquez and Franz Kafka. These were surprising literary allusions in this multitudinous context, where many *labregos* and *obreros* [farmers and factory workers] were present. Today the social base of support of the BNG, which counts on the votes of nearly a fifth of the Galician electorate, has already spread beyond its origins in rarified intellectual circles of extreme left.[11]

In 1998, Xosé Manuel Beiras opened his speech with extracts from one of Castelao's speeches dating back to 1945. To the crowd gathered in Quintana, he only identified the origin of his words after reading various paragraphs, when he said, inflecting his voice dramatically: "These words are not mine, my friends. These words that I have pronounced from the beginning until now, are, I repeat, not mine. These words, this discourse, these ideas that I am transmitting to you are, literally, Castelao's words." At issue in this passage are questions about the status of Galicia within the institutional framework of the Spanish state. The orator wanted to demonstrate the persistence of feuds and the reasons behind claims that had already been current in Castelao's day. In another passage from the same speech a replica of the *Alba de Groria* was created, taking up once again its powerful metaphors full of mythical allusions. The reiterated terms were once more about the eternity of the patria and the Galician tradition. The *Santa Compaña* of the Galician dead now included new martyrs and successes in addition to those that has already been proclaimed by Castelao in 1948:

> Because we are the future and not the past—but, yes, the tradition, that of Castelao and Bóveda, of Faraldo and Murguía, of Sarmiento and Feixóo, also of Foreiros de Nerga and Oseira, of the workers and the farmers, the industrial workers of the SOG, the INT and the CIG, of the pioneering labor unionism of Patagonia and of Montevideo's docks, of the illustri-ousness of the emigrant in Havana and in Buenos Aires. The BNG is the vanguard because it formulates in the present and projects the political energy engendered into the future, regenerated and accumulated in the unceasing tradition of this nation…

In 1930, in a speech delivered at the *Día de Galiza* celebrations, Castelao defined "tradition" in the following manner: "by tradition I don't mean a series of overlapping presents, but rather the eternal that lives sheltered in the popular instinct" (*Nós,* no. 80). On the other hand, for those who know the "old" literature on millenarian movements, the messianic meaning of many of the metaphors employed in the speeches of the *25 de Xullo* becomes ostensive.[12] In 2001 the imminence of re-demption for the fatherland of Galicia was suggested, since we were now living in the Autumn of the Patriarch, that is, of Manuel Fraga. The elections for the Galician government, in which the BNG had put great expectations for growth, were getting closer. (Ultimately, these expecta-tions were stymied in October when the Bloque experienced its first setback in terms of electoral results.) The days that had followed since the summer of the year before until that particular *25 de Xullo* of 2001 were described in the following, nearly apocalyptic, way: "So that was not more than the beginning of the period of the blackest and wicked-est of state policy since Francoism came to an end. Then the real winter weather arrived, an incessant succession of thunder and floods, wind storms that were as much climatic as they were political. And total con-fusion." Yet, as was even suggested by Xosé Manuel Beiras, the moment of definitive redemption of the fatherland and the age, of the opening of the *Alba de Groria,* dreamed of by Castelao, were already heralded. The apostolic references that bring this speech to a close, alluding to an anonymous and eternal Galicia that must be awakened in time for the redemption that will finally be fulfilled are suggestive: "Mobilize your-selves, speak to the people, go to the villages, towns, neighborhoods, places of work and leisure, the tiny corners of this country in which the Galicia that is coming lives. Do this and, I can assure you, the Dawn of Glory will rise up anew. We will win!"

The invocation of the dead would appear to be the ideal way to imagine the Galician national community; embodied here is its perpetuity, despite the contingencies of a centenarian history of subservience and offences, and the certainty that redemption is due. Likewise contained within such an evocation are all the allusions to the continuity of the anonymous Galicia of the people that was able to resist the dark centuries imposed after the so-called golden age that lasted until the fifteenth century. Those mythical times of splendor would be salvaged in the near future via the collective mobilization that the Bloque embodies by representing a nation that counts on its martyrs, evoked by name in these solemn moments to inspire the patriotic spirit (see Smith 1999 and Connerton 1989).[13] Yet, in addition to the famous martyrs, we are made aware of the existence of a depth of anonymous and eternal humus that projected into the future will guarantee the definitive *Alba de Groria*.

Manuel Rivas—who works for the daily newspaper *El País* and is a very well-known writer, the most successful among writers of prose working in Galician today—has given us a curious description of the transformations that are happening within contemporary Galician politics and of the role that the BNG plays in this context. In my judgment, the characterization proposed in his article is hardly neutral. Apparent are the author's obvious sympathies for the nationalist coalition or, at least, his strong antipathy for their adversaries in the PP of G and, above all, for its president, Manuel Fraga. Here, however, certain metaphors are used that I would like to foreground, because the imaginative choice of words maximizes the redemptive meaning of the Bloque's activism: "The world of the Galician Bloque Nacionalista presents itself as an antonym of the *fraguista* universe. Not only as a political alternative. It is a subterranean and alternative Galicia that will emerge without great convulsions just like a geological reality" (*El País* 17/10/1997).

Rivas's idea is a synthesis of many converging images employed today by Galician nationalists. But an easily identifiable inheritance can also be distinguished here, in the way in which tellurian metaphors—and ideas of radical antinomies—have forever marked the Galicianist discourse. Rivas suggests that it is an authentic and tellurian Galicia whose emergence is today imminent, liberated by the nationalist movement, agent of an inevitable "geological" movement. This manifests itself in the villages, in the *agro* [the rural world], origin of the *tractoradas* [demonstrations in which tractors are uses to block or disrupt traffic] that bring the imposing presence of the *labregos* [country bumpkins] to the city gates. It is also present, for example, in the conciliation between the young radical *rojos* with the old Christian rites in the remote localities that the priests have long abandoned. The image employed by Rivas when he contrasts the "universe of Fraga" with "world of the Bloque Nacionalista Galego" is especially curious because it echoes the famous distinction drawn by Oswald Spengler between "civilization" and "culture," with the positive connotations contained in the second term. (Spengler was read by the most prominent of the Galicianist ideologues of the 1920s.) But beyond Rivas's sympathies and the clear Galicianist enculturation that his prose demonstrates, some of the images that he uses—frequent as well in the Quintana dos Mortos demonstration—are well-defined marks of the majority of nationalistic speeches.

We might now recall the images used in *Galicia* by Manuel Murguía—"Golgotha" and "Tabor" (see chapter 1)—in order to understand the persistence of history's disentitlements in the century-old Galicianist discourse, even if the metaphors used in order to do this vary through time—successively biblical, astronomical, and geological. The nation's time-line is viewed as eternal; it does not observe multicentury contingencies and trivialities that governed the existence of "Golgotha," "rotten history" or "civilization." On the other hand, the expectations of redemption maintained are millenarian; we long for "Tabor," the "alba de glória," or the new "world." Images of this character are constant features of nationalist discourse, if we credit the suggestions of A. Smith, who speaks of the regularity of expressions of the myth of decline—and the consequent myth of regeneration—in these types of social movements. Let us quote the author himself:

> Of especial interest, from the standpoint of ethnic myths of descent, are the notions of authenticity and regeneration. The first is illuminated by myths of origins and descent, since they furnish the criteria for judging what is inauthentic or impure. ... The second, regeneration, with its metaphors of "rebirth" and "reawakening," continues this drama of self-purification, so necessary to collective salvation, by placing the act of liberation in an ideal world of heroic imagery and naturalistic metaphor. A fundamentally historical event is thereby endowed with a deeper symbolic significance, derived from the re-enacting of the early drama of liberation and the subsequent golden age. By returning to one's origins, the links in the long chain of generations are reforged. (1999: 67–68; see 57 and ff.)

The motifs of the pilgrim and of the pilgrimage are powerfully associated with the nationalist movement and its proposals for the redemption of Galicia. Galicia understood itself to be a nation oppressed, *asoballada* [humiliated]—echoing a famous title by the poet Ramón Cabanillas, *Da Terra Asoballada* (1917)—by the multisecular domination of the Spanish state in its different reincarnations. The *Terra* is considered alienated from itself and in need of redemption, and we see how strong, in the celebration of the *25 de Xullo,* are suggestions of emergence and the imminent affirmation of a true Galicia, a stranger to the de facto powers in force for the time being. The alienation of this authentic Galicia still takes its revenge just as it has done throughout the last six centuries, enduring the *doma e castración* [taming and castration] of Galicia and the present is seen as part of the *séculos escuros* [dark centuries], or of the—metaphorical as well—*longa noite de pedra* [long night of stone].[14] It is the possibility of a shared history—over centuries—that is negated by these implicit judgements. In 1982, when the democratic regime was already established in Spain, Xosé Manuel Beiras characteristically called for the unity of all Galicians. This was necessary, he said, so that "the night of stone could be converted into a glorious dawn" (*A Nosa Terra,* 30/7/1982).

Avatars of the Apostle

The Spanish state is celebrated in the Praza do Obradoiro by invoking one of the avatars of the Apostle—the *Santiago Matamoros* [St. James the Moor Slayer], or *Santiago Caballero* [St. James the Knight]—whose equestrian figure tops the enormous mass of the Raxoi Palace, in front of which the troops gather in formation for the first stages of the celebration of the *patrón de España.* Following this, as we have already seen, a procession configured around the image of *Santiago Peregrino* [St. James the Pilgrim] ends with the high officials of the Catholic Church, of the Spanish state, and of the autonomous government of Galicia entering the cathedral. The ceremonies proceed before other depictions of the seated apostle, which forms the center of the high altar and the rest of the church, and before which the *ofrenda* is realized each year. In this way the state ceremonies appropriate the three iconic depictions of the apostle. The demonstration of the nationalists is held, as we have seen, in the Quintana dos Mortos, next to the Porta Santa that is topped by an image of the *Apóstolo peregrino da Catedral* [Saint James the Pilgrim of the Cathedral].

The possible readings of each of the avatars of the apostle are, indeed, broad. Santiago presents perhaps the most plastic of possibilities as far as the discourse on Galicia and on Galician culture is concerned; in the very specific terms proposed by Victor and Edith Turner, it is a "dominant" or "central symbol" (Turner and Turner 1978: 245). One specialist on its iconography says, "Pilgrim and warrior are the two sides

which are commonly presented with the intent of molding the personality of Santiago."[15] García Iglesias refers to the fact that the figure of
Santiago Peregrino represents the anonymous and timeless pilgrim: an
interpretation confirmed by a range of legends (see reflections on this
preliminary figure by Turner and Turner 1990).

The negation of the "Galician" character in the bellicose and imposing figure of *Santiago Caballero*—identified as a symbol that is foreign
to the Galician *alma* [soul], and contrary to the very humble figuration of the Pilgrim—was, nevertheless, the object of frequent erudite
glosses. There were many of these during the first decades of the twentieth century when the guidelines of the Galician nationalist discourse
were being articulated, and today they populate the imaginative world
of many of the Galicians that I know. Allusions that update symbolic
appropriations of the apostle and its antagonistic iconographic depictions are frequent. The *Santiago Caballero,* or *Matamoro,* synonymous
designations, symbolizes that which is "Spanish," "of the state," "Castilian," "militaristic," and "imperialist." But today it also allows us to comment on a variety of themes: the repression of the arrival of thousands
of Maghrebians to the coasts of Spain, or the unhappy incursion of
politicians from Madrid into Galicia; the evocation of the humility of
the Galicians who emigrated over the centuries and their distance from
the cruel *castelá* [Castilian] history in the colonization of the Americas;
or the more recent counter-commemorations of Columbus's arrival in
Central America.

Santiago, seated in a majestic position, is the less observed iconic
depiction of the apostle, and, as well, the one that has provoked fewer
metaphorical references in day-to-day life. This particular avatar of Santiago can be interpreted as his theocratic and institutional depiction,
and, as such, associated with all of the powers structurally established in
the Catholic Church, in Galician society, and in the city over time. As
we have seen, its appropriation by the state has great symbolic importance—it is in front of this image of Santiago that the *ofrenda al Apóstol*
is performed, consecrating all of the significant temporal powers in force
in *España de las autonomías,* in which today the autonomous government of Galicia takes its place. Finally, it was in front of the seated Santiago of the Compostelan cathedral that, throughout the centuries and
successive regimes, political realities in force both in Galicia and Spain
were, in fact, consecrated.

Contrastingly, it is the liminal figure of the *Santiago Peregrino* that
comes to symbolize—in addition to those expectations for individual
redemption on the part of each anonymous pilgrim—the redemption,
as well, of the Galicia that the nationalists long for. We have seen how

on each *25 de Xullo* thousands of militants make the pilgrimage to Compostela and, next to the closed *Porta Santa,* at the Bloque's demonstration, listen to messages that speak of the eminent forgiveness of the *Terra.* In 1998, at the demonstration on *25 de Xullo,* the leader of the Bloque, Xosé Manuel Beiras, said the following: "Who are in the end the fundamentalists and the integralists ... those of us who are here, or those over there, to your right, inside of this huge boulder?" even if by that time the political, military, and religious hierarchs who had played their part in the *ofrenda al Apóstol* during the morning had left the cathedral.

Castelao, in *Sempre en Galiza*—today proverbially considered the *Bíblia do galeguismo*—defines Santiago's sovereign sitting figure in the following fashion:

> Galicia represented the Apostle Santiago in a way similar to how the Patriarchs are represented: seated in a majestic position, with a scepter in his left hand and a parchment in his right; the head is raised, the eyes looking towards the unknown West, with his lips repeating David's psalm, "Your way is over the ocean and those vast waters your paths." This is how the master Mateo represented him and how he sculpted him in the *Pórtico da Glória,* with a replica of the high altar, to receive the ancient visitors and tell them that the world does not stop with Galicia, that Galicia was not the limit of the world but rather a quay extending out from Europe toward a continent that was waiting to be discovered. (1976: 426)

The author is saying then that the *sitting* depiction was the *Galician form* among the three iconographic forms of the Santiago Apostle. However, if we pay attention to the cited description, we see that the images used suggest that in the eyes of the icon there is a kind of self-alienation and a hope placed on what is overseas. They certainly do not reflect the exploits of conquest or of the evangelizing that the arrival of Columbus initiated. They are rather, quite surely, the feelings experienced by the author himself as a transatlantic exile, feelings that, by extension, extend to all Galicians who were oppressed during these years. Based in Argentina, Castelao tried to keep the Galicianist feeling alive through political action that he cultivated among the hundreds of thousands of emigrants in Buenos Aires and up and down the River Plate basin (Monteagudo 2000). This is where the principal bastion of a *"Galiza do exterior"* was based, the only one that could be considered in those years to be free, and an open field for Galicianizing proselytism. For this reason he says that it was there over the *moitas augas* [vast waters] that one found the places of hope for the definitive redemption of the *patria* whose centuries long *asoballamento* [humiliation] *mestre* Mateo had depicted with a certain premonition in the expression of the seated apostle's gaze.

Until recently, nationalist Galicians had been precluded from the official 25 July celebrations inside the cathedral, which are held under the aegis of the sitting figure of Santiago. In 2001, a representative of the BNG participated for the first time in the *ofrenda al Apóstol.* This was a pioneering presence, resulting from procedural inertia. A BNG councilor from the Compostelan city government represented the Santiago *concello* at the ceremony as vice-president, since, in this particular year, the president of the city government exercised the function of the *delegado régio.* It is difficult to avoid the hint of irony in the wide coverage in the principal Galician newspapers of this unprecedented presence (see *La Voz de Galicia* and *El Correo Gallego,* 26/7/2001). On the other hand, the absence of references to the participation in the *ofrenda* of the *bloquista* councilor in *A Nosa Terra,* which represented a breach in the rhetoric of the nationalist movement, seemed to me a sign of the delicacy of the situation.

As a general rule, the associations that include references to the figure of *Santiago Peregrino* are apologetic. Castelao believed that this was the "European iconographic form of the apostle," and the appropriations of this icon were very frequent in the Galicianist milieu, serving to emblematize the constancy of relations with Europe that would differentiate Galicia in the context of the state. In truth, "Europeanism" was always claimed as a characteristic of the nationalist movement; as early as 1923, A. Villar Ponte (1881–1936)—organizer of the Hirmandades da Fala and first director of *A Nosa Terra*—said, "It would be welcomed if this Romantic movement of Galician nationalists—the most advanced and European of Galicia—pushed ahead tenaciously" (*Galicia. Diario de Vigo* 26/6/1923).[16] Today, because references to a "Europe of Nations" are frequent, it is also this image of the apostle that embodies expectations of the Galician nationalists, an ideal that relates to the hopes that Villar Ponte and his coreligionists maintained when in the 1920s, they hoped to see Galicia represented in the Society of Nations in Geneva. However, in order to fulfill these desiderata for the autonomy of the Galician nation, the *sedente* [sitting] Santiago must still be appropriated, though it is shut behind the Porta Santa, from where the claims of the nationalists are, each year, kept out.

In 1925 it was hypothesized that the *Día de Galicia* commemorations—still a recent event—should be held in an inhospitable and outlying place in Galicia's territory. In an article entitled "O noso ano santo. Unha peregrinación ó monte Cebreiro," it was suggested that a pilgrimage be staged that moved in the opposite direction from those, coming from all across Europe, that historically held Santiago as their objective. This new pilgrimage, with its "pantheistic" connotation, would be an expression of a new religiosity in the national sense and should aim to reach the "montaña conservadora das nosas characteristics etnográficas" [the mountain that preserves our ethnographic characteristics] (*Galicia. Diario de Vigo,* 25/8/1925). The Cebreiro is the highest pass in the mountains over which the famous *camiño francés* crosses to reach the entrance to Galicia. So it is a place of cosmopolitan transit, but it is also a threshold to the rest of Spain, a remote place that would be demarcated on a pilgrimage designed to meet the ethnic essentials of the nation.[17] Of course, as we have seen, this suggestion was not taken up, and it was close to the two tombs that the commemorations of the *Día da Patria* established themselves as traditions.

Each year, when the demonstration in Quintana comes to a close with the Galician anthem, everyone present is invited to a very special "*festa étnica*": a picnic that takes place in a oak wood at the gates of the city. There the intensity of references to the rural world is quite surprising, and we are left with an image of the plenitude of Galician tradition according to the forms of interpretation currently favored by the milieu of the nationalist left.

In the Oak Wood of San Lourenzo

At the end of the morning of the *25 de Xullo,* when the BNG's demonstration draws to a close, part of the crowd leaves for their various places of origin. Apparently, these are the people of more obvious rural appearance who leave more quickly, because of the daily obligations awaiting them with their livestock, and the long trip home to be undertaken. Notwithstanding, it is noticeable at this annual demonstration—as well as at other unconnected political events that I have attended—that references to the interests of the *labregos* and *gandeiros* [farmers and livestock breeders] have a very important place in the political activities of the Bloque.[18] Generally, in the discourse of the BNG, there are two relevant modes of referring to the rural world: on the one hand, the subjection of the *labregos* to the *caciquis* [corrupt, political bosses] of the party in power and also the constancy of their conservativism.[19] This is borne out, for example, in a recognition that each of these characteristics contributes to the fact that the majority of rural zones remain inhospitable to nationalist proselytizing. On the other hand, the fundamental importance of farming in economic terms and also as a repository of defining features for the Galician nation and culture means that it continues to receive great emphasis in the Galicianist discourse. Roughly, this has been a doubly functioning perspective from the origins of the movement at the beginning of the twentieth century. However, in my opinion, what is mainly relevant are the symbolic uses of references to the *Terra* and to the peasants by a political party that, in the end, reaps its best results in urban areas and where the middle and professional classes are more significantly represented.

A good many of those present at the BNG's demonstration lose themselves in the festive streets of the city, enlivened by the crowds at lunch time; others stick around for the fair that occupies the Carballeira de Santa Susana during the month of July. However, many of those present at the Quintana demonstration go directly afterwards to the Carballeira de San Lourenzo, another wood shaded by enormous oaks set on the south campus of the University of Santiago, beyond Alameda. That is where, starting at three in the afternoon, the Bloque's huge picnic is held. Throughout the afternoon various people that I know from Santiago will show up, coming from the beach; some consider the march and the demonstration to be too prosaic, putting on airs about not associating with the former, but appreciating the festivities in the shade of the oaks of San Lourenzo, viewed to be an authentic Galician *festa* [celebration].

In 1934, António Villar-Ponte wrote an article for *A Nosa Terra* entitled "As nosas festas" (Our Festivities), from which I cite the following passage:

> What could Galicia be without a complete Galicianist policy that involves everyone in questions connected to health and celebrations. ...
>
> And now that we are speaking of Santiago, let us believe that Compostela will be able to launch perfect celebrations in Galician style.
>
> Because of them, May contests could be held, Druidic pieces literarily inspired, revelries in traditional huts in the ancient castle of Saint Susana. ... where, to provide a good example for the people, all of the Galician aristocracy, dressed in traditional clothes, would take up the cult of the *muiñeira* (a Galician folk dance), which is the purest choreographic reflection of our pantheistic psychology. (*A Nosa Terra*, no. 341)

This description of the Bloque's picnic demonstrates that some of the expectations defended by Villar Ponte seventy years ago are still being fulfilled. Nevertheless, taking stock of the redeeming possibilities of the modes of celebrating in *galaico estilo* [Galician style] some of the impasses that mark the nationalist movement's possibilities for expression in Galicia today are once again suggested. It is still not permitted to hold nationalist festivities in the Carballeira de Santa Susana, the place that Villar Ponte imagined would be suitable for these fantastical celebrations of the *raza*. As has been suggested, all acts of community exaltation promoted by the BNG take place on the margins of locales that in symbolic terms are structurally central (Turner 1990) in the capital of Galicia. It is outside the Praza do Obradoiro, outside the interior of the cathedral and even outside the Carballeira de Santa Susana that the Galicianist militants celebrate the *25 de Xullo*. Likewise, from the succession of chronicles written about the *Día da Patria* during the last twenty-five years, we will learn about the persistence of expectations and the struggle for access to those places. We have seen how in the years of great conflict, at the end of the 1970s and the beginning of the following decade, the holding of the *25 de Xullo* demonstration in Quintana was prohibited along with access by the procession to the old city. More generally speaking, it is legitimate to presume that only the subversion of the present political context and of the symbolism by which this is justified would allow Galician nationalists access to these central locations.

On 25 July 2000 it began to rain at the end of the demonstration in Quintana; the afternoon started with constant and chilling showers that discouraged me from going down to the Carballeiro de San Lourenzo. So I remained in the center of the city where—in the shelter of the *suportales* and the bars and restaurants—the celebratory ambience continued. This was an ill-advised decision to ignore the force that traditions have, even if they are recent ones, as is the case with the BNG picnic. Later that night I ran across friends and acquaintances who were surprised that I hadn't appeared, and for whom my suspicion that simply because it was raining heavily the picnic in the Carballeira would not happen seemed naïve. In truth, as I saw in the newspapers and from my friends, the celebrations had been less crowded than usual, and had been held under tents, but they had lasted, as they always did, the whole afternoon, in spite of the inclement weather, which continued uninterrupted until nightfall.

In the Carballeira de San Lourenzo, next to the heavy buildings of the faculties constructed in Franco's day, the Bloque's picnic stands out as a surprising scenario for someone who is attending for the first time. Canopies cover long tables made with planks, and a big crowd is spread out through the oak grove where tablecloths are extended on the grass, giant *empanadas* are shared by groups of friends, large and festive groups of people eating together. Smoke from cauldrons and barbecues pours out from under the tents, the wine flows and is drunk from the small white bowls characteristic of the oldest taverns. There's also Estrella Galicia beer, *aguardente* (a clear brandy made from the husks of grapes), and other local and homemade liquors. Musicians playing bass drums, bagpipes, and accordions ceaselessly improvise, and enthusiastic

dances break out all around, surrounding the groups eating and dancing between the tables, under the canopies, and here and there out in
the woods. This continues throughout the afternoon until nightfall. In
2001 I couldn't attend the picnic, but the description given in *A Nosa
Terra* generally reiterated many of my impressions of earlier years, but
now with an apologetic note:

> The cultural invasion of strange customs and values that we are currently
> experiencing extends to gastronomy, music, and the language. There are
> moments in which the rebellion is undertaken unconsciously, the only
> drink we had to consent to was Coca-cola, which is a cultural supple-
> ment found as much in Sri Lanka as it is in Ribadavia, a small town in
> Galicia. Can you imagine a traditional festival that was supplied with
> roast beef, French champagne, and donuts? No. Traditional gastronomy,
> Galician folklore, and our own literature in our language, everyone ready
> to create a unique ambience, inviting and very much ours. (27/7/2001)

Except for the tables set up for the distribution of propaganda, the
gathering at the Carballeira de San Lourenzo, seen from afar, would remind one of the peasant bazaars in the old engravings, or a "traditional
festival," as the citation above suggests. Some of the elements of this
scenario—the canvas canopies, the cauldrons of octopus, the long tables
made of rough planks—are ones that we can find in Galicia at rural
fairs and celebrations on the outskirts of towns and in small villages.
A good example for comparison would be the open-air festival of the
famous *Feira dos Santos* in Monterroso, in the Province of Lugo, with its
stalls selling food and where the same kinds of culinary specialties are
prepared in a likewise festive atmosphere. But here, in San Lourenzo, I
know that the great part of the people whom I meet live and work in the
cities; they are high-level technicians, actors, trade unionists, university
professors, and members of the liberal professions,[20] primarily younger
people, who celebrate enthusiastically beneath the huge oak trees. In
contrast to this, in Monterroso, Padrón, or at any of the famous Galician agricultural fairs, these same urbanites arriving late in the morning often bring cameras; we could call the characteristic attention with
which they circulate among the crowds *ethnographic*. They pay attention
to the small talk or the more curious conversations, become enchanted
by the aesthetic qualities of the eyes of the livestock, the tools, and all
the agricultural products that the Galicians would describe as *enxebres*
[that is: pure, authentic, genuine, autochthonous Galician]. They stay
away from the stalls that are selling sweaters made with synthetic fibers
or those that display cassettes and CDs with the musical successes consumed all over Spain.

With a bit of irony—this was my initial impression the first time I was there, in 1997—it might seem that in the Carballeira de San Lourenzo one is arriving at a peasant celebration re-created in a film. You will see white cotton shirts, some of linen. Many of the younger women wear their hair loose; there are those with rustic straw hats. These notes help to compose the atmosphere of a timeless rural festival, which is only interrupted by the stalls selling books and music and the distribution of propaganda. Traditional music, as well as songs in Galician, are played on the typical instruments of this area—bagpipes, tambourines, a few hurdy-gurdies. Many of these songs are cunning, and their saucy allusions make the groups that form around the musicians even more jubilant. You can hear, in the loud commentaries among groups of acquaintances, especially between the men and the women, certain obscene expressions, curious instances of mimesis of the loose talk of the *labregos* and the proletariat. Also in San Lourenzo the way the majority of men and women carry themselves is more uninhibited and nimble, and they are noticeably more at ease with their bodies and attitudes than normally is the case with peasants, in Galicia as in other contexts. (see, for example, Bourdieu 1962).

The general image of the majority of those who frequent the Bloque's picnic diverges greatly from the image that we get these days at the fairs in rural Galicia—what we find in Carballeira is a mimesis of a rustic and atemporal *communitas*. At the fairs in Galicia the visitor will be taken aback by the crowd of men and women wearing dark clothing, made up mainly of the old and the middle aged, involved in their transactions or jostling at the tables set up under tents where the octopus is served. The majority of middle-aged women are heavy set, with hair cut short and almost always badly dyed, while their husbands, also prematurely old, wear jackets of poor-quality leather. Even the inattentive observer will note that in the Galician spoken by these rural couples includes Castilianisms, *castrapismos,* which are denounced in innumerable literary registers. The observer will conclude that in these haircuts, jackets, and regional speech lie the ruins of the last wave of 1960s agricultural modernization (Iturra 1988; Fernández Prieto 1992), but ruins as well of the "production of Spaniards," which occurred in the Galician countryside under Franco.

The aging of the rural population in the fields of Lugo, of Ourense, in the highlands of A Coruña and Pontevedra, brings on melancholy considerations; and this process is patent in the festivals, the fairs, and the innumerable *festas gastronómicas,* a still recent mode that has become a fixture in the last two decades. But today, in these places, we can also frequently find Senegalese salesmen selling trinkets, Portuguese Romany selling eiderdowns and shoes, Chinese selling knickknacks and toys. In the rural fairs, as I have already suggested, with each year that passes more and more curious people, coming from the cities, pass through these mercantile gatherings in the countryside, mainly those that are imagined to be more traditional or typical. But their presence is still as obvious as that of an old peasant coming from a hamlet in Ourense would be in the Carballeira de San Lourenzo on the *25 de Xullo.*

At the Bloque's picnic we are able to recognize, in the end, a nearly exemplary composition of those ethnomimetic proposals (Cantwell 1993) supported by the nationalist movement. These must be read as a mode of appropriating Galician tradition—the presumed eternity of that which is of the people and anonymous and that can be situated just this side of the contingencies of history, as Castelao suggested in 1930 (*Nós*, 80). In this festivity a greater part of the ambiguities that touch Galician society are suspended. Many of them have a centuries-old presence and for this reason it can be said—along with the simpler arguments of nationalist propaganda—that they are consubstantial with the possibilities of thinking about the history of Galicia. In the Carballeira de San Lourenzo Galician is spoken exclusively and all of the printed materials that are to be found there are written in this language. This is so despite the fact that in the urban contexts diglossia ostensibly prevails and the publishing market in Galician appears to have very obvious weaknesses.[21] As well, the presence of objects originating outside of Galicia is generally rare. In truth, since the majority of industrial products available in daily life are entirely absent, we get the strong impression that at the Bloque's picnic the contemporary "system of objects" has been deserted (Baudrillard 1968). This impression allows us to suggest that the practices of consumption as much as the stylized behavior of the guests can be understood as a ritual of introspection. This is played out around a privileged set of markers, which reveal what is judged to be essential and perennial in Galician culture as it is harvested from the *labrega* [peasant] "tradition," such as gastronomic, musical, or even behavioral references, many of which can be found registered in the ethnographic corpus created in Galicia over time. In this way, we find at the Carballeira de San Lourenzo picnic the suggestion that time, which is contingent upon history, has been suspended in favor of a new time, redeemed at the gates of the city wherein tradition is reconstituted (Benjamin 1992: 244–55; Zulaika 1996).

As I came to understand, the only habitually perceptible exceptions to the fixation on Galician tradition experienced at the Bloque's picnic were explicit references to Cuba and to Portugal. These arise, somehow, as channel markers from the outside, citations of free countries frequently referred to in nationalist rhetoric as examples of the possibility that small countries can enjoy sovereignty in spite of their proximity to powerful neighbors. As we will later see, in chapter 6, the rhetorical references to Portugal play a very large, old, and important part in Galicianist discourse. Of more recent date, and indicating ideological affinities defended by the BNG, are the mentions of Cuba and expressions of solidarity for the regime in power there.[22]

The presence of Cuba is assured by the circulation of the image of Che Guevara—a cosmopolitan symbol of the left—printed on flags or T-shirts, and occasionally by an invited Cuban musician. The two references to Portugal were also highly noticeable. In successive years I came across a man wrapped in a Portuguese flag in the chestnut grove who, when I approached him to ask about the reasons for presenting himself in such a fashion, remained speechless and smiling. Later I was told that it was someone who had come from Ourense, something of an original; he hadn't responded to me in order to uphold the mystery, which would have dissolved had he responded to my interrogations in Galician.

There is also the habitual presence of a woman dressed impeccably in the "style of the Minho" or that of "Vianeza" (Basto 1930) accompanied by a band of music-playing revelers. The presence of this woman in the festive ambience that I have described was surprising. Yet there were no Galicians playing a role that might be considered equivalent and who would, nevertheless, be shunned by all those present as "Folkloristic." These people are, as a rule, scorned as marks of *regionalismo bien entendido*—an ironic, deprecating cliché that has been used since the 1920s by nationalist Galicians in order to ape the positions of the more moderate regionalists, supposed to be weaklings, defenseless and even effectively tinged by *españolismo.* Today, manipulations of this type of folkloric image by the government of the Comunidade Autónoma, which the PP of G controls, are frequent. But their creation and initial uses had, as well, enthused the Galician nationalists at the beginning of the twentieth century, as a consultation of the periodicals of that epoch will attest to. We will find an example in the passage by Villar Ponte already cited above, but they are plentiful in *A Nosa Terra* from 1916 to 1936, where, in fact, exhortations to organize choirs, praise directed at the organization of folkloric groups, and the staging of ethnographic theatre and of other similar initiatives are encouraged.

Dressing up with stereotyped rigor, that "lavradeira minhota" [Minhotan farmwoman] obviously represented the neighboring country; in the end this image, first established at the end of the nineteenth century, is an emblem of Portuguese nationality (Medeiros 1995). Somehow, by contrast, she allowed us to attest to the "liminal" position (Turner 1967) nationalists hold in the political sphere of the Comunidade Autónoma, a fact that I have already suggested above. In nations that are states these folkloric emblems have stabilized—as mere components of the "IKEA system" that A. M. Thiesse refers to (2000)—since they were open to peaceful appropriations, as happened generally in Portugal (see for another example, Wilson 1976). In Galicia, by contrast, the illegitimacy that the nationalist movement of the left attributes to the current right-wing Galician government hampers the contemporary sharing of "eth-nomimetic" representations that predate 1936 and that the autonomous power manipulates with a ostensive facility, after having appropriated them from Franco's authoritarian regime.

Return to the City through Santa Susana

Anyone who walks through the Carballeira de Santa Susana on the same day will come across another picnic, which runs parallel to the Bloque's picnic in San Lourenzo. This is another old oak grove—right by the old city and where we find the Alameda—where a major part of the crowd in Santiago gathers. It is impossible to give a minute account of the park on this *día grande* in the month of Santiago. However, let me leave you with some telling details.

There are a great variety of amusement park rides and excited shouting coming from those who are whirling through the air. All of the icons of Disney are replicated by the hundreds in the toy stalls, in the decoration of a good many of the pavilions and on the carousels, whether modern or revivalist, surrounded by parents watching over their children on their rides. There are vendors of *churros* (a kind of cylindrical donut), of caramelized almonds and of *turrón* [nougat] from Alicante. All of the labels are written in Spanish, and it is in Spanish—or English—that all of the music that booms from the sound booths of each of the fair's concessions is sung. A large group of Bolivians dressed in ponchos have electrified their instruments; they can be heard clearly in the middle of all the cacophony. Girls who say *mi novio,* wearing black and light green lycra, linger around the most modern of the amusements. A lottery seller imitates someone from TVE [the major Spanish-language channel] to attract clients to buy raffles for his display case of fetishes of industrial society. Right by the Alameda, a stall of *los vinos de Aragón,* with two figures made up as dancers of the *jota* [a folk dance], looks like a ruin from the old program to nationalize the culture of the Spanish and hardly manages to attract any clients with its antiquated decoration. In 2000 I met some friends, a couple with their daughter—who is named after a character from Shakespeare[23]—and I offered her a toy bought at the stall of a Chinese woman whose only word in Spanish was *bonito.*

Making one's way through the Carballeira de Santa Susana on the days of the weekly fair might be described by many Galician nationalists as taking the road to Damascus. However, until 1978, this was the site of an old livestock fair—and the observations made about the place are frequently mentioned in the biographical notes of various prominent Galicianists. These are invariably descriptions of encounters with "Galicia," an "authentic" Galicia that, if we accept these presuppositions, will certainly not be recognized today at the amusement park, or in its visitors on 25 July in recent years. According to the various reports that I have read or heard, it was at the old Santa Susana fair that some of the most famous Galician visual artists of the twentieth century found models and reasons for nationalist engagement with their respective works. This is what happened, for example, with Castelao, L. Seoane, or Carlos Maside (Seoane 1969). As well, there are various fictional characters influential in Galician literature—like those created by such unavoidable writers as Ramón Otero Pedrayo and Xosé Luís Mendez Ferrín—who end up having more or less dramatic experiences at the old fair involving the revelation of the *Terra.*

Let me cite a particularly curious example of the many replications of references to the "encounter with Galicia" on the day of the Santa Susana fair. Speaking of the experience of students recently arrived in the city during the 1950s, having come from villages and then initiated into the clearly minority circles of militant Galicianism, Carlos Baliñas tells us: "And each Thursday, in the Carballeira of Santa Susana, the fair. On this day the clatter of clogs could be heard in the city streets, imparting a stupendous and unrepeatable practical lesson in Rural Anthropology" (1987: 186). Here we have a suggestion of the ways in which the forms of imagining the countryside were consolidated. This was decisive for conjuring descriptions of the essences of Galician culture that were then crystallized in the nationalist discourse. These descriptions are most noticeably mediated by a range of different art forms and, more generally, via the dispositions of more distanced ethnographic observation (Williams 1993). However, in spite of these imposed mediations, the presence of the rural in Galician society is still imposingly forceful, despite the growth of the most important urban centers that has taken place in recent decades. Those who work the fields provide a curious dimension of "cultural intimacy" in Galician cities (Herzfeld 1997a) once we understand most of the people we come into contact with in the cities nearly always have direct family connections to the countryside. This explains, for example, the quality of the products at dinners in the houses of Galician friends, in the *ensanches* [outskirts of cities] that the urban, late-Francoist *desarrolismo* [developmentalism] caused to grow, where the hosts would nearly always say that the *patacas* [potatoes], the *berzas* [kale greens], or the *xamón* [ham] served at the table had come *da aldea*—from their parents' or grandparents' houses in the countryside.

Even today, Santiago de Compostela fills each year with very noticeably rural students, just as in the 1950s, when there were far fewer of them. For many of these students, the appropriation of knowledge of Galicia and of Galician culture, codified by the references to erudite terms of the Galicianist discourse, would, at the end of the day, occur as a paradoxical disjunction with their own biographical experiences. These were the same disjunctions that the "ethnomimetic" dispositions patent in the Bloque's picnic also contained, from another point of view. I would suggest that the frequent mention of the *labregos* of the old Santa Susana fair indicates that we are observing a very well-established parable. Its ideological justification—which is similar to the way village festivals are emulated in the picnic at San Lourenzo—can be found in various passages of the works of the first generation of Galician nationalists writing at the beginning of the twentieth century.

Notes

1. A belief that was spread beginning in the ninth century. There is a vast array of historical and literary approaches to the history of the Santiago sepulcher, of the famous pilgrimages that made their way there and of the city of Compostela. I am aided here by two of the references of major literary quality, but also factual reliability: Otero Pedrayo (1991) and Torrente Ballester (1990).
2. Understandably the uses of the alternative designation *Día da Patria Galega* indicate a refusal on the part of the sectors of the nationalist left to accept the limits of the political status quo that the *Estatuto de Autonomía* imposes. The parties and political associations that recognize themselves today—and they are habitually recognized—as "nationalists" are situated mainly on the extreme left of the Galician political spectrum. This is different in important ways from that which happened in Catalonia and the Basque Country, where the big nationalist parties—who hold power—are considered right or center-right, but are above all emerging as large "national parties." The near absolute ascendancy won by the Galician nationalist movement is recent and dates back, *grosso modo,* to the 1960s, when the project for a "national party" embodied by the Partido Galeguista, composed of important and very conservative Catholic leaders and ideologues, at the start of the 1930s had already collapsed. Maryon McDonald (1989) and Sharon MacDonald (1997) give evidence of similar cases in Brittany and in Scotland, and there are, in the end, various examples in which we find such a transition, which is related to the appropriations of Marxism in the context of nationalistic demands the world over (Nairn 1997). It is important to consult a very detailed account of these mutations in the Galician case by Beramendi and Nuñez Seixas, who give us a record of the whole of

the historical course of Galicianist claims (1995). In a general way, it can be said that the institution of an autonomous political context forced the "nationalization"—or the "Galicianization"—of all the relevant parties—namely, of the Partido Socialista de Galicia (PS of G), in the opposition, and of the Partido Popular de Galicia (PP of G), who hold power presently. The terms of this obligatory Galicianization, can, however, be considered ambiguous, as they are marked by the internal tensions and constantly denounced for hardly being serious by the parties of the extreme left, which maintain more explicitly particularist positions. Among these parties, the Bloque Nacionalista Galego (BNG)—a "front" that brings together a variety of political formations—has suddenly become the political force of most significance and is responsible for the largest concentration of demonstrators on each *25 de Xullo.*

3. Otero was a polymath writer—historian, geographer, and a writer various genres of prose—in addition to being a figure of certain political prominence until 1936, when he was elected deputy by the Partido Galeguista. The conservatism of his political positions, married to his great intellectual prestige, allowed him to become a luminous figure in Galician culture, and his work is valued today across the political spectrum. The *Guía de Galicia* cited here—whose first edition dates to 1924, originally written in Castilian—went through various editions and can be seen as "the description of Galicia," shaping the imagination of the *Terra* for many of its inhabitants. Otero's preoccupations—very clear and erudite—with themes such as maps and landscape art are curious (Anderson 1991; Stanley 2000). A bildungsroman, written in Galician and published in 1930 (a work that has been reissued at least seven times since 1980, and which today is part of the secondary school syllabus in Galicia)—seems to us like the perfect guide to verify some of the more daring ideas of Benedict Anderson. There the themes of "subjectivity" and of "simultaneity" of the senses of national belonging—and the role of novels and maps in the production of these subjective perceptions—are very suggestively illustrated.

4. Today *A Nosa Terra,* the most significant historical title in the history of Galician nationalism (Ledo Andión 1982), is the only newspaper that regularly carries the positions of the nationalistic left. It is, however, a very modest weekly—with obvious editorial weaknesses—that never seemed to me to be really appreciated, not even among sympathizers. The more highly educated nationalists that I am acquainted with fulfill, paradoxically, their "daily prayer of the modern man" (Anderson 1991) by reading the important statewide daily, *El País.* They nearly always hold the daily newspapers edited in Galicia in contempt, saying that they are manipulated and impoverished in terms of content, and also attribute little importance to the articles of poor quality contained in *A Nosa Terra.* The lack of a daily newspaper in the vernacular language related to the nationalist positions seriously impedes the possibilities for communicating with the Galician community in a way that would be in accordance with the ideological lines that the nationalist movement still supports (Anderson 1991; Hagen 1997). This is a problem that has been strongly resented since the 1920s, and there have been several failed attempts to launch a daily newspaper in Galician in recent decades. Today it is the *Xunta de Galicia* that—directly or indirectly—maintains the most important means of mass communication that systematically employ Galician: the TVG and the newspaper *O Pobo Galego* (an impoverished clone of the original title written in Castilian, *El Pueblo Gallego*). *La Voz de Galicia,* a title edited in A Coruña and written in Castilian, is the most widely distributed of the dailies edited in Galicia, having a national audience equal to TVG—the most effective organ of the "imagination" of Galicia. The provincial capitals sponsor titles and have very particular audiences, who are above all the heralds

of localist interests, like "viguismo," "coruñismo," etc. For some of my informants, these localist postures carried a very strong stigma and, on a variety of occasions, they reacted impatiently to my questions about the way they manifested themselves.

5. It is important to note that Santiago's claim as being a spiritual capital of Galicia is ancient and always had importance in the most intellectually influential circles of Galicianism.

6. The PP has won growing majorities of the vote in each election since 1989 (something that was repeated once again in October 2001, when the BNG suffered its first electoral setback and the PSG was once again the party to receive the second highest share of votes). Its president, Manuel Fraga (1922)—"Fraga" to his opponents—is a very controversial figure in the world of the nationalist opposition, often referred to as the personification of many of the evils afflicting Galicia. "D[on] Manuel"—as his fellow party members respectfully call him—is one of the most important Spanish political figures of the second half of the twentieth century. He was a professor of political science, minister of information and of tourism, the ambassador to London under Francoism, and one of the architects of the process of the *transición democrática*. In 1980 he led the right-wing opposition at the state level for a year and became *presidente da Xunta de Galicia* in 1989, a position to which he has been reelected successively. In recent years internal struggles have emerged for the succession to the leadership of the PP of G, always followed very closely by the commentators and which the opposition always sardonically refers to as an implacable fight for the spoils of power accumulated by the old ruler.

7. The representatives who have come in solidarity from Catalonia, the Basque Country, Portugal, and Cuba, but also from more distant places—Wales, Ireland, Western Sahara, etc.—are normally present.

8. This route—today referred to as traditional—was fixed in 1985, after another alternative route had been tried in 1984, the first year in which access to the heart of the old city was opened to the nationalist demonstrators.

9. Throughout the years, in the pages of the most important periodicals before 1936, the references that give an account of these preoccupations are many and varied. What is mainly suggested is the influence of the readings of Friedrich Nietzsche and Oswald Spengler. Also important were references that were closer to theoreticians preoccupied with the production of new myths, such as Charles Maurras, José Ortega y Gasset, or even the Portuguese António Sardinha (see, for example, Fernández 1995; Bobillo 1995; Outeiriño 1990; see, as well, chapters 3 and 4). In the context of the Spanish state, Pedro González Cuevas (2000) provides a noteworthy discussion of the body of literature dealing with these preoccupations in the early twentieth century.

10. X. M. Beiras, parliamentarian and leader of the BNG, is the most prominent figure in the contemporary Galician nationalist movement. He was a professor of economics at the University of Santiago and an author, principally, of a work that became a key reference in bibliographies dealing with Galicia—*O Atraso Económico de Galicia*—published for the first time in 1973. His political activity, begun during the dictatorship, was early and prominent, having joined the group of founders of the Partido Socialista Galego at a very young age in 1963, of which he later became leader. The PSG—not to be confused with the PS of G—is one of the important formations in the composition of the BNG, established in 1982 and then successively enlarged (see Beramendi and Nuñez Seixas 1995 for references to the myriad parties and coalitions that composed the panorama of the Galician nationalist left during the 1970s and 1980s).

11. These citations remind me of the bitter comments of one of my Compostelan informants back in 1997, when I was trying to find out "who was who" in Galician politics. Teresa, a librarian, said to me at the time, "a eses nadie les entende," [Nobody understands these people] referring to X. M. Beiras and to the literary allusions that he increasingly employed in his speeches. By contrast, the frequent populist concessions in the language of certain leaders of the PP would be referred to with contempt by nationalist militants as *carallados* [bloody or godawful]. My suggestions—intentionally provocative—that Manuel Fraga seemed to know what the people liked to hear, or that his Galician seemed to be more vernacular than that of the leaders of the BNG, strongly irritated my nationalist friends from Santiago de Compostela.

12. The work of Juan Aranzadi (2000 [1981])—a complex and polemical approach to Basque nationalism—contains an ample and curious use of classical references from studies of millenarian movements.

13. In the nationalist calendar the *Día da Galiza Mártir,* 17 August—the date of the execution of one the most important political leaders of historical Galicianism, Alexandre Bóveda (b. 1903), in 1936—is marked as a specific holiday. This commemoration does not have, however, the same public prominence as the *Día da Patria,* or even the other important holidays, like, for example, the *Día das Letras Galegas,* which is commemorated on 17 May.

14. "Doma e castración da Galiza" is a standard phrase frequently cited in texts, but also a popularized image now used in nationalist contexts; it can be heard, for example, in the mouths of boys who have little formal education. Originally, it was used in the fifteenth century by a chronicler in order to describe the wars and repression of Galicia in the general context of the process of the unification of Spain by the Catholic kings (see a commentary, for example, in Castelao 1976). *Séculos escuros,* with its narrower meaning, designates the period in which Galician was not written, before the nineteenth century *Rexurdimento* (that is, "renaissance" or "reemergence") (see the considerations elaborated by B. Anderson to justify what he designates as the "astonishing popularity of this trope" (1991: 195) in the nationalist movements of Europe; see also Herzfeld 1986, one of a variety of possibilities for comparison). *Longa Noite de Pedra* is a famous title by the poet Celso Emílio Ferreiro, written in the dungeons of a convent in his native town, where he was imprisoned at the time of Franco's *alzamiento* in 1936.

15. J. M. Garcia Iglesias, entry "Santiago—Jacobean iconography," in *Gran Enciclopedia Gallega* (1974).

16. The references to Europe in the literature produced by the BNG, whether in the speeches of their leaders or in the programmatic basis of the party, are very relevant, even if, as a rule, they denounce the excesses in the market economy in force in the EU. In this way we can take into account the reiteration of a theme that was central in the nationalist discourse until 1936, before the passions for the "Third World," which the texts of the nationalist left displayed up until the beginnings of the 1980s had become outdated. Today in Galicia rhetorical appropriations of Europeanism and the universalism that the *Santiago Peregrino* symbolize have become widespread.

17. O Cebreiro became symbolically important at the time when Galician nationalist discourse began to emerge due to the various scholarly treatments of themes related to this location. One legend often written about by a range of Galician intellectuals suggests that the "Santo Gral" is hidden in a small local church; the variations in the symbolic readings in the national sense, which these treatments take up, are fascinating. On the other hand, the *pallozas*—a kind of rough, thatched construction, char-

acteristic of the locality and the surrounding mountainous area—were, throughout the twentieth century, viewed as a representation of the primitive Galician habitation. Today the visitors to the Museo do Pobo Galego in Santiago begin their tour with very detailed representations of the *pallozas*—using maquettes, photographs, very suggestive captions, etc.—to pave the way for a wider knowledge of Galician culture, transmitted to excursions of students or retired people. In the location of Cebreiro itself—a traditional place for pilgrims to rest—a restored *palloza* houses a small museum.

18. In these speeches it is suggested that the interests being referred to are badly defined by the present autonomous administration in the face of the EU's impositions. Union activism among nationalists in rural contexts is apparently very high and has become a regular source of news in recent years. The high points of these kinds of protests are the *tractoradas*—slow processions of agricultural tractors—on the major access routes into Santiago and other important Galician cities that have taken place on a variety of occasions over the last few years. The *agrarista* movement at the beginning of the twentieth century—even though it wasn't directly related to the claims of the nationalists who were emerging at the time—has become an important part of Galicianist memory, as it is a legitimization reference still frequently alluded to today (Cabo Villaverde 1998; Durán 1981).

19. Above all, two of the four Galician provinces, Lugo and Ourense, are today referred to as a privileged context for these manipulations by *caciques*. These are the provinces that are less urbanized and less industrialized, where there is a higher percentage of economic dependency on agriculture, higher levels of emigration, and a greater aging of the population. Today, the leaders of the PP of G in these two provinces are the figures most frequently referred to when one wants to allude to a repudiated mode of political activity, with old traditions in Galicia (Durán 1976). I will pick one example of these allusions from 1918: "Because we must take into account that even if they are noxious, nauseating, all of the *caciques* [local political bosses] that represent Galicia are especially those that the province of Lugo supports, whether out of taste, or because they are eunuchs. One day, when the future that Galicianism has been preparing is a reality, the province of Lugo will still be foreign to the citizenry, foreign to the civic reality and, so, the apostles of Galicianism will have to penetrate these lands as though they were explorers of virgin forests" (*A Nosa Terra*, no. 64, 1918).

20. As I have already suggested, the BNG has managed during the last several years to expand its base throughout Galician society. It's well known, however, that it attracts above all an important part of the professional and intellectual sectors of the urban middle class, as sociological analyses of electoral results suggest.

21. The availability of titles in Galician—originals and translations—is very important these days, the publishing of which is stimulated by a wide variety of prizes. However, any attentive bookstore goer will understand the debilities of this specific market. In addition to school textbooks and the classics, the obligatory reading in secondary school, or the reference books for university professors and students produced by local academics, the display cases in the more prosperous bookstores of Galicia are not much different from those to be found in any other Spanish city, with the exception of Catalonia.

22. In truth, expressions of sympathy for the Cuban people in Galicia—and even for the regime—overflow from the circles connected to the BNG to the other formations of the nationalist left, some of them quite touching, enough so that they call for extensive commentary. They are meshed, from various points of view, with the stories of

Galician emigration and the nationalist movement, namely, and with the paradoxes of the new culture that this has produced (see illustrations of this in chapter 6). A suggestive anecdote that was related to me on various occasions with jubilant irony by Galicians critical of nationalist positions relates to a visit that Fidel Castro made to Galicia some years ago. At that time Manuel Fraga and Fidel had begun to have a very affectionate personal relationship that left the opposition disarmed. The former, son of emigrants, had grown up in Cuba and, supposedly, the two leaders traded memories of their childhoods with quite a bit of affection during the visit. In Galicia—in many of the open air festivities in the towns governed by the PP of G, whose indifference in relation to "culture" is, for the Galician nationalists, proverbial—it is possible to see how old women dance with surprising grace to the sound of Cuban orchestras, which are always very much appreciated. They will applaud any references to *La Habana* or to Cuba—and possibly even to the resistance of the blockade by the *imperialismo ianqui*—made by the musicians on stage. Many of these people, or their parents, grew up in Cuba—and the orchestras that play Caribbean rhythms are still common in Galicia itself—and seem to find "Galician" songs with their "raiz celta" (Celtic roots) strange, the kind of music that is preferred by their grandchildren (see chapter 10).

23. These Compostelan friends of mine had not wanted to go to the Carballeira de San Lourenzo, because they had little sympathy for the majority of the positions of the nationalist left. The Galicianization of proper names is a curious aspect of the process of the nationalization of Galician culture since the end of the 1970s. Many of the people that I know, now between thirty and fifty years old, changed the way they write their name in the registry office, often to the disapproval of their parents (it is much rarer that people would change the way they wrote their surnames; apparently, this was a step taken mainly by men). Among the younger generations, by contrast, vernacular names are very common, whether taken from saints of local cults or other personalities in some way connected to the history of a Galicia thought to be more authentic. A suggestive example might be the following: a couple with names like María del Carmen and José Antonio—probably an homage to Franco's wife and to the iconic figure of the Spanish Falange, José Antonio Primo de Rivera—might come to be called Maria do Carme and Xosé Antón, respectively. Their children, still very young, or adolescents, might be baptized as Breixo, Olaia, Breógan, or Mateu, for example. González Pérez (1998) tells us humorously how out of Galicianist enthusiasm, the local government of a given town had named a street "Antón Fraguas." This eminent Galician ethnographer (see excursus to chapter 3) was conscious of the fact that his parents wanted to pay homage to the famous Lisboan saint; on the other hand, Don Antonio Fraguas knew that abbot San Antón, "the lawyer of the pigs," with a cult in rural Galicia, had nothing to do with his homonym.

Chapter 3

Precursors/Galician Culture

The initial emergence of Galicianist claims in the first decades of the nineteenth century is represented as a renaissance or awakening of the Galician nation and of its culture after *séculos escuros* of *doma e castración* imposed at the end of the fifteenth—literally, "after dark centuries of being tamed and castrated." The construction of genealogies of *precursors*—that is, the identification of protagonists who created a positive affirmation of Galicia's "being"—has been an endeavor of great ideological importance continually updated in subsequent epochs by nationalist intellectuals of major standing. Today, the recognition and the celebration of precursors and of their respective works are a very important part of the representation of national Galician culture. In the introduction of a recent book, one historian of Basque and Catalonian nationalisms affirms that he did not intend to define "culture" and proposes "a study of people that defines it [that of the nationalists] and how they do it" (Conversi 1997: 1). In my opinion, this is a pertinent point of view and deserves to be emulated; I think as well that it will allow us to take into account Richard Handler's precept cited earlier, which considers culture to be a "thing"—in the example given in this chapter—objectified by the "politics of memory" exercised in Galicia during the twentieth century in the context of the Galicianist movement (Handler 1988; Gillis 1994).

Since the beginning of the nineteenth century references to the rural world and the popular classes served to legitimate the definition of Galicia as a specific community. It was the recognition of the particularities of the Galician people and of their history that led to the first political and aesthetic manifestations of claims for regional singularity. This was a particular reflection of romantic conceptions widespread throughout the whole of Europe. Below, I will summarize certain references to manifestations of those particularist sensibilities and the way that they were defined at the beginning of the twentieth century, when they were already dedicated to the construction of a national culture. I will take into account some of the historiography now available in Galicia,[1] the knowledge of precursors that my informants possessed, as well as several texts produced by various Galician authors throughout the twentieth century. The majority of these documents can be seen as genealogical constructions, that is, as components of the Galicianist politics of memory. The generally accepted periodization, recently made more precise by two Galician historians who specialize in the study of nationalism, will be used points of reference: "provincialism, from 1840 until approximately 1885; regionalism, from 1885 to 1915; and nationalism from 1916/18 forward" (Beramendi and Nuñez Seixas 1995: 17).

From the outset, it is important to emphasize that the more impartial historiographic approximations, as much as the memories supported in the sphere of the various factions of the nationalist movement, as a rule, accept these denominations without resistance, even if the relative minutiae of respective interpretations can be very different. As such, all of these interpretations take it for granted that the names *provincialismo, regionalismo, nacionalismo*—terms used by the respective protagonists— are sufficient references for describing the limits of the phenomena in question and also that they have a progressive meaning. This way of narrating accounts constantly reinforces Galicianist claims—except in the case of the hiatuses indicated—and flows into the situation as it stands today. We saw in the previous chapter that this situation can be considered "liminal," to the extent that expectations of the redemption of the *Terra* have still not been fulfilled.

It is worth introducing an observation by John Breuilly, useful as a cautionary note in relation to that perspective which I have called unanimous:

> The narrative form, with its assumption of a beginning, middle and end, could actually become an important component of the national movement: presenting it as a form of progress with the end still to be realized in the future. Later, more celebratory and conservative narratives might be written, though equally critical forms of nationalism would continue to present the story as one still to be finished. In this way, the narrative mode could buttress liberal, conservative and radical forms of nationalism. (Breuilly 1996: 157)

This description applies well to that which is happening currently in the Comunidade Autónoma *de Galicia,* where this progressive and even epic sense of Galicianist claims is hardly debated at all in terms of its general characteristics. In one of his essays Walter Benjamin affirmed,

"In fact, one may go even further and raise the question of whether historiography does not constitute the common ground of all forms of the epic" (1992: 95), a reference that is suggestive of the inevitability of this recurrent orientation. On the other hand, disputes about the legitimacy of appropriating the ideas of predecessors, as we saw in the previous chapter in relation to the homage paid to Castelao, can become acerbic. These are sensitive questions, because each of these evocations anchors contemporary political projects. In this case we find, as anthropologists recognize in many societies "without writing," omissions and unexpected prominence placed on specific people and events and even on pious "robberies" of relics,[2] giving us a notion of the impenitent efficacy of genealogical manipulations.

Resurgence—Bards and Prophets

The meticulous documentation made available today by historians allows us to affirm that the first political efforts of Galicianists were the work of a tiny minority. These efforts were few and often disrupted. Mostly their claims are hardly clear to us, quite different from the concerns of today's nationalist movement. The particularist claims articulated by the *provincialistas* of the last half of the nineteenth century were fragmentary and scattered. This has been recognized by professional historians (for example, Barreiro Fernández 1991a, or Beramendi and Nuñez Seixas 1995), just as the most eminent figures of the nationalist movement of the second half of the twentieth century had already done: "Certainly, from our present point of view, the goal they [the provincialists] pursued had a somewhat nebulous result; also the programmatic line that they dreamed about for Galicia lacked clarity. In any case, there was a noble wake-up call in their effort, an unequaled love for the things that make us unique, a longing to encounter solutions for the problems that afflict the people" (Fernández del Riego 1983: 10–11).

It is still as a scattered and unstable reality that one of the specialists classifies the various expressions of *regionalismo* that emerged at the end of the nineteenth century (Máiz 1984: 425). It also becomes difficult to discern in the nineteenth-century proposals the political demands of aesthetic formulations, complementary and inextricable means through which a new discourse on Galicia was being created. An important biography of 1933, written by Vicente Risco,[3] recognizes the works of the most famous of Galician Romantic historians, the already cited Manuel Murguía (1843–1933), as being an encapsulation of the previous efforts of the precursors. In his own words:

Today Murguía is a historical figure of such notable prominence that he can be seen as the symbol of the Galician renaissance. A man of his time, an initiator of inquiries, a problem raiser, a pioneer of new paths, he was a bold polymath who even if he was conscious of the crushing task he had taken on, he attacked the novel, poetry, literary criticism, art criticism, archeology, history, sociology, folklore, the law and even politics, and for this reason his outstanding oeuvre, truly a Galician encyclopedia, has become a kind of synthesis of the efforts of the Precursors. (Risco 1976: 8)

This work by Vicente Risco was published for the first time in 1933, on the occasion of the first centenary of the birth of the famous Compostelan historian and polymath. It was Murguía who had introduced this specific use of the word *precursors* and, as such, can be considered the first trustee of the genealogy of the Galicianist claims, a task that has, since then, become incessant and one in which this particular term became recognizable. This was achieved in a book published in 1886 entitled *Los Precursores,* whose purpose was to invoke the first formulators of political, *provincialista* ideas, as well as the various authors who had celebrated Galicia in the vernacular language. In our days the more precise political claims formulated by Murguía or by authors that preceded him are forgotten—this is the subject of the meticulous work of contemporary historians, for whom wider recognition, or any kind of special acknowledgement is elusive. In this case, as in other analogous cases taken up by studies of nationalism in Galicia and abroad, only those who have formulated "ethnic myths"—efficacious allegories to imagine an ample and heterogeneous social space as community—are considered to be important by nonspecialists (Smith 1999: 57 and ff.).[4] Attention is drawn, for this reason, to the role of men and women of letters and artists, and the privileges contemporaneously granted to the celebration of their respective memory are special ones. A. Smith notes the following in a general reference:

> It is the intellectuals—poets, musicians, painters, sculptors, novelists, historians and archaeologists, playwrights, philologists, anthropologists and folklorists—who have proposed and elaborated the concepts and language of the nation and nationalism and have through their musing and research given voice to wider aspirations that they have conveyed in appropriate images, myths and symbols. (1991: 93; see also Anderson 1991)

If we take Smith's statement into account, we will have to recognize as well that the majority of the Galicianist literary figures of the nineteenth century created a polyvalent oeuvre, but that research by philologists, grammarians, or ethnographers was a rare thing, just as novels or theatrical pieces written in Galician were scarce. It is also difficult to identify visual artists connected with the Galicianist cause. As we will see below, there will be a range of efforts towards nationalization on the part of the sciences and the arts that will unfold later, mainly in the 1920s and 1930s, when a declaredly nationalist political movement was already beginning to succeed. This was also an epoch when, symptomatically, references to the precursors became more systematic, and the attempt was being made to popularize their memory in the most diverse ways.

Still today, it is the poets who are most remembered for their expressions of Galicianist sensibilities that gained a place in the nineteenth century, above all, those who had a role to play in the literary recuperation of the Galician language. Their activities fell under the ambit of the so-called *Rexurdimento*—or *renacencia,* the less-used term—which followed the period of the first Romantics, *provincialistas* who had written about Galicia, but in Castilian. Poetry was, in fact, the only genre that regularly employed the vernacular language during the nineteenth century, and, for this reason, it emerges as the clearest expression of the Galician "renaissance." But the romantic poets produced above all powerful metaphors to describe Galicia as a community, satisfying in this way one of the "missions" of metaphors—the emotive articulation of identity (Fernández 1986: 28 and ff.), the reason for the persistence and notoriety of the respective memory. The names of the Romantic *bardos* were familiar to many of the Galicians that I have known over time and who were often capable of citing extracts of Galician poetry or who also knew the Galician anthem, made official only in 1980, by heart—evidence of the vivacity of the process of the nationalization of Galician culture in recent years.

The great poets of the *Rexurdimento* are by consensus the most important references in the politics of Galicianist memory.[5] For example, statues were erected early on of Rosalía de Castro and of Manuel Curros Enríquez (1851–1908), financed through collections of funds gathered among the circles of Galician emigrants in South America. Eduardo Pondal (1835–1917), the author *Os Pinos* (1886), was celebrated during his own lifetime, when the words from this poem were used for the Galician national anthem. It is important to note that the works of these bards of the *Rexurdimento* were less subject to state censorship in periods of the greatest political unrest. A good example is how the *misa de Rosalía,* already referred to above, was the only public commemorative act of Galicianist import to be tolerated under Francoism.

In a text entitled *Precursores y Apóstoles del Nacionalismo Galego,* Ramón Otero Pedrayo, commenting upon what had been a "prosaic" nineteenth century in Galicia says:

But from this sad perspective great figures lit up on the desolate horizon; they were the Poets. They suffered, implored, cursed, and yet did not lose hope. They were the only ones to fulfill their duty: Curros, Rosalía, Añon, Pondal, and, above all the taciturn and distant Eduardo Pondal, from Puenteceso. Curros was the triumphant and generous revolution in Galician; Rosalía offered herself as the propitiatory host for all of the pains of Galicia. But Pondal, raised in the formidable solitude of the harsh coast, the rhythmic essence of a dreaming and prophetic race, never lost confidence, swaying above the mobility of historic shadows. He never doubted, and this is why he is our bard. (*Céltiga* no. 163, 1930)

The title of this text by Otero Pedrayo is curious for its biblical resonances. Implicitly, it is as prophets of nationalism that the romantic bards are identified, while the members of the generation of the author himself would be apostles that had already revealed themselves to be politically dedicated to the spreading of the message of nationalist redemption. I would note, in passing, that apostolic images are very frequent in Galicianist literature of the twentieth century. But there is a logical absence in Pedrayo's text: that of the central, christomimetic figure. Murguía might have been assigned this role of being the "Christ" of Galicianism if the circumstances of his biography had been otherwise and if the movement had succeeded decidedly during the beginnings of the twentieth century. But Murgía died in 1923, at the age of ninety, when a nationalist movement with clarified political positions was still only beginning to burgeon in Galicia. For this reason he received the cognomen, still biblical, of Patriarch: the nationalists who were laying claim to their heirs wanted to see in the historian the Moses of the national cause:

When during the long, sad, and tepid years of the second half of the nineteenth century and with Galicia fading into the artificial uniformity of Spanish life, it was Murguía who sustained the eternal consciousness of the Race and the *Terra*. He knew how to listen to the sad melodies of the native pioneers, the hushed voice of tradition, he opened his heart to the hope, and did not allow himself to be subdued or fall into decadent complaints, this near legendary Patriarch of the Galician people on the path to their new era. (*Nós* 16, 1923)

Today, as I have suggested, the names of the Galicianist ideologues and politicians of the nineteenth century are hardly recognized, except by scholars specializing in the respective works, or by nationalist intellectuals with broader theoretical pretensions. It was in this way that Murguía himself, or some of his other contemporaries, like Alfredo Brañas and Aureliano Pereira (1855–1906), the most articulate of the ideologues of the Galicianist discourse at the end of the nineteenth century (Máiz 1984), whose ideas were reformulated in later notions of nationalist theory, remained below the the public's radar, a public that today favor the nineteenth century "bards."

Murguía also wrote poetry, though it was only a small part—and I believe justifiably forgotten—of the varied oeuvre of the husband of the famous poet Rosalía de Castro. In a recent colloquium sponsored by the Consello da Cultura Galega, one of the organizers said, in good humor, that Murguía was remembered only as *o home da outra* [the husband of the "other one"], adding that it was also important to evoke him as the earliest and clearest historian and theoretician of Galician nationalism. This was, of course, the reason that justified this particular academic meeting convoked in his memory, one of the many initiatives that the autonomous government has used to produce a national memory during the last two decades.

In ideological terms—beyond the politics of memory exercised in Galicia today—we must give the historians of the nineteenth century who wrote "histories of Galicia" their due. These were undertakings of great import, given that they have allowed us to situate the Galician nationality in time, to a great extent an unprecedented enterprise (Barreiro 1988). For example, it was romantic historiography that identified "Celticism" as the nucleus of the most long-lasting and influential ethnogeneological beliefs of the Galician national discourse. Even today, these notions are spreading in Galicia in very surprising ways, in spite of the fact that their scientific basis has been discredited (cf. chapter 4).

Generally, the work of the historians of the nineteenth century—the most relevant names are José Verea y Aguiar, Benito Vicetto, and Manuel Murguía—became one of the most substantial references for the legitimization of the more determined political claims of the nationalists that would emerge in the future. (Barreiro 1988; Barro 1994 and Beramendi 1995). But it is the Romantic historians took an essential step in acting like "ventriloquists" and evoking the "voices of the anonymous dead," thereby retrospectively projecting the existence of a political community recently imagined (see Anderson 1991). It is worth citing a characterization of the ideas of Manuel Murguía—written by a political scientist specializing in the study of his oeuvre, R. Máiz—which corresponds to the general characterization put forth by Anderson:

> A feature characteristic of Murguía: an historical retroprojection of contemporary categories. As such, Galicia shows itself to be a 'nationality' from the beginning of time, blessed with an *unalterable essence* that runs through its history resisting the foreign and civilizing influences: prevailing over any chance factor from abroad. … The nation, definitively, con-

stitutes the core principle and reason for Galician history. (Máiz 1984: 257; author's italics)

In my opinion, Ramón Máiz has clearly proved how in the arguments of Murguía, we find solid and sufficient theoretical foundations for a national discourse, even though it had been under the banner of regionalism that the historian developed all of his civic action (Máiz 1984 and 1997). In fact, Manuel Murguía was the most resolute theoretician of the *feito diferencial galego*, still today a formula frequently used by nationalist militants as it is by autonomous institutions or social scientists.[6] These current uses confirm that the representations of Galicia as an individuated transhistorical subject have become naturalized—this is a *fact*, an incontestable confirmation (Bourdieu 1989). Murguía proclaimed in 1889:

> Galicia has a perfectly delimited territory, a distinct language and race, history and conditions that were created thanks to this same diversity, and, as such, necessities which only it can really measure in all of their intensity, and aspirations that only it can know the outer-bounds of. It constitutes, thus, a Nation, because it has all the characteristics proper to a nationality. (cit. in Máiz 1997: 175–76)

In an earlier work, and a more important one, in describing the "physiognomy" of the Galician people, the historian had given great emphasis to the timeless survival of customs among less-educated groups in the countryside and along the coast. Characteristically, he used, in a vague way, terms like "character," "personality," "spirit," "soul," "ethnicity," "civilization," "genius," "race," "traditions," and "customs" in order to define the physiognomy of the nation (Murguía 1985). Two of these terms stand out as having remained constant in Galicianist rhetoric, and their presence is still felt today: *personality* and *soul*. These expressions are still employed on various occasions: by emeritus guests at the opening of university colloquiums, by old Galicianists in editorials in the press, or by political leaders. I have also heard them from numerous people with whom I have conversed over time. Personality, or soul, have, however, an antiquated resonance; only the oldest of my informants used them. With my contemporaries another term was more frequently favored: *identity*. The reiteration of these essentially synonymous terms shows us that they are manipulated ideological precepts central to nationalist discourses. Arguing that nationalism should be considered to be an ideology of "individuated being," defined in terms of choice and property, Richard Handler offers the following assessment:

The content of national being is national "character," "personality," "culture," and "history." Yet in nationalist ideology, these are subordinated to individuated being, which is the primary reality. In other words, the existence of a bounded entity is central, whereas the cultural content within these bounds comes after the fact. The existence of a national entity is a primary assumption of nationalist ideology, rarely questioned; but the content of national being is the subject of continual negotiation and dispute. (1988: 51)

With this definition, the importance given to the precursors in the politics of Galicianist memory emerges with full justification, as first definers of the entity of Galicia, where, as we have seen, the poets' more emotive ways of imagining Galicia have preeminence. Their memory has been appropriated as a privileged reference in the nationalization of the masses. Today the dense prose with which Murguía made claims to the Celtic genealogy of the Galician nation, its "being" and expectations of autonomy, is not well known. Nevertheless, many Galicians know the verses of Eduardo Pondal by heart, a poetry in which we find the same ethnogenealogical petitions summarized and where similar promises of regeneration are inscribed. Let me cite the last lines of the Galician anthem: "The times have arrived / that announce the bards of yesteryear/ and that will finally put an end/ to your uncertainties / as everywhere gigantic/ our voice will cry out for the redemption of the good/ nation of Breogán." Various of the vague terms that I noted are patently assimilable. Between the old personality, or the soul, whose uses have disappeared, and the very recent identity, which is still gaining in popularity, there is a single argument for individuation that remains as given. The Galicianists of the early twentieth century were charged with identifying those features that defined Galicia's "being," with constructing Galician culture, as a systematic and intentional project. As we will see below, this is the principal reason for the prominence in the contemporary politics of memory of these modernist culture builders, which is of greater consequence than that of the remote "bardos" and the nineteenth-century historians.

Encounters with the People, Art, and the Irmandades da Fala [Brotherhood of the Language]

The first defined steps of the Galician nationalist movement took place in the years 1916–1918. This emerging particularist discourse solidified immediately following World War I. The end of 1910 was a propitious

time for the emergence of new nationalist movements or for the consolidation of claims against the oldest political sovereignties, various of
which were eventually satisfied. Frequent in the pages of Galician periodicals of that period are references to the successes of national movements in Ireland, the former Czechoslovakia, the Baltic countries, and
even in India where, at the time, petitions for sovereignty were particularly vigorous.[7] This "spirit of the times" certainly provided a conducive
atmosphere for the emergence of nationalist enthusiasms in Galicia. But
cases that were closer and related to the Basque Country and to Catalonia (mainly the latter), where particularist political movements began
forming during the end of the nineteenth century (Conversi 1997), were
the more directly emulated references. We can see, in this way, that the
course of Galician nationalism was very narrowly framed by the "short
twentieth century" (Hobsbawm 1994); as such, we can conclude that
this is a belated case, if we consider the history of the phenomenon on a
global level, or even in the more specific context of the Spanish state.

According to the unanimous opinions of activists and contemporary
historians, the single primordial moment in the establishment of the
nationalist movement in Galicia occurred on 18 May 1916, during a
meeting of the self-designated Amigos da Fala, which took place in A
Coruña. The convocation of various personalities—already inculcated
with regionalist ideas that had emerged from the previous century and
who had found in Manuel Murguía a referential figure—came about
through the initiative of a journalist cited above, Antonio Villar Ponte.
Two months earlier, Villar Ponte had published a manifesto in Castilian
with a somewhat ambiguous title and contents—*Nacionalismo Gallego:
Nuestra Afirmación Regional.* However, in this pamphlet it is stated that
the language (the vernacular, Galician) was the "shield of spiritual autonomy, stronger than arms" (cit. in Beramendi and Nuñez Seixas 1995:
94).

The participants of this particular meeting organized the first Irmandade da Fala,[8] an association with a local base, which was quickly redu-
plicated in various Galician cities and towns in the months and years
to follow. It is also in 1916 that *A Nosa Terra*—an already existing title—appears with new funding as *Idearium da Hirmandade da Fala en
Galicia e nas colonias gallegas d'a America e Portugal,* under the direction of AntonioVillar Ponte.[9] The use of Galician among Galicianist
activists grouped together in the Irmandades would become systematic,
as would the multiplication of attempts to create a *cultura galega,* an
expression that spread little by little and that would only become more
broadly used by the beginning of the 1920s. About the meeting of 18
May 1916, J. Beramendi and X. M. Nuñez Seixas tell us:

A new, evolved phase of Galicianism … was born, in spite of the fact that most of those present at the act probably did not imagine such, because they perhaps thought that this was one more regionalist event, since the goals of the new association were directed at the promotion of the language and other secondary cultural activities. (1995: 95)

It seems correct to consider that moment to be a key date, despite the syncretism of the terms of discussion and of the proposals that emerged, or of their supposedly "secondary" character. The intention to spread the use of Galician among the urban middle classes through the spoken and written language is notable and can be seen as a completely new initiative that contained some of the most binding possibilities for imagining Galicia as a community. Comparatively, we can recognize that the strategy for using the vernacular language on the part of the middle classes is one of the most important actions taken by nationalist movements in the European context, and well tested throughout the nineteenth century in innumerable cases (Anderson 1991; Hroch 2000; Thiesse 2000). But there are two other objectives that were mapped out in the meeting of 1916 that merit our attention:

Excursions on days of celebration will be organized to the villages of Galicia, to get to know directly the life of the life of our *people*.

On the anniversary of the establishment of the association a visit to the tomb "of the great cultivators of the language" will be made in order to keep the "cult of Galicianism alive." (cit. in Barreiro Fernández 1991b: 161)

In most widely sold titles from the Galician publishing industry there is a definite suggestion that the attendance of celebrations in rural zones was not an unusual habit among the Galician bourgeoisie in the first years of the twentieth century. On the other hand, the practice of making excursions—and many other ethnomimetic practices[10]—had already won over practitioners in a variety of bourgeois circles from Vigo, Pontevedra, and A Coruña who remained clearly disconnected from nationalist mobilizations in the years following. A notice in a 1919 periodical from Vigo makes clear the intensity of those practices and the ironies that their excesses could give rise to:

The romantic, though very Platonic, love of the region, is carrying us to lamentable excesses and a sad absurdity. Some months ago, during a village celebration a virtuoso on the chanter played the "Happy Widow" waltz on his bagpipe during the procession around the chapel, and some days before we had the bad luck to see a yokel from some regional choir, one of those types that wear patent leather shoes and a *monteira* [a kind of cap typical of rural Galicia] with a velvet tassel, go down the Avenida de los Cantones on his bicycle. And this is hardly serious, my friends.

They are very decorative and go well with our mountains and our valleys and our donkey-carts, at the end of our hedge-lined paths, and with the surplus of pine forests that Eduardo Pondal sang about; it's more important to confess that your oxcart breaks your ear drums and that its pace is too slow and tiring *for the poor peasant whom we endeavor to imitate in a highly theatrical fashion.* The oxcart is very beautiful; but we prefer the automobile. (*Vida Gallega* no. 133, 1919; my italics)

I would say that zealous incitements to behave in the ethnographic fashion of the *hirmáns* were, most probably, inspired by news of such practices employed efficaciously by other nationalist movements, namely, the Catalan and Basque movements where the practice of excursions and mountaineering were already commonplace. In Galicia, the youth excursion group connected to nationalist circles—*Ultreya*—would emerge later (in 1932). Interestingly, some of the first ethnomimetic performances in which the *hirmáns da fala* were involved took to the stage in the most luxurious of Galician hotels of the epoch, at the Mondariz spa, a meeting point for the Spanish high bourgeoisie of the belle époque. The owners, prosperous capitalists of Vigo, sympathized with the ideas of the Irmandades and, to a certain extent, became their sponsors. (This case of important financial interests moving closer to the nationalist dis-

Figure 1. *Aires da Terra* choir. Photograph by José Cao Durán, 1901.

course was particular to Galicia, and contrary to what had occurred in Catalonia and the Basque Country.) The first ethnographic museum of Galicia, whose collection has unfortunately been lost, was established in one of the rooms of the Mondariz Hotel, and the elegant seasonal magazine that the hotel published—*A Temporada*—is, in my opinion, an example, modest and marginal, but very suggestive of the initial history of Galician nationalism.

But the pilgrimages on foot around the *Terra,* to seek out the people, had some high moments and starred some of the most notable Galicianists, at the beginning of the 1920s. The most prominent document recording these walks is a book by Ramón Otero Pedrayo, *Pelerinaxes I (Itinerario d'Ourense ao San Andrés de Teixido).* There, in the prologue, Vicente Risco—illustrator and participant on this excursion of intellectuals—cites the pilgrimages through India made by Gandhi. It is worth citing a particularly suggestive extract: "You say: Galicia is very small. I tell you: Galicia is a world unto itself. ... It might be small in length: in 'depth,' as an 'entity,' it is as large as you want it to be, and from the start much larger than that which you are able to see" (V. Risco in Otero Pedrayo 1993: 10).

Generally, and in the long term, the truth is that the proposals of 1916, which were reiterated in the following years, had minor echoes. Membership in the various Irmandades was hardly widespread, however, and the number of members always remained below a thousand, until the *Partido Galeguista* was founded in 1931. Their respective base of recruitment was also narrow and predictable; mainly made up of functionaries and intellectuals, members of the urban middle class, and the petite bourgeoisie. (Beramendi and Nuñez Seixas 1995: 130; cf. Hroch 2000). It is also curious to note that the familial lineage of a significant number of the affiliates can be connected to the old *fidalguía galega* (the nontitled nobility) that the nineteenth century had brought to ruin (Villares 1997). Ramón Otero Pedrayo makes claim to these social origins in obsessive, though ideologically interesting terms that run through his important essayistic and fictional work. According to Julien Benda in a description, which is only partially correct, European intellectuals were ready to betray the cosmopolitan values that they had once esteemed for a newfound nationalistic love of the *Terra* (Benda 1969). I found Benda's work cited in the first series of *Nosa Terra.* I could not clarify, however, to what extent these references presumed a first-hand knowledge of his famous indictment. To be fair, the attempt to define nationalism as a particularist expression of universal values would be a constant theme in the texts of the most capable intellectual Galicianists during the 1920s and 1930s.

In 1918, writing in a very idiosyncratic Galician, a contributor to *A Nosa Terra* suggested the following:

> Someone has already said that what the French Revolution meant for the civil political autonomy of the individual man, this war signifies the same thing as it touches upon *the individual people*. Each nation, each group of people joined by the triple link of race, land, and blood, develops freely, according to the intimate maxims of their genius, their genuine and authentic capacities, the true distinctive aspects of their way of living a complete life. ... Through art they always represent their worries, their desires, those people who for some reason do not enjoy life's fulness. Oh art, you can be very dangerous. If I was a tyrant, I would perhaps fear the poets more than the revolutionaries. (*A Nosa Terra,* no. 31, 1917; my italics)

The uses of the term *culture* were rare in Galicia in the first years of the twentieth century, as was the case, as a matter of fact, in the rest of the world. So, in this context in particular, the term would indicate mainly the artistic or erudite interests of a minority of Galicians of the more privileged classes, who, as a rule, were readers and speakers of Castilian. These people valued their cosmopolitan references and habitually dismissed what was autochthonous from the range of possibilities for personal improvement as expressed through the cultivation of the "arts" and "letters." This cultivation was generally mediated by the standard language of the state or by foreign languages, especially French. In the citation directly above we now encounter the term "art" associated with Galicia, even if it is still only the poets who are referred to, as Murguía had already done in the previous century. However, it was during these years that, in addition to the erudite uses that the *Fala* [the Galician Language] was put to in poetry, the possibility of the existence of an art and, soon after, of a Galician culture also began to be seriously considered. Curiously, this claim will be coupled with the demand for the individuation and the full existence of Galicia, as the sentence transcribed suggests.

One of the earliest uses of the term *culture* directly associated with Galicia and the positions of the Galicianist movement that I encountered dates back to the same year of 1917. This was in a text written by the representative of the Irmandades from the small town of Viveiro that, with its title of *Fala e Estética,* is especially curious. It contains the phrase "the very erudite Portuguese Teófilo Braga" invoked to prove that Galician culture had disappeared with the end of the literary uses of the vernacular in the lower Middle Ages. It is, then, in an erudite sense that Galician culture is referred to here, confined to the erudite uses of the language. The piece contains a variety of curiosities: "The peasants' lack of culture was and still is, sadly, an open field where jokers can gather and assign to them harshness and extreme poverty for their rude work." The columnist wants to denounce an *enxebrismo podre* [festering traditionalism], or the utterly characteristic and most facile of the genre of literary and theatrical products referred to as *costumbrista* [in the Spanish tradition, a description of "popular" life], pregnant with the use of clichés that served for describing Galician peasants. And yet these clichés drew on old motifs with a long erudite tradition partly founded in the classical Spanish theatrical tradition of the *Siglo de Oro* [Golden Century]. The novella and the theater of "regional motifs" are the target here, examples of literary products that smelled of manure, which the columnist wants to anathematize. Though what follows is an appeal to refinement, and to the suitable and elevated use of Galician; to literature we must bring *that which is only literary*. The *fala* must also be of use, the columnist says,

> to express and empty into it all the ideas and all thoughts, all the truths and all the feelings, from the most subtle and delicate to the more scientific and profound. ... Our regionalism is not only economic and political. It is also an aesthetical question, one of beauty, art, perfection, and, above all, of culture, the Galician light for thought, by which we mark the path of complete and European freedom, so that a luminous day will arrive in which the old Suevian Kingdom, speaking in the language of free people can say: *I. (A Nosa Terra*, no. 29, 1917; my italics)

John Juaristi recently presented a subtle and suggestive analysis of the emergence of *costumbrista* novels in Bilbao at the end of the nineteenth century and of their ambiguous relationship with the emergence of a nationalist discourse (Juaristi 1999). Galician nationalists reacted indignantly to novels and farcical intermezzos based on "regional motifs"— normally written in Spanish, but with more or less burlesque speeches in Galician interspersed—their reaction very similar to those of the nationalist Basques noted by Juaristi. These genres—minor and strongly stigmatized among the rank-and-file nationalists—found followers over time in Galicia itself and a franker public reception than that given to "serious" theater or literature, or received by the avant-garde works that Galician authors dedicated themselves to producing during the 1920s and 1930s (Tato Fontaiña 1999).

A Manifesto in 1918

A first *asambleia magna* of the various Irmandades da Fala that had been emerging since 1916 took place in Lugo in November of 1918. In the manifesto issuing from this meeting, which is still famous today in the annals of Galician nationalism, the following declaration was loudly proclaimed:

> Since Galicia has all of the characteristics essential to a nationality, we nominate ourselves, from today on, Galician nationalists, now that the word "regionalism" does not hold all of our aspirations, nor capture the complete intensity of our problems. (*A Nosa Terra* no. 73–74, 1918)[11]

In the manifesto of this, the First Nationalist Assembly of Lugo, the co-officialism of Galician and Castilian is declared to be one of the constituent problems of the nationalist claims, on par with other more pragmatic proposals and claims of an economic and political-administrative character. Some of these proposals are surprisingly insignificant and do not merit comment. However, one last point included in the manifesto is worth looking at. Even though no direct references to Galician culture have yet been made, in the epigraph "artistic aspects" are said to be objectives of the *hirmáns* ['brothers and sisters']:

> 1) To proclaim the aesthetic sovereignty of the Galician Nation which will be put into effect: *a*) in urban and rural building projects, imposing a law that obliges owners to conform to the general style of each Galician town. *b*) In the expropriation of monuments and landscapes. *c*) In the organization of art education, with the creation of a school of Galician music.

The proposals spelled out at this point are, as we can see, modest: the preservation of buildings, vague projects concerning heritage—even though the reference to the expropriation of landscapes is especially curious—and likewise the suggestion to Galicianize the teaching of music. In 1918 exemplary practices of this type intentionally exercised in other contexts, namely, in the more powerful nation-states such as France, England, Germany, and Italy, were unending and already historical.[12] In Galicia, as well, proposals to materialize a sense of a national memory had emerged gradually even before 1918 with examples such as the statue of Rosalía de Castro in Santiago, the monument to the *mártires de Carral,* and the establishment of the Real Academia Galega and the Panteón de Galegos Ilustres.

With respect to the elaboration of the manifesto of 1918, we have Vicente Risco's commentary. In a short time Risco would become a central figure as a theoretician of Galician nationalism. He was present at the First Nationalist Assembly, about which he would write an

article that would appear in *A Nosa Terra*—"Sensaciós da asambleia."
Here he employs a range of different allusions to comment on the ideas
for the redemption of Galicia that had come out of Lugo. He speaks of
John Ruskin, as well as Hellenism, of Romanticism, of Classicism, of
the Twelve Tablets of Hindu law and mythology, and alludes to the god
Agni and the laws of Manu:

> Dr. Quintanilla proposed and the assembly accepted, unanimously, to
> declare the aesthetic Sovereignty of the Galician Nation. … The Galician
> Nation when it becomes its own, will always keep the seven lamps of
> Ruskin burning in our land, perhaps as an homage to our dead who are
> asleep beneath our ground and who constructed it with their work and
> with their flesh sewn in the earth. The dictatorship of the old Ruskin who
> was of our Race and our psychology. (*A Nosa Terra* no. 73/74, 1918)

Apparently, what moved the arguments of Jaime Quintanilla, then a
young doctor mainly concerned with the nationalization of Galician
music, were erudite aesthetical preoccupations, as he tells us in his interesting article a bit later (cf. *Nós,* no. 2, 1920). On the other hand, a
vertiginous amount of disparate intellectual references mold the commentaries of Vicente Risco, a characteristic that certainly impressed the
readers of *A Nosa Terra*. Early on, his contributions took on a polished
and memorable form, published under the epigraph "Verbas de Risco,"
an importance attributed to only a restricted elite of *guieiros* [guides].
In the passage transcribed above, John Ruskin is cited in support of the
claims made. We can also recognize themes dear to the discourse of the
French extreme right (indicated by his citation of Fustel de Coulanges)
(Sirinelli 1992). But it becomes impossible to discriminate what the
effective weight of these disparate influences in Risco's thought at this
time actually is, given the *acusada tendencia ó sincretismo* [acknowledged
tendency towards syncretism] of his readings (Bobillo 1981: 21; see also
Casares et al. 1997). As a matter of fact, Ruskin would disappear quickly
from the list of Risco's preferred sources, and the ideas of Oswald Spengler would gain prominence, his famous *Der Untergang des Abendals*
having been first translated into Spanish in 1926. Risco had perhaps already known about Spengler's book (Outeiriño 1990). He would review
the Spanish translation in a Galician newspaper, and the German author
would remain a lasting influence on his work. By the end of the 1920s,
Spengler would also be increasingly quoted by Risco's various fellow
adherents, though his ideas, cited for the prestige they could bring to a
text, were understood only in varying degrees (see, for example, Villar
Ponte 1975, and Otero Pedrayo 1982).[13]

Figure 2. Ethnomimesis: Vicente Risco, right, in a straw cap [*coroza*]. Unknown photographer, n.d.

At any rate—and this is what I would like to emphasize at this point—in that period Ruskin would already have begun to fade as a reference in the context of the founding of a nationalist movement (Williams 1993). The cosmopolitan aestheticism that the mid-nineteenth century Ruskin espoused was already out of date and irrelevant to the meanings that more directly influenced the nationalist discourses coming out of the Great War; as Raymond Geuss suggests:

> Only in the 1870s ... does the term *Kultur* begin to be used to refer to a plurality of nationally distinct ways of living, thinking and valuing. ... By the time of the First World War this kind of usage had become common. That Max Weber in 1915 could blithely write "All culture today is and remains bound to a nation" indicates the distance that has been travelled from Kant's use of the term *Kultur.* (Geuss 1996: 158)[14]

The intention to "proclaim aesthetic sovereignty" should be underscored in the founding Lugo manifesto, in spite of the fact that it is weakly formulated and underemphasized, submerged beneath a series of very prosaic demands. However, in the first place, the references to the individualized "being" of Galicia that we have already seen represented in various manners in the formulations of regionalists at the end of the nineteenth century are clearly reiterated in the manifesto. Nevertheless, these petitions for individuation now also touch upon questions of aesthetics and of property in something of a new way. Petitions for improvement and possession, which were habitually referenced to the mere individual in previous decades, were now clearly replicated in favor of the nation, according to Richard Handler, and were a defining note in nationalist discourses (1988). In the Lugo manifesto appropriations of the beautiful no longer contributed only to the private experience of separate individuals who cultivated cosmopolitan tastes, but also to the nation, now theorized as a subject gifted with specific properties that should be conserved and cultivated.

By 1918, the monumentalization of a national memory had become the deliberate preoccupation of Galicianist intellectuals and was an important part of the proposals to which the national movement gave voice in the publications that were related to it. But their realization was very modest, because the influence of nationalists in the whole of Galician society at that time was undoubtedly weak, as I have already suggested. In the few years that were propitious for direct political action that lasted until the outbreak of the civil war, and under generally agitated conditions in the context of the Spanish state, there were various ideologies that competed for the consciousness of the people of Spain (Tusell 1998, 1999a; Carr 1982; Tuñon de Lara 1992). These ideologies were also directly expressed in Galicia and, as a matter of fact, had various Galicians as proponents at the level of the Spanish state as a whole.[15] A note from 1923 in *A Nosa Terra* is suggestive of the marginal position of the Irmandades da Fala. It describes an initiative proposed with as much enthusiasm as there was lack of the means to consolidate it. We are speaking of the construction of a monument to the poet Manuel Curros Enríquez, an initiative paid for with money from donations from emigrants (known as *indianos*) and placed by the port of the city of A Coruña:

> The placing of the first stone of the monument that will be erected to Curros Enríquez has now been celebrated. It is not worth describing the act. We will only say that there were speeches in awful taste, brimming with twee Galicianism.
>
> The Irmandade da Fala attended the event because, as I have said many times, it is very much in agreement that a monument be created to perpetuate the memory of one of our great men. They did nothing else but attend. (*A Nosa Terra* no. 73/74, 1918)

However, in spite of the modest influence of the nationalists and of the rare gains achieved, there are two principal reasons that justify the emphasis that I give to their proposals from the end of the 1910s and the beginnings of the following decade. The first can be clarified by a point stressed by John Breully: "Even if nationalist movements do not have active popular support they claim to speak for the whole nation. In this sense nationalist politics is always mass politics" (1993: 19). Right at the end of the 1910s, the desire to create a "politics of the masses" on the part of the Galician nationalists will be evident after attentively consulting the pages of their *Idearium*. One will also find a sincere recognition of the scarcity of resources for the desired effect. On the other hand, the second reason is justified by the importance of the place that the founding acts of the Galician nationalist movement has in the annals of the national memory that is today cultivated in Galicia. References to the founding of the Irmandades da Fala or to the First Assembly at Lugo are found in the literature—and are even articulated by citizens of very different political leanings, especially the more educated young people—as crucial moments in the long road to affirming Galicianist ideas. However, for the majority, the recognition of the circumstances, of the claims set forth, or even of the identity of the protagonists in these founding movements is hardly clear beyond the rhetorical naming.

Whoever reads the issues of *A Nosa Terra*, published between 1916 and 1936, and concentrates on proposals for action and debates over ways of imagining the nation will understand that there was a plurality of positions and of participants that are today hardly remembered in Galicia. In fact, a good example can be found in the figure of its first director, Antón Villar Ponte,[16] the instigator of the Irmandades da Fala. On the contrary, there are frequent initiatives to perpetuate the memory of a small group of intellectuals know as the *grupo* or the *xeración Nós* [the group or our generation],[17] a name that for the majority of Galicians that I know contains the essence of the history of the Galician nationalist movement before 1936.

As we will see below, it is the name of a relatively sophisticated periodical—published in a small inland provincial city and hardly read in its time—that monopolizes the references that are made today vis-à-vis the protean period out of which emerged the Galician nationalist movement. It was a very restricted group of people, nearly all born during the 1880s and closely connected to each other, that gained such notoriety in the annals of Galicianism. This can be justified by the significance of their new proposals to objectify the representation of a national Galician culture bound together by the vernacular language. But it is also the objective result of the politics of selective memory exercised over time in the context of the nationalist movement and, to a great extent, appropriated today as an important resource to gauge the existence of a specific national culture and to guarantee its reproduction.

A Periodical from Ourense

It is the longing that Galicia feels today in living anew that makes us publish, to return the luminosity of the morning to its *true and immortal being*. We have a blind, absolute, unshakable faith in the vitality and the genius of our Race, and also in the efficacy of our effort to fulfill its glorious fate. In our *Terra* today, there exists a generation which took into account *their imperious social obligation to create a Galician culture for all times*. The magazine, *Nós,* has gathered together all of these efforts to integrate the Galician nation into its own polymorphism, which is already so rich.

Contributors to *Nós* can be what they like. Individualists or socialists, old-fashioned conservatives or futurists, intuitionalists or rationalists, naturalists or humanists, they can take up any position that touches upon the four antinomies of the contemporary mind: they can even be classicists, if they put the sentiment of *Terra* and Race above everything else, the desire to overcome, the proud satisfaction of being Galicians.

Nós should be a pious and devout study, full of sincerity, of all the Galician values: of our traditional values and of the new values that are being created daily in our *Terra*.

Nós should be the representation in the world of *the Galician personality* in its anxiousness to affirm itself as a value that is universal, autochthonous, and differentiated, within and beyond the *Terra*.

Nós should be the timeless affirmation of the *true being* of Galicia, of the Authentic uniqueness,which this personality contains, and must want to persist. *Enxebrismo* [Authenticity or Purity] is about our specific originality, our capacity for creation, our autochthonous mental dynamism. (*Nós*, no. 1: 1–2, my italics; "Terra," translator's italics)

The periodical *Nós* was published in Ourense—subtitled *Boletín Mensual da Cultura Galega* [Monthly Bulletin of Galician Culture]— between 1920 and 1935; there were altogether 144 issues. Its intentions were highly ideological, a manifesto that we can clearly see in its "*Primeiras verbas*" [First words], and whose originality resides in the choice of its principal concern—Galicia. Besides this radical choice, the rhetorical similarities with so many other contemporaneous avant-garde manifestos will be clearly evident; there are abundant examples in the first issues of periodicals of literature and of art that emerged worldwide from 1890 onwards, giving expression to innumerable movements that today we recognize as "modernist" (Bradbury and Macfarlane 1976). Primarily, it can be said that it was the desire to write novels and poetry, to do philosophy and science, and to write criticism of literature and the arts, etc., in Galician that motivated the members of the editorial board and the contributors to *Nós*—in effect, to bring into being a new "high" Galician culture (Risco 1936).

On the editorial board of *Nós* names such as Vicente Risco (1884–1963), Ramón Cabanillas (1876–1959), Alfonso Daniel Rodríguez Castelao (1886–1950), Ramón Otero Pedrayo (1888–1976), and Florentino Cuevillas (1886–1958) predominated, each of whom would become a notable figure in the nationalist movement during subsequent decades. Vicente Risco—the editor-in-chief of *Nós*—as much as the person in charge of graphics, A. Daniel Castelao, were the most recognized ideologues of Galician nationalism in successive periods, as well as being active politicians and authors of multifaceted works that displayed a Galicianizing intent. Risco was the most theoretically articulate of the movement from the beginning of the 1920s until the civil war, as has already been said, just as Castelao would take on that mantle later (after Risco had defected and fallen into silence in 1936), mainly through the influence of *Sempre en Galiza*. Ramon Cabanillas was recognized as a *poeta da raza* by his colleagues on the editorial board[18] and was occasionally involved in political action, as well as having been, indeed, a popular poet in his time. Otero Pedrayo was an historian, geographer, novelist, and also a politician and parliamentarian active in the first years the 1930s.[19] Florentino Cuevillas—the most discreet figure of the group— is remembered today as a self-taught, prolific, and erudite archeologist who produced a series of systematic studies dedicated to proving the supposed Celtic roots of the population of Galicia.[20]

Ruben Oliven examined a text by Gilberto Freyre (1900–1987), in which this Brazilian essayist recalled a "regionalist manifesto" of his own authorship, published in 1926, as "regionalist, traditionalist and, in its own way, modernist" (Oliven 1992: 33). These are qualifications that to a great extent can be linked to the manifesto that initiates *Nós*, even more appropriate when we bear in mind the ambiguities of the Galicianist movement's political demands and the type of ideological and aesthetic references that the majority of its contributors were attempting to exploit. But if on the other hand we again take up the characterization that Ruben Oliven made of the ideas of the most famous "Brazilian modernist movement" of 1922, in the state context, we will also find significant similarities with the ideas of the case we have in hand. Indeed, the possibilities of finding parallels are many: they can be found between the French regionalists of the belle époque that Thiesse (1991) dealt with and their equals in America (Dorman 1993), or between the *aportuguesadores* active at the beginning of the twentieth century (Ramos 1994), and so on. I recall a suggestive characterization that Oliven made of the Brazilian "modernist" movement of 1922: "It signifies the updating of Brazil in relation to the cultural and artistic movements which are happening abroad; on the other hand, it also implies the search for our own national roots and giving value to what is most authentic in Brazil" (1992: 32). It is very similar to what we can recognize in the ideas put forth in the contents of *Nós* in 1920.

This citation suggests—along with the variety of similar examples—the modest importance of distinguishing at this point to what extent the proponents of Galicianist manifestos at the beginning of the twentieth century were really only regionalists or actually nationalists, or, more or less, *pasatistas* or *futuristas*. It is true that there were very few futurist Galicianists and plenty of them who ignored or reacted badly to the leading projects of the vanguard that at the time were cropping up all over Europe and the rest of the world (see Castelao 1982, a significant example). The limits of their demands for political sovereignty for Galicia always remained equivocal. The proposals of the *arredistas* (that is, those seeking independence) were rare and came much later. It is, more than anything else, however, the force of those propositions that deal with the necessity of a vernacularized erudite culture that should be underlined, with emphasis also given to the range of possible appropriations left open for the future by these creations and objectivizing identifications of that which "belonged" to the Galician Nation (Handler 1988).

Three Lustra of Efforts

In a later issue of *Nós* (no. 115, from 1933) a piece entitled "A cultura galega hoxe en día" [Galician culture today] gives us the balance sheet of the results of efforts made since 1920. The epigraph at the opening uses some quite curious images, many of them evocative of Benedict Anderson's arguments:

> *Nós*, which was founded by a small nucleus of writers who essentially continue to be same ones that in 1920, live and sustain themselves thinking that there is in the Galicia of our times an autochthonous and authentic [*enxebre*] culture in full renaissance. In the name of this Galician culture, which strives to be an example and a mirror, *Nós* asks everyone who is capable to contribute their creative efforts, the greatest possible independence of spirit as well as a loyalty to the soul of the Race.

> At times it is necessary to look around us, to be able to nail the standards to the map that tell of the new conquests that have happened in the different provinces of the spiritual world.

> As a task more suited to the *Día de Galiza* [Galicia Day], let us look right away—at the measure of offerings that the Galician talents have made to the Homeland—to see in great detail that which has been gained in recent times. (*Nós*, no. 115, 1933)

In addition to this very metaphorical epigraph, the text records in detail the number of "standards signifying wins" on the Galician cultural map and their very different colors. That is, it gives an account of different literary and academic specializations that were indeed practiced and still other Galicianizing initiatives that were undertaken during the thirteen years under discussion. This is a particularly curious aspect of this text, that it not only contemplates the erudite production of the *núcleo d'escritores,* but also various initiatives geared towards the nationalization of the masses that are clearly beyond the restricted sphere of this group of intellectuals. These were approaches that did not sit together well, but they are suggestive of the concern for the various nationalizing initiatives that the author of the article supported.[21]

For most of this period in Spain the dictatorship of Primo de Rivera (1923–1930) was in power, a regime that, though it had censored the more explicit political expressions of peripheral nationalistic movements, hardly interfered at all with the other initiatives taken up by their supporters. The literary uses of a variety of minority languages, the consolidation of national symbols, and the establishment of research institutes can be viewed as examples of this relative tolerance.[22] As well, a variety of forms of entertainment, which were closely linked to nationalist militancy, spread with relative freedom. And finally we can say that during these years very significant advances in the programs of nationalizing the masses were occurring, especially in Catalonia and the Basque Country, where older nationalist movements were already consolidated and had been influencing politics since the beginning of the twentieth century.

In Galicia, the sum of results of nationalizing initiatives during the 1920s was modest, as is suggested by the article cited from *Nós*. This modesty will become even more evident if we focus on what would happen later, under the Second Republic and the Franco dictatorship, in the Basque Country and in Catalonia, where, contrary to what was happening in Galicia, forms of cultural resistance were expressed on a massive scale, due to the persistence of nationalizing programs in effect since the end of the nineteenth century (Brandes 1990; Tusell 1999; Conversi 1997). However, we should not ignore the range of efforts expended and taken note of in the above mentioned review published in *Nós,* which talks about the intentions to implement the greatest variety possible of *províncias espirituais* [spiritual provinces] in the new national culture—a particularly suggestive image (Handler 1988).

What is most glaring looking back at this relatively benign period of censorship introduced by the dictatorship of Primo de Rivera are the particularly feeble results of the diffusion of these new contents, weakened by multiple difficulties that went beyond the policies of the government. Rather, what is suggested are the lack of material resources and of effective vehicles of propaganda, which were hardly accessible to the small group of Galician nationalists with little political and social influence. But also, it is, at the end of the day, the paucity of efforts made that are notable, and that what efforts there were, were confined to a small circle of versatile producers of Galician culture. Unsurprisingly, it is the products of literature that stand out in this gamut of results; above all, it is the work of the poets that we can finally recognize as especially prolific and innovative. On the contrary, it can be said that the work of historians, novelists, and playwrights, whose nationalizing potential should be emphasized, was weak and paltry, even if conditions for the respective diffusion of their work were difficult and the public quite reluctant in accepting them.[23]

The theater provides us with a curious example of some of the dilemmas that marked the creation of a Galician culture and of the rejections that its promoters faced. "A cultura galega hoxe en día," the article we have been following, accounts for only three "serious" plays during the thirteen years under consideration. Of these, indeed only one was premiered with success that went beyond the expectations of its authors, two important personalities already mentioned above: Antón Villar Ponte and Ramón Cabanillas. A recent work about the history of the theater in Galicia—though it still came to the same conclusions found in the article from *Nós*—speaks about a wider variety of theater produced in Galicia during those years, noting how the public was drawn to these products that were less rarified and without militant intentions (Tato Fontaíña 1999).

But the 1933 article under consideration also displays advances in the *ciencias naturás* (natural sciences), in the *movementos de mocedade* (youth movements), in the *revistas, cursos e conferencias* (periodicals, courses, and conferences), in the *cinema,* in *radio,* and even in *cultura fiseca* (physical culture), perhaps rather surprising registers. Soccer and boxing are referred to, as well as the narration of children's stories on the radio—whose appearance was very recent—and even the expectation of holding the first bicycle race around Galicia, a Tour of Galicia: "The latest sporting novelty is the Tour of Pontevedra by bicycle and the Tour of Galicia which is being planned, a race from which we can expect such brilliant fruits as those achieved by the Catalonians in the Tour of Catalonia, which today is world famous."[24] During the end of the nineteenth century and the beginning of the twentieth, the attempt on the part of the Spanish state to nationalize the culture of the peasants and fishermen of Galicia was feeble; as a matter of fact, the same occurred all over Spain with respect to these occupations (Bello 1973; Fusi 2000). But the possibilities of Galicianizing this same social stratum by the nationalists of the 1920s and the 1930s were even more remote—indeed, practically nonexistent, in spite of the manifestos and rhetorical enthusiasms.

In 1930 in a surprising parable, Otero Pedrayo spoke of how narrow the ideas of Galicianization supported by the Irmandades da Fala actually were. "*A Masa Neutra e Indefrente*" is a text that is based upon a curious metaphor: the difficulty a teacher in the classroom has in sustaining the attention of most of the students throughout the year. The same thing happens with the process of Galicianization among the greater part of the bourgeoisie of the Galician cities and towns, the so-called *masa neutra* [neutral masses]. The author did not even consider the presence, in this imaginary classroom, of other less-favored social classes as equals, a fact that suggestively replicated the dynamics of recruitment for secondary education in effect at the time.[25] The peasants and the fishermen are represented in the text as merely *terra nutricia* [part of the nourishing land]; the idea was that the elite among the *reitores,* that is, the leading nationalist intellectuals, should find inspiration therein. And this descent into the countryside would be fundamental for preaching

Figure 3. Ramón Otero Pedrayo (center) at Praza do Toural, to his right Antonio Fraguas and to his left Xosé Mosquera Pérez. Unknown photographer, n.d.

the values of national culture to the *massa neutra e indefrente* [the neutral and indifferent masses] of the Galician bourgeoisie, albeit with only relative hopes of success (*Céltiga* no. 142, 1930).

Another text, by Xohán V. Viqueira, already written by 1919, would situate the difficulties created by efforts to define Galician culture from the 1920s to 1936.[26] In it he creates an equation between traffic running in two directions, between the *Campo e a Cibdade* [the Countryside and the City]—the title of the text—which would make it possible to imagine Galicia as a national community blessed with shared values. Viqueira did not use the expression *cultura galega*. We have seen that at the end of the 1910s the term was not yet in general use. However, the metaphors that he employs are quite unusual and merit attention. He speaks of the necessity for the Galicians of the countryside and those of the city to share the same sense of community and contemporaneity. For the author, this sharing can only be established through a redemp-

tive movement that would be initiated in the cities in order to create
new values on the national level; these, however, should be based upon
a previous knowledge of the countryside and of its secrets:

> See here the two examples of Galician life, two essential examples: a field,
> an immense village, nearly unknown, and a city that begins to know itself
> and to penetrate the secret of life in rural hearths.
>
> For a long time, there has been a great separation between the city and
> the village. Those who lived in the cottages that crouched in old forests
> and ramshackle oak forests, had their own kind of unique existence, they
> had their language, their ways and their manner of working the fields,
> the peasant with his Celtic plough, guarded in his soul in its most private
> part, millenary reminiscences. …
>
> One day the city began to pay attention to the words of those who
> preached a life that was seeped in its own realities. It began to become
> self-conscious, and also began to notice that which belonged to an his-
> torical unity, which in great measure was constituted by the villages lost
> among cornfields and greenery. The city began to remember the coun-
> tryside where so many noble and unnoticed things pulsed and its most
> important mission, as creator of new values, appeared to it clearly. (*A
> Nosa Terra,* no. 386, 1935)

In 1935 a Galician cultural week took place in Oporto, the largest
city in northern Portugal, where some of the select products of the new
Galician culture were proudly exhibited by an important delegation in
the Salão de Actos of the university. At the event, Vicente Risco delivered
a lecture entitled "Hipótesis e probremas do folklore galego e portugués"
[Hypotheses and Problems of Galician and Portuguese Folklore] and
Otero Pedrayo spoke about his most pressing concerns in a talk entitled
"Terra e alma de Galiza" [Land and Soul of Galicia]. But other more
unforeseen themes received their share of attention during this cultural
week; for example: "Pathological Anatomy of Some Forms of General
Paralysis" and "Viral Illnesses and Their Importance for Agriculture"
(cf. *A Nosa Terra* 9/3/1935). Taken as a whole, the lectures presented
in Oporto were the result of studies that had been hatched under the
auspices of the Seminario de Estudos Galegos. This was a very important institution through which young university students could socialize
with the members of the first generation of nationalist converts, Risco,
Otero Pedrayo and other luminaries, and could dedicate themselves to
a program of Galicianization of the humanities and all of the sciences
(see chapter 5).

Risco, the most eminent of the ideologues—and who had been, up
until the end of the 1910s, the most secure and forthright user of the

expression *cultura galega*—would assume the principal role in defining for his Portuguese audience the theoretical definition of nationalism and Galician culture. Between his texts of 1919 and 1920—when he was still working out the uses of the term *culture* and of the notion of Galician culture—and this public talk given in Oporto in 1935, on the eve of Spanish Civil War, Risco was the most lucid and purposeful user of the expression *cultura galega*. In 1919 he had already made express references to Galician culture and to the necessity of creating it based on the "special characteristics" of "tradition," "race," and the "land" (*A Nosa Terra* 15/11/1919). However, in the following year, in an article in a periodical published by emigrant Galicians in Cuba (*Galicia*, no. 30) he would speak as well about "Galician civilization"—a balancing of terms that his readings posterior to Oswald Spengler would make seem ingenuous (Casares et al., 1997; Outeriño 1990; Spengler 1991). Referring to the moments in which his conversion to nationalism took place, Risco told his Portuguese audience in Oporto, "I saw that the tradition, whose death has already been cried over so many times, in the end was still alive among the less contaminated popular classes, mainly in the rural areas, which shelter the *immortal essences of the national soul, the living root of all of higher culture*" (Risco 1936: 1–2, my italics).

Vicente Risco was, among his contemporaries—in addition to his other various skills—*the* ethnographer. Today, this part of his varied writings is seen to be crucial on the *feito diferencial galego*—the differentiating elements for what is specifically Galician. At this stage I would like to simply emphasize one suggestive point: Risco's ethnographic oeuvre is seen as a contribution not subject to polemic, free of ideology, and appropriable by all the different sectors of Galicianism.[27] In fact, this appears to be the least polemical part of his oeuvre, which allows us to put to rest Risco's reputation as a controversial person. His most important biographer, Carlos Casares noted, "As an ethnographer, he will reconstruct, wisely and patiently, the body of spiritual and material culture of the country that had been disfigured by the imposition of Castilian culture." (1997: 59).

We saw how the efforts of *piedoso e devoto* [pious and devoted] study proposed by the editors of the periodical *Nós* were taken as primary resources of a superior culture that should serve to nationalize a posteriori the references of its fellow countrymen. If we read Risco—and his contemporaries—we begin to understand how ethnographic practice was thought to be an especially sophisticated and selective activity in the context of these endeavors. Vicente Risco himself would come to suggestively clarify the point—in a bold text written in 1934—that ethnography is demanding work that presupposes a degree of criticism and whose definitive goal is the creation of a "high" culture:

> For this reason we say that nationalism was a restoration, that had to have, in order to be true, a traditional meaning, and that could only be adequately only be adequately translated by the word *engebrismo* [authenticity].

> There is a bastardized meaning of the word *engebrismo* that is important to do away with. There are still people that think that *engebrismo* is ham with turnip greens and Ribeiro wine, long-johns and rustic hats, or "*ey carballeira arde o eixe*" ["Hey your cart's on fire"] and dirty stories. And it doesn't have anything to do with this.

> Clearly these things have their importance and should be preserved, as far as possible, the cuisine of a country, traditional forms of dressing, celebrations and indigenous ways of displaying happiness, old customs, all of folklore, even when it is obscene. Yet the forms of high culture are of superior importance: language, poetry, history, science, organization and religiosity. That the people continue to make use of these forms is crucial, and men of high culture, cannot, if they want to create works of national import, in any moment lose contact with the people, who for them is often an immensely wise teacher; folklore is the living fount of all racial culture, but it is important that this culture reach those heights so that the people are among the cultured people of the world. (*Alento*, no. 5, 1934)

Of the heroic years preceding 1936, from his exile in South America, one of the nationalist militants related, "It was during the second decade of the twentieth century when the foundations our spiritual building began to be dug with more serious and precise modern techniques." Two expressions from this ostensively constructivist sentence (Faubion 1993) should be emphasized: "predio espiritual" [spiritual building] and "técnica moderna" [modern technique]. As we have seen, it was the construction of a new culture—and the fact that it was consciously erected with modern procedures—that was at issue for the first nationalist militants beginning in the mid-1910s.

Remembering(s) and Forgetting(s)

In one of the last issues of the periodical *Nós*, from the end of 1934, Ricardo Carballo Calero took stock of the productions of the new Galician culture and sought a common designation for its most eminent producers. We have already seen how the editorial board of *Nós* had declared itself—in a pioneering fashion in Galicia—as a "generation," without having been more specific. Risco, however, was more precise, though in a negative fashion—already retrospective and self-complacent—in a text that is famous among scholars of his oeuvre, "Nós os inadaptados" [We the Unadapted] (*Nós*, no. 115, 1933).[28] Carballo Callero wants, on the contrary, to find a positive designation and chooses *A Xeneración de Risco* [Risco's Generation] (the title of this short text). His introductory considerations are interesting and give importance to the context of the Spanish state as a reference for how things had previously been framed, but also as a space for the exercise of very rigorous distinctions that allow us to calibrate the full autonomy of Galician culture. Paradoxes are patent in these radical declarations of autonomy:

> For however very nationalist we might be, the reality of our integration into Spain controls many of our avatars, and Spanish life has to be the term of comparison for a good part of the aspects of our life: if we want to speak with clarity and demand at least some understanding. As such, it would be convenient and natural to establish where there might be possible parallels between the course Spanish culture has taken and that which ours has taken. A generation as interesting as Risco's is as important for us as the generation of 98 was for Castilian culture. Certainly these co-incidences depend on the role represented by each of them: the causes produced by each generation are distinct. Here there was no national and historical crisis that followed the loss of the last Spanish colonies. Risco's Generation appeared later than the parallel Castilian generation. Álvaro das Casa called the Galician artists and thinkers that I am referring to the "novecentististas."

The use of the adjective *castelá*—that is, Castilian—in this context would suggest a curious plea for autonomy and separation, even more so since in the so-called generation of 98 we recognize the impetuses for the production of a Spanish national culture created by a group of intellectuals recruited at the state level and, naturally, as well, in Galicia. On another note altogether, A Coruña was one of the emporiums of the Spanish colonial economy of the nineteenth century. Galicians fought in Cuba and in the Philippines. Patriotic indignities were resented in the most important Galician cities in "'98"; the empire and colonialism drew on protagonists from among the masses of Spanish people from peripheral regions like Galicia.

In this claim, coming from a Galician and autonomous generation, we should take into consideration—according to Raymond Williams, who cites Dilthey—the plea "of commonly experienced time" (Williams 1988: 141); this, in the end, is also a central plea for the imagination of nations. For this reason, the overlapping of suggestions about difference becomes especially appealing, in the fusing of the claim for an autochthonous and completely distinct generation with that of a nation that wants to distinguish itself. These are aspirations that are completely clarified in a later passage by Ramón Otero Pedrayo, which recalls his friend Florentino Cuevillas, the master of nationalist archeology, also a member of the editorial board of *Nós*: "One day the book that is essential for Galicia will be written, about the origins and rise of the Galicianist movement. ... Galicianism served—and this is enough to make it worthy of the respect of its adversaries—to discover disinterested and uplifting vocations, *and bring together in daily and affectionate unity all of the cities and districts of Galicia*" (Otero Pedrayo 1980: 49–50, my italics; compare with Anderson 1991).

In a recent article I found a curious statement in favor of the recognition of another group of protagonists in the history of Galician culture, in addition to the restricted gamut that is most commonly the object of contemporary commemorative politics:

> The more we deepen our historical knowledge of the period running from 1916–1936, the more important the Generation of 16 will be perceived to have been in the cultural and political reconstruction of Galicia. The fact that the authors belonging to the "*Grupo Nós*" were always privileged, contributed to the exclusion of figures of the second order from historical-literary research, without whom we cannot have an accurate picture of the generation that played a role in the cultural modernization of Galicia since the foundation of the Irmandades da Fala. In our opinion, the denomination *Xeración Nós*—that is part of the Generation 16, a more precise term proposed by Ramón Villar Ponte in his ingression speech before the Real Academia Galega—contributed what still today seems to be a history of Galician literature which does not adequately represent what was brought to our culture by Antón Villar Ponte, Roberto Blanco Torres, Luís Peña Novo, Leandro Carré Alvarellos, Johan Vicente Viqueira, Victoriano Taibo or even Ramón Villar Ponte. (Capelán Rey, *Luzes de Galicia* no. 18: 53)

These opinions of Antón Capelán Rey, appearing in a review of a recent book entitled *Camilo Díaz Baliño: Crónica de Otro Olvido Inexplicable* [Chronicle of Another Inexplicable Forgetting] by José Antonio Durán, are interesting. In the book under review a painter, set-designer, and graphic artist is evoked who was—along with Castelao—the author of a widely disseminated graphic oeuvre and one of the few effective popularizers of nationalist ideas outside of the restricted circle of the influences linked to the Irmandades da Fala (Durán 1990; Sobrino Manzanares 1996). What I would like to note in the first instance, with the citation above and with Durán's title, is the recurrence of these "forgettings" in the contemporary Comunidade Autónoma. They are also present in Capelán's argument, which suggests including recognizably secondary figures, but which supports, however, a system of exclusions: that of Galician culture considered to be written in Galician by a restricted circle of authors.

During the beginning of my stay in Santiago I was surprised by the lack of recognition of Galician authors that at the time contained references for some of my knowledge of rural Galicia—for example, Emilia Pardo Bazán or Ramón del Valle Inclán. Still, these were authors who were practically contemporaries of the Irmandades da Fala and of the period when the periodical *Nós* was published, whose literary qualities could have been appreciated by my interlocutors. However, the identification of the respective oeuvre as *part* of Galician culture was always considered ambiguous, or, more often, denied, mainly by those who were more involved in nationalist militancy. At a certain moment they explained to me—irritated with my naïve insistence on the descriptive merits of Emilia Pardo Bazán—that she had been a *bourgeois* and *españolista* writer who didn't have *anything* to do with Galicia; this was the unanswerable opinion of a supporter of the nationalist left with a degree in the social sciences. I would emphasize that the memory of this author—just as, indeed, that of other Galicians who wrote in Spanish—is scarcely promoted by the principal autonomous governmental institutions, which practice the kind of exclusions argued for by Carballo Calero in 1934.[29] Some years ago, at a dinner to mark the closing of a colloquium of specialists, one of the most important Galician anthropologists—in an almost euphoric tone, justified by the good mood of all present and by the implicit transgression of saying such a thing—said: "Shh, shh, Pardo Bazán was the one who best described rural Galicia ... in Castilian ... but we can't really say this, shh, shh!"

Today, proposals that emerged from the editorial board of the periodical *Nós* are taken to be the most prestigious and solid basis of national Galician culture. Its most notable contributors might also be referred to occasionally as precursors, as a short-hand. However there is a more concise and frequently used form that is recognized by many Galicians: *a xeración Nós*. This expression, which has become widespread, can be recognized as the result of a politics of lineage, a constant preoccupation in Galicianist discourse. As we can see, Carballo Calero's suggestion that put forward the designation *xeración de Risco* never caught on.

Memory of *Nós*

In contemporary Galicia we will eventually be able to find republished facsimiles of all of the periodicals and texts written in the vernacular language during the first half of the twentieth century. Choosing and defining the monuments of Galician culture (Le Goff 1984) is an undertaking that receives substantial support from the autonomous government. The republication of the periodical *Nós* occurred especially early, in 1979, right at the time that the debate over the *Estatuto de Autonomía da Galicia* was being initiated. Its appearance owes itself to the initiative of the Editorial Galaxia, a publishing house in Vigo that is considered to be a noteworthy institution by anyone who knows anything about the history of the Galician nationalist movement during the period of Franco.[30]

In a certain way, it could be said that the Galaxia publishing house was the most visible face of the resistance and of Galicianist ideas from its outset in 1950 until the end of the dictatorship. Today, many references are made in academic journals and papers to the *xeración Galaxia* and to the *anos de Galaxia* [Galaxia years], which alludes to the Galicianist intellectuals whose work was either first published or came to maturity there. Such an important figure as Otero Pedrayo was a director and an editor there, but there were also younger personalities, such as Ramon Piñeiro and Francisco Fernández del Rego, who had already been involved in politics before 1936. Otero was, as we have seen, a prominent member of the so-called *xeración Nós;* Piñeiro (1915–1990) and Fernández del Riego (born in 1913), for their part, would have already belonged to the second generation of its disciples, the *xeración Galaxia,* which would have followed an intermediate generation, the *xeración do Seminario (de Estudos Galegos),* still habitually distinguished today.

We have seen that it was the members of the editorial board of *Nós* who were the first of Galicia's intellectuals who thought of themselves as a "generation," a local echo of a Europe-wide phenomenon as the nineteenth century passed into the twentieth (Bradbury and Macfarlane 1976; Williams 1988). As to the cultivation of Galicianist memory and the contemporary process of the nationalization of Galician culture, we now understand the varied efficacy of these precise attributions of identity, which had hardly been clear in their time. There were get-togethers and common projects that united or divided individuals of different ages; but these generation gaps were only sketchily represented in the pages of periodicals that were hardly read. However, in our own times, these divisions, having become rigid, allow us to formulate a narrative—still somewhat unfulfilled—of the gradual emergence of a true Galicia.[31]

Francisco Fernández del Riego and Ramón Piñeiro should be recognized as eminent curators of Galicianist memory, alongside a variety of other relevant names.[32] In this same group, we could also cite the names of Ricardo Carballo Calero (1910–1990), Xosé Filgueira Valverde (1906–1996), Antonio Fraguas (1905–1998), and the youngest, Isaac Díaz Pardo (born in 1920). This group of personalities, all of whom had come to age before 1936, maintained the memory through writing—namely, in the form of biography and memoir—but also through drawing, collecting "Galician art," gathering dispersed artifacts and creating museums for them, establishing recognized literary canons, or staging civic events. All of this was accomplished from different political positions and with different emphases. However, from a broader perspective, it can be said that all of them became significant figures in the creation of Galician culture of the last five decades and that theirs was the work of managing memories. After 1975, each one of them led important institutions that were charged with the representation and preservation of autochthonous culture within the Comunidade Autónoma.

The notion of Galician culture towards the end of the 1910s was employed in only the vaguest of terms, and only readily appropriated by the Galicianist intellectuals of major prominence, those who in the years following the 1920s produced the most decisive proposals for its objectification. The uses of this term were already decidedly absorbed into the prose of their closest disciples, those just mentioned above, all of whom were still quite young in the 1930s. It is worth comparing the citation already made from the "Primeiras verbas" of *Nós* with an extract from another more recent text, the "Presentación" that opens the 1979 facsimile edition of this periodical:[33]

All of the cultural and political endeavors that the precursors carried out in the nineteenth century picked up new energy and a new look with the creation of the Irmandades da Fala on the 17th of May 1916. We can say that this is the date, and that it is because of this initiative, that our twentieth century begins. ...

The recuperation of the language brought with it a chance for educated Galicians to reencounter Galicia's true culture. ...

The periodical *Nós* represents, from the start, a transcendent achievement in the recuperation of our personality—because it was the orienting organ of our cultural Galicianization. ...

In republishing a collection of the periodical *Nós* in facsimilie, Galaxia is taking it upon itself to circulate one of the most significant monuments in our cultural history. And, as well, at the same time to pay homage to the exemplary efforts of the members of the *Nós* generation. (*Nós* facsimile edition vol. 1, "Presentación": 2)

The editor of the facsimile of *Nós,* Ramón Piñeiro, was a personality who had a unique influence on the Galician nationalist movement from the 1940s onwards—a Galicianist politician, a man of the *tertulia* [the often clandestine discussion groups mentioned above], a great publisher, and an essayist of philosophic bent, even if his written oeuvre is thin. This was poured mainly into an elaboration of a "philosophy of *saudade,*" Galician-style; it makes for difficult reading and has noticeable affinities to the homonymous current—equally hazy—to have emerged earlier in Portugal (Piñeiro 1995).[34] He was also involved in bringing young university students into the ranks of Galicianist militancy, who later spread into all of the different political quadrants (Baliñas 1987). Ramón Piñeiro epitomized the *Galeguismo do interior* [Galician resistance] during the Franco years. His actions were characterized by the general defense of culturalist positions and by the observance of a timid *posibilismo* [a strategy of incremental steps designed to avoid confrontation] in the area of political action. The positions taken by Piñeiro certainly would have been justified by the ferocious constraints imposed by the dictatorship. Nevertheless, they were little understood, both in Galicianist circles in exile as well as, soon after, by the younger militants active from the 1960s onwards. The latter were already strongly influenced by Marxist ideas, disposed towards the mobilization of the masses and even towards the undertaking of armed actions (see, generally, Beramendi and Nuñez Seixas 1995).

Culturalismo—or *piñeirismo,* a frequently used neologism—is a term that, in the circles of the nationalist left, carries pejorative weight. It is used to disqualify the preoccupations of those who concentrate on "cultural" questions, who appear to be indifferent to the defense of the *people's* interests and, more broadly speaking, those who appear to be unaware of the uncompromising claims for the sovereignty of Galicia. This type of disqualification, which the appellation *piñeirismo* represents today, is not new, and can be said to thread its way through the whole history of Galician nationalism. In 1922, Lois Peña Novo, a lawyer and a relevant figure among the Irmandades, argued with Vicente Risco in the following way:

> With respect to this coexistence that Risco would agree to, I proclaim the most absolute incompatibility between the Spanish state and the nationalist ideal. This is why Risco gives no importance to political action. For my part, I would say that until now I have not felt the necessity to

count the stones of the arch of the church where I was baptized, but I have often felt deeply anxious about the full tragedy of our unredeemed citizenry. ...

The goal of culture is not to pull superior men away from the consciousness of the people who later are alienated from that consciousness, but rather to forge a collective spirit, a spiritual principle that harmonizes their efforts so that the people become intellectually that which they already are by nature. (*A Nosa Terra*, no. 174, 1/12/1922)

We have already seen how those positions, which were known as *arredistas*—that is to say, separatists—were always in the minority, or at best ambiguous, in the Galician nationalist discourse of the twentieth century; in fact, they didn't even find expression in 1922, in spite of the occasional discursive reprisals, like the one cited above. Today, however, Lois Peña Novo is a forgotten figure, just as are so many of the politicians from his period who were even more dedicated, while the *contadores* of the *pedras do arco da Irexa* (those who "count the stones of the church's archway") denounced in 1922 are today the object of constant commemorative initiatives. In recent years we have been able to conclude that the recognition of Galician culture and its celebration are values that are shared by both autonomous institutions, which the Popular Party of Galicia (PP of G) controls, and the organizations that make up the nationalist left. Paraphrasing Peña Novo, we can say that all of the different sectors are committed to seeing that "o pobo chegue a ser intelectualmente aquelo que xa é por natureza" [the people become intellectually that which they already are by nature,] a phrase that would delight the late Ernst Gellner and that seems to bring together all of the paradoxes of the different nationalist discourses. This is a task that for everyone is marked out by the references to an erudite modern culture, imagined initially by the writers of the periodical *Nós* and later patiently objectified through the work of its closest disciples.

In recognizing the *precursores*, the *xeración Nós*, the *xeración do Seminario*, and so on, we are confronting a genealogy molded over time— with the characteristically forgotten—and one that has full political intentionality. In the sphere of today's politics of memory exercised in the Comunidade Autónoma, the lives and the works of the members of the *xeración Nós* are the subject of many initiatives, now more frequent than those that involved the great poets of the *Rexurdimento*, like Rosalía de Castro and Curros Enríquez.

The commemorations of that *xeración Nós* have indeed become systematic, played out in the erection of statues, busts, and commemorative plaques and in the naming of streets. There are various literary and

research prizes, study foundations, and initiatives to republish its respective literary works; and also there is great variety of academic studies—as
well as television documentaries—dedicated to its works and biogra-
phies.[35] But these are also frequently recapitulated in quite summary
fashion. Examples of this are the innumerable pages that can be found
on the Internet—set up by anonymous authors, private associations,
or institutions of the autonomous government—and quick references in
the editorial pages of the most widely read newspapers. There are also allusions in the pamphlets or other publications of many different political parties. Certain prominent members of that *xeración* of Galicianists,
whose memory today is certainly conspicuous as a reference in the representation of Galician culture, have as well been distinguished by being included in the Panteón de Galegos Ilustres. This was the case with
Ramón Cabanillas, with Castelao, and would affect, as well, the mortal
remains of Ramón Otero Pedrayo, as twenty-five years have passed since
his death.

However, obscured beneath such a celebrated collective designation,
we can see that the memory of Vicente Risco has become singularly subdued. His mortal remains (as I have been assured by the people whom
I have consulted about this very issue) will not be awarded a space in
the Panteón. Today, for the majority of Galicians, Risco is an unknown
figure, or only vaguely recognized. The less sophisticated of the nationalist left refer to him as a *fascista* (fascist) or a *traidor* (traitor), a comment that I heard on a number of occasions; in the more right-wing
sectors, on the contrary, the difficulty in promoting his memory is as
much justified by the implicit radicalism of some of the passages in his
nationalist theses, as it is by his past as a collaborator with Francoism.[36]
In Spain, where there was a slow process of *transición* between regimes,
these kinds of memories that the majority prefers to forget, particularly
in the sectors of the right, are particularly inconvenient. Today there is
a research grant and a foundation that carries his name, which curiously
enough is supported by intellectuals considered to be of the nationalist left—Risco was an extremely dedicated and conservative Catholic
throughout his whole life.

We have seen, on the contrary, how Castelao's memory is celebrated
by the Xunta de Galicia and whose biographical course after 1936 was
symmetrical to that of Risco: a secessionist and *rojo* [a leftist] in Francoist propaganda, and for Galicianists a martyr for his love of Galicia.
Then the process of autonomization brought the possibility of erasing
the first form of identification, providing us with an exemplary story
that emphasizes the force that certain symbols have for representing peripheral national cultures in the *España de las autonomías,* as Carmelo

Lisón Tolosona did so astutely in 1977, even if he was speaking merely of "regions" (Lisón Tolosana 1977: 27). Castelao became a symbol of Galicia and of Galician culture, which allowed him to be appropriated by all of the sectors that participate in the political life of the Comunidade Autónoma, a process that is a source for the constant recycling of disputes, as I have noted above. In a characteristic passage—which appears in a widely used textbook—Francisco Fernández del Riego defines Castelao by employing Christomimetic metaphors: "Alfonso Rodríguez Castelao, 'man,' draughtsman, writer, achieved self-realization through Galician expressions as much as Galicia expressed itself in him, he became Galicia through transubstantiation" (Fernández del Riego 1984: 105–7). Even today similar suggestions are still prominent in many of the appropriations of the memory of Castelao: his tomb can be found in the Panteón de Bonaval in the chapel of Cristo Redentor [Christ the Redeemer].[37]

Recently, at one of the very frequent homages to which the celebration of Galician culture gives rise, Ramón Piñeiro was evoked by one of his contemporaries, also a celebrated figure in Galicia, Domingo García Sabell (1909–2003)—doctor, essayist, and a curator of the memory of historical Galicianism. In the fragments of his very elegant piece of oratory we can see how the expectation of *A Nosa Terra* was fulfilled at the end of the 1910s: that the *Fala* would serve to express *toda-las ideias e todo-los pensamentos* [all ideas and all thoughts], even the most *prefeundos* [profound]. García cites some of Piñeiro's influential definitions, letting us see how, in spite of the denunciations, the terms of the debate that the question of culture raised are "piñeiristas" and that this is a fulcral political question in contemporary Galicia:

> How do we make sense of the Galician people's manner of being through their language? What is the creative virtue of this—in the sense of an activating force? And, finally, how can the correspondence be understood, the intimate correspondence between language and a manner of being, the profound anthropology of the Galician man?
>
> Serious questions, all, pregnant with light and the power of future projection. Having gotten this far in our conversation, it is important, in accordance with the diamond-like differentiations proposed by Ramón Piñeiro, to create a path with three features; knowledge of the people, the culture and the language. "Man"—Piñeiro affirms—"is a social being. His individuality is created through living with other men. From there the natural form of human self-realization would be these units of shared experience that we call peoples. The people is the natural unit of shared experience, culture is its form and language its vehicle." (García Sabell in *Lembranza de Ramón Piñeiro: Catro Discursos,* 28)

We could go through the various influential formulations that the theorization of Galician nationalism has given rise to—and I wanted to identify its proponents in this chapter: Manuel Murguía, Vicente Risco, A. D. Castelao—in order to recognize their affinities with this proposal by Ramón Piñeiro. It is the strength of the naturalizing statements that should be more strongly highlighted, invoking, as Handler says, the presence of the individuated "being" of the nation as petition for incontestable fact (Handler 1988). We could also underline various differences in emphasis, differences of terminology, and so forth, but I believe they are less significant in ideological terms than the essential similarity that I have brought to light. I would like to point out that in present day Galicia, "*cultura*" and "*língua*"—*forma* and *vehículo* of the nation, as Piñeiro suggested, and these words should be emphasized—are themes of constant political disputes.

Excursus: A Polymathic Galicianist, Ethnography, and the Presence of Death in Galicia

1. I personally met Don Antonio Fraguas in the autumn of 1997 on the ground floor of the Instituto de Estudios Gallegos "Padre Sarmiento." He was a venerable figure to whom everyone referred with great respect; for me, this was an emotional encounter. I had already heard Don Antonio on a variety of occasions, when he regularly officiated as honorary president at the opening of events linked in some fashion to ethnographic questions. At that meeting in 1997 the old Galicianist polymath said to me: "Ah, the gentleman is a Portuguese anthropologist! I knew another young man well who also spent some time here, Ruy Serpa Pinto." This gracious mention of recognition became surprising when I checked on Serpo Pinto's biographical data in order to confirm my impression that he had died quite a long time ago. In fact, Serpa Pinto—archeologist and a scholar of Oporto's prehistory, who had worked with some of his Galician counterparts at the end of the 1920s—had passed away at a young age in the distant year of 1933.

Don Antonio Fraguas graduated in *Filosofía y Letras* in Santiago in 1928, and received his doctorate in history in Madrid in 1950. Throughout his academic career he taught history and geography—sporadically between 1928 and 1933—at the university level, as well as at a variety of high schools. His career as a teacher in secondary education ended in 1975, as a full professor at the Rosalía de Castro Institute in Santiago de Compostela. His life during the first decade of Franco's rule was tumultuous when he was forced to leave official teaching and obliged to live

Figure 4. Young D. Antonio Fraguas, posing as a peasant. Unknown photographer, n.d.

discreetly, due to the fact that he had emerged as figure suspected by the new regime because of his earlier Galicianist activities. Born in 1905, Don Antonio was one of the rare survivors of the group of scholars and artists of the two adjacent generations, the *xeración Nós* and the *xeración do Seminario,* collective designations to which I have already made reference, and with which we identify the Galicianists already active in the period before the civil war (see chapter 3). Don Antonio Fraguas died in Compostela in December of 1999.

Those who have studied anthropology at the university level might consider Don Antonio Fraguas to be a man of the "old school," a folklorist or ethnographer. Yet, on many other occasions he could be referred to as an anthropologist tout court, or even a social anthropologist, or cultural anthropologist. The possibilities for recontextualizing his work have only been consolidated in the last few years. I believe that all of the characteristics mentioned are reductive; each of them is marked by a perspective imposed by the development of the specialized areas of social and cultural anthropology in the universities, a belated phenomenon in the whole of the Iberian Peninsula (see chapter 4). Nevertheless, we cannot underestimate the usefulness of these perspectives, as far as they suggest to us a clear proof of the power of reading the past from the vantage of the present (Cohen 1996). They demonstrate, namely, the importance attributed today to anthropology when it comes to defining Galician culture and identity.

Don Antonio was a prolific researcher of distinct themes. What we consider to be his ethnographic work composes merely a part of a varied and extensive oeuvre. However, during the last decades of his life he became, by antonomasia, the anthropologist—or ethnographer—of Galicia; these were the studies that justified the recognition that crowned the last years of his career. I suggest that a part of his prestige was justified by his extreme longevity. It was only in recent years that Don Antonio

Fraguas became the patriarchal figure of ethnography as it is practiced in Galicia. Other contemporaries of his had already died, polymaths as well, with relevant ethnographic works; people like Xaquín Lorenzo (1907–1989), Fermín Bouza-Brey (1901–1973), or Xesús Taboada Chivite (1907–1976). These are authors who had also been disciples of the personalities of major intellectual standing in the history of Galician nationalist movement, like Vicente Risco, Ramón Otero Pedrayo, and Florentino López Cuevillas.

2. Don Antonio's acceptance of the affinities of the work of anthropologists (which is how I was introduced to him), archeologists, and ethnographers is suggestive. Indeed, these affinities could be broadened to take in still other specialties, like history and geography, which Don Antonio practiced throughout his life. It is difficult to strictly define what ethnography was considered to be in the Galicia of the twentieth century, or anthropology (a term that was less used until recently, unless it was being applied strictly to physical anthropology). On the other hand, I believe that we should consider these practices, ill-defined as they were, by associating them with the nationalizing efforts of those who exercised them. One of Don Antonio Fraguas's contemporaries, the above-mentioned Xaquín Lorenzo, would describe as foundational—even if he used the well-known metaphor of "revitalization" (Smith 1999)—the academic disciplines involved in the affirmation of Galicia as a cultural entity:

> Some years ago, in that small and loving city of Ourense that some still remember, three men got together, still boys, who one day would become luminaries of our culture: Ramón Otero, Vicente Risco and Florentino Cuevillas. They analyzed the existing curriculum and came to the conclusion that there were three disciplines missing in Galicia and that it would be important to bring them to life: Geography, Ethnography and Prehistory. They divided them up between themselves, and Cuevillas dedicated himself to Prehistory. (Lorenzo 1957: 135)

In order to clarify this citation, it should be specified that in this extraordinary division of labors in Ourense at the beginning of the twentieth century, ethnography was assigned to Vicente Risco and geography to Ramón Otero. In this way, we can understand the full nationalizing intent of this foundational act. If we add to this the practice of history—and Otero himself, for example, was an eminent historian, while Risco also occasionally worked as a historian—we will have before us the complete range of the central disciplines regularly brought into play in the processes of the nationalization of culture (Thiesse 2000; Smith

1991; Díaz-Andreu 1996; Graves-Brown et al. 1996). But we have already noted in the previous chapter the variety of works produced by these personalities and their coevals.

The more specific undertakings in academic research inspired by nationalizing commitments were mainly practiced under the auspices of the Seminario de Estudos Galegos.[38] This institution was organized in 1923 through the initiative of a group of students from the University of Santiago. They received the tutelage of the ascendant generation, of which Risco was a part. He, himself, became the director of the ethnographic section. It is worth citing Joan Prat, who sees the Galician case as an example of the historic relations between ethnography and the political projects in the Spanish state prior to 1936: "The paradigm that we have come to note could be the Seminar on Galician Studies, along with its variety of disciplines—prehistory, history, archeology and history of art, philology, history of literature, geography, ethnography and folklore, social sciences, law and economics, natural and applied sciences, etc., making up the complete study of Galician culture and civilization" (Prat 1991b: 27). The seminar's objects of study were restricted to Galicia, and Galician was the language adopted for the communication of the results of the multidisciplinary research conducted there. On the organizational chart of the old Seminario de Estudos Galegos, the practice of disciplines such as biology, geology, and astronomy—or at least the intention to practice them—are referred to along with a variety of other disciplines that were taken in under the auspices of the progressive unfolding of its sections until 1936.

In 1998 I had the opportunity to attend a lecture given by Don Antonio in the town of Melide, in a session commemorating the fieldwork that led to the publication of the collection of studies entitled *Terra de Melide*. This is the work most emblematic of the multidisciplinary research undertaken by the Seminario de Estudos Galegos. It is a volume composed of a series of thematic monographs (geographical, archeological, ethnographic, etc.), the result of research conducted in the *bisbarra*[39] of Melide and published in 1933. In the long-ago summer of 1929, Don Antonio Fraguas worked with the expanded teams that did research in Melide; he was young and newly graduated, and the beginning of his involvement with the Seminario was recent. Today, *Terra de Melide* is an important reference in the conversations that arise concerning the ethnography and culture of Galicia. I would say that it is more cited than actually read, beyond a small circle of scholars who might have a specific interest in one or another of the monographs that the volume contains. What is important to emphasize is the relatively fluid form in which citations from this monument of Galician culture circulate (Le Goff

1984). *Terra de Melide*—as we saw occur with the magazine *Nós*—was republished in facsimile form early on, directly following the hinge year of 1978. Other collaborative works of similar character were published before 1936, yet *Terra de Melide* is—due to its size, and the scrupulous and solid quality of its component parts—the document that clarifies most completely the impetus behind the work of the Seminario de Estudos Galegos from the years 1920 to 1930.

It is worth paying attention to the justifications for two of the research projects conducted through the Seminario de Estudos Galegos by two of its participants, but separated in time, one by Ramón Otero Pedrayo and the other by José Filgueira Valverde.[40] Otero Pedrayo, one of the mentors of the research team, wrote about the geography of the district of Melide, the first piece in the volume, providing its principal ideological justification (Bourdieu 1989: 107 and ff.). Don Ramón talks about the lack of "individuality" of the "*terra de Melide*" and finds an advantage therein: exemplariness. He says: "So the whole of the life of the Galician *soil* can only be understood in a harmonious way that includes the richness and the variety of its manifestations. Only in this first sense can the unity of Galicia be explained. And the undifferentiated *terras* comprise the great telluric mass from which others—…—are not more than further developed affirmations of the general theme."

Filgueira Valverde did not write any of the monographs included in *Terra de Melide;* like Don Antonio Fraguas, he was one of the young col-

Figure 5. Another scientific journey to the heart of rural Galicia, *Xeira da Terra do Deza*. Unknown photographer, 1929.

laborators on the work teams brought together at the time. Yet he would write the prologue to the 1978 reedited facsimile. Don José's evocation is sweeping, speaking of the times and the heroic works of the Seminario and of the projects of knowledge production conducted there. He says the following:

> They were conceived as group studies—tearing down, in a humanistic way, the walls imposed by specializations. In this way Prehistory would not be something distant from those that catalogued plant life or birds; the paleographer would be able to converse, in the field, with the geographer; the architect would have something to learn from the historians, and from all, from the artists and poets. By foot, over the difficult mountain paths, in coastal village taverns, in the eating locales of the markets, we went to discover our people, studying Galicianism. (Filgueira 1983: 7–8; cf. Smith 1991)

In the commemorative colloquium held in Melide in 1998, scholars of various disciplines participated, academics as well as autodidactic specialists. There, Don Antonio would be the only remaining survivor from the times being evoked and the figure most anxiously awaited by all. The audience was mainly made up of local inhabitants, teenagers from the local high school, parents, teachers, and cultural activists from the association that maintained the town's small ethnographic museum. The arrival of the old ethnographer provoked comments and whispers since he was a known figure beyond academic circles. Don Antonio had become well known in the past for his walks through the *Terra,* and in more recent years from his participation in any number of public talks and events that celebrated national culture. However, for the majority of Galicians, recognition of this figure came from Galician television (TVG) where he had his own program. In Melide I began to understand his popularity when a group of modest-looking middle-aged women became excited when the old Galicianist arrived, saying "Xa ven Don Antoniño" [Don Antonio (with the affectionate diminutive suffix –*iño*) is arriving] and began to compare his appearance in the flesh with the images of him on the television. They then followed him inside the auditorium to listen to him speak about old festivities, past modes of courtship, the properties of herbs, and proverbs. It was through this that Don Antonio spoke of Galician popular culture; in the end it was as anthropologist and gifted guardian of knowledge of everything Galician that the organizers of the event had presented him.

Throughout his life, Don Antonio Fraguas was a member of some of the most important Galician cultural institutions. In addition to the historical Seminario de Estudos Galegos, he became, over the years, a member of the Real Academia Galega and director of the *sección de etno-grafía* of the Instituto de Estudios Gallegos "Padre Sarmiento,"[41] where he succeeded Vicente Risco. With the end of the autocratic regime, he also came to be director of the Museo do Pobo Galego [Museum of the Galician People], *cronista xeral de Galicia* [general chronicler of Galicia], an important member of the Consello da Cultura Galega, and president of the Real Academia Galega, among other positions, all of them invested with a strong sense of national symbolism. It is in recent decades that public recognition of Don Antonio as an anthropologist has been consolidated. This has occurred for various reasons, mainly through his extreme longevity, because of the publications or republications of certain of his titles with more explicit ethnographic content, but as well because of the appearance of new institutions that have brought visibility to anthropology in Galicia—and the fact that anthropology itself has become a subject area of study that is now seen as playing an important role in the Galicianization of culture. The Museo do Pobo Galego was established in 1976. A bit later the Ponencia de Antropoloxía Cultural was created as part of the Consello da Cultura Galega under the direction of Don Antonio, and anthropology also slowly gained a place in the Galician university system (Pereiro Pérez 2001). In a more indistinct way, allusions made to "ethnographic" or "anthropological" questions on the programs of TVG and various unrelated practices recognized throughout Galician began to occur with more frequency.

Figure 6. Inauguration of the Museo do Pobo Galego; D. Antonio Fragua is standing at the center of the second row. Unknown photographer, 1976.

In the mid-1970s, José Filgueira Valverde wrote a laudatory bibliographical article on Antonio Fraga that opened with the following: "A very prominent figure in contemporary Galician letters for his work as a professor and in cultural institutions and for his copious and rigorous studies and publications on various aspects of history, geography, social anthropology ..." (entry: Fraguas, Antonio, in the *Enciclopedia Gallega*). The ellipsis employed by Filgueira in his statement about his companion's writings is certainly justified—indeed his work contained an even greater variety than stated. We must at least count his archeological work, the various contributions of which are registered in the enormous bibliography that accompanies this biographical sketch. However, what I would emphasize is the curious and very incisive "presentist" updating (Stocking 1968) of Don Antonio's career, which occurs when Filgueira identifies a part of the studies that he undertook as "social anthropology." In Spain of the middle 1970s social anthropology was a very recently introduced discipline that was being pioneered in a limited number of universities and whose practitioners very explicitly defined the boundaries between their own practices and antecedent ethnographic practices. One can easily suggest that it was his encounter with the prestige of this emerging academic discipline that caused Filgueira Valverde to designate the older interests of his subject in the way that he did.

We will find more definitive proof of this suggestion by looking in this same *Enciclopedia Gallega* at the entries, which Don Antonio Fraguas himself wrote, for "Ethnography" or "Ethnology." These contain definitions that should be linked to the entry for "Anthropology," which was written by another author and deals exclusively with an appreciation of questions respecting physical anthropology. It is in the very dated and theoretically unsubstantial proposals of José Leite de Vasconcelos (1858–1941)—a Portuguese archeologist, ethnographer, and philologist—that Don Antonio mainly finds authority, while references that he also made to German authors from the beginning of the century, like Graebner, father Schmidt, or Ratzel, are hardly clear at all. These are apparently second-hand citations, or at least inattentive ones, such that they are given little importance as trustworthy examples. Also important are the citations originating in the works of Vicente Risco, who was the author of some of the clearest and most influential works of Galician ethnography from the 1920s onward (González Reboredo 1996).

The truth is that if we look deeply at the theoretical references that Risco himself used, we will recognize the same vagueness, in spite of the omnivorous bibliomania that marked his work as a whole.[42] Risco had attended the classes of Luís Hoyos Sainz (Ortiz and Sánchez 1994), when he was a student at the Escola Superior de Magisterio in Madrid, though the weight of his influence is not entirely clear. Later, in 1930, he would travel to Germany with the idea of deepening his ethnographic studies. A very curious report came out of this journey and was published in successive issues of the periodical *Nós* (no. 79 and ff.), in which Risco discusses much of what he saw on his trips to Berlin, Vienna, and Prague, yet, because of a series of set-backs, he was never able to make contact with the teachers he was seeking. However, at an already mentioned conference held in Oporto, Risco demonstrated an extraordinary clarity in his proposals with respect to the nationalizing uses of the ethnographic collections that he had undertaken (Risco 1936). It was the foundation of a Galicianized *cultura popular* that had motivated his proposals and justified his compilations, which were done with simplistic criteria and very few theoretical references. His influence is mirrored in the work of all of the most relevant Galicianist ethnographers of the nineteenth century—Fraguas, Jesus Taboada Chivite (1907–1976), Xaquín Lorenzo (1907–1989), Fermín Bouza Brey (1901–1973)—none of whom concerned themselves with theoretical speculations or looked for justifications beyond those that Risco's oeuvre provided.

More recently, we can say that Don Antonio Fraguas has been officially recognized as an anthropologist. For example, an institutional pamphlet produced with the establishment in August 1999 of a foundation that took the name of the *antropólogo e historiador* says as well that the intentions of the Fundación Antonio Fraguas Fraguas are for "the popularization and conservation of Galician 'sites of memory.'" The appropriation of this concept "sites of memory" that was introduced in the mid-1980s by Pierre Nora (1986) is especially curious because here it is projected onto the personality of a famous person and his legacy, which become references for the process of the nationalization of culture underway in Galicia. In recent years, those who know the history of the nationalist movement and its anecdotage would be able to repeat, with respect to Don Antonio, what had already been said of the "patriarch" Manuel Murguía—"*ali vai Galicia*" [there goes Galicia]. This was a phrase that I had seen written in evocations of the famous nineteenth-century historian, so that it was a surprise to hear it repeated by one of my friends from Santiago de Compostela, now with respect to Don Antonio. It was the winter of 1997 and we saw Don Antonio pass by, his figure shrunken with years, in front of the famous Colegio de Fonseca, along the Rúa do Franco, his umbrella in his hand and his cap on his head. This was a curious replication of a recurring expression, demonstrating how topics based on the recognition of the existence of Galician culture as a distinct entity are reproduced, even subject to being personified by the iconic figures of its most representative intellectuals.

3. Don Antonio began his ethnographic writings in 1930, with the first relevant article being fairly lengthy and full of highly detailed descriptions. It was published in no. 77 of *Nós* and was entitled "O entroido nas terras do Sul de Cotobade" [Carnival Celebrations in the Land of South Cotobade] (84–94). Let us look at a passage that continues to emphasize the "salvage mode" impetus (Marcus 1986) that was very characteristic of the entire corpus of ethnographic publications in Galician anthropology geared toward nation building: "In some of the (parishes) many of the notes of these days of happiness are disappearing, and yet in all of them there still remains a typical and traditional air and they hold great interest for ethnography" (84). This text ended with the catch phrase of the Galicianists of that time period: *Terra a Nosa!* [Land of ours]. The second group of four contributions by Don Antonio published in *Nós* was titled "O culto dos Mortos" [The Cult of the Dead] and appeared the following year (*Nós*, no. 87, 1931). The space of reference is now Galicia in its entirety. Once again, the prose is simple, illustrated by the transcription of stories, sayings and pictures, short anecdotes, and by the absence of any theoretical justification whatsoever, characteristics that would be maintained in Don Antonio's ethnographic texts throughout the more than six decades of his career.[43]

These thematic choices are quite interesting; in them, one can recognize two topics that are quite pronounced in the anthropology produced in Galicia in the twentieth century. Much later the author himself reiterates similarities between Carnival and the cult of the dead in certain longer works that appeared—*La Galicia Insolita: Tradiciones Gallegas* [The Unusual Galicia: Galician Traditions] (1973) and *A Festa Popular en Galicia* [The Popular Celebration in Galicia] (1996). It is important to note as well that there were plenty of earlier examples demonstrating an interest in these same subjects. We will find them treated in the works of Don Antonio's "*mestres*" [masters] in the Seminario de Estudos Galegos, above all in those of Vicente Risco, who had already contributed significant work to *Nós*, precisely in relation to Carnival, the cult of the dead, and the unusual beliefs of the Galician peasants. These would have been the more direct influences on the young ethnographer, even if they were themes that could be traced to earlier authors that had described Galician peasants, mainly Manuel Murguía, Alfredo

Vicenti, and Nicolás Tenorio (Murguía 1985; Durán 1984). On the
other hand, if we were to analyze the work of some of the most significant contemporary academic anthropologists or those who influence
Galician cultural institutions, the presence of these themes would still
appear conspicuous to us. What I would like to suggest is that in these
thematic recurrences we can recognize the presence of a "tradition of
ethnographic writing" (Fardon 1990), a "tradition" that is much more
interesting when it does not arise out of the mere reproduction of some
academic context, but rather through the dynamics of a long process of
the nationalization of culture (Ferro n.d.; Lema Bendaña 1990–1991;
Pereiro Pérez 2001).

In Galicia the prominence of references to death and the notoriety
of funeral practices in daily life made a great impression on me. Above
all, in recent years these practices are no longer simply an automatic
expression of contemporary life, only capable of catching the attention
of foreign travelers or local scholars, as is proven by the innumerable
older literary references. On the contrary, many of the Galicians that
I met were convinced that this was a relevant characteristic of their
cultura; for example, on various occasions I was reminded that it was
a tomb, that of Santiago the Apostle, around which Compostela was
organized and, by extension, Galicia. As I have already suggested, for
a long time the practices and the beliefs that have to do with death in
rural contexts have been a relevant object for the attention of Galician
ethnographers until this day. On the other hand, the type of fieldwork
that I did led me to understand the relevance of this theme in the actual
seat of the autonomous government of Galicia. There, as I have already
noted, *ofrendas florais* [offerings of flowers] and the *misas de cabodano*
[annual masses given to commemorate the dead] are frequent. Nor are
the machinations of the "political lives of dead bodies"—to cite the suggestive title of a book by Catherine Verdery (2000)—at all unusual.

In 1885, the writer Emilia Pardo Bazán described the surroundings
of the Termas [hot springs] de Mondariz, located near the city of Pontevedra as "el país de las benditas ánimas" [country of the blessed souls]
(1984: 219). It was the restricted French sense of *pays* that Doña Emilia
had in mind in referring to the profusion of small votive niches dedicated
to the "almas do Purgatório" [souls in Purgatory] in that area close to the
border of Portugal, the proximity of which she took to be an explanation for the presence of these constructions. I found that the phrase had
been appropriated by Galician intellectuals in recent years, but used to
designate the whole of Galicia. This is a suggestive synecdoche, as it can
be used to account for how necrophilic themes were objectified as part

of national Galician culture, a longstanding process for which there are no significant parallels on the Portuguese side.

Vicente Risco confirmed the "the affectionate coexistence that Galicians have with the dead" in 1926 (*Nós*, no. 34). These kinds of observations have had a long history, however, dating back at least to the lucubrations of Murguía in *Galicia*, where they appear wrapped up in Celtophilic ruminations. Yet, in addition to the erudite and little-read speculations of Risco and Murgía, it is also true that the Galician periodicals with the greatest circulation at the turn of the nineteenth century and into the twentieth had already established the *paisanos* and their affectionate intimacy with macabre themes as suitable topics. Supporting the diffusion of these stereotypes were caricature, illustrations, and legends, or characteristic anecdotes appearing in periodicals directed at the "*americano*" market that frequently contained comic-pathetic references to *noso defuntiño* [our little dead one], to the fabulous *Santa-Compaña*,[44] and to incredible scenes at wakes.

In the Galicia of recent years there have been, for example, cases in which famous architects were hired to design cemeteries, and, with an eye towards the newspapers and the television news programs on TVG, local governments as well as architects emphasize their conviction that these works and endeavors are justified by characteristics that are specific to *cultura galega*.[45] In Santiago I attended various performances by "story-tellers"—*conta contos*—given to theaters full of students where old stories were retold, about wakes and with all the typical references to the "hands of the dead," caskets that open, etc. These are themes that have been covered very carefully by ethnographers—a recent very vivid example is a book by Gondar Portasany (1989)—but on those occasions they were part of the whole celebratory and conscious sense of *cultura galega*.

Very recently, plans by the *Xunta* to construct the Cidade da Cultura de Galicia [City of Culture of Galicia] were received with indignation among left-wing nationalists, but as well they were the source of macabre jokes. Indeed, the construction of this complex—"the most important construction site in the world today" (*El Correo Gallego* 4/4/2001; Zulaika 1997)—implies a huge investment much argued over by various sectors of the opposition. Jokes and other ironic insinuations about its "pharaonic" character circulated around Santiago, and that it would become a memorial to Manuel Fraga, the aging president of the *Xunta*—now a senator—whose state of health provoked constant speculation at the time. Curiously, a defender of the project felt obliged to write the following: "From the cultural and architectonic point of view, the *Ciudad de la Cultura* ["City of Culture"] is probably the most ambitious

Figure 7. *Velatório* [wake] at a peasant house. Photograph by Joaquín Pintos, ca. 1905.

project that Galicia has faced *and without being subjected to the so-called deifying obsession to render tribute to the immortality of memory*" (Luis Pousa, *El Correo Gallego,* 16/2/2001, my italics).

4. In the program for the "Simposio de Antropoloxía—Etnicidade e Nacionalismo. En Homenaxe a Manuel Murguía," scheduled for April of 2000, Don Antonio Fraguas was listed as honorary president; this additional honor was, in the end, posthumous. Friends from Santiago informed me of his death in November of 1999, and from them I also heard reports of how emotional the various phases of the funeral had been in the Boisaca cemetery and at the mass held in San Domingos de Bonaval, the church that contains the Panteón de Galegos Ilustres. Even Curro, one of my local informants, who did not personally know the ethnographer and was neither an anthropologist nor a militant Galicianist—rather, he was a critic and always ready to ridicule what he thought of as the ticks of nationalist militancy—become emotional during the various acts of homage. Many other ordinary Galicians reacted similarly, as was suggested by the news reports and other publications, registers that invariably suggest that the death of Don Antonio marked an important moment in the history of Galician culture.

It is as much the post mortem evocations of Don Antonio Fraguas as the public recognition that his oeuvre and his personality received in the last years of his life that allow us to see a familiar process in operation. I speak of the recognition and celebration of great national figures registered by a range of scholars of nationalism in a wide array of contexts (Thiesse 2000; Nora 1986–1992; Verdery 2000). An obituary of Don Antonio that appeared in a newspaper widely circulated throughout the whole of the Spanish state (especially curious for this reason)[46] said the following: "It was as though he was the living memory of Galicia, a knowledge that he shared with some of the greats of Galician culture of this century, among them Castelao and Ramón Otero Pedrayo" (*El Mundo,* 6/11/1999). All of the civil authorities and academics were present at his funeral, according to the report from Curro and from the Galician newspapers.

Don Antonio's mortal remains were not immediately interred in the Panteón de Galegos Ilustres. In fact, they have established statutes for this Galician "site of memory" wherein twenty-five years must pass after the death of whatever personality for any transfer to occur. However, in the opinion of my informant, Curro—and this was only supposition that was not based on a knowledge of any political plans and had nothing to do with the instituted principles—the passage to the Pantheon should occur as soon as the organic process of decomposition of the cadaver of the famous Galician ethnographer was complete. My Compostelan friend's suggestion quite surprised me. It seemed really a bit macabre to me, in its simplicity and pragmatism, but then it occurred to me that it might be an especially interesting point for reflection. It suggested not only the understandable inevitability of consecrating the memory of an ethnographer in contemporary Galicia, but it also alluded, in a less direct way, to the prominence that death and the cult of the dead have as a social phenomenon in Galician society. Today, in the Comunidade Autónoma these two dimensions are interwoven as expressions of a nationalized culture.

Notes

1. Barreiro Fernández (1991); Máiz (1984, 1987); Beramendi and Nuñez Seixas (1995); Bermejo (2000). It is not always possible to trace a clear line between historiographic products that make reference to the course taken by Galicianism from a sympathetic perspective and others that are established on the basis of more securely critical dispositions. The references cited here can generally be considered to be of the second type, even if they occasionally revert to certain apologetic notes more characteristic of Galicianist memorialism.
2. The historians of the Compostelan church designated a remote episode involving the famous Bishop Diego Gelmírez (1059–1139) with the expression "pío latrocínio"

(pious larceny). In 1101, making use of deceptions, the truculent prelate appropriated a group of relics of saints from the Cathedral of Braga, which he then brought to Compostela. We saw that the nationalist left viewed the transfer of the relics of Castelao from Buenos Aires to the Panteón of Bonaval by the autonomous authorities as a cynical and abusive appropriation—or robbery or kidnapping !—still today referred to with resentment.

3. Vicente Risco (1884–1963) articulated the most influential and cohesive corpus on the theory of Galician Nationalism of the first half of the twentieth century. These contributions were successively refined (Bobillo 1981) and maintained a practically uncontested influence in Galicianist circles until the first half of the 1930s. In addition to being an ideologue, Risco was an imaginative polymath of many merits, whose importance is difficult to express in the space of a footnote (see, among others, Carballo Calero 1934; Beiras 1968; Bobillo 1981; Beramendi 1981; Casares et al., 1997; Beramendi and Nuñez Seixas 1995; Filgueira Valverde 1995 as well as the variety of allusions made as this chapter develops).

4. In addition to Smith, and his varied and influential production, other general references will suggest clarifying comparisons, for example, Hroch (1985), Anderson (1991), Eagleton (1999), and Thiesse (2000).

5. A. M. Thiesse (2000) documents how the glorification of the great poets as the nations' emblems was a generalized phenomenon in Europe at the beginning of the nineteenth century. In each case, "bards" who were more or less remote in time were taken as the epitome of "national genius" (França 1993 provides curious illustrations of the destiny of the memory of Camões in Portugal in the nineteenth century; see generally, Gillis 1994, and Nora 1986–1992).

6. A long cycle of conferences was inaugurated under this title at the Museo do Pobo Galego at the end of the 1990s, giving birth to various and voluminous publications that identified the *feito nacional galego* [differentiating fact of Galician] in the context of history, music, and anthropology and which hosted the collaboration of many of the most well-known specialists of these disciplines (indeed, the fixing of the *hechos diferenciales* [differentiating facts] was generalized for all of *España de las autonomías*).

7. See Hroch (2000), Mazower (1998), Hobsbawm (1985 and 1994), and also Eksteins (1999) (a very curious and personalized testimony). In 1919 the League of Nations was founded in Geneva in an attempt to respond to the variety of claims that the end of the Great War provoked (Mazower 1998).

8. *Hirmandade* was the first way of writing it, the use of which I maintain; however, the alternative *irmandade* rapidly replaced it and today has become the norm. The idiosyncrasies of Galician in the prose of the decade of 1910 are patent and curious, as in the subtitle itself, *A Nosa Terra,* for example. In that period, the capacities for inventive orthography were evident in each text, given the absence of any rules and the scarcity of prose models.

9. It is not known with any precision what the print run of *A Nosa Terra* was during the long period from 1916 to 1936, during which time its periodicity varied and the journal suffered a few short hiatuses. The most optimistic suggestions speak of 2,000 copies, numbers that are debated by other opinions. One of these suggests that only in 1934—a year of great activity from the Galicianist Party, established in 1931—it had reached the level of 1000 copies (Beramendi and Nuñez Seixas 1995: 64–65). At any rate, these are very modest numbers that speak of the insufficient capacity of this principal "voice" of Galician nationalists to influence Galician society (Ledo Andión 1982).

10. One especially curious case can be illustrated by the figure and the actions of Perfecto Feijóo (1858–1935), a pharmacist from Pontevedra, who founded the first Galician choir, Aires da Terra, at the turn of the century. Feijóo was a very handsome man, a bagpiper player, who delighted in dressing in elegant regional costumes. Curiously, it is possible to find a variety of illustrations in books—or on illustrated postcards, Spanish and well as foreign—where the portrait of Feijoo carries the caption "Galician man," "Galician," "A Galician," "A Galician bagpipe player," or "a Celt" (Scherer 1988). One of Perfecto Feijoo's admirers was the famous writer Emília Pardo Bazán (1851–1921), under whose direction El Folklore Gallego would make its appearance in 1884. This gathering of intellectuals—which included Manuel Murguía—supported projects, which were not always brought to fruition, for ethnographic studies that were inspired by the pioneering actions in Spain of the *folklorista* Machado y Álvarez, the spirit behind *Folklore Andaluz* (Ortiz and Sánchez 1994; Aguilar Criado 1990). The nationalizing actions of the choirs, which began to multiply in Galician cities in the first years of the twentieth century, would be applauded in a range of articles appearing in *A Nosa Terra* and later in other publications related to the nationalist movement.

11. See Barreiro Fernández (1991) who details the precedents for this *asambleia magna dos persoeiros das irmandades da fala* held in Lugo 17–18 November 1918.

12. Verify, for example, the documentation on these practices in France throughout the nineteenth century in Nora, who is exemplary for his exhaustive variety (1986–1992); see as well Tobia (1998), Hobsbawm (1985), Gillis (1994) and Mosse (1996). Alöis Riegl's title, *Der moderne Denkmalkultus: Sein Wesen und seine Entstehung* [*The Modern Cult of Monuments*], dating from 1903 [1999], is a particularly suggestive document on the importance of these preoccupations in Europe at that time.

13. On the contrary, *Der Untergang des Abendals* was a best-seller read by thousands of people in North and Central Europe during the beginning of the 1920s. In his memoir, Elias Canetti tells of how in a rooming house in Vienna there were arguments caused by the then very popular work of Spengler (1999: 291 and ff.).

14. As well, Raymond Williams suggests that in England there was a similar processual shift in the accepted meanings of what he refers to as "one of the two or three most complicated words in the English Language" (1988: 87). As a reference to the transformations undergone by the term *culture* he points to Tylor's famous definition of 1870, saying that it gained influence later and only gradually, serving to refer increasingly to societies. We saw in the first chapter that Stocking (1968) proposed a different version, with interesting nuances that relativized the role that we must attribute to Tylor's proposal.

15. Some of the important protagonists in the political life of the state were Galicians during the period in which the first successful outbreak of nationalist movement lasted—until 1936. Although not by any means exhaustive, this list would include Pablo Iglesias (1850–1925), Salvador de Madariaga (1886–1978), José Calvo Sotelo (1893–1936), Santiago Casares Quiroga (1884–1950), FranciscoFranco (1892–1975), and even the shadowy figure of José Millán Astray (1879–1954), *el novio de la muerte* [death's groom], the founder of the *Legión española*; see Preston 1998).

16. He is an especially curious figure, as is revealed in the texts of *A Nosa Terra* and a variety of other newspapers to which he contributed (Villar Ponte 1975). Hardly talented, in my opinion, as a novelist or playwright, areas in which he held ambitions, Villar Ponte showed himself to be consistently well informed about the nationalizing policies exercised in other parts of the world. With great enthusiasm he proposed their adaptation to Galicia and he was, among his contemporaries, apparently, the

one who had the most lucid views on the importance of the use of the mass media to steer the Galicianist discourse. He touched upon such a variety of different themes such as the importance of natural reserves (or parks), the nationalization of celebrations, the construction of sculptures, the uses of caricature, the encouragement of landscape painting, the popularization of texts in Galician, the nationalization of music and theater, etc. An admirer of Yeats, and especially concerned with the nationalizing uses of the stage arts, Villar coauthored a "drama in verse," *O Mariscal* (1926). The subject was drawn from the fifteenth century and created a hero out of the figure of an eminent aristocrat Pedro Pardo de Cela—supposedly a resister to the process of political unification promoted by the *reyes católicos*. Villar took as examples analogous figures that nationalist memory had mythologized all across Europe, for example El Cid, Du Guesclin, etc. (Thiesse 2000). By 1936 Galician nationalists had still not gathered sufficient funds to erect a monument to Pardo de Cela, and Villar's drama had very little success with the public (*A Nosa Terra*, no. 296, 1932). In recent years in Galicia *O Mariscal* has been staged by the Centro Dramático Galego; this work has become the most significant public reminder of Villar Ponte.

17. *Xeración* is the normative form accepted in the recent *Diccionario da Real Academia Galega;* however, *geración* and *xeneración* appear in texts of different periods cited below.

18. That was the cognomen that at the time was disputed by other Galician poets and, as a matter of fact, was distributed with a certain freedom (the frequency of mutual compliments between the writers of *Nós* was notorious; also praising those associated with the Irmandades was systematic in *A Nosa Terra*). The uses of the term *raza* and the adjective *racial* in Galicia merit consideration. They can be spotted frequently in the texts of the first three decades of the twentieth century, but became increasingly rare after the Second World War (although sometimes old Galician expatriates still employed them in the 1960s). In these uses, it is the reach of their meanings that stands out over the connotations—also vague in many of their uses—and which the *cultura* came to know starting in the 1920s through Galicianist prose. A common cliché was *racial essences,* used at the time with respect to a wide variety of themes.

19. Later on, after the most difficult years of the Franco regime, Otero became a university professor in Santiago and an influential intellectual figure for successive groups of students (see a fictional example in Méndez Ferrín 1999; see as well in Quintana and Valcárcel 1988). We have already seen that he was the author of novels, wherein Galicia is represented as an exemplary community.

20. Cuevillas was a graduate in pharmacy who made his career in the public administration in Ourense (Otero Pedrayo 1980).

21. This is an unsigned article, from the "editorial board." The greater part of the pieces and articles "from the editorial board" of *Nós* carry the unmistakable personal mark of the literary editor, Vicente Risco. Notwithstanding, in this period Risco was absent in Germany, where he had gone with the suggestive purpose of deepening his ethnographic studies. The authorship of this article—written by one hand and so attentive to literature—could by chance be Ricardo Carballo Calero, at the time a young lawyer, writer, and critic of strong nationalist convictions. Carballo Calero would become the great historian of Galician literature at the University of Santiago de Compostela; he was also one of the most enthusiastic and articulate of the Galician *lusistas* (cf. chapters 4 and 6).

22. As happened in Galicia with the Seminario de Estudos Galegos, established in 1923 (see chapter 5).

23. Notwithstanding, preoccupations over the diffusion of the new national culture were notable. We find an expressive example of this in the establishment of various publishing houses throughout the 1920s—like Lar, Céltiga, and Nós, all dedicated to producing low-priced books written in Galician. Incentives for the production of novels written in Galician were favored in the respective publishing programs. But, suggestively, other works appeared as well, good examples of which are *História Sintética de Galiza* by Villar Ponte, and *Geografía Sintética de Galiza* by Otero Pedrayo, both in low-priced editions.

24. These hopeful notes on the destiny of cycling in Galicia—where the Galician nationalists would not have had any type of direct influence—emerged alongside the reference to modernist poetry. This new poetry is shown, praiseworthily, to be inappropriate to the process of nationalizing the masses: "This class of poetry, that which is presently written world-wide, sifts to create a poetic super-real universe, full of rules other than those of the living world. In order to immerse the reader in this poetry you have to substitute the ordinary mind for another, special mind: that which presides in the poet through the creation of his poems."

25. As one informant from Santiago told me, "a cultura galega foi unha obra de profesores de instituto," (Galician culture was the work of high school teachers). Indeed, the greater part of the ideologues of the 1920s were secondary school teachers. (Hroch 2000). On the contrary, university professors who were close to the Galicianist movement were few and only two names stand out: Lois Porteiro (a professor of law) and Salvador Cabeza de León (a professor of literature). Functionaries of the state administration were also well represented; for example, Castelao or Florentino Cuevillas practiced bureaucratic professions.

26. Xohán V. Viqueira (1886–1924), a psychologist trained in Germany and a high school teacher in Santiago, can be considered a kind of John the Baptist of the Galician nationalist movement, for the way he died young and for the prophetic meaning given to his highly metaphorical texts. *A Nosa Terra* printed the *verbas* of this *guieiro* of the nationalist movement throughout the years before his death.

27. See, among others, Beiras (1968), Lorenzana (1979) and Piñeiro (1978 and 1995).

28. "Nós os inadaptados" remains an interesting reference—perhaps not completely trustworthy—to Risco's readings that preceded his "conversion" to nationalism. There he cites, for example, Ruskin, Carlyle, and Dante Gabriel Rossetti, though Mathew Arnold is absent! These would be particularly treasured English authors for him, all of which he read in translated versions.

29. I didn't find a single text written in Galician on the Internet about the author of *Los Pazos de Ulloa*. This seems to be a suggestive example, since it is possible to find hundreds of documents about literary figures of very doubtful merit published by the Consello da Cultura Galega, or by commercial publishers.

30. Following the orthographic rules observed in the periodical *Nós*, it was the orthography of the editions of Galaxia that became the most important for the standardization of written Galician in the twentieth century. In 1982, with the seal of approval of the Real Academia Galega and of the Instituto da Língua Galega, an official normative orthography was established and soon became the source of innumerable controversies. The variety—and the quality—of the titles to emerge from the various collections published by Galaxia over time is huge. Also, some of the most important Galicianist periodicals of the second half of the twentieth century were published there, among which *Grial* stands out. The editorial activity of Galaxia created a phenomenon that had been very sketchy before 1936: a "community of readers"

(Anderson 1991) in Galician that was stable and spread out over the whole of Galicia, even if the number of those involved remained relatively modest (Beramendi and Nuñez Seixas 1995).

31. The *Xeración do Seminario* and the *xeración Galaxia* are still not widely used designations, as has happened today with their more famous antecedent, *Nós*. However, their use has begun to spread due to the intensity with which Galician culture is currently celebrated; for example, on TVG it is common for random references to be made to these two *xeracións*.

32. Great is the personal merit and the charisma, recognized by various sources, of Don Paco and Don Ramón. Both of them were politically active, as well as being the driving force behind the literary and political discussion groups held during the decades of living under Francoism (Baliñas 1987; Franco Grande 2000). Within the Galician resistance, these gatherings were significant spaces for socializing—and, in the main, the only ones and very restricted—and for the survival of nationalist ideas in the post-1936 period.

33. In the unsigned "Presentación" we can recognize the style and the ideas of Ramón Piñeiro that were already present in one of his texts of the previous year (1978).

34. Piñeiro became the first president of the Consello da Cultura Galega [Council of Galician Culture] directly upon its establishment, in 1983, a position he held until his death.

35. Knowledge is also transmitted in secondary education through obligatory readings.

36. However, Risco's theoretical contributions are valued by academics and certain politicians; this has occurred in spite of the course he took prior to 1936, when he silenced himself as a Galicianist and became close to Franco's new autocratic regime (Casares et al. 1997; Bobillo 1981; Lugrís 1963). The extent of Risco's "collaboration" is a subject of intense speculation among specialists of his oeuvre; I think the approach proposed by Carlos Casares is particularly interesting for its sensibility (Casares et al. 1997); see, as well, the proposal that has emerged from the extreme left, from the hand of Xosé Manuel Beiras, whose appraisal of the unequaled force of Risco's nationalist formulations, in spite of his controversial biography, seems very significant to me (Beiras 1968).

37. Religious images were frequent as well in the evocation of Rosalía de Castro during the first decades of the twentieth century; she was often referred to as *a nosa santa Rosalía*.

38. In vol. 3 of the *Cuadernos do Laboratorio de Formas de Galicia* (1978) a commemorative monograph appears on the old Seminario de Estudos Galegos that brings together exhaustive documentation on that Galicianist institution. The directors and contributors are identified, oral testimonies of survivors are collected, the flow chart of the sections transcribed, and publications and other activities undertaken are registered. *A Nosa Terra* and, to a lesser extent, *Nós* were regular repositories for news about the activities of the Seminario de Estudos Galegos.

39. *Bisbarra*, according to opinions that I heard in Santiago, would have been one of those terms invented ex novo by the Galicianists of 1920, supposedly a poor interpretation of a vague local expression taken as a synonym for *comarca* [a kind of district, or county]—the first word, supposedly more vernacular, would have been preferred.

40. José Filgueira Valverde (1906–1996) was, in 1923, one of the young founders of the Seminario de Estudos Galegos. Connected to an ephemeral conservative Galicianist group during the Second Republic—the Galicianist right of Pontevedra—he was able to have a political career during Franco's dictatorship, a unique case among

Galicianists of greater notoriety. He was a talented and erudite polymathic writer; under his direction the Pontevedra Museum became famous in Galicia for the variety and richness of its collections. Filgueira Valverde was the second president of the Consello da Cultura Galega, succeeding Ramón Piñeiro.

41. The Instituto de Estudios Gallegos "Padre Sarmiento" emerged in the period 1942–1944 as a concession granted by the new authoritarian regime. Since then the extent to which the Institute could be considered the legitimate heir of the old Seminario has been a source of polemic. Censorship controlled tightly not only the number of disciplines offered but the impetus behind the orientation of the research of the earlier project; all of the publications also began to be written in Castilian. Don Antonio had a place in the new institution—having been its first librarian. This is similar to the case of Vicente Risco, F. Cuevillas, Bouza-Brey, and Otero Pedrayo among other Galicianists active during the earlier period (Ortiz and Sánchez 1994). Even today, critics of the institution draw attention to the fact that the double "l" in "Gallegos" to account for their lack of appreciation for the Institute (which depends on the funding agency that supports scholarly research at the state level in Spain, the CSIC or Consejo Superior de Investigaciones Científicas). In 1978, a group of nationalist intellectuals reestablished the Seminario de Estudos Galegos, and their approach copied the multidisciplinary character of the original project. Even today, the activities of the resuscitated Seminario are carried out discreetly. I imagine that this is due to a weak level of support and material resources. Don Antonio was involved as well in this highly symbolic reestablishment (Díaz Pardo 1990).

42. One of Risco's most curious texts about anthropology and ethnography appeared in *A Nosa Terra,* in an article that carried the expressive title "O que todo o galego ten que saber" [That Which Every Galician Must Know], which contained expressive *resumes d'etnografía galega* of his colleagues (see, for example, *A Nosa Terra,* no. 231, 1926). However, I would emphasize that Risco's ethnographic oeuvre is voluminous and extremely interesting, given the author's vast curiosity and intellectual liveliness. His ethnographic texts were published in a variety of Galician, Madrilenian, and Portuguese publications and were condensed by Risco in his collaboration on the monumental *Historia de Galicia,* edited by Otero Pedrayo (Risco 1962).

43. These first fruits of his ethnography are written in Galician. Later texts were written in Spanish, generally all of those publications that were coetaneous with the authoritarian regime; texts published after 1976 were again published in Galician. This raises a curious question because, though an important part of his oeuvre is written in Spanish, today he is, without any significant hesitations, considered to be a contributor to Galician culture. The same did not happen—as I have already noted—with respect to literature, whose authors writing in Spanish, even if they were writing about Galician themes, were not habitually recognized.

44. See, for example, Lisón Tolosana (1998), Gondar Portasany (1989), Risco (1946) and Murguía (1985), among a large *etcetera* of ethnographic approaches to the fantastical "processions of the dead" already referred to in chapter 2.

45. The most relevant—and beautiful!—example can be found in the small town of Finisterra, where the commission for the creation of the new local cemetery was awarded to César Portela, the most famous contemporary Galician architect. A comparison of available ethnography allows us to suggest that there are strong similarities in the group of beliefs surrounding the cult of the dead in many communities both in the Minho and in Galicia. In the Minho, however, I never noticed the type of reflexive appropriations that are so conspicuous in Galicia today. Even if in the Minhotan parishes that I know best local government investments in cemeteries

always have an enormous political significance, I never found that this was justified for "cultural" reasons; nor is it so in the larger cities. Literary, ethnographic, or
graphic valorizations of necrophilic themes in the descriptions of the peasantry are
also hardly prominent in the Portuguese case.

46. Curiously, I didn't find a single obituary of Don Antonio in the Portuguese newspapers, an absence that suggests the Spain of the Autonomous Communities is akin to
a space of specific "flows of meaning" (Hannerz 1992).

Chapter 4

Indianos, the Country of Bagpipes and the Nation of Breogán

Until the end of the 1970s nationalism in Galicia was a minority phenomenon, feeble in terms of political expression. It is only during a very short period—in the fleeting years of Spain's Second Republic in Galicia—that historians identify a significant spreading of Galicianist ideas. However, this process of diffusion, still incipient, was quickly repressed and only continued in highly censored form under Franco's authoritarian regime. Thus, the mass dimensions of the Galician nationalist movement have become relevant only in the most recent years at the end of the last century. These weaknesses in the historical trajectory of the Galician nationalist movement can be seen as intricately linked, if we follow the suggestions of Ernest Gellner (1983, 1998), with frequently noted frailties in the modernization of the economy and society in Galicia. For example, in the present day autonomous region there have continued to be, until quite recently, very low levels of literacy, urbanization, and industrialization, the kind of statistics to which all analysts inevitably point.[1]

Along with Gellner, I would suggest that the insufficient modernization of Galicia—and of its correlatives "mobility" and "anonymity"—can be seen as important reasons for the fact that only a minority of the population became interested in nationalist proposals. He defines nationalism as a "political principle which maintains that similarity of culture is the basic political bond." This principle has recently been generalized, relying upon processes of modernization mainly dating back to the nineteenth and twentieth centuries. Gellner says categorically that "nationalism is rooted in modernity" (1998: 3–13) and even affirms that the appearance of new and homogenous erudite cultures distinguished by a concern for rural roots is a distinctive mark of the "idiom" of nationalisms. It is for this reason that references—for the most part ironic—to the "mysticism of roots," to pretentious *narodniks* and to the more or less anecdotal *ruritanias* that are so dear to the collective imagination of nationalists in a whole range of contexts are so frequent in his work. These are characteristics reiterated in the new, more educated cultures that the nationalist movements have produced in an array of cases easily recognized in the Galician context, as I have already suggested in the previous chapter.

The majority of people that I met in Galicia held the conviction that they shared a common culture the composition of which was indisputable and based upon rural and popular origins. More-educated informants, or those who had a greater affinity with the political parties of the nationalist left, would defend this point of view with greater clarity, but at any rate it is an already widespread conviction that tends to be universally held in the Comunidade Autónoma. However, and paradoxically, there are frequent debates over the references to "ruralism" as a stigma of national culture; indeed, these mentions go all the way back to periodicals and newspapers from the 1910s. During the 1920s, the necessity of "a large and important Galician city" was a much-commented upon topic; for those that defended this idea it was the success of *catalanismo*, centered in Barcelona, that provided the principal inspiration (see, for example, Villar Ponte 1975; Leandro Carré, *A Nosa Terra*, no. 191, 1923; R. Blanco Torres, *Nós*, no. 5, 1921). From this perspective, Vigo—and its hypothetical metropolitan destiny—appeared to be the most viable Galician emulation. Apparently, in these discussions the way ruralism also marked the representations of national culture in Catalonia was not taken into account (Marfany 1995; Brandes 1990; Martí 1997).

In the Galicia of our times the mutual denunciations of ruralism m entioned above are still frequent, found among the various sectors of the political spectrum in a curious way; for the most part, the term appears as a stigma linked to the positions of supposedly less-sophisticated adversaries who defend atavisms. However, if we take into account what Ernst Gellner affirms, we will understand that the stylized reiteration of atavisms is essential for the construction of national cultures. In my opinion, the possibilities for systematizing new and alternative representations of Galician culture that are based on definitive critiques of its ruralism are limited. As has already been noted, this would have the character of a matrix—an effective sign of its modernity and an indispensable reference for its existence.

I believe it is worthwhile to keep in mind the features suggested by Benedict Anderson when he refers to the ferocity of Gellner's denunciations of the "inventions" that nationalisms presuppose (Anderson 1991:

6). Even if various of Gellner's arguments are considered to be good references, I recognize the problems that lead to his implicit supposition of the authenticity of "cultures" or "communities" other than the national ones. As Anderson proposed, I believe it is also worth praising the imagination and the creativity in the case of Galician national culture, which had already invented its clearest definitions by the beginning of the twentieth century. However it is also important to refer to other more diffuse and less-recognized registers, through which Galicia was also imagined as a community during a period that preceded or was contemporary with the publishing of the periodical *Nós* and with the first activities of the Irmandades da Fala.

I would note that the most prominent history of Galician nationalism usually takes the successes that have occurred in Galicia into account. As I wanted to demonstrate in earlier pages, it is habitually theories proposed by well-known individuals or fleeting political initiatives attracting few among the general population that receive the greater part of the attention in historiography, in memorializations, and in commemorative initiatives, all of which today are assiduously pursued. As will have become clear, I also valorize these perspectives, given the fact that the analysis of contemporary expressions of the nationalist phenomenon is important to me. It is in these materials that the politics of memory play a part that is extremely relevant to the possibilities for reproducing a particularist discourse. Nevertheless, the available theory suggests alternative modes for thinking about dimensions of the imagination of a national Galician community, to which the small intellectual circles referred to above did not contribute significantly. In the first place, I intend in this chapter to look into some of the expressions of the senses of national belonging that specifically thrived very early in the process outside of Galicia in the most emblematic and cosmopolitan destinations of Galician emigrants. Then I will discuss some specific examples of manifestations that are presently employed to demonstrate a nationalized culture. I will pay close attention to the discrepancies and disputes over meaning that divide the representations proposed by elements of the autonomous government from those supported by the nationalist movement. In doing so, I will attend—in addition to the most salient disagreements—to the respective convergences that I believe to be, in great measure, inevitable.

Doing the Inappropriate, Some Andalusian Caprices

At the beginning of the twentieth century Buenos Aires and Havana had many more Galician inhabitants than any of the Galician cities. Before

1898, when Cuba gained autonomy from Spain, Havana had a larger population than either Madrid or Barcelona. On the other hand, in subsequent years Buenos Aires—*Bós Aires*—would become a great metropolis on a world scale. There were tens of thousands of Galicians that lived or moved to each of these distant cities at the turn of the century and in the years following. Nuñez Seixas (1998) notes that the Centro Galego of Havana had a maximum of 50,000 members in 1919, while the Centro Galego in Buenos Aires reached a peak of 39,118 members in 1932, this in spite of there being other competing associations in each of these cities. In general terms, the same author draws our attention to an impressive array of quantitative data for the whole of transatlantic emigration in this period. Between 1910 and 1930, 733,000 emigrants had left Galicia, not to mention the fact that the end of the previous century, from 1890 onwards, had been a period of emigration en masse to the Americas.

In the first decades of this long cycle of mass emigration, Cuba was the most significant destination, while by the end of the 1910s and in the following decades, Buenos Aires would become the great center for Galician emigration in Latin America. There, in the Americas, and especially in the large cities, the Galician-born were able to acquire referents of belonging to large supralocal communities. These were possible to imagine through new forms of sociability and through new and varied patterns of consumption. Due to the fragile bond of citizenship maintained by the majority of emigrants in relation to the Spanish state, it became possible for individuals subjected to new conditions of mobility and anonymity to transcend identifications that were originally limited to the boundaries of their parishes or districts of origin and to absorb new meanings linked to their condition as Galicians (Gellner 1983). At an already late date, in 1933, a correspondent from *A Nosa Terra* raised questions that I would now like to look at in very explicit terms. After having remarked that "there was always Galicianism among those Galician emigrants who live in Argentina" and referring to the importance of their monetary contributions to various Galician causes and institutions, he says:

> As can be seen, it ends up being a bit difficult to find a city in Galicia that is so concerned and does so much on behalf of Galicianism than the city formed by the Galician community of Buenos Aires, and it seems to us that neither Vigo nor A Coruña can be compared to it, perhaps because they still lack the spirit of being cities. (*A Nosa Terra*, no. 316, 1933)

The creation of new solidarities on the other side of the Atlantic happened through a variety of associative movements. Recreational associations and mutualism in Galician émigré circles in the Americas were lively phenomena (Nuñez Seixas 1998). These new senses of supralocal solidarity were also stimulated through the consumption of books, newspapers, and periodicals published there or arriving from Galicia, where their publication was justified, for the most part, by the existence of this significant transatlantic market. Equally important was the publication of books on Galician themes in Buenos Aires, which started at the beginning of the twentieth century and continued until the 1960s. According to Nuñez Seixas the first newspaper written completely in Galician came out in Havana, in 1885; this was the satirical weekly *A Gaita Gallega* (Nuñez Seixas 1992).

On the other hand, by the turn to the century in Havana and Buenos Aires, a few more sophisticated periodicals that dealt with Galicia had appeared, with better graphics, more varied illustrations, selling more and thus widely circulating the emblematic aims of the *Terra*. What stands out in the composition of these periodicals is the reproduction of paintings and photographs of "Galician landscapes," of "Galician traditional dress," and also of the caricatures of the *paisanos retranqueiros* [ironic peasants]. Suggestively captioned illustrations took their place next to transcriptions of the poems of the great bards of the *Rexurdimento,* the news of the *Terra,* Galician *triunfos* [triumphs] and *triunfadores* [winners], or—constantly!—criticism of the factionalism of a localist nature that would weaken the representation of the *raza* [race] in Latin America. These were some of the more characteristic contents of periodicals for which, it is also important to note, the newest technical means were used relatively early on in the production of images. This was the case with the important *Almanaque Gallego,* which began to be published even before the end of the nineteenth century in Buenos Aires, or later with the *Suevia* or the *Céltiga,* but also with the *Revista del Centro Gallego,* originating in Montevideo, and *El Eco de Galicia,* from Havana.

Along with this production in Latin America, the *Vida Gallega* began to be published in Vigo in 1909. But it too was mostly sold in Latin America, the reason for its obvious prosperity. In 1930 70,000 copies of this illustrated magazine were sold, with its great variety of photogravures recording Galician themes, these numbers and characteristics being unprecedented in Galicia. Its director, Jaime Solá, was an *españolista* of conviction—in his own words, a *regionalista* who was *sano* [wise] or *bien entendido* [enlightened]—as a consequence of which *Vida Gallega* became a repository of scathing criticism of nationalist positions beginning to emerge at the time. Since it provides us with such a rich register of alternative modes of imagining Galicia to those that appear in *Nós,* or in *A Nosa Terra,* it is an excellent counterpoint for studies on the history of Galician nationalism; nevertheless it is hardly ever cited in academic papers and in today's evocations in Galicia itself about the history of nationalism.

For example, caricatures by the young A. D. Castelao, at the time just beginning his career as an illustrator, appear in *Vida Gallega* containing images of Galician peasants with amusing captions, some of them adorning the cover of the magazine in 1909. Curiously, the most common references that I found to *Vida Gallega* were scornful, made in the context of Castelao's later comments that it was a magazine full of "dirty jokes" for "Americans," which he was sorry to have collaborated with as an illustrator in his younger years. Even today, Castelao's later and more dramatic caricatures provide us with a resource for the nationalization of references that are highly manipulated in Galicia. Successively reproduced in various media—often as graffiti in the streets of Galician cities—they have become the object of intersecting citations that many Galicians recognize. Even though we cannot pursue the subject here, it is important to take into account the uses of caricature—a genre that became highly developed in the Galician press at the outset of the twentieth century—as a way to create especially powerful depictions of a community. This was most effective when they represented virtues and habits supposedly common to each nation, depicting them through types of rural origin. Before joining the nationalist cause, Castelao's caricatures in *Vida Gallega* had these characteristics, which he later repudiated for being frivolous (Durán 1972, 1976), even though they were characteristics that he took up again in his later, militant productions.

Given certain of Benedict Anderson's ideas, it is possible to argue that imagining Galicia as a community was particularly helped by the large illustrated magazines bought by "Americans" at the start of the twentieth century. These efforts seem to be the first significant expressions of "print capitalism" (Anderson 1991) specifically targeting a reading public comprised of Galicians and providing images and texts that spoke of *A Terra.* This point of view is still defendable even if the majority of texts were written in Castilian and their commitment was ambiguous—and often even acrimonious—in relation to regionalist, and later nationalist, political positions.

In contrast, we see how the first doctrinal texts of nationalism circulated initially through titles whose editions numbered in the hundreds, a recognizably inefficient way to mobilize masses of adherents or even the bourgeoisie of the Galician cities. Already, by the 1920s, some of the large-circulation Latin American periodicals began publishing articles by the more important nationalist ideologues. This would be the case of

Céltiga in Buenos Aires, *Galicia* in Havana, and *Galicia* in Montevideo. These were, doubtlessly, the highest moments of their circulation, equal to the relative influence that nationalist ideas took on in the editorial departments of the two largest "modern" daily newspapers that were not organs of particular political parties and maintained a large circulation, appearing in Vigo during the 1920s: *Galicia* and *El Pueblo Gallego*.[2]

It was above all among the emigrant masses of the principal cities of Latin America that new symbols and habits of consumption were most expressively established. This successfully contributed to the imagining of Galicia as a community. It was among the emigrants of Havana and Buenos Aires that certain of the most relevant symbols, which allowed for the identification of Galicia as a nation, were produced early on and remain in place today—some of the indispensable pieces in the "do-it-yourself-kit of nationalism," to cite the memorable expression of Orvar Löfgren (1989: 7). The Galician national anthem was composed in Havana and introduced to the public in 1907. At around the same time and in the same city an academy of the Galician language was proposed, an idea that attracted sponsorship,[3] and even the founding of the Panteón de Galegos Ilustres was aired. It was also emigrants who for the first time adopted the white and blue flag, which today is official and has been recognized through the twentieth century by a variety of different Galicianist factions. Baldamero Cores Trasmonte gives a touching version of the invention of this insignia: "Vaamonde Lores said that it was the flag of the Navy Command of A Coruña and that it was copied by a certain association of emigrants who believed that it was an authentic regional flag. ... In spite of the lack of tradition and centuries of consecration, white and blue were imposed among Galician émigré associations and among those who began to construct nationalism, like the Irmandades da Fala" (Cores Trasmonte 1986: 59–60).

It was, respectively, in Havana in 1921, and in Buenos Aires in 1930, that the most radical and the earliest claims for independence in the history of Galician Nationalism arose (Beramendi and Nuñez Seixas 1995; Cores Trasmonte 1983). These were *arredistas* positions that were not explicitly echoed in Galicia at the time and that even today are infrequent, or, at least articulated with a surprising lack of clarity in the discourse maintained by the Bloque Nacionalista Galego and only formulated by small radicalized political associations, like the FPG (Frente Popular Galega) or the AMI (Assembleia da Mocidade Independentista). Suggestively, it was under the aegis of one of the *bardos* of the *Rexurdimento*—the Pondal Nationalist Society (SNP), active between 1930 and 1938—that these *arredista* formulations arose in Buenos Aires. Some passages from the SNP newspaper, *A Fouce*, will indicate the radicalism of their positions. But, at the same time, they will make clear the paradoxes that the American experience presented—principally the new senses of belonging that these emigrants felt now being subjected to different and more intense references of nationalization, as Galicians, but also as Argentinians and Spaniards:

> We are nationalists and *arredistas* [those calling for independence]. And we know that our people are unaware of our anti-Spanish feelings. ...

> Some think that our attitude of Galician intransigence is the product of the many kilometers that separate us from our country, that we live on the moon and that we know nothing about the lamentable and shameless state of renunciation that possess (the spirits) of the Galician people.

> And those who think that we do not take into account that we were born in Galicia and that we live far away but are in contact with thousands of Galicians who have become as Spanish and as unworthy as those who live in the *Terra*.

> But we are not men of resignation. We don't join up with the Spanishness of our people, and if anyone could convince us that Galicia will never be itself, we would continue to be the way we are, because we cannot return to being enslaved, our being is free; we are Galicians! (*A Fouce*, no. 69, 1934)

In an earlier issue, *A Fouce* would denounce the "miseries" of Galician associationism in quite suggestive terms, well worth transcribing:

> Certainly the Galicians that have emigrated to this city, who add up to some thousands, are those who most frequently patronize the most truculent and immoral events and proclaim to the four winds their servile, contemptible, gloomy and alienated condition.

> "Cultural" societies, in order to support an anti-Galician school in the *Terra*, promote the prostitution of women, and organize dances to make money, where pimps, thieves and neighborhood toughs end up.

Still, in the same issue the "sociedades" are once again reproached:

> In Buenos Aires there are a large number of Galician societies who undeservedly exploit the name. To better understand their activities we must divide them into two groups; the first group has to do with recreation and sport and its goal is to host dances and festivities; the second are educational and cultural and their goal is to create schools in their respective districts.

> It's hardly worth taking the "*milongueiras*" [parties and dances] seriously, as they're normally ridiculous. ...

Those who intend to educate and do cultural work, these indeed should be taken seriously for all the harm they do to Galicia. As far as I know there is not one that does anything for the advantage of its *Terra*; the schools maintained in our homeland by the so-called societies are only capable—due to the ignorance of their directors—of making brutes out of our pure children and opening the doors of emigration to them, already opened sufficiently by the Spanish state that, so we don't make any demands on them for the liberty that is ours, oblige us to emigrate. (*A Fouce*, no. 45, 1932)

Both the exasperated declarations of *arredismo* by these expatriates who wrote for *A Fouce* and the denunciations of the social relations and support that drove the majority of emigrants are suggestive, and it is worth commenting in detail on their implicit variations, namely, those that are related to the strict moral values that the above passages reveal. George Mosse proposed a systematic and clarifying approach to these questions in *Nationalism and Sexuality* (1985). In fact, in much of the comparative literature that I have read, I have found nationalists expressing preoccupations about "slow dancing"—denunciations of the corrupting influence of tangos, fox-trot, "negroid" songs, etc.—even if in Galicianist literature these kinds of moralizing preoccupations never seemed especially prominent.[4] Less anecdotal and also very suggestive are the preoccupations of columnists vis-à-vis the advances in literacy in Castilian, which the emigrants favored for their own villages and towns of origin through the donations collected by innumerable *sociedades de instrucción* that have suggestive names with a localist basis, of which many examples are to be found in one of the works of X. M. Nuñez Seixas (1988). At this point, however, I would simply like to emphasize how, for the majority of Galician emigrants, their social experiences in the contexts of their transatlantic havens produced new experiences—for most of them—of overlapping and intersecting references of nationalization.

In the photographs of, and reportage about, the celebrations that took place in the context of the "recreational societies" we will recognize many palimpsests in the use of the symbols of belonging that Galician emigrants in Argentina, Uruguay, or Cuba came to appropriate. For example, the same photograph might show their children dressed up as *sevillanas, manolos,* as *rapaciñas* or *gauchos* [traditional dress of the young]. In the backdrops for the *verbenas* [popular dances]—or on the covers of the magazines themselves—to the *Giralda* [cathedral tower in Seville], we can see motifs like *pinos* [pine trees] and *hórreos* [granite or wooden structures for storing crops such as grain], or *paisajes de la marina gallega* [Galician seascapes], joined together. These syncretic overlaps can also be found during the same period in Galicia, considering the intense exchange of these stereotypical signs of nationalization between both sides of the Atlantic.

It would be impossible, on the other hand, to create an exhaustive list of the relevant personalities in the history of Galicianism who were emigrants or exiles, or who experienced both conditions in consecutive periods.[5] It is important to note that emigration to Cuba and to Argentina around the turn of the century also attracted various intellectuals and artists in addition to the more characteristic masses of illiterate or partially literate peasantry that swelled this intense migratory current. As the various personal stories of famous Galicianists suggest, it was easier to make a living as a musician, journalist, or even a poet among one's compatriots in Havana during the years 1880–1910, or in Buenos Aires and Montevideo between 1910 and 1930, than in Galicia itself. It was, in the end, the movement of ideas and images produced in the metropole—with the greatest part of their consumers residing on the other side of the Atlantic—along with other similar productions by expatriated intellectuals in Latin America who returned to Galicia, which more decisively influenced the notion of Galicia as a national community. This happened in Cuba, Argentina, and Uruguay, and to some extent also in Madrid, Mexico, Puerto Rico, and Venezuela, where emigrants, and later exiles from Franco's regime, projected images from this *Galiza do exterior* that became important for political action in the homeland.

During the 1920s, Galician culture began to be deliberately objectified by an elite group of intellectuals (of whom we spoke in the previous chapter), articulating it in an increasingly refined fashion. I believe that this process unfolded through a process of explicitly censoring marks of alterity and cosmopolitanism that, in their opinion, corrupted the purity of the old customs of the Galician *labregos* [farmer or peasant]. Above all it was the Castilian influences that were targeted and, generally, all of the sundry *flamenquismos* [Andalusian and, thus, Spanish stereotypes] that found expression in the daily lives of the Galicians. Over time, especially starting in the final decades of the nineteenth century, these *flamenquismos* had become important references in the nationalization of the culture of a growing number of Spaniards. Their appropriation by the greater part of Galicians of the lower classes were blocked in Galicia itself, but they were given freer rein in the transatlantic centers of Galician emigration. It was there, that many—perhaps the majority—became fluent in the Spanish language. Occasionally, in the case of the most successful, they began to identify it, according to the cliché, as the "language of Cervantes." For their children, they could afford to buy *maja* and *manolo* carnival costumes to be used at celebrations in the Galician centers in Latin America, or, upon returning to the homeland, in the *casinos,* news of which so often appeared in *Vida Gallega,* known as the magazine of the *"triunfadores"* and that reported on and photographed these events on both sides of the Atlantic.

It was also likely that many of these emigrants consumed Spanish products of high quality in the Latin America for the first time in their lifetimes. The extent of the impact of gastronomic consumption is not inconsiderable, especially since in this context it is also possible to discern the presence of many nationalizing references. For example, in the magazines directed at Galician immigrants in Argentina, the advertisements for better-stocked delicatessens told of *vinos de Jerez, cidras asturianas,* and *jamones extremeños* [wines of Jerez, ciders from Asturias and hams from Extremadura] along with products coming specifically from Galicia and even of an assortment of local foodstuffs, like *charque* [a form of jerky] or *mate* [a bitter tea]. For the recently wealthy son of a day-laborer from the Galician province of Lugo, buying these products, which would have never been available to him during his childhood in Galicia, would be a practical lesson in the references of nationalization. Likewise, there is the rather novel fact that *grelos* [turnip greens], *castañas* [chestnuts], and *unto* [lard], which were nearly inexistent in Argentina and other American countries, or very expensive, would for the first time be associated with Galicia—with the homeland—after having been components of the monotonous diet of generations of his ancestors.

The indications of a recent access to new mass cultures that we find among the emigrants who belonged to the recreational societies of Havana, Montevideo, or Buenos Aires also began to make an appearance in festivities all across Galicia. *Flamenquismos* are recognizable in the festivities, paid for by *Indianos* [returning emigrants] in their villages of origin; likewise, there is an belated interest in bullfighting, which suddenly became popular at the beginning of the twentieth century among the city dwellers of A Coruña and Pontevedra. It is unfortunate that in the periodicals the peasant costumes were not *enxebres* [authentic], or that they had abandoned the *muiñeiras* [a Galician folk dance] in favor of slow dancing. New customs subverted the *labregos* in the most remote localities of Galicia, where they were singing *saetas* [traditional Andalusian songs] in their processions, if we are to believe in the scandalized denunciations that occasionally turned up in the pages of *A Nosa Terra* during the 1920s, a period in which there was no place in the definition of Galician culture for the *mantóns de Manila,* the *peteneras* [a form of flamenco dance], the theatrical *giraldas, toros,* and *picadors* [the various accoutrements of bullfighting].

Under Franco's long dictatorship the restriction of all peripheral nationalist propaganda was imposed (Tusell 1999b) and practically all of the possibilities for proselytizing representations of Galician culture were disparaged. In Galicia, contrary to what occurred to a certain extent in the Basque Country and in Catalonia, the censorship that the Franco regime had imposed had particularly grave consequences, even more so because the recognition of the new national culture had not been accepted on a widespread basis before 1936. The ways in which it was expressed since its recognition barely survived, so the reproduction and defense of earlier representations was played out on a small scale until 1975, as we saw in the previous chapter. The American circuits of emigration remained the only places—relatively speaking—open to the Galicianizing catechization. Even there, however, over the long term the results of this process had little effect on the majority of emigrants and was met mostly with indifference (Cores Trasmonte 1983; Monteagudo 2000). The change in the editorial line of certain emigrant magazines suggests that the new regime was viewed sympathetically abroad, and that it was not squeamish about spending funds on propaganda. But it is also true that on a global scale the "apogee of nationalism" had passed (Hobsbawm 1992).

It was only starting with the years of the *transición democrática* (1976–1980) that the recognition of a common Galician culture allowed for the possibility of disseminating nationalist ideas to the mass public. Its more cohesive figuration would coalesce around the contributions of the *xerácion Nós* and, more distantly, on the cultural inheritance of the precursors, as Ramón Piñeiro would say during the hinge year of 1978 (*Grial*, no. 59: 8) when the new post-Francoism state constitution was drawn up. Starting in 1982, the government of the Comunidade Autónoma gained legal capacities to defend itself according to the *Estatuto de Autonomía de Galicia*. Today the expression *cultura galega* includes many new meanings that were absent or badly articulated, as the uses it was put to at the beginnings of the twentieth century were very limited. As Richard Handler has indicated, it is necessary to recognize to what extent the registers in which Galician culture is objectified have multiplied (Handler 1988). Today, given the particular political circumstances that dominated in the Comunidade Autónoma, the possibilities for dissidence surrounding certain national cultural referents are high. The heterogeneous and hybridized conditions under which working-class emigrants with little formal education contributed to making it possible for Galicia to be configured as a community on both sides of the Atlantic seem to have been generally forgotten.

Country of Bagpipes

One morning in the winter of 1997 I went to work at the library at the Museo do Pobo Galego; in my distraction I missed an opportunity to attend a rousing event that was shaking up the center of Compostela. In order to celebrate the recent reelection of its president, the Xunta da Galicia brought together thousands of pipers dressed in colorful folkloric garb in the Praza do Obradoiro. The surprising and multitudinous gathering made the newspapers and was covered by international television. According to what was said in Santiago, the event even gained a place in the *Guinness Book of Records*. In the following days sardonic jokes multiplied; likewise the enthusiastic reports in the official newspapers, ostensible disdain, embarrassed smiles, and reactions varied according to people's political sympathies. Still today, calculations about the quantity of pipers at Obradoiro vary widely. The promoters adopted a triumphal position, declaring that their greatest expectations had been surpassed and that there had been nearly 8,000 pipers present in the square. A friend, disconcerted for having to give importance to something that he wanted to present with contempt and even shame for Galicia, stuck to his guns, however, in affirming that there had not been more than 3,000, and few of them were anywhere near the Praza de Obradoiro. Surprisingly, this was a reaction common to a variety of my informants connected to the BNG.

In 1995 a periodical linked to the nationalist movement published a suggestive thematic issue entitled *No País das Gaitas* [In the Country of Bagpipes].[6] By that date already two of these large gatherings of pipers—even though more modest in size—had been organized by the president of the Xunta under the same pretext. This is clearly a case of consolidating an invented tradition in line with the famous definitions of Hobsbawm and Ranger. The publisher of *No País das Gaitas*, in spite of emphasizing the importance of being critical of all attempts to take advantage of traditions for *legitimación política* (political legitimation), also suggests that there is an intimate relationship between this instrument and the history of Galicianism. He is, perforce, associating the flourishing of this instrument with periods of political and cultural rebirth in Galicia.

Today tens of thousands of children—girls and boys—are learning to play the bagpipe in associations and schools around the *Comunidade,* a major part of these lessons being subsidized by the Xunta. But on the other hand, there is also a variety of *talleres* [workshops] devoted to teaching the bagpipe that are supported by circles in one way or another connected to the nationalist left. We saw in chapter 2 that the march organized by the Bloque on the *25 de Xullo* was opened by two pipers dressed quite formally in traditional garb. The multiplication of the number of pipers in today's Galicia was described to me by a nationalist friend—in a very funny fashion—as an inexorable cloning that takes the famous Real Banda de gaitas da Deputación de Ourense as its most important model.[7] This musical group—whose costumes, accessories, and poses are similar to Scottish regimental bands—is an obligatory reference for those who would cast the political culture of the Xunta de Galicia in a contemptuous light. A bumper sticker in circulation some years ago in nationalist circles referred to the said group with following parodic caption: *The Famous Royal, Clerical, and Scot Pipe Band of the Deep Utation.*

In 1935, Alexandre Bóveda—a Galicianist politician and one of the mortal victims of the Franco uprising the following year—wrote a suggestive *Envio as Mocedades* [Dispatch to the Youth], subtitled *Temos que crear o noso Baile Nacional* [We Must Create Our National Dance], in which he had the following to say:

> Since we already have a National Anthem, a Flag and songs … we have to rapidly create our National Dance.
>
> Does this exist? Yes. Our *Redonda,* which can be danced to the same rhythm, and at the same pitch by hundreds or thousands of people. …
>
> One day, during our great festival, we will come to Compostela from all the points on the compass, thousands of young people who will consecrate our dance. (*A Nosa Terra,* no. 396, 1935)

Today, regular meetings of expert dancers—or *pandeireteiras* [tambourine players], and *conta contos* [story tellers], etc.—are common, not to mention the overwhelming proliferation of pipers in recent years. What I would like to emphasize is the similar concerns shared by these two examples so separated by time and by the ideological positioning of their proponents. These days these activities are a way of spreading modern—nationalized—mass culture, founded on objectivizations of that which is Galician and popular, and open to all sectors of Galician society under the new conditions that the *Estatuto de Autonomía* has made possible.

During the 1920s Antonio Gramsci was already making accurate observations about questions similar to those that Alexandre Bóveda was taking up, and which I would say are still open to debate in Galicia (Gramsci 1985: 188 and ff.). They are fascinating, especially his opinions about what he designates as the range of "arcadian conventions" and the possibilities for styling them in such a way as to create a "popular-national culture." Using Gramsci's terms, we can say that between the performances of the young *pandeireteiras* at the Bloque's picnics and those that the Xunta recruited in the villages of Ourense or Lugo there are merely conventional differences. In both cases the common objective is to use cultural markers to develop nationalist meanings. Coming from the urban middle classes, the performances of the Bloque's *pandeireteiras* are generally looser and more creative; those from the villages are more rigid and conventionally interpreted and the performers' costumes rigorously follow the in-vogue folkloric traditions. But it is a national culture that in both cases needs to be represented, even if, in the second case, the same folkloric outfits and performances were used to represent an "agreed-upon regionalism," having received the dedicated patronage of Franco's government, which is why such folklorisms remain suspect to the nationalist Galician left to this day.

In 1997, I asked an eminent Galician academic, off the record, who, in his opinion, had contributed more to the Galicianization of culture in Galicia.[8] After a moment of reflection, he said that it was the current president of the Xunta de Galicia, Manuel Fraga. As we have seen, Fraga was an important minister during the Franco regime and, from 1990 to 2005 he was consistently reelected to the position of president, winning increasing majorities of the vote. That unexpected response stayed with me for a long while, and I ended up mentioning it in a variety of conversations with sympathizers of the nationalist left, for whom the said response seemed laughable or simply provocative.

As a rule, among those connected to the BNG or other even more radical Galicianist groups, references to the Xunta, and above all to its president, are very acerbic and derisive. But in the Spain *de las autonomías,* each of the autonomous governments has found it necessary to "prove the originality of its culture," as James Fernandez has suggested (Medeiros 1997), through separate projects that have the approval of the Spanish state. This constitutional and statutory imposition is observed in a particular way by the government of the Xunta de Galicia in terms of the special attention given to processes of "folkloricization" (Martí 1996; Bausinger 1990). The opposition, the parties of the nationalist left, tend to see these processes as anachronistic manipulations as tainted by the habits of the anterior regime, and so susceptible to parody. And yet, more ambiguously, they also see them as unjustified appropriations of a heritage of references that they imagine they should be able to claim as their own.

In fact, it was the work of various generations, in the context of the nationalist movement, that put together the most legitimate resources available today for creating a pedagogy suitable for the making of a national Galician culture, work that today finds its most prominent protagonist in the autonomous government of Galicia. In this process, those in the government have appropriated cultural productions that were created over time—most often in the bitter conditions of repression, exile, and censorship—by Galicianists with a wide range of political sympathies. The most resounding example is the way in which the cult of the memory of A.R. Castelao and his body of work has been officialized.

This process cannot be considered to be either completed and fixed or even exactly easy to trace to only specific dates; on the contrary, it is a very active and ongoing project to this day, touching on many different registers, whether literary, musical, or ethnographic, among others. As such, we can see it as the continuous movement of objectification that serves as a "proof" that Galician culture is perpetuated and that it is closely linked to both official institutions and the nationalist movement, in spite of their mutual contempt. Those proposals that emanate from the nationalist circles of the left seem to be more creative because they are situated in an "antistructural" position (Turner 1990), on the margins of those in power, whose legitimacy as a Galician government they contest. Thus, they are constantly involved in the production of a redeeming discourse out of which emerges an expanding "version of the world" in Galician (Goodman 1995) whose destiny, quite inadvertently, is institutionalized under the jurisdiction of organs supported by the autonomous government, as various examples will suggest.

Other Pipers

On one occasion I was told that if I went to Cangas do Morrazo—a proletarian town inhabited mostly by fishermen and workers, which is located across an estuary from Vigo—I would be able to see the performative updating of an interesting story. It is very simply told. In the display case of a bar there is a bottle of whiskey called 100 Pipers. A fisherman comes in—the proverbial fellow villager—who says in a thick voice: "Dame un cen jaiteiros" [Give me a 100 Pipers]. This cheap brand of whiskey is very popular in the bars of Galicia; on a variety of earlier occasions I had the opportunity to hear this request that had become so "intimate" (Herzfeld 1997), a request made as often by intellectuals inspired by the circulation of the story and disposed towards using it ironically as by ordinary people who used the expression without reflecting on it.

I have heard this story recounted to intellectuals on a variety of occasions, always in an ambiguous and very particular manner, mixing mockery of the provincial uncouthness of the seafarers or workers with a note of particularist pride. What is illustrated is a certain frankness and vivacity of the villager that serves to collectively identify the Galicians, their *génio* at using an outdated term, which we could take to mean *spirit*, or *character of a people or a place*. The story of the *cen jaiteiros* is curious because it is a parodic expression of an instance of "banal nationalism" (Billig 1986). What is in question here are the recent practices of consumption among the lower strata and the recognition of one of the regional varieties of Galician pronunciation (*jaiteiros* for *gaiteiros*). But, at the same time, one of the most well-nurtured myths of Galician nationalist discourse is alluded to, that of the supposed Celtic origins of Galicia and the affinities maintained between Galicia and the "Celtic nations" of the periphery of Western Europe.

The reasons this anecdote has become a favorite among nationalist intellectuals seems clear to me. To a certain extent only the knowledge of more imaginative references that delimit the production of national Galician culture—a work of the well-educated classes as I have already suggested—allow us to carry to the limit all of the ironic implications implicit in it. Here, as James Fernandez argues with another case in mind (1986: 130 and ff.), it is in a special "semantic field" in which this account can be fully developed. In this case we have the meanings delimited by the multiform references of an erudite culture. For this reason, in a bar in Compostela when my nationalist friend—an essayist and Seamus Heaney's Galician translator—asked for a *cen jaiteiros* in a hushed voice, he did so with complete irony and self-consciousness, even mimicking the "nebulous" melancholy of the Celts (Chapman 1982) for my benefit.

Another informant and friend, Xurxo,—a nationalist anthropologist who was the first to tell me the story about *cen jaiteiros* in 1997—insisted on several occasions that I should go to the Morrazo peninsula, perhaps settling in Cangas, and do some serious "participant observation." This was well-intentioned advice from someone who had seen me lose time available "for fieldwork" walking around urban centers like Vigo and Santiago in the company of intellectuals, spending time in libraries and museums and—sometimes—with other anthropologists, far from the *pobo* [the people]. In the end, if I intended to understand Galician culture and to study the contemporary expressions of the nationalist movement, Cangas and the Morrazo peninsula were the most advisable destinations. It is there that the Bloque Nacionalista Galego (BNG) had a substantial percentage of voters and support for the party was enthusiastic; also the associative movement between the workers and the fishermen was a spirited one. At the time I was given this bit of advice, Cangas was one of the four municipalities throughout Galicia that the BNG governed, a fact that brought with it a demand for exemplary management.

Expressions of nationalist activities described enthusiastically by Xurxo would be more animated and authentic in Cangas. He referred, for example, to the Galicianist fervor of the wives of fishermen and the workers in the fish canning factories in Cangas, sometimes expressed in outcries directed at Galician politicians whose positions vis-à-vis Spanish centralism were ambiguous. Curiously, when I finally had the opportunity to travel to Cangas, it was in the company of an anthropologist, a foreigner who was very familiar with Galicia, where she had lived. For both of us it should have been a trip to meet the *pobo*. Fiona wanted to gather additional documents about the workers' struggles at a large canning factory that had been, in the meantime, closed—the sequel to a project begun years earlier, and she told me enthusiastically about her expectations surrounding her return. As it happened, however, we mainly spoke with local intellectuals, people distanced from work in the factories, old acquaintances working in the nationalist movement. They were conversations conducted inter pares, from Fiona's perspective; she knew these people and who they supported. She asked them about what was new in Cangas and Galicia, which she had been away from for a number of years.

Though I had still not had the opportunity in Cangas to see exactly how the proletarian population had appropriated the nationalist ideology, it was interesting to find the topics and circumstances of so many conversations that I had already had in Compostela, Vigo, and Ourense reiterated by Fiona's friends. They spoke in Galician of the scandal over the linguistic policy of the Xunta, of the affinities between Galician and Portuguese, of the various demands being made. I even recognized the expression of an interest for the *pobo* in the collection of "popular art" that one of the hosts had at home. In one of the other conversations it was the politics of a theater production that were center stage, namely, the cross-border projects between Galicia and the north of Portugal, the kinds of initiatives that have lately become more common. The meals we ate were very Galician, like the excellent *alvariño* wine with which they were accompanied. The relationship between the consumption of wine and the process of the nationalization of culture in Galicia merits further comment. Later, in Vigo and in Santiago, I had the opportunity to speak with the owners of wine stores, who held well-informed opinions about the habits of their customers, which they related directly to their respective political leanings. Retrospectively, I believe that their curious theories would be borne out in Cangas as well.

At the end of the day, nothing in particular happened at the time on the peninsula of Morrazo that could have given me any idea of the local influx of Celticism, beyond the music that was playing in one of the restaurants in Cangas where we ate; in fact, I didn't have the opportunity there to see anyone asking for a *cen jaiteiros*. It is true that on a variety of occasions, in demonstrations in Santiago, I saw people from Morrazo, identifiable from their banners behind which they gathered singing the Galician national anthem with great emotion—like everyone else who was present—in which one part speaks about the "nación de Breogán." But the reference to the mythical colonizer of Ireland, or to the verses of the nineteenth-century "bard" Eduardo Pondal, is a small part of the widespread Celticism that plays a role in the representation of Galician national culture, a theme that I would like to speak about below (see chapter 10).

Given his position as a nationalist supporter, Xurxo's reference to Cangas as the best place to carry out the research that I wanted to do was interesting. Unintentionally, it was the social composition of the nationalist movement and the respective weaknesses that were referred to, because the disaffection of the majority of the Galician *labregos* and *mariñeiros* [agriculturalists and fishermen] from the political positions of the BNG and the rest of the nationalist extreme-left is especially highlighted in their voting patterns. Yet in Morrazo, the disfavored stratum—in the end, legitimate representatives of a *Galicia mariñeira,* an emblematic and discursive reference used to speak of the *pobo galego*—had already been won over to the nationalist cause. Xurxo's allegation implicitly contained the suggestion of an "in it for themselves" positioning on the part of the working classes—a positive version of the more common behavior: alienation from the values of Galicianism on the part of those who are taken as repositories of the essences of national identity.

But, as the capital of the Comunidade Autónoma, Santiago is, in the end, a favorable place to learn about expressions of nationalism in Galicia and of the new national culture. It is possible to attend frequent celebratory events, parades and public gatherings, lectures and conferences, and to spend time in libraries, *hemerotecas* [libraries for magazines and newspapers], and well-stocked bookstores. I would say that the Galician language tends to be more robust and correct in the classrooms, in the speeches of politicians, among conference-goers, or in chance conversations, even if this is sometimes taken as a polemical opinion. I was criticized on various occasions for suggesting this and told that in other places—normally in the *aldeas de Lugo*—the Galician would be more valued for its purity and authenticity. Yet Santiago is, precisely, the most appropriate place for these kinds of discussions about the areas where Galician is purer or more beautiful. The Real Academia da Lingua Galega is also a natural setting for these discussions. It is very common in Santiago for academics to deliberate on the subject. Jokes circulate about the old academy that was born in a bookstore in A Coruña and nicknamed the Cova Céltica. The theories and the politics of nationalism have also gained surprisingly reflexive expression in Compostela; for example, it is not uncommon to hear about the "invention of traditions" and of their necessity to people who are engaged supporters or have institutional responsibilities.

The "cidade do apóstolo" is the seat of the government, of some of the principal official institutions and of some of Galicia's most important organs of social communication, namely the Televisión de Galicia (TVG), one of the institutions created under the shelter of the *Estatuto de Autonomía*. For this reason, gossip—always of interest to the anthropologist—is intense. And it is highly present behind the scenes of the production of representations of Galician culture. In academe, in artistic and scientific circles of the autonomous administration, rumors constantly circulate over who will be nominated or who will be dismissed, who won a grant, who will direct a given piece by a Galician author or organize the most daring colloquium. Also, the variety of events held to celebrate Galician culture is extensive: lectures, exhibitions, concerts, performances, gastronomic events, etc.

Towards the end of 1998 and into 1999 I traveled sporadically to the Comunidade Autónoma, as I had already left Santiago, where I had lived until July of 1998. On one of these trips, during the summer of San Martiño of 1998, I spent some days in one of the most "remote" localities of the Ancares Mountains (Ardener 1989). It was a very small village, built in schist, which had been the target of a program of reconstruction sponsored by the Xunta, construction whose recent completion was marked by a visit from Manuel Fraga and by enthusiastic reportage on TVG in which the Galician character of these kinds of places was emphasized. Only three families live permanently in this village, the youngest of which included María, José, and Suso—their son, already an adult. They ran a "rural bed and breakfast" where I stayed. María and José had spent more than half of their lives in the Basque Country, where they had been factory workers. This was a common experience for thousands of Galicians in recent decades, nearly always indicated in the smallest villages of the provinces of Ourense and Lugo by the presence of automobiles with license plates from Bilbao or Vitoria, cars that were usually of modest makes and very old. This is because it had already been many years since the metalworking industry of the Basque Country underwent its "reconversión" [restructuring], which caused the majority of emigrants to return to Galicia with their small savings earned over a good part of their lives.

In their *casa de turismo rural*, María's most frequent clients were relatively young, middle-class couples who lived mainly in A Coruña or Vigo. She told me that they were normally Galician speakers, above all interested in going for long hikes, relaxing, and appreciating the "*enxebre*" [authentic] cooking. I could not ascertain the political affiliation of these visitors, but was able to recognize by her description of one of the most characteristic types of those who sympathized with the BNG, which I had met every year at the Carballeira de San Lourenzo picnic and here and there throughout Galicia over the years. María spoke to them in Galician—"*moi acastrapado*" [close to a form of Castilian spoken in Galicia that relies heavily on Galician vocabulary and syntax]—as she served them rich and abundant meals. These included the bread, honey, meats, and chestnuts of the *Terra,* and the tapas, of *jamón Serrano* of Extremadura, all of which her guests ate in prodigious quantities. With her guests, María had perfected her Galician over time—most of them were "educated people"—as she also told me.

I returned to Santiago in time to participate in an event that had been publicized for a long while and that I did not want to miss. It was a literary protest in the old Casino on Rúa do Vilar, which Ramón Otero Pedrayo described in the following way in the *Guía de Galicia:* "The casino, one of the societies that preserves the old ways, has been in this street for many years. On the night of the 25th of July a dance is celebrated which draws the best of Galician society" (1991: 508). The Casino had long faded and certainly the "Día de Apóstolo" balls were no longer held for the "best of society"; decades had gone by and the changes in Galicia were many, as well as changes in the composition of this particular stratum of high society. A crowd of people were sitting in the Casino's worn-out cushioned leather chairs taking turns throughout the night to participate in this singular protest.

The Centro Dramático Galego had been given a grant by the Xunta de Galicia to stage a series of pieces by the famous modernist Galician writer Ramón del Valle Inclán (1866–1936), who is one of the glories of twentieth-century Spanish literature. Valle Inclán only wrote in Castilian, but his works mostly take place in Galicia of the nineteenth century, which is described in an utterly original fashion that brought numerous Galician words into the Spain of that period. We saw in chapter 2 how Castelao had, in 1940, invoked the *not completely fleshless* Ramón del Valle Inclán in his nomenclature of illustrious Galicians. In 1999, the question that was in the air was whether the Centro Dramático Galego should put on the plays in the original language or translated into Galician. This question had already taken up a lot of space in the newspapers, with many different arguments, some serious, others ironic, coming from both sides, and was already thriving by the beginning of 1998.

At the *velada* [literary event] in the Casino members of the nationalist left and sympathizers came together. I was able to meet old friends and acquaintances once again. Late that night Xosé Manuel Beiras, the leader of the BNG, arrived. His entrance provoked a certain excitement in the hall. In a previous address, Beiras condemned the anti-Galician cultural policy of the Xunta, then gave emotional readings of some of Valle Inclán's poems that he himself had translated. Performances of this same general character followed, guaranteeing to the audience the possibility of effectively translating the plays and the whole of his works. There was also much condemnation of the abuses perpetuated by the official institutions responsible for the safeguarding of Galician culture. I took advantage of the end of the evening and the next day to learn about the conclusion of another of the curious stories that had upset the artistic world and involved some of the autonomous institutions at the beginning of the previous year.

I am speaking about the replacement of Gloria Moure in the directorate of the Centro Galego de Arte Contemporánea (CGAC), the institution that she had run since its inauguration in 1994. The building that held the CGAC, as I have already noted, faces the Panteón de Galegos Ilustres and the Museo do Pobo Galego, in Bonaval. It is an elegant building designed by Álvaro Siza, the famous Portuguese architect. It is one among other recent prestigious commissions intended to symbolize Galician identity and culture. One of the stories that I heard, but which I could not confirm, suggested that the architect's first intention was to cover the whole construction in glass. At the request of the owners of the project—the Xunta de Galicia—he had agreed do the outside walls in granite to stress the "Galician" character of the building. Gloria Moure, on the other hand, is a Catalan academic and curator with an international reputation. She had accepted her position at the CGAC from Manuel Fraga, who had personally requested her, with the guarantee of generous funding and the freedom to exhibit according to her own agenda and to make essential acquisitions. Prior to the crisis that I am speaking about now, the fact of Gloria Moure being of Galician descent—evident in her surname—was emphasized with a certain suggestive insistence in the newspapers and on TVG.

The reasons that led to the dismissal of the director of the CGAC were never completely clarified; apparently it was a personal decision of the *Director Xeral de Patrimonio,* but had counted on the support of the *Conselleiro de Cultura,* the highest level politician responsible in this emblematic instance of political action in the Comunidade Autónoma. Nevertheless, there was wide speculation about the reasons: mention of irresolvable personality conflicts, or unhappiness about money spent and even supposed atavistic reactions of more *enxebrista* members of the PP of G [Partido Popular of Galicia, Fraga's party], displeased with the cosmopolitan directions of the programs favored by Moure. On the other hand, interpretations about what role Manuel Fraga had taken in this case were varying. It was wondered whether his actions were due to his personal discontent with Gloria Moure's work, or if he acted as a politician under the gun, letting her "fall" in order to appease the predominant sensibilities of his governing party; at any rate, no one apparently believed that Fraga had not been involved in the final decision.

Once the dismissal had become news, various attempts were made to mobilize the citizens. On one of the following days a small crowd of demonstrators that was gathered in the vicinity of the CGAC was blocked by the police from gaining access. The names most criticized were those of the *Director Xeral de Patrimonio* and the *Conselleiro de Cultura,* and, most of all, the *Presidente da Xunta de Galicia* himself. The night of the same day one of the best known bars in Santiago filled up with those who had been present at the demonstration and others who had decided to show up—what took place was a kind of informal redress of Gloria Moure, who was present herself.

The owner of the establishment, a friend, and informant when he was not too busy, was exultant because there were a number of well-known artists and intellectuals in his bar. Later, X. M. Beiras arrived. Many present that night had been, in earlier days, regulars at Fran's bar, before getting older and taking on responsibilities that brought them notoriety in the culture of contemporary Galicia. Yet even here, beyond the celebration of solidarity and apparent unanimity in favor of the work of the former director of the CGAC, I heard that there were many complaints about her tenure. In the end, there were resentments in the artistic community—people more or less well recognized had failed to see their work represented at the Centro, because the program had favored exhibitions of the work of international artists compared to only a small number of that of Galician artists.

Even if Manuel Fragas had initially been silent on the issue, thus corroborating the official version of the story that it had been a normal administrative decision, he ended up feeling obligated to say something in public once the crisis became an issue in the news. He said that it was felt that it was necessary that the program of the CGAC be more Galician, though he did make known his personal appreciation for the work and the person of the dismissed director. It became, and for some time remained, a burning issue in the editorials in Galician newspapers, all of which minutely examined the episode and its consequences and the possibilities for interpreting it. The larger state newspapers also attributed some importance to the episode that was agitating the Galician intelligentsia, yet they portrayed the question as an obscure episode typical of any other *ruritania*. This is exactly what happened in a report in *El Mundo* on 6 February 1998. This is a point of view that I feel merits a closer look, since we are dealing with a newspaper connected to sectors of the center-right, with an affinity to the party in power in Galicia. But even so, the most striking result was the tone of mockery directed towards the vernacularizing sensibilities that reign in the PP of G.

People That Know a Lot in Various Places

Cultura galega is an expression that is used frequently in contemporary Galicia, and the notions that give weight to its representation are conspicuous. As I would like to suggest, its familiarity is spread through a process that is at the moment lively and multivocal. However, many of the references that allow for legitimate uses of that notion are hardly accessible to a good part of Galicians. This is the case with many older people and with the less educated, with those who constitute a significant part of the rural population, precisely where it is imagined that those elements that define national culture are preserved with the most integrity—that is, in rural Galicia. It is common to hear old peasants say, "I'm not cultured," or that they don't have a good command of Galician, or that they speak a corrupted form of it. I have heard this in the small villages of Lugo, for instance.

These are opinions that show a degree of resentment towards the influence of the conception of culture that Roy Wagner called the "opera house sense of the word" (1981: 21). However, it is often now possible to understand these expressions of the old peasants as small provocations, uttered by those who are expecting to be misrepresented by people from the cities or by the anthropologist—interlocutors that they imagine would like to valorize their role as putative retainers of the foundations of the new national culture. It is common in these situations, as well, that anyone else present—a son or daughter, grandchild or neighbor, normally younger and better educated—will guarantee that the *xente vella da aldea sabe moito* [the old people of the villages know a lot], or carry on with a discourse about the importance of the vernacular language preserved in these rural spaces in the definition of Galician identity.

Language and *culture* are terms that normally appear together when we are speaking about Galician "identity," a much-used expression but one that only became common in Galicia during the 1990s. We find an early and suggestive use by Ramón Piñeiro in 1978 that refers to "the Galician consciousness in search of its collective identity," in a passage already cited (*Grial,* no. 59, 8). But these uses only really began to multiply in Galicia from the mid-1980s on, when the notion began to be enthusiastically accepted by local social scientists—as happened, as a matter of fact, in other academic contexts in the Iberian Peninsula and in the rest of the world (Prat 1991a, 1991b; Handler 1994).[9] But these days, in fact, its use is spontaneous and generalized in cities, towns, and villages. I've had the opportunity to listen to sermons about Galician identity in some very unexpected places, like in Limia and Monte Cebreiro, outlying localities in the Comunidade Autónoma, distant from major cities, where only during the last two decades has it been increasingly consolidated.

Identity, culture, and language—as well as "tradition," a word that, as we noted in chapter 2, is so central to nationalist rhetoric—occur as terms that are overlapping and interchangeable in their daily use. When we discriminate more precisely, we will understand that language and culture are thought of as guarantors or foundations of *identidade galega,* today the term with the strongest and most inclusive uses. In its turn, *cultura galega,* is also a frequently employed and very inclusive term—a phrase that we have seen used with holistic, "anthropological" meanings (Handler 1988; Clifford 1988), since the middle of the 1920s. This expression would have a crucial dimension in the Galician language, whose defense and promotion appear to be the most important guarantors for the possibility of the survival of Galician tradition, culture, and identity. The Galician language and culture are understood as being constantly under siege and their survival threatened. Notwithstanding, an observer from the outside could easily think that recognition of the Galician language and its prestige has never been so great, and its prospects for the future never so secure.

The relative familiarity that a growing number of Galicians demonstrate in relation to the representations of their "culture" can be understood as the result of a widespread pedagogic effort through which references are popularized, ones that until recently were only debated in intellectual circles. Various are the social agents that today exercise a role as pedagogues promoting Galician cultural representations. We can point to the importance of the involvement of not only teachers, writers, artists, performers, and anthropologists, but also politicians, journalists, television announcers, and functionaries in the autonomous administration. These—the most conspicuous mediators—can be understood as specialists in the production or the spreading of representations of Galician culture, but active participants in this process are increasingly numerous, a process that, each day, seems to be gaining more strength. I met unemployed young people of irregular habits and with very little schooling who saw themselves as supporters of Galician culture and identity, even if their capacity to influence others was restricted. What is important, however, is to note that their appropriation of this group of discursive references—even if they are limited, gotten from bars while enjoying themselves with more well-informed friends—inform, to a large extent, their vision of the world.

On a program on TVG, *As Tardes con Ana* [Afternoons with Ana]— broadcast every afternoon and directed mainly at women in their domestic settings in the towns and villages of Galicia—stereotypes about a Galician culture are reiterated with great frequency. Guests speak about a variety of subjects, such as drug addiction among the young, diets, or personal stories of emigration. But it is also frequent to have one of the guests—middle-aged women with little schooling for the most part—give their personal opinion by referring to illustrations of Galician culture that they consider relevant. Even if the more rigorous and well-informed references are the purview of Ana, the host of the show, the guests often speak of the old customs, the concentrated use of vegetables in cooking, or the respect that the young had for the old, all of which today is lost, and so on. They suggest a variety of things in which Galician culture is manifested; "Galician culture" is the expression used increasingly by those invited to appear on the program.

A Story of Automobiles and *A Fala*

We saw in chapter 2 how the different designations for 25 July accounted for the lack of unanimity when it came to writing down Galician terms. I also noted that these dissonances were old, justified by the relatively recent literary use of Galician, which was "reborn" only at the end of the nineteenth century. Orthographic forms have crystallized significant political discussions in Galicia to this very day, providing a mirror for the ambiguities imposed by the political context that the Spanish Constitution of 1978 created. It makes sense to allude first to disputes about how to write the name of the country itself; this is a relevant dispute because of the ideological implications to which it relates.

Galiza was the written form used by personalities as relevant as Vicente Risco and A. D. Castelao. But in the context of the Galician nationalist movement, in its first phase from 1910 to 1920, we find curious indecision about how to designate *A Terra*, ones that are registered in important publications such as *A Nosa Terra* and *Nós*. However, just a short time later it would be *Galiza* that became the standard form in both periodicals, even if other publications and titles of books in Galician continued to use *Galicia*. One more example of these fluctuations—and their simultaneous use over time—can be found in the first volume of the facsimile edition of the magazine *Nós* from 1979. In the introduction *Galicia* is used, according to the rules of the Editorial Galaxia that, beginning in the 1950s, regularized how Galician was written until official rules were established in 1982, which in turn preserved Galaxia's standards. In the first six issues *Galizia* was used, which changed to *Galiza* in the rest of the issues, but there are still a range of forms, like *Galiça* and even *Galisa*.

Nation—a key term—can also be written in different ways; I was able to find four alternatives in recent texts: "nación," "naçon," "naçom," and "nação." It should be emphasized, however, that the relationship between the way one writes the name of the country and one's political orientation is not completely linear; this follows, more generally, in the case of any kind of normative reference. As such, as important a writer as is X. L. Mendéz Ferrín (b. 1938)—connected to a group of the extreme left that supports irredentist positions of the most radical kind—fiercely defends the form *Galicia* and the official orthographic norms now in place. On the contrary, other personalities of more moderate politics can appear to defend the form *Galiza* and position themselves on the side of alternative standardizations of the written language.

There are, basically, three norms in confrontation with each other: the form that is the current official one (having the support of the Instituto Galego da Lingua and the Real Academia Galega), the norms of the *reintegracionista de mínimos* and those of the *reintegracionista de máximos*. The *reintegracionistas* take Portuguese orthography as their general reference—this is more or less agreed upon. The differences are only uncovered in the habits of reading. But the gamut of discontent with the official version are many, even for one who is not a *reintegracionista*, and idiosyncratic orthographic usages are very common.

One example of the use of the designation *Galiza* can be found in cyberspace, in a chat room in which one of the most notable figures of the Galicianist movement participated, Isaac Diaz Pardo (born in 1920).[10] In this context he is speaking in a thread with the children of Galician emigrants in Canada: "[16:11] <Isaac> Another question.../[16;11] <francois> Señor Issac do you not believe that the first thing to recuperate the memory of Galiza begins with its name /[16:13]<Isaac> Francois, the name of Galiza is Galiza: Galicia is the Castilianization of the toponymy Galiza."[11]

The name *Galicia* is, however, the established form in all official uses: in institutions like the Parlamento de Galicia or the Xunta de Galicia, and in all of the official publications. *Galiza,* on the other hand, is the form used in the documents of the BNG and generally by the nationalist left. Notwithstanding, acquaintances of mine in Santiago—Bloque voters—use the form *Galicia* in their daily lives, always pronouncing it very clearly—as do almost all Galicians—and even writing it. Indeed, for some of them, the fact that the party uses *Galiza* in its publications or that the official norm is not observed in *A Nosa Terra* seems now to be hardly appropriate and even prejudicial in strategic terms. The official norm is that which is used in the mass media and in the majority of books published. The possibilities for reverting to the older state of affairs are few from the perspective of the most pragmatic nationalists. This is a good illustration of the hegemonic potential held by official institutions to link given forms with Galician national culture. In fact, many of the ways this imposed conditioning occurs are utterly prosaic. One example will show this clearly. Very few are the books that are published with the designation *Galiza,* in spite of the sympathies of the better part of their authors, among whom a good many would defend the use of that form as ideal. This happens because only titles that observe the official orthographic norms will receive publishing subsidies, indispensable in a market in which there are more books published than there are consumers to buy them. Accommodating the official norm was considered by the said critics to be an additional factor of accreditation for a party that was broadening its social base and expressing ambitions to govern. But these opinions are perhaps too naïve and far too pragmatic. In the end there are other ideological reasons that underlie the positions of the BNG, as we have already seen in chapter 2.

Recently in Santiago a new civic movement was formed called Proposta Galiza, constituted by a small number of intellectuals in whom I see a proximity to the positions of the *lusistas.* Their primary objective is the launching of a campaign to recuperate the name of the country. The respective manifesto reads as follows: "*Galiza* is our own name, it constitutes the mark which differentiates us as a group, it symbolizes our will to be authentically ourselves, and our way of being and relating ourselves to the world" (*La Voz de Galicia,* 24/07/2001). This is a recent and timely initiative, remarkable for the notoriety of its proponents and for their apparent conviction that this desire can be achieved through a growing civic mobilization. Here, in spite of the dissensions that run through the nationalist movement—and which even include ways of designating the country—I would suggest that the use of the name *Galiza* is an especially efficacious symbol of the expectations of redemption that the discourse of Galician nationalists implies.

The ways in which *Galiza verdadeira* is emerging out of the ruins of an officialized *Galicia*—like a "geological reality," according to the metaphor we saw in one of the previous chapters—can be surprising. An isolated episode in the history of one of the most well-known multinationals—SEAT (Ford-Volkswagen Group)—will serve to illustrate the central place of orthographic policies in Galicia and the surprising paths that the nationalization of cultures in *España de las autonomías* can take.

In the spring of 1998 an informant enthusiastically recounted how he had become involved in an argument over recent projects at SEAT. The company was getting ready to produce a new utilitarian model called *Arosa,* a Castilianized Galician toponymy, like so many others in place in Galicia until recently. For two decades the designations *Villagarcía de Arosa* and *Ría de Arosa* were official.

Toponymic Galicianization is one of the processes resulting from the *Estatuto de Autonomía.* It provoked extremely curious disputes that occurred in many localities of the Comunidade Autónoma during the 1980s and that, sometimes, were not completely resolved. One of the cases with the greatest media attention involved the establishment of the Galician name for the important city of A Coruña, which followed the previous official designation. However, other alternatives were suggested: *A Coruña* (which was made official), as well as *Coruña, Cruña,* and *A Cruña.* Further suggestions were aired, including *A Corunha* and *Corunha,* which were put forward by the more fervent *lusistas.* Even today, Francisco Vázquez—the local socialist *alcalde* [mayor] and one of the bêtes noires of the nationalists—insists on using *La Coruña* in government publications and also continues to move slowly on the Galicianization of the municipality's street names.[12] In the case of Vilagarcía, as far as I understood, when they proceeded to establish the Galician name of this small city, there was absolutely no room for the disputes that sometimes disrupt toponymic Galicianization: the Galician name is unequivocally *Arousa.* As such, *Vilagarcía de Arousa* is the city's new official designation. The same occurred with the denomination of the estuary that the city borders, referred to frequently in the newspapers because of the activities of gangs of drug traffickers that operate there.

Initially, it was through the newspapers that I learned that SEAT's proposals were being contested in circles connected to the defense of the Galician language. I was happy to learn that Xusto was directly involved in the so-called contestation, which took place while he was a member of the Mesa pola Normalización Lingüística [Committee for Linguistic Normalization].[13] This was merely one more aspect of a constant struggle on many fronts that in Galicia involves various organizations for the defense of the language that were out of step with each other. At Mesa, a group had formed for the purposes of fighting this small battle, and Xusto became a relevant figure on the committee.

My friend told me that there had already been an exchange of correspondence with SEAT's department of public relations. Significantly, in *España de las autonomías* these protests staged by certain young people seemed sufficiently relevant or threatening to the interests of the very powerful multinational. It was an administrator at the highest level on the peninsula that became the interlocutor in an intense exchange of correspondence. This fact made my friend proud, even more so because he was a supporter of the extreme left and the expectation of winning in this confrontation with a large multinational enthused him. He seemed convinced that the subject would be resolved to the contentment of the petitioners. Understood in this way, this would be a victory in the process of broadening the recognition of the language and culture of Galicia.

Beyond the various appeals for the observation of the letter of the law regulating the Galicianization of toponyms, which, according to the petitioners, would be applicable in this case of an isolated commercial use, there was the threat of a boycott of SEAT's products in Galicia. More precisely, these were threats against the distribution of the new utilitarian car model, at the time about to be launched. I realized that this possibility would have caused much worry on the part of the company, even if Galicia comprised only a small part of the market. The SEAT representative arrived to explain the technical and commercial reasons to justify the improbability of reversing the decision on the name of the new model. He also argued that naming the contingent of automobiles set to be distributed in the Comunidade Autónoma "Arousa"—Mesa's minimal request—would not be viable for the same order of reasons.

Sometime later the small, brightly colored utilitarian vehicles were already circulating in Galicia—and a bit later in Portugal—going by the name of *Arosa*. This fact led me to think that the demands for vernacular rigor that had incited the Mesa pola Normalización Lingüística did not echo widely among Galician consumers. It is impossible to quantify to what extent the Castilianized name dampened sales of the model in Galicia. However, most of the time, according to what I could understand during my stay there, protests of this type often carry a restricted echo and confine themselves to sectors of supporters already sensitized to the defense of the language. It seems difficult, on the other hand, to broaden this kind of mobilization because the access to the mass media that the left-wing nationalists actually have is insufficient.

It is important to note here that the scant preoccupations with "political correctness" initially demonstrated by SEAT in this commercial initiative—and the apparently trivial consequences of this confrontation among the general public—reveal more than anything else the lack of recognition of the particularities of Galicia and the Galician language in the rest of the Spanish state. But it also gives us an indication of the weakness of particularist sensibilities among the majority of Galicians with respect to the defense of the language, constraints recognized with varying degrees of disappointment by the supporters themselves. *Marbella, León,* and *Toledo* are the names of some of the recent SEAT models, all of which "Castilianize" the Spanish-built products of a large multinational.[14] The *Arosa* model would have seemed to be able to be added without consequences as one more designation potentially attractive on the global market and not susceptible to being polemicized. On the contrary, it is important to account for the fact that in more recent years that SEAT would probably not risk naming models after San Sebástian or Lérida rather than the Basque name Donostia or the Catalan Lleida, as they would run the risk of offending more intense and widespread nationalist sensibilities, not to mention more important markets—the Basque Country and Catalonia, respectively (Conversi 1997). As to Galicia, I believe that this risk was not even taken into account; and this is due, I repeat, to the weakness of Galician nationalism in the Spanish context.

At that point I was not that familiar with the ups and downs of linguistic claims in Galicia. So I suggested to my friend that the best way to solve the question in favor of the petitioners would be to demonstrate to SEAT how much more suggestive the name *Arousa* was. I said that it seemed more poetic to me, because of all the lyrical associations with medieval Galicia, and that this could be demonstrated with scholarly arguments. Perhaps it would be possible to convince the multinational company that their own interests were undercut by the more prosaic and hardly evocative choice of the Castilianized *Arosa.* This was a bit of a joke on my part: I went on about all of the possibilities of creating "Celtic" associations with *Arousa*—with the mists and the mysteries and so on—which would create fantastic possibilities for the sales of the automobile. I do not think my friend saw the humor in this advice.

This small battle was forgotten by the Mesa pola Normalización Lingüística; apparently it seemed a lost cause. In any case there are many other debates over the autonomous government's linguistic policy. But I still wanted to consult the opinion of the old intellectual and nationalist supporter, Don Mendo. He was a well-known essayist and, in recent decades, a protagonist in the process of the Galicianization of various institutions. D. Mendo habitually used Galician in his texts and spoke in the language almost exclusively on a daily basis, even in situations in which the circumstances might have called more for the use of Castilian, when, for example, his interlocutors were less competent in *A Fala* (Galician language). I always understood his stance, justified as it was by pedagogic intuition, given that Don Mendo was habitually the oldest person with the most stature among those present.

His answer to my question was quite disdainful. His sense of things might be summed up in the following way: these kinds of conflicts did more damage than good to Galicia. He said to me, for example, that a huge event for the launching of the *Arosa* model planned for one of the large hotels has already been cancelled, so that the *moitos millóns* [many millions] will not come to Galicia because of the protests of the members of the Mesa, which seemed to him puerile. I was witnessing at first hand the posture of a conservative who knew—because of the nature of some of his professional responsibilities—many of the economic interests that were active in the region. In spite of my appreciation for Don Mendo, his argument seemed too prosaic, even if he went on to formulate more abstractly the damage caused to Galicia—and not the sundry hotel owners as might be too easily suggested. What I would like to say is that in his response there was, at the end of the day, the proposal for an abstract community that transcended the atomized interests of economic agents.

In spite of occasionally downplaying linguistic questions for the practical reasons that I have noted, Don Mendo's notions about Galicia were very similar in ideological terms to the examples cited by Richard Handler in relation to Québec: "These images of the nation as living individual—a tree, a friend, a creature with a soul—convey first of all a sense of wholeness and boundedness. They establish the integral, irreducible nature of the collectivity as and existent entity" (Handler 1988: 40). Considering these positions, the fact that Don Mendo is viewed contemptuously by Xusto as a *culturalista* was particularly intriguing. In the end, the language and the culture are springboards for the political action of the most lively groups and parties of the Galician nationalist left. For this reason, being identified as a *culturalista,* as well as Don Mendo's opinions about this particular case, suggest an apparent subversion of roles. But this would represent a rather alacritous reading. In fact, culture tends to forcefully join all sectors in the process of nationalizing the Galician masses. This is a determination inscribed in the statute of autonomy, because the Spanish constitution in force legitimizes and overrides, by its binding force, all political contentions of detail.

The Xunta de Galicia is obligated to observe and disseminate the use of the Galician language in the public administration, schools, mass media, and in the books that it subsidizes. It does so according to the standardized orthography that was made official in 1982 and that we have seen provoked serious discussion. By spreading the use of the language in such a fashion—even if the process is thought to be weak and the method is bitterly criticized and debated—there has been a noteworthy increase in its use. Standard Galician is disdained and has become the object of jokes and constant caricatures in Santiago. It is often referred to as *invented* Galician, or *TVG* Galician, which is, in the end, the most dependable and influential source for the diffusion of the recently standardized language. However, invented Galician is used systematically in schools and in the publication of books and is likewise subject to various and continuous institutional uses; for this reason, the social effects of these new practices are noteworthy.

The practices make the initiatives and the patronage of the Xunta especially relevant in the diffusion of the *Fala,* the spoken language, through the publication of books or the contents of television programs—mainly these, given the popularity of some of TVG's programs (*Luar, Galeguidades, Tardes con Ana,* etc.). The standardized uses of the language bring with it a tendentious homogenization of the spoken and written language throughout the autonomous territory with a force that cannot be equalized by any of the other competing alternatives. For example, one informant, whose parents lived in an isolated valley in the Ancares mountains in the extreme east of Galicia, told me that in the last few years his mother had started to use new Galician words. These had come from standard Galician, which had the effect of replacing Castilian as well as local Galician forms and expressions, *castrapismos,* as they are called according to my informant, who was hardly convinced of the linguistic purity of the Galician that his parents spoke in the Ancares. In spite of not having access to TVG broadcasting due to the difficulties in reception in the isolated valley in which she was living, this woman extended her lexicon simply by getting together with her friends in the next village on Sundays. They regularly watched soap operas on TVG or *Tardes con Ana:* in this way they learned about the new Galician culture.

One day I wanted to clarify with my friend—a truly dedicated *arredista* who had studied philology—what the true name of Galicia was. He spoke about medieval texts, about forms used in these texts, and was inclined towards *Galicia,* against his own will. The truth is that I have seen and read equally erudite arguments in favor of *Galiza* and have also come across civic movements to make the latter official. As a matter of fact, recent news suggests that this might actually be about to happen, as its legitimacy was approved by the Instituto da Lingua Galego and the ratification of the Real Academia Galega appears to be near. This decision will surprise many people in Santiago that I know, for whom this was a very distant objective. I also learned recently that the denomination *Arousa* had been adopted by SEAT. In an e-mail, Xurxo told me that cars baptized with this Galician name were already in circulation in Galicia. I have not had the chance to clarify the reasons for the change, but this was simply an exemplary story of *España de las autonomías.*

Notes

1. Historians, like X. Beramendi and Nuñez Seixas (1995), or even X. R. Barreiro Fernández (1991b), provide quite expressive quantitative data about the weaknesses of the nationalist mobilization in Galicia during the Second Republic. The notes that Barreiro Fernández presents on the general panorama of the Galician press are particularly suggestive. They refer to the relatively strong expansion in the circulation of magazines, other periodicals, and newspapers during the first decades of the twentieth century and give, in passing, an account of the weaknesses—in terms of the number of titles and their circulation—of that part of the press devoted to nationalism (see also Ledo 1982; Durán 1981, the latter being especially interesting, even though its focus is somewhat scattered). The "backwardness," the "lack of development," and the "peripheral character" of Galicia have been the object of a good number of well-documented studies, debates, and denunciations in recent decades (see, for example, Beiras 1997; Carmona Badía 1990; Barreiro Fernández 1991a, 1991b).

2. The number of periodicals named *Galicia*—and variably subtitled—that appeared throughout the nineteenth and twentieth centuries is quite large; they were published mainly in the most important emigrant destinations, like Havana, Buenos Aires, and Madrid, a fact that is immediately suggestive of the ways in which references to belonging to a large community were spread through print media.

3. After being founded in La Coruña in 1905: the Real Academia de Lingua Galega, the regulations of the "Asociacón Iniciadora y Protectora de la Academia Gallega" are transcribed by Nuñez Seixas. There it stipulates that, among other things, that a new institution should give "unidad al idioma gallego por medio de una Gramática y de un Diccionario" [unity to the Galician idiom through a new grammar and dictionary] and also "recoger nuestros cantos populares y nuestros monumentos arqueológicos" [recognize our popular songs and our archaeological monuments] (Nuñez Seixas 1992: 365–66).

4. See, meanwhile, some of the contributions to *Guieiro,* the publication of the Young Galicians, published as a supplement to *A Nosa Terra* during the 1930s. There are denunciations of "slow dancing" in many of the articles and books published at the time, and yet the subject was not a particular obsession with the Galicianists.

5. Castelao can be seen as an emblematic figure: he emigrated to Argentina as a child, accompanied by his parents. This would be the place of his last exile as well. There were also émigré poets such as Curros Enríquez, one of the "bards" of the *rexurdimento*, and the *poeta da raza* [poet of the race] Ramón Cabanillas, both mentioned previously. Indeed, there is an ample list of these transatlantic circulations of Galicians who would become famous.

6. Cadernos, "*A Nosa Terra,*" no. 20; this is an occasional supplement to the historical title already referred to at various times.

7. In addition to these anecdotes, see the very suggestive reflections of Michael Herzfeld of the production of "iconicity" in the Greek context (1997).

8. Presented by a nationalist autocrat in a curious way—saying that his name had already been in the *Enciclopedia Galega* (Llobera 1998) for quite a while. The *Enciclopédia Galega* is a *lieux de mémoire* [realm of memory] in Pierre Nora's famous evaluation (1986)—and an important research tool. It was compiled by a large group of Galician intellectuals, many of them from the nationalist left.

9. A good example can be found in the volume entitled *I Coloquio de Antropoloxía* (VVAA 1989). In the first volume—containing texts from 1982—none of the titles contain the word *identity*. On the contrary, it is present in seven of the twenty-nine titles of the lectures delivered at the second event of 1984. This data provides us with a certain sense of the chronology in the wave of enthusiasm that the notion of "identity" raised in global anthropological circles during the middle of the 1980s. It seemed to lose this impetus in the following decade, exactly when the use of the term became popularized.

10. He is an unavoidable figure in the Galicianist movement, one of the most fascinating, in my opinion. D. Isaac was engaged in projects involving the Galicianization of the various arts through his own practice as a visual artist, and through important entrepreneurial initiatives in Argentina and Galicia. His father was Camilo Diáz Baliño—a visual artist dedicated to the production of a Galicianized art as a graphic designer and a set designer. He was assassinated in 1936 by rebel soldiers at the start of the civil war. (Durán 1990).

11. *Galizacelta* (http://www.simil.com/galizacelta) is a *lusista* site where the normative *reintegracionista* of *mínimos* is employed.

12. In A Coruña they are still fighting against street signs written in Castilian, which maintain designations such as *calle* instead of *rúa* for "street." Homage paid to figures of historical Galicianism is rare, contrary to what has occurred in other localities, where their respective names already dominate important arteries. Another controversial and curious case was the establishing of the Galician name of Puebla de Caramiñal. An extract from a commentary by R. Carvalho Calero will give us some indication of the terms of these kinds of arguments: "The technocrats of the autonomous power did not include the form *Póvoa*—...—among those they proposed as a correction for *Puebla,* because they did not think it was documented locally, and did not play a sufficiently ample part in the concept of the system. But the magistrate of the town also did not accept the forms *Proba*—or *Prova*—*Pobra, Pobla* justified by Galician documents and of the same toponomy. He simply wanted the Castilian form" (1990: 113). This passage from Carvalho Calero is a paradigmatic example of the *reintegracionista de máximos* orthography. The author even Galicianized his last name (Carballo), a less common step, contrary to what occurs with first names. Someone who knows Carvalho Calero well assured me that the famous academic only spoke Castilian at home with his children; this gap between the private and the public is common in Galicia, something I myself witnessed.

13. One of the various—and boldest—associations for the defense of the Galician language.

14. Today SEAT forms part of the Ford-Volkswagen group. From the 1950s to the 1970s the brand nearly held a monopoly on the Spanish market, where it was distributed exclusively under license by FIAT. In the past the models were numbered—600, 850, 124, etc. Curiously, the introduction of famous Spanish toponyms, or ones that were suggestive of a certain part of Spanish geography, occurred when its distribution was internationalized.

Chapter 5

In the Skin of the Bull

State and Locations of Anthropology

The mutual lack of awareness between Portuguese and Spanish anthropologists is evidenced by the absence of a comparative history of their respective practices. If we want to interpret something in common or recognize affinities in these centuries-old developments, there are only two recent articles that will help us. They were written by Luis Ángel Sánchez Gómez (1994, 1997). But as has often been suggested, in addition to the political relationships that result from their contiguous borders, we also see sociocultural affinities between the respective populations of Spain and Portugal, which are thought to be especially marked between neighboring regions. These are putative similarities that available ethnographies might have gauged if they had been compared in a systematic fashion, or if scholars had crossed each other's borders with any frequency. However, these actions never resulted in consequential outcomes: to this day there are no relevant systematic comparisons and collaborative scientific projects that were outlined at specific instances that have succeeded. When it happened that Portuguese and Spanish anthropologists actually did get together, at the time the work was always governed by the centripetal interests of the scholars involved and by their respective autonomous developments—breakdowns in cooperation still notable today.

In theoretical terms, attempts at collaboration are much more interesting when they have failed; they will be valuable when the history of the period comes to be written. In my opinion, these systematic disagreements mainly confirm the existence of ideological similarities in the development of the various focuses of anthropological research on the peninsula. The presence of two states and of various nationalist discourses are the most important references to consider in explaining the indifference as well as the ideological affinities that justify them.

In the first part of this chapter I want to outline, in general terms, the principal characteristics that have marked the study of anthropology in Portugal and Spain from the middle of the 1960s to the present. That was the point at which significant transformations took place in the way ethnographic interests were practiced. Until then they were above all influenced by their proximity to a range of nationalistic projects that varied in scope. The proposed description is impressionistic, lacking solid comparative references, simply because this type of work that crosses the borders does not exist. What I am proposing is a summary portrait of a "family" that sees itself as being more heterogeneous than it is—even when confined to one or the other of the two states. In the second part of the chapter I will comment upon certain aspects of the contemporary practice of anthropology in Galicia and of the relationships that it maintains with the production of a national Galician culture. This is already an historical process, but one that today has entered into a decisive phase of consolidation due to the post-1978 political context. I would like to suggest in this second part that we pay greater attention to the commitments that exist between the two traditions of research, which the recent historiography of this discipline has habitually separated: those ethnographic interests justified by nationalist discourses that are now out of date, and anthropological studies, recently based in the universities.

Types and Places of Anthropologies

A suggestive text by George Stocking distinguishes between three types of anthropology: "nation-building," "empire-building," and the more recent "international anthropology" (Stocking 1982). The practice of this last category is today disseminated in various academic contexts on a global scale. I believe that the explanation for the absence of contacts between the two peninsular states would be simplified were we to take this proposed typology into account. In this way, the impasses that result from the use of different classifications could be gotten around concurrently.[1] Following this typology, we can suggest that various anthropologies concerning "nation construction" arose in the Iberian Peninsula beginning in the final years of the nineteenth century. In the same period, this process would find abundant parallels in the rest of Europe, where the number of states then in existence obscures the variety of particularist discourses (see for example, Hroch 2000; Cocchiara 1981). Likewise, on the peninsula, various ethnological discourses developed in parallel. The variety of particularist discourses that came into being can be seen—beyond the most well-known cases, like the Catalonian one, the Basque, the Portuguese, and even the Spanish case—in regional contexts, like the Azores, Galicia, the Canaries, Andalusia, and Valencia.[2] These cases differed in terms of their significance and persistence. What happened on the Azorean archipelago—a unique case in Portugal for being an autonomous ethnological discourse below the level of the state (Leal 2000)—is a good example of the fragilities and hiatuses that have influenced ethnographic studies in Iberian regional contexts where clear and persistent nationalist discourses have not been consolidated.

Borrowing from the arguments that Benedict Anderson used to characterize the "modular" mechanics of the expression of nationalisms (1991), I would suggest that there is an essential ideological similarity between each of these "anthropologies" and that there is likewise a similarity in their development in the more persistent cases. By this logic, we will find the best way to explain the development of a variety of points of focus in the studies that were conducted in the peninsula and the distance that their authors maintained between themselves for more than a century. From many points of view, this separation could be contextualized from within each one of the states—specifically in Spain where there are a real plurality of cases—but it would be made conclusive by the border.[3] In the Spanish context the possibilities for the autonomous affirmation of "national" or "regional" anthropologies that thrived with more or less strength over time were never complete. On the other hand, it is also true that an uncontested ethnological discourse about the state in its entirety never flourished. From the end of the nineteenth century there were various projects of identification of nations that gave substance to discourses at a substate level. This happened with particular clarity in the context of the so-called historic nationalities—Galicia, Catalonia, and the Basque Country. A nationalizing discourse concerning the whole of the Spanish state prospered in parallel. In the century following, and up to this day, this coexistence has been maintained, changing in important ways in correspondence to a succession of various regimes.

Briefly summarizing, we can say that in Spain the more ample conceptual space proposed by the state—and by the dynamics of nation building that we have seen in operation at this broader level—always appeared as a logical antecedent, the necessary counterpoint to various processes of objectification of "peripheral" national cultures that grew within its context. One Galician anthropologist, suggesting a localized illustration of these persistent dynamics of interdependence at the state level, has the following to say: "Visions of Galicia implicate in their turn visions of Spain, it would never have been possible to formulate representations of the first (created from within) without thinking at the same time of the second" (Rodríguez Campos 1994; see also Lisón 1981). Generalizing once again, we can say that this is an essential tension that is still detectable today and that the nationalizing intentionality of these mutually conditioned anthropological practices is of enormous interest.

A close reading of a sampling of the introductions of some of the most important works (for example, Ortiz and Sánchez 1994) where ethnographic practices and active institutions in Spain are investigated will suggest the persistence of a tendency towards autonomy that marked many of the scientific initiatives that arose in various parts of Spain starting at the end of the nineteenth century. These would include a variety of projects like the formation of study centers, museums, and collections that represented important watersheds in the articulation of nationalizing discourses. These were in force above all in Catalonia, the Basque Country, and also Galicia; in each case we find clarity and specific chronologies. Let me cite a strong reading of an autonomous scientific discourse from the nineteenth century:

> The ethnographic installations *in situ* want to say that that which science has discovered was, more than anything else, a *totality*. ... To Basque nationalism of the end of the century— an ideological "totality" based in identifying the Basque in complete exclusion from the non-Basque—anthropology provides the arguments that corroborate its worst traces of xenophobia. Self-identity is raised over the impregnable tower of racial, linguistic and cultural difference. (Zulaika 1996: 23, author's italics; cf. Azcona 1984)[4]

On the contrary, it is easy to recognize what happened in Portugal, where the state and the nation seem to overlap perfectly in terms of the ethnological projects that were being proposed; this is an anomaly in the Iberian context. And it is something that is mirrored by the most significant Portuguese academic institutions. Over time these institutions have become centralized and hierarchical, due, above all, to the lack of disputes over the identity of their object of reference. The same can be said about museological systems in Portugal, which clearly do not mimic the recurring disputes in Spain.

> Through the museums established there over time the *Praça do Império* materializes the pith of intellectual aspiration in two isolated fragments arising out of the latter parts of the nineteenth century: to construct a major museum of the Portuguese people. ...

The foundation of the *leitiano* museum, its establishment at *Jerónimos,* its consolidation and continuous functioning up to the present, in terms of the symbolic representation of the nation, marking the square and indirectly the country, are a pillar erected to mark the *nationalization of the people* in national political life. (Branco 1995: 168)

After these incontestably argued passages on the persistent representativeness of an old archeological and ethnographic museum whose program dates back to the nineteenth century, Freitas Branco comments on other museological proposals, competing alternatives in the symbolization of the country and the people. However, the subject of the discourse under question will be maintained without ambiguities, without any demands for more specificity in any of the proposals mentioned: the Portuguese state, whose legitimacy for nationalizing the people was never contested. The terms of questioning regional diversity beginning in the nineteenth century (Leal 2000: 27–61) make it sufficiently clear that it always was an exercise conducted from the center (see also Sobral 1999).

Two Precursors of Circumstance

If we again take Stocking's typology into account, there are certain identifiable analogies that exist between anthropological studies in Portugal and in Spain during recent decades. In addition to being a place where various "anthropologies of nation building" have occurred since the end of the nineteenth century, even more influential anthropologies of "empire building" have inspired a certain point of view. In Spain this approach was taken by English or North American anthropologists during the second half of the twentieth century; Portugal has hardly been focused on, which has created an intriguing difference. Nevertheless, I do not believe that the various foreigners who worked in Spain, in the wake of George Foster, Julian Pitt-Rivers, and Michael Kenny, had a direct or decisive influence. These were references taken into account later in an unsystematic way by local anthropologists—emulated as examples, for compiling bibliographies and finally being repudiated, at times overemotionally, from which we can draw several curious examples.[5] However, they did become a direct or decisive factor in the transformation of the research practices that we saw later in the peninsula, which were mainly subject to endogenous dynamics. With few exceptions, foreigners who did field work pursued careers in their respective countries of origin, and it was from there that they could be influential, participating in international debates as specialists in their areas as Hispanists or *mediterranists*. Recently Portuguese and Spanish anthropologists who have done field work in their respective societies of origin have also joined the international debate.

In the mid-1960s there were local anthropologists developing projects in the peninsula who took the most influential theories coming out of the British academy as guiding references more than three decades ago. The appearance of two doctoral dissertations out of Oxford, roughly contemporary to each other, by Carmelo Lisón Tolosana and José Cutileiro, anticipated to a certain extent the very rapid transformations that occurred in the study of anthropology in Portugal and Spain from the mid-1970s onwards. Today I believe that we would be safe in saying that the most prominent academic anthropology on the peninsula would find a familiar reflection in each of those works, esteemed as references of indisputable prestige. More ambiguous, however, is the status ascribed to the extensive studies—inspired by a range of theories that nearly no one evokes today—written by Iberian authors who were recognizably important in their day, such as A. Jorge Dias, or Julio Caro Baroja (1914–1995), or even Claudio Esteva Fabregat (b. 1918).

The individual initiatives of Lisón Tolosana or of Cutileiro appeared disconnected from the traditional methodologies exercised until then on the peninsula and had the support afforded by academic prestige. In a recent and relatively marginal discipline within the academic context, the expression of what we might call an "anxiety of lineage" obsessed with the search for prestigious precursors, is recurrent. It is in this way that the initial works of Lisón Tolosana and of Cutileiro help us to effectively mark out an impressionistic interpretation of the anthropology of the two states. In truth, the routes followed were less linear in both of these contexts. They demand a highly detailed interpretation of the various personalized versions—always subject to dissent—and that, above all, account for the character of a process that is too recent to see retrospectively with any objectivity.

It is clear that the multipolar panorama of anthropological practice in Spain does not facilitate linear generalizations about its history. Rather, the contrary is the case, as the diversity of works available, the contradictory oral versions, and the works of interpretive synthesis to appear in recent years have made clear. However, from a narrower academic perspective, it seems to me that this identification of predecessors is the only possibility we have for illuminating, as a group, the individuals who created the anthropology of the Iberian Peninsula, with respect to the recent period during which the institutionalization of the teaching of anthropology at the university level has occurred. This process is still only a quarter of a century old.

Beyond the metaphors, I believe that this late institution of the centers of anthropological studies in the two states was mainly brought forward by the growth and modernization of the university system during the 1970s and because of the political pluralism institutionalized following the fall of the authoritarian regimes of Franco and Salazar. These were transformations that brought about a notable flourishing in the various social sciences in the contexts of both states. They were broad processes that I believe should be understood as independent of personal influence.[6] In spite of everything, we can refer to certain hinge moments that were dramatized. In the following passage Lisón Tolosana describes two such moments that occurred at the beginning of the 1970s in which he played a part as a protagonist.

> Three years ago, in this same space, at the end of a paper on our discipline, I suggested that we commemorate in a *modo anthropologico* the first hundred years of the *Sociedad Antropológica de Sevilla*. We are witnessing and cooperating in the second *take off* of Spanish anthropology. As this is a moment that could be decisive, I would suggest a pause in the short path already traversed in order to refresh our imagination and, during this morning and afternoon, conjure up the evocative power, that prompts anthropology in relation to the unknowns that our peoples and cities present to us anthropologists today. (1981: 7–8)

In truth, the individual influences of Lisón Tolosana or of Cutileiro in the processes of modernization and the institutionalization of new university disciplines are quite different and, as I have suggested, both of them can be seen in relative terms; they should, I would emphasize, be taken simply as parts of broader processes of political and social transformation. It is the relative precocity of the respective works that provides us with the strongest reason to attribute the role of predecessors to them. To verify this we can consider the very similar chronology of the institution of the study of anthropology in Portugal and Spain, in spite of the fact that Cutileiro never came to exercise a significant influence on academic policy, since he never engaged in a career in research or in teaching.

Taking the Portuguese case as a reference, I will make my argument more specific by suggesting that it was the later growth of departments of anthropology—parallel to that of the other social sciences—that brought importance to the work of Cutileiro. In the absence of this set of transformations, his work would have remained an isolated exercise. Interpreting the Spanish case will certainly be more problematic, since

Carmelo Lisón Tolosana's influence was so prominent there; however, in this case it is by reference to the variety of expressions and developments in the study of anthropology in recent decades that the importance of individual contributions can be contextualized.

In the Iberian Peninsula, anthropological works completed in more recent decades find their legitimacy mainly in the theoretical influences originating in the anthropologists of "empire building" according to Stocking's typology. This seems to be very clear today in the peninsula, just as it was with the first important works by Carmelo Lisón Tolosana and José Cutileiro. The use of these kinds of exotic references has justified a privileged status for the studies that universities recognize. However, in spite of these references, the anthropologists of Portugal and Spain have conducted their fieldwork for the most part within the boundaries of their respective states—apart from one exception in the doctoral thesis of Portuguese anthropologist Luís Polanah, which was not widely circulated—and without, it is curious to note, visiting their neighboring country of the peninsula.

In the end, this characteristic method of working "at home" is a differentiating mark of the work of Iberian anthropologists in relation to the traditional methodologies of the exoticist vocation whose theoretical principles they emulate. Recognizing this fact allows us to test the limits of Stocking's typology. In the context of his classification, anthropological studies conducted outside of the universities of the two Iberian states in more recent decades can be seen as hybrids. Lacking an "imperial" vocation, the possibility that we might identify these more recent studies under the strict scope of "nation building" would also seem ambiguous.

In general ideological terms, the suggestions of a similarity between anthropological studies produced in recent decades in Portugal and in Spain can be made if we still keep in mind *Belmonte de los Caballeros* and *Ricos e Pobres no Alentejo*. The latter title takes its opening epigraph from the poet, Alexandre O'Neill: "Portugal questão que tenho comigo mesmo" [Portugal a question I really have about myself.] It seems quite obvious to me that "Spain"—and its recent history—was a question that Carmelo Lisón Tolosana would pose, taking "Belmonte" as a microcosmic reference. To study "in villages"—according to Clifford Geertz's famous phrase—remained a common characteristic of many ethnographies done later in the peninsula by natives. The highly detailed ethnographic surveys in rural contexts—"communities," as they are nearly always called—or sometimes among marginal groups in the cities have arisen with the idea of mirroring broader entities. Studies conducted "in villages" stand for Portugal or Spain and any of the "historical nationalities"—Catalonia, Basque Country, and Galicia. The range of examples can be enlarged to include any of the different *comunidades autónomas* established today in Spain, each of which became the object of a specific ethnographic discourse gaining its own characteristics and became a focus of academic research in an important number of cases. In this way processes of cultural objectification have taken form, all of which is fascinating to outside observers.

We could suggest that the type of academic anthropology conducted in Portugal and Spain in the most recent years—which mandated a "social" or "cultural" orientation at the start in order to mark out clear origins and borders (see, for example, Prat 1991a; Lisón Tolosana 1977)—originated "internationally." We could go so far as to say that the tendency to work "at home" was anticipated in the peninsula, something that only became evident in the United States of America and in Great Britain at the beginning of the 1980s (Jackson 1987); in the end, Stocking's typology is sufficiently elastic to support this formulation. But, besides the more or less capricious identifications that one can make, I believe that only a very detailed approach will allow us to weigh up all of the ambiguities that an obligatory coexistence between new and more dated ethnographic practices presumes in this context. Taking into account some of the illustrations of Galician origin, we will see that today the possibilities of identifying these practices through the exhaustive use of a typology are quite diffuse.

The presence of nationalist ethnographic discourses is an unavoidable point of reference on the Iberian Peninsula, but these should not be seen in isolation from the importance of recent anthropologists in the production of new national cultures beginning in the 1970s. As I have already suggested, this type of involvement is multipolarized and especially demanding in the context of the Spanish state, where the current constitution provided for the sudden appearance of new political entities endowed with competences and resources for proceeding with the nationalization of their respective cultures. These are processes that are ongoing and in which old and new ethnographic materials are seen as pertinent resources.

Mythical-Mystic Elaborations and Atlantic Myths

In 1977 Carmelo Lisón Tolosana published a book entitled *Invitación a la Antropología Cultural de España*. This collection of essays opened with an interrogation oft repeated by other Spanish intellectuals in a variety of epochs—"Que es España?"[7] However, Lisón Tolosana's interrogation does not cite a single example from this ample tradition; it introduces itself, ex novo, from a disciplinary perspective of which the author presents himself as a pioneer. He suggests that there is an urgent task of gaining knowledge that should fall to all anthropologists: "As long as we do not lay out a sufficient amount of objectively gathered primary ethnographic data, obtained from all of the national geographic contexts, it will be difficult to respond to the questions that the anthropologist formulates about the pluricultural reality of Spain" (1977: 13).

Lisón Tolosana goes on to consider all the different levels of identification that he recognized as key in Spain. In the first place, he would investigate "la región," so that he could then follow a kind of descending scale, until he arrived at the level of the "casa" [household]—to the "patrilineal" and "matrilineal" family—using illustrations from various rural contexts, principally in Galicia.[8] What most interests us here is what this author had to say about the region—*la región,* a name whose use is still maintained, even though it is now seen as an anathema in a range of contexts, because the term has since been overtaken by the term *nation* (Lisón Tolosana 1977: 187); substate nationalisms, whose manifestations the Franco regime repressed brutally, reemerge in this period. In considering the region, the author firstly examines the importance of the strategy that he has established—the urgent and cumulative gathering of "primary ethnographic data":

> The ritual, the mystical-mythic elaboration and symbolic creation are the sources or springs that nourish regionalism. In specific and crucial moments regional flags and symbols appear (the tree of Guernica, the Pilar, Castelao, Montejurra, etc.). They condense abstract notions such as independence, group solidarity, power and force, all ideas of great importance for them and which are not easy to represent directly nor to be spoken about in another manner. Values, ideas and ideals that champion co-existence at the regional level, belief in mystical and ontological essences, union and mutual aid, are part of the message that these symbols communicate and inculcate. When these are ritualized or dramatized in order to demonstrate what they have to offer in the face of forces or external pressures, that is, when these symbols are deployed most fully, the region flourishes. (Lisón Tolosana 1977: 27)

This collection of essays nevertheless closes with two short texts— "*Panorama programático (nacionalidades)*" [The main points of an overview (nationalities)] and "*Panorama programático (ultimidades)*" [The main points of an overview (final points)]—which are full of key questions that at the time were extremely opportune. Here we find the re-emergent nationalisms that cast a shadow over all of the questions that Carmelo Lisón Tolosana leaves suspended.

In a 1994 article, Joaquín Rodríguez Campos—professor of anthropology at the University of Santiago de Compostela—opens by questioning the impact of the conditions affecting anthropological practices in very general terms in order to then produce more contextualized considerations. Rodríguez Campos uses the most recent anthropological activity on the Peninsula, in Spain and in Galicia as examples to specify arguments about the more recent expansion of the discipline. Galicia and the way in which anthropologists have worked there are what most interest him. The interpretation of this text, which is full of references and inconclusive questions is risky; nevertheless, some of the questions already introduced in this chapter and Lisón Tolosana's proposals are repositioned through this curious contribution:

> I will analyze the different views which are given of Galician culture and that of the North of Portugal by intellectuals and anthropologists. ... The intellectuals' views have only occasionally been taken into account by anthropologists; they created myths that exercise a powerful influence over society. The views created by the anthropologists can be divided into the views of foreign anthropologists and views of native anthropologists, because the two types clearly differ in their focus in the studies that have been done up until now. The different views of the anthropologists do not simply comply with what is happening in the context of different anthropological theories, but above all they are motivated by different myths, which leads to very particular views of the same culture. (1994: 209–11)

Through what we can call meta-anthropology (White 1973), both consensuses and recognizable tensions have suddenly arisen in the Iberian context—now thought of as a space for the circulation of "myths" of various origins and concomitantly as a reference to the endeavors of anthropologists. In this reading the relational dialectics between interior and exterior, belongings and discrepancies, are recognized casuistically. Rodríguez Campos proposes a wide net for considering these belongings and endeavors and the circulation of myths that give them meaning. As such, he considers peninsular anthropologists to be "natives" in various phases—only those anthropologists whose origins are from beyond the Iberian Peninsula, but come here to work, are considered foreigners. He says that the cosmopolitan myths in circulation support the analyses of the "foreigners" as much as they do those of the "natives." Moreover, at the end of the day, it would be the circulation of other "myths"—now at the restricted level of the peninsula—that will give legitimate meaning to the work of native anthropologists.

I believe that this argument can be understood as a justification for the involvements and endeavors that have proceeded according to a segmentary logic; in the final analysis we have already seen that this was efficacious, in broad strokes, for comparing the history of peninsular anthropological practices, even after they had begun to be reformed by the beginning of the 1970s. Rodríguez Campos provides a reflexive proposal conscious of these dynamics in which he wants to take note of new reasons to study what until today has been scarcely examined. In his article, Rodríguez Campos denounced the fallacies and the "naïve realisms," examples of which he has found in some of the arguments of Ernest Gellner. By analogy, this qualification can be broadened to include the more empiricist arguments in the program for the recognition of Spain that Lisón Tolosana suggested in 1977. Moreover, when we consider the possibilities of thinking theoretically of Spain as a nation-state, we can see that Lisón Tolosana has also already shown himself to be convinced of the power of "myths" when we examine what he says about the regions, certain as he is of their erudite origin, historicity, and latency and potential for rupture.

The consequences of the threats presented at the time as latent are illustrated soberly and without any sense of alarmism by Rodríguez Campos. The author is informed as to what has come to pass in the most recent decades under the rule of the "Estado de las autonomías"; as such, he speaks of the emergence of new phenomena and of their unpredictable directions:

> In the cultural dynamic of contemporary Spain we see that the regional elites reproduce and produce myths, generating images of a dismantled nation-state, as though it were a mere fiction of the past, strengthening symbols and old founding myths of ethnic identities. The working classes do not always participate in these myths, and when they do, they do not participate to the same extent as the intellectuals and other elites who proposed them; at times they participate by pursuing social practices that contrast with the strategy that the elites pursue, strengthening, among themselves, identities that are different than those that were proposed to them. (Rodríguez Campos 1994: 229)

Rodríguez Campos gives us an account of some recent disagreements between the "elites" and the "popular" classes and how the space of the state was the primordial space for the circulation of "myths," which afterwards were appropriated on the regional scale. This is what would have happened with that which we designate as the "myth of Atlantic culture," which was created by Spanish elites at a state level at the end of the nineteenth century, even if its complete appropriation only occurred much later, in the context of the Galician nationalist movement and also in the north of Portugal, as the author surprisingly suggests.[9] With respect to the "myths" in circulation in the academic settings of "international anthropology"—theoretically dependant on the "anthropologies of empire building," as Stocking suggests—a similar mechanism of modular appropriation in the practice of anthropology in Galicia and in the North of Portugal would be reiterated. These are contexts that Rodríguez Campos once again groups together. Thus: "The persistent influence by the old anthropology of the primitive world on Galician and Portuguese anthropological investigations resulted in, among other things, the neglect of the dialectic between the rural world and other dominant elites of provincial, regional and national culture" (Rodríguez Campos 1994: 224). In addition, the destinations of these works would have been highly contextualized, shaped by cosmopolitan theories.[10]

> However, with respect to Galicia, anthropological analysis was at times capable of proposing new myths to society (new visions of Galician society that would come to be actually experienced by its members) that remained fully justified. … Other Galician anthropologists … have contributed effectively towards the idealization of rural life, which had always been very marginalized by public authorities, and on which political and intellectual reflection focused in part when the time came to think about the problems of Galicia. (Rodríguez Campos 1994: 224)

It is clearly suggested that in Galicia native anthropologists reified rural life by using theoretical and methodological precepts that were in international circulation. In the opinion of the author, the verisimilitude of some of the proposals would be questionable. He suggests, for example, that the dynamic relationships that rural communities always maintained with the outside and its ideologies could appear to be clouded over. However, what seems most significant is the suggestion that these contributions are, in the end, efficacious and could be appropriated locally as contributions to the process of constituting a new culture, one that is nationalized.

Inheritors/Inheritances

Joan Prat suggests reasons for the discovery—belated as it was—and the revalorization on the part of anthropologists of the traditions we refer to as "folkloristic" in the context of the autonomous communities that exist today in Spain. He says that this movement should be understood as a necessity imposed by the political process that created the *Estado de las autonomías*. In each of these it would have been known that "nineteenth-century anthropologists and folklorists came to occupy in a more or less conscious way the role of ancestors and precursors and began to be understood as the link that was lacking to guarantee the historical legitimacy of the professional practice itself" (1991a: 48). There are various chronological nuances that the author suggests could be used to reference these contemporary articulations that have affinities and differences with the historical legacy of older ethnographic interests. In another text, Joan Prat broadens his discussion on the force of the distinct "anthropological and folkloric traditions—of a regional and national character—that were initiated during the second half of the nineteenth century, continued in some cases until the Civil War, or until the 1960s in other cases" (1991b: 13). Understandably, the claims to these inheritances were more prestigious or pacific in relation to the period before the civil war.

The chronological adjustments successively suggested by Prat are well thought out and explain the burden of the mistakes that can remain intact as a result of these processes of identifying with the past. With respect to Galicia, all of the chronological contextualizations suggested can be confirmed. The reliance on the past is also seen as dominating and long lasting when we examine how the modes through which "international" anthropology is exercised today are enmeshed with the memory of the "anthropology of nation building" that over time came to be a facet for expressing Galician nationalist discourse. In the Galician case, it is difficult to consider the civil war to be the high point for the recognition of worthy predecessors, given the weakness of ethnographic practice exercised there up until that date. In fact, publishing activities and research done after 1936 are considered to be an extremely significant part of the resources that are used today in the process of nation building. As such, the limited context in which ethnographic interests were practiced, the chronology of their occurrence, and the biographical circumstances of their practitioners necessitated persistent intergenerational commitments that have lasted up to our own times.

J. Prat also remarks on how social anthropologists trained in Spain during the 1970s were sometimes collaborators—enthusiasts as a rule—with the projects for the nationalization of culture that emerged out of each one of the new *comunidades autonómas* as they were established (1991a, 1991b). It is also important to underscore—I take the Galician case as an example—that the academic anthropologists were hardly ever objective interpreters of these rapid processes of nationalization of autonomous cultures. Knowing this, it is not the extent of anthropologists' complicity in new political projects that is important to evaluate. It is the all-encompassing expression of these social phenomena that were so capable of concentrating the undertakings of anthropologists—providing them with unexpected possibilities for work—that becomes the important focus of interest.

In Galicia the old ethnography that documented the reasons behind the "differential" claims put forth by the nationalist discourse from the beginning of the twentieth century onwards is not embodied merely as remote outdated references viewed from a distance. It would be difficult to represent it as mere memory in order to articulate the lineage of precedents for those who are interested in a detailed history of the discipline at a local level. In a recent text by one of the Galician anthropologists most active in the last few decades, a useful illustration of these questions is proposed. Directly inspired by certain well-known texts—by James Clifford (1988), Clifford and Marcus (1986) and Clifford Geertz (1988)—X. M. González Reboredo analyses the "rhetorical" resources used by two very different authors who had done prominent ethnographic studies in Galicia in different periods: Vicente Risco and Carmelo Lisón Tolosana.[11]

Let me take up the portrait that Joan Prat draws of Risco: "As we had seen, the double condition of being the most important ideologue of Galicianism between the 1920s and the Civil War and the verifier, through his position as ethnographer of his own political ideology, converge in the person of Vicente Risco" (1991b). This is an overly succinct and rather ironic presentation, but I believe it to be pertinent. Carmelo Lisón Tolosana, for his part, is, for a variety of reasons, a reference point in Europeanist anthropology, namely, for having been a pioneering practitioner of social anthropology in his society of origin (Davis 1977); on the other hand, the ethnographic corpus resulting from his research activity in Galicia is voluminous and very influential. Lisón Tolosana is Aragonese; thus, the first figure is a self-taught, native ethnographer, while the second is an academic from outside, practicing in a context that could in some ways be described as exotic. González Reboredo attributes importance to these facts, just as one of the commentators on his text does.

After summarizing the precepts and their respective theoretical foundations, González Reboredo looks at each author in isolation. He identifies the theories that both authors depend on, followed by the explanation of an analysis taken from certain of their texts in order to expose in detailed fashion the "rhetorical strategies" that each of them employs. From Risco, he chooses a gathering of short texts to analyze: *O Demo na Tradición Popular Galega, Notas en Col do Culto do Lume* and even *Notas sobre las Fiestas de Carnival en Galicia.* Lisón Tolosana's text, *Antropología Cultural de Galicia* (1971) is included in this volume that brings together the results of an extensive survey in which the author tried to demonstrate the existence of certain sociocultural constants throughout rural Galicia against a backdrop of localist variations.

In my opinion, González Reboredo's demonstration of the "rhetorics" of ethnographic authority employed by Vicente Risco and Carmelo Lisón Tolosana, is, in the main, detailed and precise. However, any reader, even those not warned ahead of time, will note the lack of sympathy and even the asperity of González Reboredo's critical reading of Lisón Tolosana. On the other hand, Risco's texts are treated with tolerance, relativism, and notable praise. The article's epilogue is short and reconciliatory, emphatically valorizing the qualities of the works and their authors, after having pointed out certain cracks in their respective arguments.

González Reboredo's text was published alongside two additional "commentaries," both of them brief, written by other Galician anthropologists (González Reboredo 1996).The first is by X. R. Mariño Ferro—a professor at the University of Santiago—and the second by F. Calo Lourido.[12] Though Mariño Ferro's contribution is neutral and extremely well informed, what Calo Lourido has to say is more interesting. His *comentario* is the more extensive, and he is also quite virulent about Lisón Tolsana's contributions to Galician ethnography. Calo Lourido tells us first-hand about the circumstances of González Reboredo's training, drawing our attention to the fact that González Reboredo began his career in ethnography and archeology under the guidance of Fermín Bouza Brey (1901–1973). Bouza Brey was a poet, archeologist, ethnographer, and an active Galicianist influenced directly by Vicente Risco in the context of the Seminario de Estudos Galegos, in the years that proceeded the civil war. In fact, Risco as well as Bouza Brey remained active as ethnographers several decades after 1936, confirming themselves as the figures most recognized in the practice of these kinds of interests—among the various interests that made up their respective multifaceted oeuvres—in the Galicia of their time. Citing a passage or two from Calo Lourido's commentary will give us a better idea of the sensibilities in question, while at the same time it will let us conjecture certain of the commitments and debates that occupied the small Galician anthropological community, where prominent positions are shared among people with varied training, as we have indicated above:

> We are not going to get into commenting on each assertion, but the attentive reader will note, as we have, that Don Vicente comes out better in comparison, even if Xosé Manuel notes that his Galician work inclines more towards sentiment than towards reason and that, if he was a great

observer of *Mitteleuropa*, in Galicia he did not show much interest in "participant observation. ...

I recognize (without too much effort) that I liked Xosé Manuel's veiled criticism, or rather I could understand such a "rite" as participant observation, and that this more elegant skill applies to Evans-Pritchard (after the fashion of "I'm speaking to you son, understand me daughter-in-law") so that what he has to say about the second author analyzed is not so strong. But as we start to read the dissection that he performs on the work of Lisón (Tolosana), we see how, little by little, the negative criticism begins to grow ... and ends up overflowing in words and phrases that make reference to "authoritarianism," "excessive manipulation," "of the Indians on their reservation," of the "primitives," of "the nobles savages" ... in a word, that Lisón is for the Galicians the paradigm of the English school which was left without Africans and (that) conducted Mediterranean anthropology "a bit" diverted towards the Northwest. (in González Reboredo 1996: 73)

The contents of this commentary could be seen as an extreme reaction. Today the terms of this denunciation would not be publicly accepted—as much as I could gather after listening to various comments—by a full range of Galician anthropologists.[13] However, it would be wrong to think that this is simply a marginal reaction of two "native" ethnographers whose training is antiquated and hardly relevant in the institutional system that sustains the possibilities for undertaking anthropology in Galicia. On the contrary, as a local informant told me, these are "xente que corta moito bacallao" [big-shots] (cf. Chun 2001). As I noted previously, González Reboredo, even if he is not a university teacher today, is one of the most important figures in that institutional system. It is also true that in his oeuvre he deals easily with the highly prestigious theoretical references of contemporary international anthropology. Beyond all the localist vehemence contained in the two cited texts, it is important to note that this is as well a reckoning of accounts with a way of doing the ethnography of "antropología modernista" [modernist anthropology]. These are the terms employed in González Reboredo's critique, in which he uses recent resources that have notable legitimacy in international anthropology (Marcus 1998: 230 and ff.).

This is an example of how slippery it can be to apply Stocking's tripartite typology. We have scholars that claim the inheritance of an "anthropology of nation building" using resources from "international anthropology." They do this as a way of denouncing what is considered to be an outdated, "modernist" form of working in which they recognize affinities to a posture linked to those that mark, in the most negative ways, the "anthropologies of empire building." Apparently, with this example, a circle is closed, demonstrating the prudence with which we should employ the typologies, even the more suggestive ones, in the *España de las autonomías.*

The critical reading of the other text by Vicente Risco, undertaken by José Antonio Fernández de Rota,[14] suggests a very different set of perspectives than the ones that we have commented on above. In a text entitled "Releyendo 'Una Parroquia Gallega' de Vicente Risco" [Rereading 'A Galician Parish' by Vicente Risco],[15] Fernández de Rota comments in the following fashion on the objective and expository strategy of this text by the famous theoretician of Galician nationalism:

> His theme and focus escape the molds of traditional ethnography, dominant at the time in our country and intuitively looks beyond to the theoretical sources of Social Anthropology. …
>
> Already, the mere act of selecting a parish, the basic communitarian unit of the Galician countryside and converting it into the core object of his research provides the author with important possibilities and advantages with respect to other approaches. The central thread becomes the social unit and a social unit existing on the other hand due to the conviction of the "subjects of study" and verifiable for the researcher in empirical behavior patterns. With this approach, the social dynamic can play an important role and, above all, the pieces of the culture are not isolated from their framing context outside of which their meaning cannot be understood. (*Cuadernos de Estudios Gallegos,* no. 100: 585)

It is easy to recognize the unilateral praise in this excerpt for what Bernard Cohn was calling, already in the 1970s, an *island model.* This is the expression through which Cohn assembles such relevant names as Bronislaw Malinowski, Alfred R. Radcliffe-Brown, and Meyer Fortes and their influential methodological approaches (Cohn 2000: 80 and ff.) In his short text, Fernández de Rota will cite in succession Mary Douglas, Edward E. Evans-Pritchard, Edmund Leach, Carmelo Lisón Tolosana, and Victor Turner—more recent names, but prominent in the lineage of "British Social Anthropology"; this profusion of references serves to legitimate the explicit valorization of Vicente Risco's proposal. It is the sum of affinities that he views between Risco's work and that of the "sources" of social anthropology—especially their methodological guidelines—that sustains this intentional praise. After all, as we have seen, references to British social anthropology came to authorize the first steps taken to institutionalize anthropological studies at the university level throughout the Iberian Peninsula, as did the unilateral praise interposed by Fernandéz de Rota.

I think that some of Fernández de Rota's commentaries are faithful to the spirit of certain of Vicente Risco's convictions; Risco was the ethnographer who proved himself to be most attentive to and knowledgeable about Galicia. In a variety of cases, Risco demonstrated the importance of the parish as a social unit and reference for ethnographic observation (Risco 1920, where we find an early and categorical affirmation of these convictions; see also Otero Pedrayo 1922). However, I think that Fernández de Rota's praise is excessively dramatic for the way he valorizes the theoretical inferences and exogenous methodologies as though he wanted to gain prestige for his own reading of Risco. With such a broad point of reference, he neglects paying attention to other dimensions that were central to Risco's ethnographic process, mainly his more constant ethnological preoccupations. Using a cliché common in the English writing that Fernández de Rota seemed to cherish, this is like "throwing the baby out with the bathwater." In fact, for Risco, the nation stood out as the most determinant reference for all of his ethnographic concerns. Such that the "household," now the parish, the town, or even the judicial district, were subject to a detailed analysis and were tactical objects that were part of a conscious strategy that led to imagining Galicia as national community.[16]

The decisive framing of nationalist support on behalf of the articulation of a new Galicianized culture, in which Risco and his colleagues were involved, could easily vanish with a reification of the importance of the study of small local communities. These studies had fed off the fact that they imitated the longstanding sources from the tradition of British social anthropology, so celebrated in the piece by Fernández de Rota. I believe, however, that the set of practices and motivations involved in the anthropology of nation building conducted in Galicia throughout the twentieth century is much more suggestive than this very focused reading of one of Risco's texts implies. To clarify, it is worth citing the evidence of one of the few survivors of the group of nationalist intellectuals active in the period preceding 1936. Recognized as one of the disciples of Risco, Francisco Fernández del Riego tells us the following: "It was Risco who defined a Galicia that those who were young then dreamt about. He was not just an ethnologist who rigorously analyzed the material and traditional life of the people. He was, above all, the theoretician of a political-cultural movement that tried to encourage and foment the specific originality of Galicia" (1996: 425). We can also see in these attempts, precisely, the impulse to turn Galicia into a social unit that "exists in the conviction of the subjects of the study," using the phrase applied by Fernández de Rota to praise the parish as *the* frame of observation.

Parishes

One of the strongest arguments in Gonzaléz Reboredo's critique of
Lisón Tolosana was, curiously, the attempt to demonstrate how the importance of the "parish" as a social unit became mystified in the book
Antropología Cultural de Galicia: "In the construction of the text an
emphasis is placed on all kinds of people, geographical spaces, objects
(like the church bell) and the places through which the parish is made
evident through a plurality of messages. The reader is convinced that the
parish is a firm pillar of social-territorial segmentation of Galicia; its material, social and symbolic borders are irrefutable" (González Reboredo
1996: 52). By underlining cracks in this argument and relativizing it
in various ways, González Reboredo ends up recognizing the marks of
authoritarian and, finally, primitivizing rhetoric in Lisón Tolosana's proposals. This recognition is highlighted later in even harsher terms in
Calo Lourido's "commentary." Calo Lourido uses a curious phrase—
"fáloche fillo, enténdeme nora" [I'm talking to you son, understand me
daughter-in-law]—certainly fascinating for someone who is interested
in questions of kinship and marriage in Galicia (but as well for the use
of ruralist tropes among Galician anthropologists). This phrase makes
us suspect that there are other quite contemporary tensions that are
revealed in González Reboredo's text, tensions that are being debated
indirectly through the strongly worded critique of Lisón Tolosana's old,
and, in several ways, now outdated text.

A move to set up an equation for the "existence of indicators" of a
"Galician identity" was recently proposed by Xosé Manuel González
Reboredo (2001b)[17] in a text in which certain positions of José Antonio
Fernández de Rota become specific targets of criticism, and in which it
is clear that the two authors hold different understandings of Galicia
and the "ethnonationalist" phenomenon. The reiteration of strong ideas
already present in the previous criticism of the *Antropología Cultural de
Galicia* can be seen here:

> Could we accept, for example, that the inhabitants of the Ancares river
> valley, in adjoining *terras* between Galicia and León form an ethnically
> defined group? … And, to a certain extent this is what certain anthro-
> pologists who love ambiguity do in terms of the ethnic and national
> identities referred to; an example of this can be found in a recent text in
> which one of them, using ways of speaking as a reference, affirms that the
> isoglosses of the Romance languages vary every fifteen or twenty kilome-
> ters, which allows for the construction of one nation just as it would a
> hundred (Fernández de Rota, 1998, pp. 359–360).

The interesting *reductio ad absurdum* neglects that in the cited Romania, as in the rest of Europe, ethnic-national delimitations are a fact that simply permit the exercising of centuries-old ties of belonging to supra-local units: historicity. In effect, we should never lose sight of the dimensions of the historical construction of European ethnic identities up to the 18th century, and, from that date on, the construction of nations and of nationalist theory. (González Reboredo 2001b: 210)

In this text, in which the adjective "interested" is key, the author bases his argument on enough and sufficiently significant references from recent and prestigious studies, such as those that can be found in texts by Fernández de Rota. I have already emphasized this characteristic in the respective texts. Yet, it is not the prestige of the theoretical references cited, nor even the correctness of their use that I want to discuss here. With these examples, I would simply like to emphasize the force with which the debate in contemporary Galicia over national culture focuses the preoccupations of anthropologists who work there. Beyond the different postures—and we have noted one example of disagreement—we have to take into account that these debates are played out in a specific political context in which each of the post-1978 autonomous governments is obliged to "prove the originality of their particular culture," as James Fernandez suggested, processes in which anthropologists have been recruited as specialists and in which they seem to work according to their political convictions.

In a 1991 text, Enrique Luque drew a distinction—roughly—between the two principal moments in the work of anthropologists in Spain of the previous two decades: "Simplifying the not so lengthy trajectory of our contemporary ethnography, it can be divided into two stages. The first, lasting until the middle of the 1970s was taken up almost exclusively with community studies. From this period on a second phase begins which went way beyond the limits of municipalities: studies of regions, countries, nations and nationalities. ... The dividing line is not arbitrary, but quite clear. Whether we like it or not, it reflects the political trajectory of those years: from the innocuous municipality to autonomous plurality" (1991: 71).

The institutionalization of anthropology in Galicia—including university positions—was consolidated only during the second period indicated by Luque. And it wasn't until the 1980s that the first doctorates earned by the most well-known anthropologists (teaching today in Galicia) were completed. These were pioneering studies in their invocation of "international" theoretical concepts (Stocking 1982), following a completely different line in methodological terms than that taken by

Galician ethnographers during earlier decades of the twentieth century. It should be noted that academic consolidation and a general renewal of the anthropological discourse very much paralleled what happened in the autonomous government institutions following the promulgation of the *Estatuto de Autonomía de Galicia*. We can use Luque's citation to gauge the relative typicality of this case, even if its manifestation came late—what is absent is the so-called stage of "studies of the community"[18]—compared to what occurred in the more significant poles at the state level.

If we again take up Joan Prat's historical studies, we will see how typical what happened in Galician anthropology during the 1980s was. Prat demonstrates that at the time politically autonomous regional spaces polarized the undertakings of the majority of anthropologists throughout Spain, leading the way to the very characteristic studies "*sobre la identidad*" [on identity]. This is a general definition under which, according to Prat, three principal lines are subsumed beginning in 1977–1978—"histories of folklore and anthropology," "the study of 'popular culture,'" and "studies of celebrations, rituals and popular religiosity" (1991a). If we were to produce a summary of the ethnographic publications that have appeared in the last twenty years in Galicia, we would recognize, generally, how the picture adjusts itself to that painted by the overview works of Enrique Luque and of Joan Prat. We will clearly recognize the occurrence of the themes listed above and the extensive formulas of recognition, nominally broadened to include the *Comunidade Autónoma*, which Prat noted were typical. A good indication of these characteristics would be the incidence of the term *Galicia* in published titles. (Lema Bendaña 1990–1991; Mariño Ferro, n.d.).

In Galicia J. Rodríguez Campos and X. M. González Reboredo are the two most active figures in describing the history of ethnography from the end of the nineteenth century until today. It is worth citing from two texts by the first author, who, because of his training and the path that he took, can claim minor, yet direct, affinities with Galeguista [Galicianist] ethnographers. Once again, these extracts serve to illustrate the contingencies imposed by the anthropologists' condition as natives—a significant question for this author, as we have already noted.

In a 1991 text entitled "La etnografía clásica de Galicia: ideas y proyectos," Rodríguez Campos maintains, "Classical ethnography, unlike anthropology, did not claim to put to the proof principles of social life to defend a general theory of culture, but rather aimed to discover and explain popular customs, ideas and beliefs, responding to the intellectual, social and political preoccupations of the society during the historical moment in which their defenders lived" (1991: 99). He then alludes to the various "projects" that have stood out in the history of Galician ethnography since the end of the nineteenth century. This text appears in a collection that opens with a contribution by J. Prat that defends the coexistence in Spain of an "anthropological discourse"—"in the strict sense" and the various "folkloric discourses" (1991b: 13). As a matter of fact, the Galician case is used as an exact illustration of this second, supposedly minor, type. In his contribution, Rodríguez Campos generally observes the boundaries formulated by Prat.[19]

In a more recent text, written in Galician and part of a volume organized as a homage to one of the "classic" Galician ethnographers,[20] Joaquín Rodríguez Campos has already taken up a significantly new approach:

> It seems advisable, in the first place, to make clear to whom we are assigning the name of "Galician romantic anthropologists": with this name I refer to the founders of the *Seminario de Estudos Galegos,* known also as the *"Xeneración Nós"*: A. R. Castelao, R. Otero Pedrayo, V. Risco, F. Bouza Brey, F. Cuevillas, R. Cabanillas, A. Villar Ponte. I believe that they should be recognized as a group of anthropologists because—as will be seen throughout this paper—their fieldwork (archeological, geographical, folkloric and historical) was always guided by a theory of culture that they themselves created with the goal of showing that the original culture of Galicia was a reality that existed in the period, and not a collection of survivals killed off by the past. (1994b: 41)

The terminological affinities of this text with the other contribution by the same author that we spoke about above are patent. In that one, the expression "romantic anthropology" was valorized and defined in the following way: "A romantic anthropology is therefore defined as that which would try to understand the force which 'myths' acquire within a society" (1994a: 210). Apparently this "romantic" position was assumed by the author himself, who dedicated himself to the analysis of "myths" created—or adopted—by Galician intellectuals at the beginning of the twentieth century, at the same time that he showed himself conscious of the fact that the production of anthropology was also about the observation of "myths." If we read the texts of the most articulate ideologues of the famous *Nós* generation, we will find a wealth of references they made to myths, to their collection, but also to the necessity for their ex novo creation, in order to be able to impose the project of collective identification that these ideologues aspired to. On the other hand, it does not seem to me at all problematical to identify the ethnographic works of that generation as an "anthropology," as J. Rodríguez Campos proposes, distancing himself from the distinctions that he formulated in 1991. In the end, this is a designation that is sufficiently supported by Stocking's classification (1984).

The suggestion implicit in Calo Lourido's "comentario" (from which I have already cited) is much more radical. There he states that the self-sufficiency that is denied to the parish—against the views of Carmelo Lisón Tolosana —could be granted to Galicia and to Galician culture. This proposal is worded in surprising terms, which are worth citing:

> I want to introduce here a small and arguable discrepancy between my-self and Xosé Manuel. I think that Risco does not intend to engage in participant observation because, among other things, he has "always been" immersed in the "spiritual culture" of our *terra*. He forms a part of it so when Xosé Manuel speaks of the ethical perspective in Risco I think more about the profound immersion in the culture that he is describing. I well know that calling this the "Stockholm Syndrome" would perhaps be excessive, but I think that something like that happened to Risco, the same as happened to Xosé Manuel ... and to me. Not to Lisón. (in González Reboredo 1996: 72)

What is suggested is that it is possible to delimit a "Galician culture," and the ways to gain access to it are questioned. It is implicitly suggested that there is a cognitive border that would be difficult to cross by nonnatives, or that this crossing would be barred to them. In fact, the strange image of the "Stockholm syndrome" employed by Calo Lourido contains a radical suggestion: the knowledge of "Galician culture" is gained in proportion to one's "immersion" in its "spiritual culture." An innate and privileged condition is alluded to, a quality that would even allow for the disqualification of the legitimate and methodological precepts of academic anthropology used to validate the knowledge of other cultures.

"Spiritual culture" is a curious term, one that is fairly dated. We see this when we look at the history of the discipline from an ecumenical perspective that includes various types of anthropology, following the proposal of George Stocking. In the Iberian Peninsula, in the context of the anthropologies of nation building, which underwent more than a century-long evolution, "spiritual culture" was taken to be synonymous with "folklore" and, as such, normally put on the level of "ergology," as components of ethnological studies (Risco 1962). With the example of the use of this dated term—which appears paradoxically in the context of a discussion that includes some very up-to-date terms—I would say that the complexity of the contemporary practices of studies of Galicia is more than suggested. In Portugal, in more recent years, I believe that these surprising coexistences are rarer, even nonexistent today. The reasons for the difference, in my opinion, can be found in a different history with respect to the forms of state organization and the respective importance of the presence of nationalist discourses in each of the two countries.

Notes

1. In this way, for example, the bipartite typology proposed by J. Prat (1991b)—which distinguishes between folkloric and anthropological discourses in Spain—seems to me to be less agile, in spite of certain notable capacities for clarification contained therein. I note Prat's typological terms to classify the nineteenth-century context, but as well a posteriori, as is inferred, the respective inheritances.
2. See for Spain the commentaries and the bibliography suggested by Prat 1991b, as a clarifying reference. Other important general references can be found in Aguirre Batzan (1992), Ortiz and Sánchez (1994) and Prat, Martinez, Contreras, and Moreno (1991).
3. The presence—a common occurrence—of Galician ethnographic texts in Portuguese ethnographic periodicals in the mid-twentieth century could be viewed as a flagrant contradiction to the argument I am now pursuing. One could prove that there were constant motivations in the Galicianist nationalist discourse that justified this movement of intellectual relations that crossed state borders in one direction only (see chapter 6).
4. A text that dates from the years of Franco's rule, entitled *Representación de Galicia en el Museo del Pueblo Español*, will furnish us with a curious counterillustration of these dynamics of autonomous affirmation through the medium of museological discourse (Hoyos Sancho 1961). The institution of a national museum came late in Galicia, which, due to various circumstances, was not consolidated before the establishment of Franco's authoritarian regime. However, and very significantly, this was one of the first initiatives concretized once the authoritarian regime began to crumble, in the form of the Museo do Pobo Galego in 1976.
5. These are repudiations that can also be identified within the Spanish state itself, a curious type of segmentary replica that illustrates above all the force of the various nationalist sensibilities in play in this context. I illustrate one of these cases in detail later in this chapter.
6. It is important to note that *Belmonte de Los Caballeros* (Lisón Tolosana 1966) was not translated into Spanish; *Ricos e Pobres no Alentejo* [The Rich and the Poor in the Alentejo, *A Portuguese Rural Society* in its original title] is a relatively late translation from 1977, appearing three years after 25 April 1974 (the Portuguese revolution).
7. Research of this type was as intense in Portugal as in Spain, with chronological and ideological similarities that are clearly significant. Britain's ultimatum to Portugal in 1890 had effects comparable to Spain's loss of its colonies in 1898. These were dramatically resented successes; and they reinforced beliefs about the "decadence" of the peninsular societies. Also, therefore, intellectual proposals directed toward redemption intensified (these are topics in innumerable historical studies available for this period in both countries); here are some general references: for Spain, Fusi and Niño (1997), Tusell (1998) and Carr (1982); for Portugal, Catroga (1993) and Ramos (1994).

8. During these years it was the *casa* [household] that provided one of the main sources of fascination for Europeanist anthropologists. We can recognize it in this text and in all of the ethnography of Galicia that Lisón Tolosana carried out.

9. However, it still remains to justify one of Rodríguez Campos's suggestions that the "myths of Atlantic culture" have taken a common course in Galicia and Portugal. At this point, a detailed critique of this point of view is not viable. I would like to simply suggest that there are other erudite "myths" of Portuguese national culture, and these are articulated in specific ways and with singular histories that, in fact, are not linked to those of Galicia. It is, on the contrary, justified to suggest the mythical versions of "Atlantic Culture" were influential for some of the anthropology conducted in the North of Portugal—we find their echoes, more or less explicit in different cases, in the work Sally Cole (already referred to) (1991), Caroline Brettell (1986), Brian O'Neill (1982) and João de Pina-Cabral (1986), works that J. Rodríguez Campos refers to. However, these references are derived exclusively from their affiliation with "international anthropology" and not—as occurs in Galicia—from domestic "mythical" representations.

10. The author proves that this lack of awareness was also significant in the case of foreign anthropologists who worked here, such as Caroline Brettell (1986), Sally Cole (1991), and Heidi Kelley (1991). In these cases, in addition to the observance of the usual methodologies and theories (in the end, the heavy mark of the "old anthropology of the primitive world" was there and took form through more general "academic myths"), ideological motives of North American feminism would be at work here and subject to being illustrated by some of the unvarying topics of the "myth of Atlantic culture." With respect to Portugal, Joaquín Rodríguez does not provide substantive clues about the role of the local consequences of the practice of an anthropology conditioned in such a way by the theoretical precepts that originate in the prestigious anthropologies of empire-building and are simultaneously deployed in national political projects.

11. The work is entitled "La Construcción del Texto Etnográfico a Través de Dos Autores: Aportación a una Historia de Etnografía en Galicia" (González Reboredo 1996). González Reboredo used translations into Spanish of the titles referred to here by the dates of their original editions in English. The author has a doctorate in *Filosofía y Letras* from the University of Santiago and is a full professor at the high school Instituto Rosalía de Castro. He is the director of the ethnography section of the Instituto de Estudios Gallegos "Padre Sarmiento" (where he succeeded Vicente Risco and António Fraguas, two unavoidable names in the area of the ethnography practiced in Galicia in the twentieth century). He is responsible for the committee on cultural anthropology reporting to the Galician government's Consello da Cultura Galega [Council on Galician Culture] and a patron member of the Museo do Pobo Galego. He is also an advisor for the Galician television station TVG (a supporter of the nationalist left told me that Reboredo is one of the people responsible for the creation of the "imaxe ruralista" [ruralist image] of Galicia sponsored by TVG, a polemical theme in the context of the disputes that have to do with cultural policy in Galicia today). He is one the most active Galician anthropologists whose published work is extensive (see, generally, in the context of institutions connected to anthropology in Galicia, Pereiro Pérez 2001).

12. F. Calo Lourido is an archeologist and ethnographer, with a doctorate in archeology. He is a member of the Instituto de Estudios Gallegos "Padre Sarmiento" and of the Consello da Cultura Galega. He is the author of a small number of texts about coastal localities and the anthropology of fishing in Galicia and a member of the

"ponencia de antropoloxía cultural" of the Consello da Cultura Galega. In his public appearances he is usually presented as an anthropologist.

13. Contemporary echoes of Lisón Tolosana's work in Galicia are, curiously, few (with one exception that I refer to in the following note). This fact is surprising given that Galician anthropologists do their research in primarily rural contexts, using themes often first broached by Lisón Tolosana. Apparently his work remains in limbo in local anthropological circles. As to this, one Catalonian anthropologist told me with some sarcasm, "For a long time now the Galicians have been killing the father." In 1989, Marcial Gondar—now a full professor of anthropology at the Universidade de Santiago de Compostela—responding to the question, "So what is the panorama of anthropology in our country?" said, "Not much has really been done. The qualitative leap forward came with Lisón Tolosana and we have to thank him for this leap forward, but now it is necessary to undertake a broad revision of his approach" (*A Nosa Terra*, no. 400: 10). Frankly speaking—beyond the omissions or polemical attacks—I believe that this revision never occurred explicitly or convincingly.

14. J. A. Fernández de Rota (1940–2010) was a professor at the Universidade de A Coruña. His most important work, *Antropología de un Viejo Paisaje Gallego* is solid and interesting, and little known in Portugal (an example of the lack of interrelatedness referred to in the first part of this chapter). Fernández de Rota is one of the most important disciples of Lisón Tolosana in the state context. In Galicia, among senior academics, it is Fernández de Rota who most explicitly emphasizes the ideas of Carmelo Lisón Tolosana. These ideas should already be more known locally, as I stated in the previous note.

15. *Una Parroquia Galega en los Años 1920-1925* is a late text by Risco, dated 1959.

16. This could take place freely until 1936, mainly within the ambit of the Seminario de Estudos Galegos. On the other hand, it is true that it was the judicial district—or the *"terra," "bisbarra," "región natural,"* equivalent terms in the prose of the Galician nationalists from 1920 to 1930—which on the majority of occasions was taken as the basic unit for a knowledge of Galicia that Risco and other contemporary scholars considered to be a politically engaged task (strongly influenced by the theories of German and French geographers about "natural regions" that had won prestige in Europe at the turn of the century) (Otero Pedrayo 1978).

17. The text under discussion is entitled *A Construcción de Referentes de Identidade Etno-Nacional. Algunhas Mostras sobre Galicia.*

18. The most characteristic of the community studies available in the Galician case would be the work, already referred to, of J. A. Fernández de Rota, *Antropología de Un Viejo Paisaje Gallego,* that came out in 1982.

19. J. Rodríguez Campos speaks of the Galician case and clears up rigid and distancing distinctions when he tells us, "This is not a reflection of anthropology for its own sake, or its past, but to see the interpretations of culture from the intellectual movements themselves which are generated by them." He mentions the works of Lisón Tolosana as pivotal and the "new vision" that they contain.

20. *Actas do Simposio Internacional de Antropoloxía: In Memoriam Fermín Bouza Brey.* In Galicia, commemorations of Galician intellectuals have taken on a great importance in recent decades, seemingly part of the process of objectification of Galician culture.

Chapter 6

Portugal in Galicia

On the morning of 25 July 1999, a group of people were singing in the middle of the crowd that was heading down the Rúa do Franco, in Compostela. The outpouring of voices was enlivened by someone playing the concertina and by a variety of percussion instruments improvised from soda cans. Everyone was wearing white T-shirts and a light yellow baseball cap with a sticker that identified them as coming from a rural parish on the outskirts of Braga. They seemed to be factory workers, but there were also people still connected to farming, "part-time peasants," a stratum of the population of northern Portugal that during the most recent decades has attracted notable attention from the social sciences (see one of the most recent examples in Silva 1994). As one of the celebrators told me, they were "from Portugal" and had come here on an excursion "with the priest." Their singing became even more spirited with the arrival of a Galician boy who joined the group and sang *A Laurindinha.* He knew this joyful song from beginning to end and not only the refrain, which we would be remiss in not noting for its ethnographic interest: "Vai, marinheiro, vai, vai, vai dizer à Laurindinha, vai, vai, ela é tua, não é minha" [Go sailor, go, go, go, go tell Laurindinha, go, go, she's yours, she's not mine].

Various renditions of the same song followed, increasingly united and enthusiastic, which caught the attention of the passers-by. Some of them stopped, and the circle of spectators grew and held up the crowd moving through the street. After a certain amount of time the Galician began to conduct the choir with sweeping gestures while at the same time singing louder than all of the others. Suddenly, when the singing began to wane, after many renditions, the Galician boy shouted out loudly: *Viva Galiza Ceibe!*[1] *Viva Portugal!*

The event came to an end, the group of Portuguese broke up into three or four smaller groups remarking on what had happened; they were still distinguishable because of their yellow caps in the middle of the crowd that continued to flow along. Suddenly one of these groups surrounded me, and I could better hear their conversation. It was the priest who seemed more upset about the Galician boy's unexpected outburst, perhaps because he was worried about the "political" implications on a day when the king of Spain and the president of the Republic of Portugal were both in Compostela. I heard the people on the excursion asking what was wrong with the *espanholito* [little Spaniard]. They said things like, "What does this man want?" or "The little Spaniard seems crazy," while the priest tried to bring the group together again and get his parishioners away from the spot as quickly as possible. I lost sight of their yellow caps in the mass of people that filled the Praza Obradoiro.

The fact that the nationalist movement in Galicia is relatively less known outside the autonomous community is recognized by its various sympathizers. For example, on various occasions I have been asked how I became interested in such an inconspicuous phenomenon that had not before attracted the attention of foreign social scientists, contrary to the case of Catalonia or the Basque Country. These places have attracted important, varied, and already historical interests of foreign as well as Spanish social scientists, in particular, anthropologists. The number of studies about the Galician nationalist movement is, on the contrary, more modest, and such studies are, for the most part, written by Galician academics.

As with the tourists from the Minho, the slogan *Viva Galiza Ceibe* would also surprise tourists or pilgrims coming from other parts of the country who have paid little attention to the multiple political and culture claims of a nationalist character that have arisen across the whole of contemporary Spain. Within the *Estado de las autonomías,* recognition of the Galician nationalist movement is always in a state of flux. This fact can be attested to in the daily press or on television at the state level by the absence, on a practical level, of references to Galician questions as specifically *national* questions; this, for a variety of reasons, is contrary to that which happens with the Basque and Catalonian cases.

The recognition of the various nationalist movements existing in contemporary Spain is segmentary. As I have already suggested above, the process of Galicianization of the culture is largely centered within the Comunidade Autónoma; however, given the variety of similar cases, only a certain virulence or a state of conflict will produce a recognition on the state level. I never found people in Compostela especially well informed about the nationalist claims in the Canaries, in Valencia, or even about the particularist tendencies that find expression in the *Principado* of the Asturias, a region adjacent to Galicia (Fernández de Rota 1994). Contrary to this, the majority of Galicians that I know have some sort of opinion, more or less emotional, about the successes achieved through violence that mark expressions of nationalism in the Basque Country, or even, for example, about Jordi Pujol's (the nationalist leader in Catalonia) frequent positions on the use of force.

In contrast, references to Portugal have been notable in defining the Galicianist discourse throughout various epochs. In this chapter I would like to examine certain of the more salient characteristics that we can identify in these references—one of the more constant motifs that serve to mark the particularities of Galicia within the ambit of the Spanish state.

Kinship and Affinity

The epithet *espanholito* used by the Minhotan tourists was ridiculously *flamenquista* and could be suggestive of various ironic interpretations (Fernandez de Rota 1988); these would be quite obvious for those who know about the most prominent topics in Galician nationalist discourse. It was certainly malicious to direct it at the man singing *A Laurindinha,* who simply wanted to denounce the presence, which he believed to be oppressive, of the Spanish state and to celebrate the fraternity between Portugal and Galicia on the corner of the Rúa do Franco and the Praza do Obradoiro. The communion surrounding a playful moment with people who had come from south of the Minho River would have seemed just the moment to celebrate and denounce the state. The rounds of *A Laurindinha* could be narrated as constituting a moment involving the resurgence of old voices, or of the momentary suppression of time, as well as the strangeness that political borders imposed. These could be thought of as artificial and recent, a possibility given by the timeless character that ethnogenealogical discourses frequently imply (Smith 1991, 1999). I think it is worth applying these potential interpretations to that isolated episode. I am undertaking this because I have been inspired by ideas from a variety of epochs that speak of similarities between Portugal and Galicia and that are still repeated today, more or less transparently, in a range of forms.

One recent and appropriately nebulous example (Chapman 1982) comes from Portugal and is contained in a text by the writer Mário Cláudio entitled: "Endovélico: continuidade cultural de uma mística reprimida na periferia atlântica" [Endovelicus: Cultural Continuity of a

Repressed Mysticism on the Atlantic Periphery] (Ledo 1996: 379–82). This is a text that is difficult to interpret, full of citations of famous ethnologists, which appears in the acts of one of the many international colloquiums held in Santiago with the support of the autonomous government of Galicia. The subjects taken up at this particular conference were all questions of contemporary relevance related to the management and the study of the media, an unexpected context, yet certainly suggestive of the present and future potential of these formulations of affinity in our times.

For one indoctrinated in certain of the ethnological arguments debated on both sides of the border beginning in the nineteenth century, the situation on Rúa do Franco would seem to provide a privileged register of the reasons behind the Galician-Minhotan community, of its everlasting marks. This was a folkloric demonstration that could be enjoyed by the natives of the two parts of the ancient *Gallaecia* in an intense moment, even more suggestive because it occurs in the context of a pilgrimage (Turner and Turner 1978). The principal interpreters were (still) peasants, a class that an old erudite tradition—reinforced by Romantic sensibilities and even more so by ethnographic literature—determined to be the most reliable documents of the perennial nature of collective identities (Williams 1993; Herzfeld 1986).

In 1949, Fermín Bouza Brey began to consider a curious theme—"The lizard in Galician-Portuguese folklore," affirming in a revealing fashion, "But in *costumbrismo*, in tradition, in agricultural practices, in religious rites, there is still much to compare, although we certainly do not need to engage in such labor to know that historical Galicia as far as the river Douro, is the same people, with the same traditions and with the same longing in their soul." In this citation, from one of the most well-known Galician ethnographers of the twentieth century, we find "certainties" for the reasons behind the transborder community proposed in a phrase that seems to skirt history (Fabian 1983), though someone more familiar with the subject would easily recognize the ideological marker of a period that can be precisely dated in the reference made to the "longing soul" supposedly common in those who have lived to the north of the Douro River.[2] This citation, coming, as it does, from a highly reputed author, as an example of a monumentalizing assertion (Herzfeld 1992), can be seen as a snippet of erudite common sense, an example of the Galician discourse in relation to Portugal.

In order to attribute meaning to the episode on Rúa do Franco and to contextualize Bouza Brey's sentence, we must keep in mind the place that the references to Portugal occupy in the definitions of Galicia as a nation, which began to form in the nineteenth century (Máiz 1997; Beramendi and Nuñez Seixas 1995). These definitions prominently defend the existence of a latent and continuous Galician-Portuguese solidarity that is founded on affinities of a historic, linguistic, and ethnological character. In the better-informed versions—rarer and formulated by scholars—it is suggested more precisely that there are decisive affinities in relation to the two provinces adjacent to the north of Portugal. However, even in these types of more accurately referenced formulations, the attribution of importance to the regional differences that exist in the neighboring country, or an effective knowledge of them, does not always appear clear, which would suggest their eminently rhetorical character.

There is a famous sentence by Manuel Murguía among the early forms of these affirmations of affinity; it is curious because it makes an insinuation about an "arredista" [secessionist] threat and presents an image of political convergence between Portugal and Spain. As early as 1888 the famous historian of Galicia had the following to say:

> This is why the Spanish state runs the danger that the differences that separate us become deeper, and that the relations that at present unify the different nationalities of which it is composed convert into a marked hostility that is much more serious as Galicia finds itself constantly solicited by Portugal, which could at any given moment come to its aid and take it for itself, without harming us, far from it. (cit. in Torres Feijó 1999: 302)

The expressions and the importance of references to Portugal in the Galicianist discourse were analyzed in various recent texts by Galician authors; standing out, among others, are the contributions of Piñeiro (1982), Vázquez Cuesta (1991), Villares (1983), Nuñez Seixas (1991), Torres Feijó (1999), Álvarez and Estraviz (1999) and López Mira (1998). The variety of critical approaches that this theme has attracted explains the prominence that has been attributed to it during the most recent decades in Galicia, and the role it has played in affirming the nationalist movement and consolidating the process of the construction of a national culture.

Today the lack of attention paid to relations between Portugal and Galicia among Portuguese scholars is clear, since the preoccupations that have inspired so many prominent academics in Galicia are without parallels in Portugal. It is true, however, that various nineteenth-century ideologues of Portuguese nationalism have reflected upon ethnic and linguistic relationships between Galicians and Portuguese. To generalize, I could point to some of the more important names, such as Teófilo Braga (1843–1924), J. Leite de Vasconcelos, and Oliveira Martins, whose interests were recently illustrated by Elias Torres Feijó (1999), who offers us a very clarifying selection of citations from these authors about Galicia. With the end of the Great War, we have the general impression that there were many mentions in passing of Galicia on the part of Portuguese authors holding various ideological positions. These were references that are to be found in magazines of the period, like *A Águia, Nação Portuguesa,* or the *Revista de Guimarães.* But they can also be found in the daily press, mainly in the most important newspapers from Oporto (Ledo Andión 1987).[3] This was a crucial period marked by a growing sensibility towards national questions, while for Europe many of the political borders were being redrawn and the League of Nations had been established (Mazower 1998; Hobsbawm 1994).

In spite of the fact that the greatest incidence of references to Galicia in the Portuguese press occurred around 1920, in terms of the larger picture they were few. They echoed opinions formulated at the end of the nineteenth century, with some original contributions arising, but mainly, I believe, responding with greater or lesser generosity to solicitations for literary collaboration with periodicals close to the Galicianist movement. Even today, these contributions are still the best mirror as to how irrelevant were preoccupations with Galicia on the part of Portuguese intellectuals, who above all understood the phenomenon as a mere irruption of literary regionalism in the image of the then famous provincial *félibres* [nurslings of the muses] of Southern France (Roche 1954; Thiesse 1991). It was in this sense worthwhile to respond to the appeals for guidance and to the obsequious dispositions across the Minho.

For intellectual Galicianists, Portuguese collaborations—and the general references to Portugal—appeared as a factor of prestige and a corroboration of differentialist theses, whose production was vigorously and imaginatively put to the test in that period. In spite of the importance locally attributed to these exogenous collaborations—still today reified as a prestigious memory[4]—I would say that the majority of contributions were fragmentary and of low quality. Authors like Leonardo Coimbra (1883–1924), Teixeira de Pascoaes (1877–1952), and even António Sardinha (1887–1925) are cited as venerable references, even though their collaborations are sparse and summary and not always clear in their misguided speculations.[5] Other Portuguese authors, many of whom are completely unknown today, were also—overgenerously—gathered as references.[6] One of the first issues of *Nós* says the following:

> From that time until today, the movement has been emphasized. ... *A Nosa Terra* has happily gathered the writings of José Joaquim Nunes, António Sardinha, Luis d'Almeida Braga, Novais Teixeira and many other Portuguese writers. ...

A Nosa Terra initiated, quite some time ago, a study, up to our present period, of the newest manifestations of Portuguese literature and art. In Portugal, the most elite of the new generations draw attention to our efforts to reconstruct the "Patrea Galega" and, looking at us with *agarimo* [with affection], even with curiosity, they gave us wings with their words full of fraternal sentiment. They were Teixeira de Pascoaes, Leonardo Coimbra, Pina de Moraes, João Peralta, Armando de Basto, Manuel de Figueiredo, João de Castro, Alexandre de Córdova, José Cervaens Rodrigues, Orlando Marçal, A. Pereira Cardoso and many more. (*Nós*, no. 7, 1921: 4)

We can recognize, as a structural characteristic in the history of these references (which both Galicians and Portuguese made about the other), the temptation to perceive what was happening on the other side of the border as redemptive of their own predicament. This characteristic, which is more perceptible in some of the Portuguese speculations, also marks a variety of the propositions made by Galician authors (López Mira 1998), even if the formulations in either case are quite vague.

It is worth citing a passage from Jaime Cortesão (1884–1960) that, though much later, would express well some of the contours of the Galician question as they were imagined in Portugal in the "age of nationalisms." His words are significant because they come from a man educated in the "war of nations" and who was one of the most relevant ideologues of republican nationalism of the left: "Thanks to the Minho and its people, creating a body with Galicia—*the Portuguese Alsace*—we had a tradition of lyric poetry, inspired and graceful and an entire plastic dialectic sculpted in the capitals of granite altar-pieces of the national baroque" (1966: 17, my italics). This sentence could be compared with, among others, an earlier one from Galicia that speaks at the same time about the organization of poetry and music festivals, of the facilitation of the book trade and even, in the same sequence and with equal emphasis, about the restoration of a "Galician-Portuguese civilization": "*NÓS* wants to have a part in this movement that carries these two brotherly peoples in the direction of the other, in this movement full of glorious promises" (*Nós*, no. 2: 8).

In fact, in most cases, it was in vague formulations of this character—which were also basically equivocal with respect to the interpretation and the dispositions in place on the other side of the border—that proposals or expectations of a growing Luso-Galician closeness occur. This theme was interpreted using more or less poetic and rather undefined formulations (Villares 1983), involving curious classifications of great emotional power where the use of vocabulary of kinship occurred frequently—"sister," "mother," "daughter," "son," "boyfriend," "fiancée," "husband," "wife," etc. An illustrative and particularly dense example can be found in the citation of extracts from a letter written by Teixeira de Pascoaes to his Galician friends: "Galicia is the sister and the mother of Portugal. Portugal emerged from the breasts of Galicia; later it abandoned its mother and left for the high seas; escaping like the prodigal child." In another paragraph Pascoaes adds, "The tempest that shook the world of Galicia and Portugal has calmed, and they appear as spiritually married to affirm to the world their healthy and redeeming spirit" (*Nós,* no. 1: 18, 1920).

But the consequences of these types of declarations of kinship and affinity that were so frequently made have been, until today, inconsequential in terms of practical results. This certainly was the case with respect to some of the more trivial dimensions of the expectations of Galician intellectuals at the beginning of the last century, who hoped for the growth of the book trade in both directions. For example, I was able to verify by going around to the best bookstores in Lisbon in 2000 that it was impossible to find any of the Galician dictionaries in print today; as a matter of fact, my search seemed to astonish the store employees questioned.[7] It is important to note, in addition to these ironies, that references to Portugal have remained constant in the Galicianist discourse. They survived circumspectly during Franco's dictatorship and have vivaciously sprung back to prominence in recent decades, having become popularized and flourishing in often surprising ways, as I would like to demonstrate below.

At the end of the 1930s, with the consolidation of the "Estado Novo," a cycle of interests centered on Galicia on the part of Portuguese intellectuals that had begun in the last decades of the nineteenth century came to a close. Lively and politically plural expressions of nationalism, which came to their full force during the years of the First Portuguese Republic when interests in Galicia were at their peak, were incited by solicitations for recognition emanating from beyond the Minho. It was, however the *Alzamiento* of 1936 (Franco's coup) that finally marked the end of curiosity maintained in Portugal about the "Galician Question." This lack of interest has persisted to this day.

During Francoism the relationships that various Galician intellectuals had with certain erudite circles in Oporto and Guimarães became paradoxically firmer, or at least more substantial than they had been up until 1936. They arose out of academic collaborations written in Castilian—tolerated because any explicit political content was expunged—and appeared in various Portuguese periodicals with notable regularity throughout the decades. These substantial collaborations sent from Galicia to periodicals like the *Douro Litoral, Trabalhos de Antropologia e Etnologia, Revista de Guimarães,* and later to the *Revista de Etnografia* contrasted with the fragmentary character of the texts that had served for interlocution between Galicians and Portuguese in the period before the civil war.[8] Until then, what most often occurred were bouts of mutual praise and congratulations. There were also more or less radical declarations of affinity that appeared in forms as poetical as they were inconsequential.

For example, for a Portuguese reader the scarcity of references in Galician periodicals to the radical transformations that political life in Portugal underwent during the 1930s is surprising. After all, an authoritarian regime was being imposed, and this absence of attention that is quite evident in publications linked to the nationalist movement underlines the eminently rhetorical character of the references made to the neighboring country. On the contrary, after 1936 the movement of texts from Portugal to Galicia became negligible and as well, more generally, academic interest in Galicia on the part of Portuguese scholars, a discrepancy that seems to a large extent to have continued to this day.

It is important to stress that references to an affinity with Portugal were always useful resources for nationalist Galicians for articulating ideas of differentiation from *Castela, centralismo,* or *Espanha.* These terms are used as synonyms and are the most common rhetorical references of alterity in the Galicianist discourse. According to Ramón Villares, what was being sought was to configure "the neighboring country as a 'founding myth,' a defining factor and something that gave character to Galician identity" (1983: 302).

In this way, mention of Portugal—usually in an abstract and thinly substantiated fashion—can be seen as a way to underline the reasons for Galicia's difference in the context of the Spanish state. These kinds of mirroring exercises had already been practiced in nineteenth century Galicia and became better defined in the first decades of the twentieth century, surviving, as Pilar Vázquez Cuesta suggested, as a "an asymmetrical dialogue" (1995). However, it was only in more recent years that they became gradually popularized and recognizable as part of the shared knowledge of many Galicians, especially those who are more sympathetic with militant Galicianist positions. It is this range of perspectives that I would like to bring into focus.

In the presentation of the programmatic principles of the most important of the nationalist political formations, the Bloque Nacionalista Galego (BNG), the point that refers to "relations with Portugal" is as highly emphasized as other prominent sections like the "organizational principles" of training, its "alternative to the government," and its "European policy." This very contemporary presence of *"filolusismo"* accounts

for the continuing importance of this question, one that has been present throughout the historical development of Galician nationalism, as I
have said above. Below I cite clarifying extracts that originate in one of
the items cited above, which is entitled "As relacións con Portugal como
diferenza nacional galega" [Relations with Portugal as a Point of Galician National Difference]:

> The political border between the two states was one of the determin-
> ing causes of the political, linguistic, economic and even geographical
> marginalization of Galicia. During the nineteenth and the twentieth
> centuries the search to re-encounter Portugal was a distinctive sign of
> Galicianism. From Murguía, to the *Manifesto das Irmandades da Fala* at
> the Lugo Assembly of 1918 and to the establishment of the Galicianist
> Party, the history of Galician nationalism is replete with statements in
> favor of a decisive cultural and political re-encounter with Portugal.

What is curious in the formulations proposed by the Bloque is a qualification made at the end of this same item: "In all cases, independent of
the specific human and economic relations which are produced between
Galicia and the North of Portugal, the BNG situates Galician-Portuguese
relations vis-à-vis the whole of Portugal" (www.bng-galiza.org).

On the contrary, the interests currently maintained by the autonomous government in its relationship with Portugal seem to be very
secure. Economic transactions have now become very important, and
meetings between Manuel Fraga and the president of the Coordinating
Commission of the Northern Region are frequent, for example. In this
context, as well, in addition to the "myths," affinities between Galicia
and Portugal are increasingly common due to new government capacities and in dealing with the construction of a "Europe of Regions." To a
great extent, the expression of *filolusismo* of the nationalist left remains
ethereal.

It should be pointed out that only in the most recent decades have
propitious conditions emerged for the realization of academic studies
comparing Portugal and Galicia. It will be the result of these studies yet
to be undertaken that in the future will allow us to gauge what there is
of substance in these putative affinities that are invoked once again in
the citation above. In spite of the fact that some transborder studies have
already made relevant and historical contributions, mainly in disciplines
like philology, literary history, and archeology, I believe, however, that
in the majority of cases stubbornly held assumptions about Portuguese-
Galician affinities are more or less imprecise products of passion.

One of the historians of Galician nationalism said that "the subject
of *political* and *cultural* relations between Galicia—or more exactly, the

Galicianist movement (from its provincial phase in the middle of the nineteenth century until the *nationalist* one, beginning in 1916– and Portugal have been, if you like, an overexploited terrain with respect to political and socio-linguistic perspectives which have been clearly projected" (Nuñez Seixas 1992: 61–62, italics in the original). Núñez Seixas wants to emphasize the necessity of being certain of the meaning and the reality of those relationships independent of the actual political appropriations that inflate the retrospective perception of their importance. These notes seem to me to be appropriate. They are, after all, comparable to those already present in the 1983 text by R. Villares that, in my opinion, can be considered the most precise reference to these discussions.

Galician Stories of *Lusos* [Portuguese]

One current example of the spreading of Galicianist *filolusismo* in summary formats can be found on a "personal page" on the Internet maintained by an unknown person. There, immersed in a simplistic text with rather curious orthographic manipulations, we find a series of citations from a variety of the most relevant ideologues of Galician nationalism about recognized affinities and what the destiny of the Galician language should be. An excerpt attributed to Ramón Otero Pedrayo appears among them. I will transcribe the passage in full to illustrate the difficulties the author would have in recognizing himself and his work in this excerpt:

> Ramom Outeiro Pedraio (1888–1976)
>
> The best Portuguese and Galician spirits are citizens with a complete sense of ancient Galicia. ... the language should go back to being the same, in order to strengthen the transcendent being of Celtic Iberia.
>
> Galicia, as much ethnographically as geographically and including the linguistic aspect, is a prolongation of Portugul; or Portugal is a prolongation of Galicia, it makes no difference (1931–1932).[9]

Some initiatives of Galicianist indoctrination—mostly enthusiastic, like this example from the Internet—popularize lusophilian opinions and inspire a variety of declarations that might surprise those Portuguese who visit Galicia or who have some kind of contact with its sayings. But, in addition to the articulation of lusophilian declarations made by scholars over time—or to their contemporary reiterations, justified for reasons of contemporary political proselytism—references made in daily life about Portugal and the Portuguese are numerous and varied. These are not always positive, as one will come to know once familiarized with daily life in any number of Galician localities.

Observations made in the context of daily life easily allow for the opportunity to relativize erudite definitions of the relationships of Galicia with Portugal that rise out of the Galicianist discourse. As a rule, these make reference to a time without separations and are unwitting of the contingencies of history, invoking the existence of ethnographic similarities as guarantees of fixed and latent affinities; or they affirm the existence of primordial communities in remote and little-understood epochs. They also allow for the imagining of a time in the future that would redeem the current borders, as though they were accidental, even though they were established nine centuries ago.

At the beginning of my fieldwork in Santiago, I attended a lecture given in the Faculty of Philology; I entered an auditorium full of young and enthusiastic students. One of the famous personalities from the most radical nationalist circles, one of the few people in Galicia who had been involved in the *loita armada* [armed struggle] of the 1970s, was going to talk about orthographic reintegration. This ex-guerrilla's credentials for speaking about the scheduled topic, if I understood correctly during his talk, were limited to the enthusiasm of his *lusistas* convictions, a fact that did nothing to diminish the reverence with which the students held his words. He spoke rapidly of megalithic civilization, of Celts and, following that, in some detail, about D. Urraca, about D. Tareixa, about Afonso Henriques and the Count of Trava.

The details given about the separation of "Portugal and Galicia" and the brief evocation of those medieval figures lost in time created, from my point of view, a surrealist atmosphere in the auditorium. It seemed to be a recycling of the history lessons that he had been subjected to in primary school, even though there were certain differences in the valorization of the roles that some of those personalities had played. The lecturer even spoke of the *mariscal* Pardo de Cela before referring to the current struggles against the rules of official orthography and the future of the Galician language, that only the *reintegraçom* [reintegration] could redeem. When I decided to ask a question, I did so in Portuguese, trying to stress the characteristic pronunciation of Viana do Castelo in order to facilitate its understanding by the people present. I believe the lecturer did not understand very well what I was asking because of the response he gave. After this impertinent quid pro quo, the lecture continued. The entire audience seemed enthusiastically convinced by this synthetic history of Galicia inspired by the *problem of the language*.

On the contrary, in day-to-day life, there will always be reasons for finding something different, or worthy of disparagement, with respect to

Portugal. This is justified by biographical experiences, or by the repetition of ethnocentric judgments that specific occurrences help to corroborate. Examples of this might be the detention of Portuguese prostitutes in a roadside bar, the collapse of a bridge in Portugal, or the death of a Portuguese sailor in the port of Vigo who had never paid his social security. In the end, in Galicia ambiguities and contempt are often directed at Portugal and the Portuguese. It is worth suggesting certain examples in order to understand how these different versions of modes of imagining the neighboring country can coexist, but also to understand how they mutually fall into place and are in transformation. These are modifications that will account for the process of the construction of a national Galician culture, where a very positive image of Portugal is replicated. This is part of the legacy of historical Galicianism and was, as has already been stressed, an important source of its ideological justification, conforming to the perspectives of many Galicians that I know of their neighboring country.

At another lecture that I attended in Compostela, a member of the audience, a Portuguese, made mention in passing of the fact that in northern Portugal indices measuring economic development were lower than in Galicia. This observation has a factual basis; that is, it could be documented by comparing the economic indicators of both regions. It is also something that would be evident to any attentive tourist who traveled on both sides of the Minho River. This person's statement was indeed a product of circumstance and should have had little consequence; however, it provoked curious reactions in the audience of young university students. Some of them began to say that, to the contrary, the neighboring country was much richer and evidence to the case began to unfold about this supposed prosperity, in which it became evident that the participants had a very spotty knowledge of Portugal. One of the students began, more articulately, to elaborate the reasons for the backwardness and poverty of Galicia, all of which could be summed up under a litany of denunciations directed at the centralist impositions of Madrid.

An interpretation of this unusual defense of the relative prosperity of the Portuguese would have to take into account the subtext of nationalist ideology and the way it is circulated in contemporary Galicia. This so-called prosperity is one of the principal subjects of the propaganda used in this nationalizing ideology: the denunciation of the plundering of Galicia on the part of "Castela" [Castile] or of "Madrid," presented as a constant factor throughout the centuries during which this region has suffered from political dependency. It was this topical image, updated by references to the theorization of 1960s colonialism, which was the strongest reason for idealizing the realities of Portugal's economic situation. In the eyes of these young people sympathetic to the nationalist movement, Portugal was a country that was able to remain free of these depredations, and was made unquestionably the richer for it.

By contrast, in the street, for Galicians who are indifferent to luso-philian sympathies at work in Galicianist circles, opinions about the neighboring country are commonly different. This is true principally among the older generations who still remember the difficulties of the postwar period, who became adults at a time when the *desarrollismo* [developmentalism] of late Francoism prevailed and who benefited from the continual economic growth of the Spanish economy during the last few decades. These were more characteristically people of the middle classes, with right-wing, rural origins, often the parents of the young university students with nationalist sympathies who attended lectures about Portugal in Compostela.[10] As such, one of the most common reasons for disdain of the Portuguese would be, precisely, their "poverty" and "backwardness," opinions that on various occasions I was able to ascertain in conversations that resulted from the curiosity of Galicians in this camp who attempted to confirm their impressions that average salaries, retirement pensions, or unemployment benefits were much lower in the neighboring country.

On various occasions I listened as café employees or the owners of other establishments commented on their very low expectations about the civility of the most characteristic Portuguese visitors. In fact, the people who mainly go to Vigo to shop or to Santiago as religious tourists, usually on rapid excursions by bus, are often poor and of rural origin. In Vigo you hear the proverbial expression: "Portuguese Thursdays," which refers to the most intense commercial day of the week, when they expect to be left with the public gardens and the shopping areas strewn with the trash from their visitors' picnics.[11] On a variety of occasions in Santiago, I observed how the approach of a tour group of Portuguese tourists could make the employees of more sophisticated shops worried and irritated. Once they had gone, there was a sense of relief and an outpouring of some very expressive comments filled with contempt.

In the pages of the press during the first decades of the last century it was not unusual to come across information that, in the police logs, the most likely subjects of crimes and questionable incidents that happened all across rural Galicia were Portuguese. "A Portuguese citizen was detained as a suspect" was an expression frequently repeated in the old copies of newspapers, like *El Pueblo* or *La Voz de Galicia* from the 1920s and 1930s. This could be found in the pages next to editorials and the articles on politics that were of more immediate interest to me. What can be concluded from this type of news item is that the suspects would have been manual laborers of various types or vagabonds, and that their passage through Galicia had been noticeable throughout the twentieth century.

Little is known about the presence of the Portuguese in Galicia, given the lack of specific studies. Though, as a countercurrent, this displacement certainly did not have the generalized characteristics of the arrival, en masse, of Galicians to Oporto and Lisbon during the same period. The most notable descriptions of the movement of workers in the direction of Galicia seem to suggest a scattered and random mobility of individuals. It would also strongly suggest the ease of integration, strengthened by the very real instrumental affinities of language and customs. Through stories heard from older people in different places in Galicia, it seems that teams of loggers and stonemasons were a relatively common sight and that some of them remained permanently. As a matter of fact, we can still find Portuguese journeymen and farmhands in the remote villages of Lugo. In the Minho I was told about recent cases of this sort, sharecroppers, farmhands, and girls that become prostitutes, people of a variety of rural occupations of whom it is said that "they went to Spain" (Galicia) and often fell out of contact.

These different kinds of movement, the ethnocentric contempt for the Portuguese on the part of the Galicians, but, as well, the real affinities that allow for the humbler classes of Portuguese to establish themselves in Galicia in such a discreet fashion, are the parts ignored in the references made about Portugal in the Galicianist discourse. In Santiago it is possible to come across those who had been emigrants to Portugal, very characteristic of the first third of the twentieth century, or, more frequently, the children and grandchildren of these emigrants. Likewise, it is frequent, when going to Lisbon, to find owners of apartment buildings in the streets of the Bairro Alto who come to collect the rents and to deal with bureaucracy related to their inheritances. But the destinies of the Galician emigrants to Portugal in a variety of epochs are a forgettable chapter in the history of the nationalist movement in Galicia, in spite of the *filolusista* rhetoric that has marked it so intensely.

In a previous chapter we saw that the histories of Galicianism and emigration are inextricably linked, intersecting in so many different aspects, and yet following a common pattern, as some of the comparative literature would suggest. The recurring importance of the influence of expatriates in the "invention of traditions" of Galician nationalism is salient in these studies, as Eric Hobsbawm (1985) has already noted. Portugal and, primarily, the community of Galician émigrés in Lisbon seem to us to be more on the sidelines of the process that the political organization and the proselytizing of Galician nationalism would follow.[12] This example confirms the still "monumental" (Herzfeld 1991) character of the time in relation to which knowledge of Portugal—and the quality of references that comprise it—is defined in the Galicianist discourse.

A Song Gathered in a Remote Place

Rafael, one of my frequent fellow diners at lunchtime in Santiago, grew up between Lisbon and Salvador da Baía, since he was the son of Galicians who had started businesses in each of these cities. On various occasions we discussed characteristics of street life in Portas de Santo Antão, in the center of Lisbon, or tricks for cooking rice, a product that is little used and for which there are few recipes in Galician cooking. Among our tablemates all of them were in favor of the Bloque's positions, more or less engaged, and had a great knowledge of the history of Galicianism. Conversations on this subject were frequent and especially interested me. For Rafael, his biographical experience of Lisbon and of Brazil raised a very different sort of question, free of the monumentalizing expressions characteristic of Galicianist *filolusismo.*

Despite its rhetorical importance, references to Portugal found in the literature that gave voice to the Galician nationalist movement are very narrow and predictable. The opinions of many of the more dedicated Galicianists that I knew in Santiago de Compostela were, as a rule, guided by those references, a fact that accounts for the effective spreading of an ideology in which the mention of Portugal has an enormous prominence. On the other hand, the possibilities are frequent for contrasting this with the daily experience in a city that is a tourist destination for many Portuguese, or with the real biographical experience of the many thousands of Galician emigrants in Portugal.

References to the neighboring country that occur in the Galicianist discourse can be characterized as appropriations of very selective aspects of Portuguese culture. They are mostly stereotypical perceptions, invariably positive, yet, as a rule, quite apart from what is familiar and judged to be relevant in the daily life of the natives of the neighboring country (see comparisons proposed by O'Neill 1995 and Herzfeld 1991). There is a dated yet still influential example of this, in *Sempre en Galiza,* the so-called bible of Galicianism. After many years had gone by, the author denounced the parodic mimicry of trivial aspects of Portuguese culture that his more thoughtless fellow students had engaged in (those who were uninterested in Galicianist preoccupations) during their return from a student trip to Coimbra in 1906. Here is what Castelao had to say:

The Galician students—*señoritos* [well-off and spoiled] raised in ignorance of themselves as Galicians—made fun of the sweet Portuguese
courtesy, of French importation, and the sibilant music of their language, and with the return of the *tunas* [student groups of troubadours]
they started to imitate the oratory and the kindness with which they had
been received in Portugal. In this way, the members of the tunas made
use of all kinds of antics to make their companions laugh. Recalling the
"*pés de cabalo,*" the "*contos dos reis,*" the "*vinho verde*" … and, sometimes,
the frenetic love of some mulatto servant … , but it was certain they
didn't stick their noses into a single *cátedra* (university class), nor appear in a single bookstore, nor learn the name of a single writer. (1976:
360)

Another kind of interpretation might suggest that those imitations
were, in the end, forms that were especially suited to understanding a
strange society (Taussig 1993) or for achieving a more "intimate" understanding (Herzfeld 1997a), given outside of the lessons of the *cátedra*.
In the lusophilist nationalist circles one can hear serious references to
the *lusos* and meet young people capable of citing Guerra Junqueiro
(1850–1923) or Teixeira de Pascoaes. Also frequent are the neutral colloquial references to the *revolución dos claveis* (Carnation Revolution),
a designation that will sound rhetorical to the Portuguese and is used
infrequently these days. On some occasions, I heard, to my surprise,
detailed explanations of the annexation of Olivença by Spain, an occurrence that dates back to the eighteenth century, seen with indifference or
ignored by the majority of Portuguese. This so-called Olivenza question
is more frequently referred to on web pages maintained by Galicians
than by Portuguese, who, ironically enough, use the Spanish designation, *Olivenza,* most of the time.

It is possible to produce many other contemporary examples that are
even more trivial of this type of an appreciation for what is Portuguese,
but which vary, as I have suggested, from the commonplaces and valorizations that today are observed on a daily basis in Portuguese society.

In Santiago, among the people that I came to know, I was often made
aware of how an emotional appreciation for the music of the neighboring country would bring together, syncretically, products that Portuguese
consumers would habitually separate. It was also curious to understand
how common and exorbitant was the taste for roast chicken, a specialty
that was taken as an emblem of the excellence of Portuguese culinary
traditions by various of my Compostelan acquaintances who traveled
less frequently to Portugal. This is a taste that would seem bizarre to the
Portuguese of the middle classes, for whom this recipe is a kind of local
example of fast food most appreciated by children.

One of my Galician friends possessed such a knowledge of Portuguese literature and history—and of even miniscule aspects of recent political life—that it was almost an embarrassment to me. Like other less sophisticated Galicians that I knew, Xosé Bieito was someone who appreciated roast chicken and the Fado singers Dulce Pontes and Mísia. So I didn't anticipate his reaction when one time when we were talking, I brought up a play of words cited from the most popular comedian of the last twenty years in Portugal, Herman José, leaving my interlocutor quite perplexed and wondering at the meaning of what I'd said. My explanations were necessarily plodding: first I had to let him know who this comic was, how he had become so successful in Portugal, why he had such an unusual name, etc.—in many ways odd tasks, especially since I had thought that I knew this friend so well. Xosé Bieito, in spite of never having heard of Herman José, knew the works of Camões well, and the history of the publication of *Clepsidra* by Camilo Pessanha, the films of Manoel de Oliveira, and even the minutiae of the destinies of some of the "capitães de Abril." (The "April Captains" were the protagonists of "Carnation Revolution," of 25 April 1974, that brought about the end of authoritarian regime in Portugal.)

Curiously, I was able to clarify the subject by referring to the programming of the channel Televisión Española (TVE), where another comedian performed whose success was analogous with Herman José's. There was no humorist on Televisión de Galicia (TVG) as charismatic and easily recognizable, yet neither did Xosé pay much attention to the channel of the Autonomous Community, because, in his opinion, the daily information was manipulated and hardly objective, the general quality of the programming was low, and the Galician spoken on air was artificial. This example certainly indicates that I would find it hard to talk about other widely recognized Portuguese topics or personalities.

Lila Abu-Lughod recently suggested the importance of "elasticizing creatively" the "dense" descriptions that we habitually get from anthropologists as they pursue their objects of study, whose lives are permeated by the influence of the media (Abu-Lughod 1997).[13] She even points out the relevance, when looking at "cultural texts," of considering a "national system" disseminated by television, the form of mass communication that she takes as an example. I believe that these suggestions are somehow obvious; nevertheless, in paying attention to media there is a risk of seeming unusual and even impertinent in a field of knowledge marked by valorizations based on collecting "local" data, mostly in the field—a proverbial job performed in "villages," according to Clifford Geertz's famous play on words. We are speaking of data whose character, in a somehow arcane manner, are implicit not only in their exposition but in the references to the respective circumstances of collecting them.

In the "field" (and keeping in mind the interests of the study that I was engaged in) it was clear that I needed to be attentive to the programming of TVG and the ways that official Galician national culture was represented in it, as they were significant, as we have already seen, for so many Galicians. Yet it was also important that I be minimally attentive to the television channel of the central Spanish state. Its pertinence is suggested by the paragraphs above that raise doubts about which "national system" should be more relevant in terms of media impact in Galicia.

I was often surprised when watching TVG at how new possibilities for thinking in the Galician language were nourished. It was possible at dawn to see John Wayne on TVG in a mad rush through Monument Valley, speaking pure standard Galician, a situation that creates surprising palimpsests out of rustic lexicons. It is important to note at this stage, however, that those possibilities were, even just a short time ago, unavailable in a mass media context, which until recently had been dominated almost exclusively by Castilian.

As I have already suggested, many nationalists held the majority of the Autonomous Community's television programming in contempt and kept themselves informed through the channels of the central state. The same thing held for the print media, since they believed that the contents of the newspapers published in Galicia were manipulated and of inferior quality.

Anxo, another one of my acquaintances, was a devoted reader of the Portuguese weekly *O Expresso*. He spent Sunday afternoons and even part of the beginning of the week reading it in the café we customarily went to. With the help of examples of the reading he had in hand, he'd often make ironic comments about the news on TVG or TVE. The more infrequent customers, who knew nothing about how eccentric he was, often feared for his sanity when he loudly proclaimed decontextualized analogies between aspects of the political life of both countries. One day I asked him why he didn't read the Portuguese daily newspaper *Público* instead, giving him my opinion about the superior quality of this newspaper. Anxo agreed with me; as a matter of fact, he bought it sporadically. However, as he explained to me, this created a pertinent problem: *Público* arrived a day late in Santiago; for this reason Anxo's morning prayer of modern man was consummated under the rubric of *El País* (Anderson 1991). This famous Madrilenian newspaper is designated "intimately" in Galicia as *O País* and was for Anxo—and for nearly all of the nationalist intellectuals that I knew—an obligatory daily read.

In July 1997 I was at concert of "traditional" music, promoted by the city government in one of Santiago's squares, Praza do Toural. I was accompanied by another one of my Galician friends, also a sympathizer of the BNG. Antón was studying Portuguese literature. It was a second degree for him, a choice that was only justified by his lusophilia, since he already had a stable job and there were, in his opinion, very few practical possibilities for utilizing this new qualification. He was as unconditional an admirer of Eça de Queirós as I was of Camilo Castelo Branco. With these literary references to the most famous of nineteenth-century Portuguese novelists, we had a very droll and lively friendship right from the start.

The spokesperson from the group onstage presented each of the songs with real rigor, giving an account of the places and the circumstances of where it was found and emphasizing the merits of rescuing such a piece of heritage. These old songs had been gathered, on the brink of having been lost altogether, in the mountainous zones on the border between Portugal and Galicia. One of the specimens was presented with even more drama. It had been uncovered in a very remote and old-fashioned zone of Portugal near the border close to Verín, coming from the mouth of an extremely old woman. It is worth transcribing the first lines of the song as it was presented in the Praza do Toural: *Água fria, da ribeira / Água fria que o sol aqueceu / Três corpetes, um avental* [Cold water, from the brook / Cold water that the sun warmed / Three bodices, one apron].

My companion was left very confused when I began to laugh out loud at the first line. It was really quite difficult to express in that moment all of the ironic sides to such an anticlimax, inevitable for anyone who was Portuguese and had paid attention to the dramatic set-up that the recounting of the circumstances of the song's discovery had inspired. This was none other than one of the emblematic popular ditties of one of the most well-known comedies of Portuguese filmography from the middle of the twentieth century. In Portugal, since the film is often shown on television, each line is automatically recognized. Their parodic use in daily life is frequent for a wide range of allusions or for the repeated mimicking of the performance of the hugely popular actress who first sang them. This citation can be considered a topic of shared Portuguese popular culture—completely nationalized throughout all the regional contexts—easily recognizable by children and adults of different socioeconomic statuses in Portuguese society.

The Free Voices of Galicians and Minhotans

In the Minho, as soon as we put a few kilometers between ourselves and the border, the perception becomes widespread that there is no difference between the Galician language and Castilian. Its existence is even frequently ignored. This is a fact that is often painful for the more lu-sophilian Galicians that I know, who frequently lament the fact that, paradoxically, the Portuguese understand their language badly, find it very strange, and that, most of the time, respond to them by mimicking Castilian. The Galicians inevitably find this mimicry parodic, given the flagrant mistakes that are made. These quid pro quos can often be veri-fied in Minhotan localities close to the border, for example in Caminha, Ponte de Lima, and Barcelos, places where my informants want to feel brotherly connections with the natives and not face obstacles in com-munication when they use their own vernacular.

These unmet expectations were, in Santiago, frequent topics among my group of friends. Many of them had questions about the name of some object in Portuguese or the exact pronunciation of a certain word. Normally, these questions were about terms that had created some im-passe during conversations on one of their visits to Portugal. The most characteristic situation would arise when the Portuguese interlocutor made the effort to speak Castilian with someone who responded to him in Galician, thus multiplying the obstacles to comprehension, which can be hilarious, depending on how funny the narrator of these imbro-glios actually is.

It frequently happens that the Galician words and expressions that have provoked impasses can be found in old Portuguese texts or in use in certain localities of the rural Minho; the same could be said of prac-tices recognized in both contexts, but that, nevertheless, can also lead to mutual incomprehension. As an example, I want to suggest below the difficulty in accounting for these parallelisms out of context and at-tributing restrictive meanings to them, without taking into account that differentiated processes of "objectification" of national cultures impose on the respective understanding (Handler 1988). Acritical valorizations are, then, problematic against a backdrop of ahistorical similarities, and only defensible when vague recollections are made that ignore the his-torical period and the observable social practices.

In a work that explains the official symbols in force in the Comu-nidade Autónoma (Cores 1986) there is a curious remark concerning acoustic symbols in Galicia and, particularly, of their use in the history of Galicianist activism. He says the following:

> Galicia is rich in acoustic symbols or sounds of an ideological and politi-cal type. The cries or shouts are many and are used with great frequency, as often in typical festivities as in patriotic acts. Some of these shouts indicate an endorsement of what is taking place, as with *Terra a Nosa!* Or *Galicia Ceibe!* But more than being shouts or cries of identification, ad-hesion and proselytizing they are instruments of affirmation that deepen

the communitarian spirit manifested at banquets, at political acts and in cultural acts. (1986: 101)

In this text the reference made to "typical" practices of the lower classes are underscored. The author shows how they are selectively adopted and used as instruments of nationalist engagement—the passage above highlights the adoption of *berros* [shouts]. These were characteristic of historical ludic practices in rural contexts, or in small towns, at festivals, evening celebrations, collective tasks, all of which can be found mentioned throughout the ethnographic bibliography of Galicia (Lema Bendaña 1990–1991; Mariño Ferro n.d.). Only some of these *berros*—*berros secos* or *aturuxos*, the designations usually employed—are appropriate to new and prestigious uses, whether in political demonstrations, in literature, in erudite music, in the theater, or for the appreciation of ethnographers who comment upon them. Thus, for example, the *aturuxo* "u ju juu...!" would be appreciated for being archaic and earthy. It has often been commented upon by academics and used in sophisticated vanguardist performances, and even provided the title for a futurist poem by Vicente Risco. Yet another of the frequent *berros* used by groups of male youth, *Ei Carballeira!,* is considered uncouth and vulgar and is repeated periodically by columnists to exemplify some kind of rude behavior committed by lower-class individuals (as Castelao did in a conference during the 1920s!).

Baldomero Cores notes as well that the mottos chosen by the engagé *regionalistas* of the nineteenth century were still Latin phrases—*Deus fratesque Gallaeciae,* for example, was used by Alfredo Brañas, one of the most famous precursors. This would have been comprehensible to the traditional intelligentsia beyond the borders of Galicia. *Berros* in the vernacular were legitimized in the second decade of the twentieth century in the political arena, in the context of the nationalist movement. Following this they were recycled in political acts and also fixed in writing, for example, in the headings of periodicals and pamphlets, or to close articles by activists—all examples of a recognition and expansion beyond their original restricted and impromptu usage. The example cited above gives us a supplementary reference to the processes of vernacularization of the Galician language in which literate groups of Castilian-speaking Galicians took part; that is to say, supplementary to a process of the "nationalization of culture" and the creation of a "imagined community" in which the press played a very important role.

The recognition of the instrumentality of the *berros* as an "instrument for the affirmation and deepening of the communitarian spirit," as Cores implies, is suggestive. However, as we saw at the beginning of this chapter, one of these *berros* had paradoxical consequences, upsetting the harmony that the group interpretation of *A Laurindinha* had created between Galicians and Portuguese on Rúa do Franco. The word *ceive*—or *ceibe,* a strange term in the ears of urban Castilian or Portuguese speakers—used to qualify the shout, *Viva Galiza,* would quite probably be understood by those rural people coming from Portugal and participating in the *rusga* (a typical dance enacted during pilgrimages). Nevertheless, it would hardly be probable that they would completely understand the implications of its use in the specific context described above, given the general ignorance of nationalist claims beyond the borders of the Comunidade Autónoma.

Ceive and *Ceivar* are defined in the *Dicionário de Morais* (1999) as "provincianismos minhotos" [words peculiar to the Minho province]. *Ceivar* is illustrated in the following way: "Ceivar os bois, soltá-los do jugo. Destapar, soltar" [Free the Oxen, loosen them from the yoke. Uncover, loosen]. According to my experience, this word is infrequently heard today and still more rarely written in the provincial context. In Galicia—written in two ways, as *ceive* or *ceibe*—in rural contexts it had approximately the same meanings as those attributed to it in the entry in *Morais* (which it records as "ceive," even though it is, as rule, pronounced as "ceibe").

In Portugal *ceive* is increasingly restricted to erudite uses as a highly stylized word—of interest to ethnographers or linguists working in isolated rural areas, or used in soap operas, in historical films and in ethnographic performances, and so on. In Galicia the same word has similar rural origins and was also mostly used orally. Today, however, its written form is widespread and it is used to voice the aspirations of the masses at large urban rallies and other commemorative acts staged by the nationalist movement. What is more, *Galicia Ceibe* or *Galicia Ceibe, poder popular* [Free Galicia / Free Galicia, Power to the People] are frequently written as graffiti on the walls of major Galician cities, or even in Portugal in areas near the border. These ostentatious uses replace the word *livre* and the terms derived from it, which are also Galician. Less used today in their original contexts, they are restricted to the process of the vernacularization of the Galician language. This phenomenon touches everyone who now speaks and writes in urban Galicia, a practice that had been exclusive to the small groups of elites that embodied Galicianist proselytism from the beginning of the twentieth century up until the 1980s.

In the Minho there are certain types of *berros* similar to those uses that Baldomero Cores noted in Galicia as "typical," although in Galicia they have been revived for current political purposes, giving them prestige and leading to their use as well in mass politics. In one of the parishes in the district of Braga, where I did field work at the beginning of the 1990s, I learned that the young men who participated in collective work or in confrontations between groups of young people would "afoutar." *Afoutar* consisted, according to the explanation given, in yelling out stereotypical shouts of jubilation affirming the group's solidarity using onomatopoeias that would be difficult to transcribe. This remote memory was discussed in detail by people who were around forty years old and was a complete novelty to their younger brothers and sisters in their early twenties. The latter, with more schooling behind them, had grown up in more prosperous times marked by great transformations, namely, concerning practices of socializing among young people.

These illustrations suggest that the word *ceive,* when it is associated with mass political demonstrations, would greatly surprise Minhotans of rural origins. In the same way, many of the words used casually by educated urban Galician speakers, words loaded with obvious rural associations, would also surprise them. For a Minhotan listener they would be familiar, but also surprising at the same time, because of the obvious status of those who use them, as when a waiter of rural origins is listening to a Galician doctor or university professor in a restaurant in Barcelos or Ponte de Lima.

The word *ceibe* (*ceive*) is associated with already outmoded practices in the parishes of the rural Minho that I know and has always seemed foreign to the vocabulary of the majority of inhabitants of the towns and cities of this province. In rural contexts, the term alludes to times long past, when, for example, it was a real drama when excessive rainfall would break through the dams holding water for the purposes of irrigation, or when oxen would escape at full speed during an accident, and even when the children would take the cows to graze, unsupervised—with fewer responsibilities and more time for play—in the months of April and May before the plowing. In the same way, the expressive *berros* with which one would *afoutar* evoke struggles between neighboring places, collective tasks that are no longer engaged in and localist solidarities that no longer hold sway or have been taken on via other expressive forms.

These are, in a certain way, pastoral evocations; they contain ethnographic registers and were part of the experience of the older generations still present in the rural areas of both the Minho and Galicia. However, it was a younger, educated culture that in the second context reanimated their use, attributing new meanings to them and new forms of employing them. Paradoxically, it is these expressions of a younger culture that can stymie comprehension between Galicians and Minhotans. This is demonstrated through the example above of the use of words whose contemporary usage is quite different in each of the cases.

There are various examples that could be illustrated with respect to the use of words. One especially curious example—and perhaps one that is perhaps more inspiring in terms of ideological transcendence—would be the word *saudade*. It was used by Rosalía de Castro, the most emblematic figure of the *Rexurdimento*, and later appropriated by the Galician nationalist discourse under the influence of the speculations of Portuguese intellectuals who, as we have seen, have left behind a lasting influence in the rhetoric of Galicianism (Álvarez and Estraviz 1999; Piñeiro 1995). In current Galician, *saudade* has been practically lost, both in its oral and written forms in favor of the vernacular term *morriña*, which is less refined (and which, as a matter of fact, was used for literary purposes during the *Rexurdimento*). This is also a word used in rural contexts in the Minho—taking the form *morrinha*—where it means weakened, debilitated, sick—meanings that are partially close to those meanings that the uses of the contemporary term has recovered in Galician. Yet in the Minho the term applies mainly to animals, particularly to dogs. When it is applied to people it is considered rude and takes on very strong disrespectful connotations; it could be used for example, to say, behind the back of a drug addict, "That guy goes around like a "cão morrinhento" [a sick dog]. We can see that, since the mid-nineteenth century, these kinds of uses of a term in the Minho correspond proportionally to its accumulation of positive and uplifting meanings when used in Galicia. In this second context, the references to *morriña* are used to this day to talk about positive qualities of the *alma* or spirit of the Galician nation.

Where Is Portuguese Identity?

When Guadelupe returned to Santiago after having spent some time with her parents in the Campos Góticos, in a village near Palencia, she told her group of friends that she was returning full of *morriña* for Santiago and Galicia, even for the rain. Guadelupe was a tall, red-haired woman whose profile and bearing had, surprisingly, many similarities with the "Goths" stereotyped in the comic strip *Asterix among the Goths*. She had grown up in the "austere" Castilian landscape, an emblematic reference for painters and writers, whose works had contributed to the nationalization of the culture of the Spanish elites towards the end of the nineteenth century (Pena 1998; Álvarez Junco 2001). She was a producer of Celtic music and had lived for more than twenty years in Santiago in a village house on the outskirts of the city where she grew vegetables in her garden. Guadelupe spoke a Galician punctuated by spirited vernacular expressions, as did many other women who sympathized with the nationalist left whom I knew in Santiago. She told me one day that there were certain sounds in Galician words that she wasn't able to pronounce correctly, the consequence of having grown up in Castile—but she felt Galician. I open *Sempre en Galiza,* and go to a citation from the inspired myth maker that Castelao was. There I come upon a paradigmatic passage that, like many other contemporary Galicians, my informant knows well:

> A long time ago I wrote a story: there was once an "Habanero" [an emigrant who had returned from Havana] who brought a little black boy with him, as though he were bringing a parrot, or a phonograph. ... the "Habanero" died and the black boy became a young man, and, like any other Galician, he felt the need to see the world. He emigrated to Cuba: but his *morriña* [homesickness] did not let him stay there. And sick of crying he returned to his *terra*. He didn't bring any money, but he brought a new suit, an empty trunk and a great amount of happiness in his heart. That black man was a Galician. (Castelao 1976: 41)

In the autumn of 1998 I attended a talk in Santiago de Compostela organized by the students of one of the city's university residences. A professor from the neighboring country teaching, at the time, in the city's university had been invited to speak about "Portuguese Identity." The audience's interest was very evident, and the room was full. The speaker launched into an argument that interested the audience for its novelty, though it would have been quite familiar to a Portuguese audience of the same makeup. He relied solely on Eduardo Lourenço's influential theses on "Portuguese identity" (Lourenço 1978), describing them in abbreviated form but very faithfully, without introducing nuances or attempting to problematize their validity.

A certain lack of intellectual alacrity was noticeable in the speaker's manner; this must be one of the reasons for the false step that led to an error at the end of the talk, when he tried to inspire the involvement of the still timid audience to engage in a debate. He suggested that since he was from the north of Portugal, that his affinities for those present were probably greater than what he might feel for someone from Lisbon, a *lisboeta,* or for an inhabitant of the extreme south of his country, someone from the Algarve, an *algarvio.* Quickly this suggestion was challenged by one of the more attentive members of the audience who found a certain incompatibility between this observation and the whole argument of the lecture. In the end, Lourenço's notions characterized the Portuguese in absolute terms as sharing a common "identity," a fact that didn't allow for the exceptions that the speaker now wanted to introduce. This momentary embarrassment was patched up in a benign fashion, as people began to discuss the affinities between Portugal and Galicia.

Let me, once again, cite *Sempre en Galiza,* but also at the same time Murguía, because Castelao paraphrases descriptions already proposed in *Galicia:* "When a Galician reaches the plains of Leon or of Zamora, he feels like he is in a foreign land, invaded by the sadness that deserts produce in us. When he reaches Asturias he has to get his eyes used to a new type of landscape. But when he crosses the Portuguese border, he feels at home, and gives no credit to the arbitrariness of historical politics" (Castelao 1976: 45).

Notes

1. *Ceibe* or *ceive*—this is the normative spelling, but both forms are used—is a term that signifies "free," "unbound," or "liberated" (some of its recent uses are discussed later on).

2. A theme referred to in the interpretation of the ethnic psychology of the Portuguese and the Galicians clearly influenced by the formulations of Teixeira de Pascoaes during the first part of the twentieth century (Leal 2000). The poet and the author of *Art de Ser Português* was widely read and cited in Galicia by nationalist intellectuals who wrote for *Nós,* of whom Bouza Brey was a direct disciple (see the correspondence sent to Teixeira de Pascoaes collected by Álvarez and Estraviz 1999). *Saudosismo* marked the work of the influential Ramón Piñeiro, as I have already suggested, as well as other contemporaneous authors.

3. The Galicianist publications of the period provide—for obvious reasons—a better source for those items about Galicia that appeared in the Portuguese periodicals and the literature of the period. For example, these mentions are especially rich under the heading for book reviews "Os homes, os feitos e as verbas [Men, facts and words] kept up in the periodical *Nós* by Vicente Risco.

4. See an enthusiastic example with Ledo Andión (1982) and another one, more sober, with Sánchez Rey (1992).

5. Sánchez Rey's article, "O eco de alén Miño na generación Nós," efficiently summarizes the nebulous syncretism of some of these collaborations (and the harsh criticism that the respective interpretation would impose on Galician readers). To this extent it remains a document on the products of the so-called Portuguese philosophy in its most splendorous period—contemporaneous with the activities of the group known as the "Portuguese Renaissance"—from the curious point of view of its reception in Galicia.

6. See the article entitled "Portugal e a Galiza" published in *Nós,* no. 2, 1920, and the article entitled "A embaixada spiritual de Leonardo Coimbra" (*Nós,* no. 7, 1921); see also Sánchez Rey (1992). M. Ledo Andión summarizes the Portuguese collaborations in the periodical *A Nosa Terra* (1982).

7. Contrary to this, in Galicia the better bookstores are better stocked with Portuguese books, even though the variety of this selection is quite relative. There are well-known historical examples of attention having been paid to Portuguese publications, as has already been referred to in a previous note.

8. Beginning in the 1930s Galician archeologists and ethnographers began to submit articles to periodicals in Oporto. In this period we can point to names such as Xaquín Lorenzo, Florentino Cuevillas, Fermín Bouza Brey, and, less frequently, Antonio Fraguas. Their texts were even published in Galician. This movement consolidated itself later, mainly in the 1940s and during the following decade. Texts by more important personalities such as Ramón Otero Pedrayo or Vicente Risco also began to appear with some frequency along with lesser-known folklorists. Galician intellectuals were a presence in certain celebrated moments of Portuguese archeology and ethnography, starting with the "homage to Martins Sarmento" in 1933. They were also present at the Congresso do Mundo Português in 1940, at the 1st Congresso de Etnografia e Folclore in 1956, at the Colóquio de Estudos Etnográficos Dr. Leite de Vasconcelos in 1958, or at the Congresso Internacional de Etnografia of 1963. We have seen how early in 1935 a *Semana Cultural Galega* [Galician Cultural Week] had been held at the University of Oporto, a moment that would have been important in the reinforcement of personal relations, which would be maintained during the following three decades. On the Portuguese side, there were some important players in this conversation, such as António Mendes Correia, Fernando Castro Pires de Lima (1908–1973), and the archeologist Mário Cardoso (1889–1982), all of whom were largely responsible for the periodicals where archeological and ethnographic articles by Galicianist intellectuals were published.

9. Cf. http://XMCM/galizalivre/reintnosideologos; here we have an example of the application of the *reintegracionista de máximos* orthographic norm. It was in texts that observed this rule—mainly those that applied a more imaginative form, mimicking Portuguese orthography as much as possible—that I found some of the more intricate difficulties in the comprehension of Galician.

10. This is a very curious question in contemporary Galicia, providing an updated illustration of the solidarity between alternating generations, famous in the annals of our discipline. Young Galicians—mainly between the ages of 20 and 30, closer to nationalist ideas—tend to see their parents as a kind of "lost generation," de-Galicianized, and finding, on the contrary, their grandparents as bearing notions of Galician identity that they hold in high esteem. The grandparents, however, even though they feel flattered, recognize the limits of their formal education and the corruptions of the Galician that they habitually speak, but they are proud of their grandchildren, of their superior education that allows them to write in Galician— and in Castilian—with facility.

11. Curiously, *portugueses* is a deprecating term used to provoke the fans of Celta, the most important soccer team in Vigo, by their rivals, fans of the Deportivo da Coruña. *Portugueses* can also be used to designate the group of inhabitants of the province of Pontevedra in a disdainful fashion. As a matter of fact, the allegiance to certain soccer teams is very curious to observe, to the extent that they reconstitute the pertinence of the Spanish state as an imagined community and become a motive for the manifestations of a "banal nationalism," inevitable even among unwavering Galicianists.

12. I believe that this fact can be explained by the social constitution of the contingents of emigrants who shared this destiny—Lisbon seems to have never been the destiny of intellectuals or qualified professionals, as were, at various times in the history of the Galician diaspora during the nineteenth and twentieth centuries, Havana, Buenos Aires, and even Madrid. I did not find any significant references to the nationalist movement in the minutes of the executive or in the memorabilia housed in the library of the important association of Galician emigrants in Lisbon, the Juventud

de Galicia (today Xuventude de Galicia). Curiously, in this same location today, one can learn not only to play the bagpipe, but also learn the dances of Galicia and Seville, as well as Flamenco (or eat paella in the restaurant), all of which suggests that among Lisboa's Galician emigrants or their descendants there is some confusion over the politics of the nationalization of culture in which today all of the political sectors of Comunidade Autónoma are involved.

13. Concomitant suggestions were proposed, for example, by Llobera (1998), Appadurai (1996), Clifford (1997), and Hannerz (1992).

Chapter 7

The Minho and the Painting of the Customs of Nations

One afternoon at the end of the summer of 1993, I decided to pose a question to one of my informants that surprised him: I asked him where the Minho was. This was during S. Miguel, the period of harvest, and it was hot, yet a large trellis covered the *eido* [patio or small yard]. Wasps hovered about the ripe grapes as we prepared the *dornas* [wine barrels] for the *vindima* [the grape harvest]. A large roof stood out in the distance where we had calibrated the press, burning sulfur fumigators in the casks—"men's" work (Pina-Cabral 1989). The women of the *casa* had gone to work in the distant cornfields; every once in a while one of them would call out, sharply slicing the air. The cows ruminated in the *corte* [stable typically beneath the house on the ground floor], within our sight. They were my friend and informant's passion, an old farmer in modest circumstances and also a livestock *contratador* [trader]. The bucolic notes were abundant that afternoon; that was how work went during the days of September in the Minho. This was a *minhoto* ambiance. The use of this adjective could be justified by innumerable old citations, literary and cinematographic.

It was then that I asked my informant where the Minho was. We were drinking sparkling wine from a huge bowl, just as is described in the anthologies about the region (Trigueiros 1967). The man, his hat on his head, wearing a white shirt, lowered his eyes and said: "Look, I don't know how to answer that question, professor." He insisted upon using such an academic title, much to my embarrassment. This extreme deference often made me think about ethnographic descriptions of Java and Bali (Boon 1990).

Figure 8. Visiting Manuel Cruz Azevedo (right) in the early 2000s. Photo by Rosa Areal Medeiros, n.d.

My informant, wanting to clear up the unexpected question, suggested, "Perhaps Augusto would know." Then he shouted out for his son: "Gusto, come over here, the professor wants to ask you a question." Augusto arrived; he was friendly man in his forties, a salesman of agricultural chemicals who worked in a city in the District of Oporto, thirty kilometers to the south. Better educated than his father, he knew everything about the farmland to the north of the Douro river where he traveled by car to advise his clients. I decided to embellish the question I'd asked his father: "Gusto, are we in the *alto* or *baixo* [upper or lower] Minho?" He laughed and said: "That's a difficult question, António, I don't know, I think we're in the upper Minho, the lower must be to the south, below Póvoa [de Varzim, the city where he worked]." And the question that had seemed bizarre to my interlocutors died there. For my part, I already knew the official answers, not always clear, but described in books. We continued to drink the wine from the enormous white bowl—afterwards it took the strength of all three of us to budge the huge *balseiro* [tank for crushing grapes].

In a relatively recent article Arjun Appadurai suggested a conceptualization of the term *locality* that I believe to be suggestive for the analysis of the two cases we have in hand. Firstly, I would like to suggest that it might be suitable for considering the conversation about the Minho as a province and the fact that a portion of its inhabitants do not know it as one. Appadurai has the following to say: "I view locality as primarily relational and contextual rather than as scalar or spatial. I see it as a complex phenomenological quality, constituted by a series of links between the sense of social immediacy, the technologies of interactivity and the relativity of contexts" (1995: 204). Following this, the author puts forth the idea that from the beginning of modern age the production of nation-states as localities became favored. On the other hand it was necessary for states to produce "localities" on a smaller scale in their hinterlands as an important part of the task of constantly updating this process of place making. "The nation-state relies for its legitimacy in the intensity of its meaningful presence in a continuous body of bounded territory. It works by policing its borders, producing its 'people' [Balibar 1991], constructing its citizens, defining its capitals, monuments, cities, waters and soils, and by constructing its locales of memory and commemoration" (Appadurai 1995: 213).

I have pointed out various historical expressions of nationalism in Galicia; we have seen how its construction as a "locality"—and of its locales of memory—was created in a variety of moments against the will of the Spanish state. But I also wanted to account for how the recent granting of capacities of self-government has magnified that process of localization in the different registers pointed to in the citation. In that which has to do with the Minho—and the vast majority of Portuguese provinces—state interventions arrived late and have remained to this day only fragilely connected and weakly pedagogical, as I have already suggested in a previous passage. On the contrary, the work of scientists, artists, and men of letters were all relevant in the articulation of the ways of naming that province. Marketplace phenomena that have sustained the spreading of products or the use of the Minho as a tourist destination likewise contributed in similar ways. These dimensions, which are inextricably interlinked, became significant facets in the process of nationalizing the references of the middle classes in Portugal, or, in other words, their *aportuguesamento* [Portugalization] (Ramos 1994).

Valorizing the interpretations of Appadurai and taking what happened in Galicia as a counterpoint, it is in the absence of interventions by the state that we are able to find explanations for the weaknesses in the recognition of the Minho among the less-favored levels of its population. Appadurai also distinguishes "localities" from "neighborhoods," defining the latter notion in the following fashion: "I use the term 'neighborhood' to refer to the existing social forms in which locality, as a dimension or value, is variably realized" (Appadurai 1995: 204). Staying with the terms of Appadurai, there is still room for reflection on the stories of the "production of localities" and their contemporary appropriation in "neighborhoods." Let us follow this line a bit further.

An Early and Imaginative Theory of the Provinces

In the first pages of Oliveira Martins's *History of Portugal* we see a new type of sensibility at work on the interpretation of the differences one finds in the territory of the Portuguese state. In this work of 1879, the so-called differences are referred to in an absolute fashion as provincial divisions, stressing, in the respective categorizations, ethnogenetic distinctions. Each province is considered individually in terms of its geographic characteristics, and their dissimilarities are viewed in absolute terms: determinations imposed by very specific mesological conditions are discussed, a justifying factor in the great ethnic variety understood to exist between the respective populations (Corbin 1997). On the contrary, the author deemphasizes—firstly, and in a relative way—the role of ethnic and geographic determinations with respect to the national whole, the nation and its respective history.

I believe that it is in Oliveira Martins's proposal that the earliest and most explicit formulation of the existence of a Portugal of differentiated provincial entities occurs—it is a theory of the nation that justifies such well-defined discriminations. To the provinces—which had been vague topographical divisions without any independent power in the administrative context of the old regime, that is, the extensive period before the 1820 Liberal Revolution—the historian now attributes a "natural" physiognomy. Almost a century later, Orlando Ribeiro would observe: "The reader will be perplexed ... to see that there are natural borders to the provinces (older than the state itself) while the borders of the state are not natural" (1977: 36). It is worth comparing this with another more recent and significant opinion: "No one as much as Oliveira Martins has given us a 'theory' of Portugal in space and time, a theory which is certainly open to discussion, and really quite provocative, yet without a doubt rich in suggestions that still today are not fully explored" (Saraiva and Lopes 1989: 922).

Oliveira Martins suggests a new reading of the countryside, where the presence of architectonic ruins of the Middle Ages or of the different mountain ranges, valorized as referents of memory by the Romantic authors, is erased in the conceptualization of the landscapes of the different parts of the country (Medeiros 1995). Now it is the inhabitants of the provinces—inscribed in a natural space, "terra e homem" [land and man]—that have become the topic of reflection and documents/monuments of remote eras (Le Goff 1984). This historian's proposal is extremely significant; through him we have the monumentalization of the provinces and their respective inhabitants. It is they who are given the role of document of a very remote past, explaining the antecedents of the nation, and it is upon the representation of their static plurality that the nation might arise as a synthetic organism. We have a "being" (Handler 1988) dynamically involved in the flux of its own history.

Oliveira Martins's ideas are filled with anachronistic suggestions. For example he refers to a Minhotan peasant, one of his contemporaries, as a "galaico" [a Galician], the beirão [someone from the center of Portugal] is a "lusitano" [a Lusitanian], and the "algarvio" [someone from the Algarve] a "turdetano" [a Turdetani]. The author portrays these provincial types by postulating their invariability in an undifferentiated timelessness and as though inside spaces that are identified definitively. Characteristically, each of these provincial types is depicted in a rural context. As Michel de Certeau says, the peasant is chosen to be the "savage of the countryside ... the density of history here replaces geographical distance" (1993: 48)

With his imaginative rationalizations, Oliveira Martins tries to formulate a conceptual centralization for Portuguese history. He reconciles the political history of the construction of the state—in which he stresses a founding act, the process of "reconquest" from the north to the south—as the definitive and incontestable justification for the "nation." Lisbon as the political and symbolic capital becomes the reference for the resolution of this dilemma: "The taking of Lisbon gives form to the birth of the Portuguese nation, until then caught in the limbo of its genesis" (Oliveira Martins 1942: 95). In this way, the central swathe of the territory can take on an anachronistic prominence in the identification of the "being" of the nation; we can see a teleological resolution of the whole of the argument. On the slopes of the Estrela mountain range, among the supposed descendants of the *Lusitanos,* Oliveira Martins recognizes a praiseworthy ethnic "heart" as well as a more virile countryside. With a convenient metaphor he reflects this centralization that the Tagus river defines: "Via the Tagus maritime Portugal embraces agricultural Portugal fusing the two physiognomies typical of the nation" (1942: 58).

The suggestion is implicit in these arguments that it is from the capital, from the exercise of powers concentrated therein, that the most effective organizing principles will emanate—that is, those which allow for the act of imagining, in the broadest sense, the internal division of the country (Bourdieu 1989; see also chapter 1). These are prerogatives that include, namely, the legitimacy to connect provincial peculiarities in a symbolic cartography. The moralizing landscape is justified through reference to the nation and centered upon a reference to its capital.

The work of Oliveira Martins should be considered a select reference for the task of identifying the country imposed in the "age of nationalisms." In his analysis of the Minho and the Minhotans, *"a terra e o homem"* are singularly disfavored, against the current of broadly spread stereotypes, still at play and which are eminently lovable. We can explain this discrepancy if we keep in mind the theses of the *decadentistas,* which Oliveira Martins shared with other Iberian (and European) intellectuals. In Portugal, these theses were emblematically articulated in a famous lecture by Antero de Quental entitled "Causes of Decadence in the Peninsular Peoples" (Quental 1970; Catroga 1993b; cf. Álvarez Junco 2001; Pick 1989). In the landscape allegory proposed by Oliveira Martins, the most peripheral parts of the territory become polarized as images of the limits of the nation in space and time, touched by some essential ambiguity.

The Minho is described negatively with adjectives more often used in the pejorative descriptions of Galicia and the Galicians, but also, more generally, in descriptions of the *"génio celta,"* in a curious amalgam of references of different provenance (Vásquez Cuesta 1991; Chapman 1992). The metaphors used in order to characterize this province contain suggestions of germination and feminization, of excessive luxuriance, and also of death and corruption. In this imagistic argument the suggestion is of the recessive ethnogenetic characteristics of the nation: in its coming into being, Oliveira Martins senses an unavoidable destiny of decadence and submission. This teleology would be inscribed in the "large dose of Celtic blood" that would touch the nation as a whole, but principally the Minho. In the disproportionate parable that the historian draws, the Minho stands as a metaphor for the beginning and the end of the nation—the site of its remotest origins and maintained as the atemporal mirror of its predictable agony. In *Portugal Contemporâneo,* a later title by the same author (1881), we find even livelier illustrations of these teleological interpretations. There, "Maria da Fonte" and "Patuleia" occur as central episodes in the narrative structure. In the description of these *jacqueries* [peasant revolts], the attention to the ethnic stigmas of rural Minhotan plebeians confirms the historian's pessimism vis-à-vis the future of the nation (Oliveira Martins n. d.).

It is in the description by Oliveira Martins that we find the strongest of the deprecatory versions of the provincial image of the Minho. This same sensibility can be recognized among other authors who describe the province and its population and share the same decadent sensibility, like the novelist Fialho de Almeida (1857–1911) or the important ethnographer A.A. Rocha Peixoto (1866–1909). However, it is difficult to identify these same negative versions of the provincial image of the

Minho in the more popularized texts and images that were produced starting at the end of the nineteenth century. This should be read in light of the affirmative nationalist discourse that began to circulate during this period due to the influx of various aesthetic currents that can be grouped under the rubric of a single adjective (which first appeared at the time): *neogarrettistas* (Coelho 1976: 711–13; see later in this chapter). The Minho had already been a "favored province" in the imaginative world of the first nationalist romantic authors (Medeiros 1995). However, it was with the spreading of an evolutionist ideology—of which Oliveira Martins was an influential proponent—that a lasting canon of description of the Minho (an amalgam of fin-de-siècle scientism and a romantic taste for the picturesque) began to hold sway. The mechanical reproduction of texts and works of art (Benjamin 1991), intensified by the enormous social and technological transformations during the final decades of the nineteenth century, helped the spread of a range of characteristic knowledge about the Minho. This, as we have already seen, was a period in which the invention of traditions was favored (Hobsbawm 1985).

O Minho Pitoresco, by José Augusto Vieira (1856–1890), is a curious document about the ways that people at the time came to know this province. The book brings together a sensibility for the picturesque with a vague ethnographicism tinged with evolutionist references. In this voluminous description, published in 1886–1887, with its profusion of illustrations, the author is attracted by "*os tipos*" [characteristic types], the traditional clothing, the monuments, local practices, everything that is considered picturesque in this loveably exotic province, the "garden of Portugal," where "men are carnations and women are roses" (1887: 769). *O Minho Pitoresco* was a work directed at the more well-to-do classes throughout the whole of Portugal. This is suggested by the text's accessibility, by the variety of the images, and by the resulting luxuriousness of the two large volumes.

José Augusto Vieira was born in the Minho; nevertheless, in his book's opening he emphasizes that a trip to this province is analogous to a trip through time, to coming face to face with the beginnings of the nation: "The Minho has been the sacred tabernacle of our ethnic traditions. ... there the spirits preserve the affective qualities of this Celtic temperament, which was our genetic fiat, and of that Greek spirit which was our artistic beginning" (1886: III).[1] Throughout the text, the author would cite some of the prestigious contemporary Portuguese authors, who considered themselves the pioneering ethnologists, to assert his identification of "archaisms" or "surviving remnants," because, as he assures us, "ages follow ages, traditions flow—light gondolas on the people's soul."

Vieira's monumental work can be compared to *Galicia,* Manuel Murguía's contemporaneous title, introduced in chapter 1. The major difference between them, echoing one of the expressions commented upon in the passage, is the absence of a "statement of being" in the explanations of J. Augusto Vieira, but also of performative claims, and of a geography, history and culture belonging to the Minho (Handler 1988; Bourdieu 1989). These are the suggestions of partiality (Williams 1988) that predominate in *Minho Pitoresco,* as, as a matter of fact, in all of the abundant literature describing the Minho up to our own days, and that the phrase "sacred *tabernacle* of our ethnic traditions" (my italics) exemplifies so well.

An Improbable Lineage

Recently, James Clifford questioned the terms of reference that form the professional identification of anthropologists at the present time, recognizing that their practices have become systematically diversified and that their objects of study have multiplied. The historian questions whether it is possible to recognize an open border between anthropology, cultural studies, and other analogous traditions. His response: a rigorous no (1997: 63). This response might be inconvenient for those who would like to consider, with a certain depth and latitude, the history of this interest in "describing the people" in the Portuguese context (or the Galician), or in recognizing valuable antecedents in the works of nationalistic polymaths who produced these types of descriptions with a certain rigor and persistence. As I wanted to suggest through the various Galician and Spanish examples from recent years, the expressions of nationalist discourse and the processes of the nationalization of culture are susceptible to the introduction of surprising syncretisms and agreements. This would account for—I would underscore once again—the vitality of those processes and the interest in studying living ethnographic practices through which this vitality is allowed to flourish. We saw in chapter 5 how the application of such a suggestive and elastic typology as that proposed by G. Stocking hardly stood up to the classification of anthropological practices that have recently arisen in *España de las autonomías* and to the way they remained committed to older ethnographic interests.

According to Clifford, it is possible to say that an approach carried out according to the criteria used by Raymond Williams in *The Country and the City*—a key text in cultural studies—could clarify the situation in terms of our understanding the ethnographic practices generated from the nationalist discourses of the nineteenth century. On the contrary, absent here—or only sparsely detectable—are the observation of and record of the social practices of a "participant observer" ethnographer, which are more similar to the academic practices on which we place a greater value. It would be easy to conclude that today's anthropologists recognize themselves with greater facility in the writing and in the type of observations registered by the "naturalist" novelists of the end of the nineteenth century, for example. These writers made field notes with great assiduity and had a decided interest in the detailed description of social contexts (see, generally, Geertz 1988); the same could be said, from another perspective, of the reports of politicians and administrators.

Some of the representatives of the generation that was involved in the institutionalization of anthropology as an academic discipline in Portugal have tried to establish the most important coordinates in the history of ethnography as it was practiced in the country until the end of the nineteenth century. The most important texts in this endeavor are those by Jorge Freitas Branco (1986 [1985]), João de Pina-Cabral (1991) and João Leal (1988, 1993, 1993b, 1996 and 1997). The differences in emphasis and relative depth that characterize each of these works are not discussed here; though I would like to point out a preoccupation that they all share. They all attempt to discern points of contact with older yet valued theories in the annals of academic anthropology in polymath authors recognized as ethnographers or ethnologists in the last decades of the nineteenth century. This research is mainly concerned with the degree of relevance in the work of these polymaths to the terms of debate that held sway at the beginning of the most famous of the "anthropologies of the construction of empire," English social anthropology. Special emphasis was given to the memory of figures like Consiglieri Pedroso (1851–1910), Adolfo Coelho, Teófilo Braga, Rocha Peixoto (1866–1909), and, more equivocally, the extensive activity of Leite de Vasconcelos, which continued into the 1930s.

We should remind ourselves that the possibilities for recognizing such affinities are extremely scarce, affected, as they are, by syncretisms that were irrelevant or only ephemerally expressed. This became gradually clearer after the initial enthusiasms. What is more, I believe that this research into antecedents was not justified and lasted too long. The discernment of a rousing object of study—nationalism—and the relevant place of disseminated ethnographic practices that embodied it remained obscured.

We can say that contemporary Portuguese anthropology is not, in theoretical terms, nationally anchored: its most significant conceptual references are imported. The recognition of this fact should not be unduly exaggerated; and I believe, as a matter of fact, that no one in Portuguese universities is preoccupied with doing so. It is for this reason that Portuguese anthropology's past engagement with nation building could become the object of pure research more easily than it could—for reasons that I would now like to explain—in Galicia.

The approaches to the history of works of ethnographic interest in Portugal cited in the penultimate paragraph suggest a hiatus that lasted for some decades, which is marked by the absence of proposals for work thought to be significant, aside from certain isolated contributions by Rocha Peixoto and Adolfo Coelho that came about relatively late in the day. Starting in the 1910s, we would have observed a process of degeneration—or to use an even stronger word that I happened to hear, of *cafrealização*—a "going progressively native," contextualized, from the beginning, by certain important works produced in the nineteenth century wherein some—though few—references deriving from anthropological theories circulating abroad can be found.

Leaving aside this play on words, or at least its derogatory connotations, I believe that this process of "nativization" was indeed an observable phenomenon, if we see it as a manifestation of the intense nationalizing process experienced during the first half of the twentieth century, in which the uses of ethnography were particularly concentrated. Indeed, the disappointment over the quality of the ethnography conducted in Portugal in the beginning of the twentieth century is longstanding. As a comparative reference let us look at the perspective of Ernesto Veiga de Oliveira in a text from 1968. Here he wants to account for the first twenty years of the activities of the Centro de Estudos de Etnologia Peninsular, presented with the systematic intent to impose academic rigor on a corrupted field of study:

> Without even speaking of this irresponsible amateurism, the ethnographic research itself practiced by scholars with academic training (though not specialized), based on antiquated and out-of-date theories and molds, did not respond to the demands of a discipline that was in the vanguard of the social sciences, enriched with all of the discoveries that were emerging from this field. ... And primarily not only in the old masters—and justifiably so—but also for those who follow them (and who never go beyond them), ethnography continued to be merely a descriptive activity whose object was the study of the "tradition" conceived statically and as an end in itself, and which depicted the culture of enclosed societies isolated in space, doing so under the influence of their localist conditioning. (Oliveira 1968: 35)[2]

At the head of the so-called movement of renovation was the figure of Jorge Dias, the director of the Centro de Estudos de Etnologia Peninsular, whose training was undertaken within the context of the anthropology of "nation building," *die Volkskunde.* Later, Dias attempted to bring his references up to date when confronted with the influential canon represented by the American tradition under the tutelage of Franz Boas. This *aggiornamento*—as proposed by Oliveira in the 1962 text—with the anthropology of "empire building" was marred by a range of equivocations, as João de Pina-Cabral (1991) has so reasonably concluded.

A note by the influential geographer Orlando Ribeiro in the preface of one of Dias's first relevant works sheds some light on some of the questions at hand: "The discontinuity of a university tradition, which was never able to organize itself, explains the appearance of a young ethnographer who owed nothing, in terms of his initial impulse, to the Portuguese school. Dr. António Jorge Dias, also a university professor, began his studies in ethnography at the University of Munich, where he received his doctorate in *Volkskunde*" (1948: x). The absence of academic institutionalization is noteworthy when it comes to its consequences for ethnographic research; notable as well is Dias's later commitment to the "Portuguese School," a commitment that we see clearly expressed in a 1952 text, *Bosquejo Histórico de Etnografia Portuguesa,* where he presents a genealogical reading of ethnographic research in Portugal, recognizing the few "masters" most deserving of praise. At the end of the lineage, outlined as it is, the author can present himself as a modernizer, resolving to embody the rupture himself. However, he is obliged—despite his criticism—to recognize the importance of the commitments to the history, the institutions, and the institutional ethnographic practices indeed still then in existence in Portugal. The following phrase is significant: "The second Lisboan organ is the Secretariado Nacional de Informação, represented by the 'Museu de Arte Popular' which while without scientific intentions, constitutes a great event within Portuguese ethnography" (1952: 36). For those who know the "Museu de Arte Popular," untouched since its foundation, the meaning of this phrase can only be viewed as ambiguous. However, the more rigorous scientist in J. Dias brings him later to question the curious posture of Luís Chaves, an influential figure during those years: "After this brief and generalized portrayal, it is important to understand what is happening in our country. Is the present phase simply using ethnography for exhibitions, concerts, competitions, etc., in order to maintain national characteristics and to recuperate ... as Luís Chaves intends. I do not believe so, it would be the negation of science itself" (1952: 36).

By 1952, the practical uses of ethnography had been underway intensively for some decades and (relatively) successfully for the purposes of nationalization. It was later, under the authoritarian regime (after 28 May) that the state began to finance and support pedagogic events that had an ethnographic cast, now instrumentalized for political ends. As Rui Ramos amusingly said (1994) it was "a lack of money" that often hampered already clear nationalizing intentions in the final years of the constitutional monarchy and during the First Republic (1910–1926). The Estado Novo demonstrated itself to be more capable and ready to support these initiatives early on during the first stages of its institutionalization.

We can give examples of other versions of the lineage of ethnographic interests in addition to the proposals of Jorge Dias and Veiga de Oliveira, or those of contemporaneous academic anthropologists. Comparable, for example, is the approach of José Leite de Vasconcelos—one of the recognized "masters" of the "Portuguese school"[3]—who links the period of "scientific" ethnography to the studies carried out by the Grimm brothers.[4] With respect to Portugal, Vasconcelos brought attention to authors from a somewhat earlier period—who had little to do with ethnological specialization per se—like Almeida Garrett (1799–1854), João Pedro Ribeiro (1758–1839), and Alexandre Herculano. This is the period in which the author, quite familiarly, situates himself. (1980: 232 and 250). I believe that we should take this opinion into due account, since not only is this a register of the first romantic manifestations of nationalist sensibilities, but the career of Leite de Vasconcelos unfolds between 1870 and 1930, which coincides exactly with the "age of nationalisms" and its intensification.

The suggestion made by Leite de Vasconcelos at the end of his career will be taken up a bit later by a more recent figure—also surprisingly, hardly known today—who is unavoidable in the history of the practice of ethnology and ethnography of the first half of the twentieth century, António Mendes Correia.[5] Correia synthesized some of the most prominent characteristics of the studies that were inspired by nationalism soon after its first wave at the beginning of the nineteenth century. In 1933, the author has the following to say about Alexandre Herculano and his pioneering *História de Portugal*:

> The science of ethnic origins had already been born when in 1846 the first volume of the *História de Portugal* appears. … This led to the first steps in the modern academic studies of Anthropology, Linguistics, Pre-History, Ethnology, etc. "*História Militante*" was about to begin, an appropriate expression with which Henri Berr designated archeological excavations as understood in the broadest sense. (1933: 10)

In interpreting the passage just cited we should take into account the periodization proposed and draw attention to the use of the adjective "*militante*" as much as we do to the "archeological" character attributed to the intertwined group of disciplines mentioned as having come out of the nineteenth century. The similarities recognized to exist between archeology, ethnology, and linguistics were commonplaces. For example, in the phrase transcribed by Correia, various disciplines are linked in a way that would be perceived as obvious to any educated European of the nineteenth century; even in 1933—an epoch of newly intensified nationalist activity—these disciplines could hardly be considered anachronistic and, for example, in Galicia could be understood to be implicitly supported even today.

The practice of a *história militante* [partisan history] imposes criteria of legitimization that are internal, nonuniversal, and specific to each nation-state. It suggests terms of truths that only exist on "this side of the Pyrenees," to paraphrase Pascal's famous line.* But we should also take into account the observations of Löfgren (1989) and of Thyssen (2000) on the international similarities that the do-it-yourself kit of nationalism has imposed as a counterpoint to this ironic perspective. Here, what results—if we take into account simultaneously the plurality of the social uses of the term *ethnography* throughout more than a century—is the imposition of very diffuse limits when it comes to the possibilities for working out its history, which should be guided mainly by the attention to its uses as resources of nationalization. The extent of ethnographic practices that are recognizable in the context of processes of the nationalization of cultures is extremely fluid: they extend even to the tradition of bucolic poetry, to novels and to painting, as well as to the ethnomimetic practices of various social strata, to cinematic scripts and those used for ethnographic processions, etc. In general, it is necessary that analysts are familiar with the aesthetic criteria that predominate in a given epoch so that they can trace the manifestations of ethnographic dispositions and their consequences in the objectification of new national cultures.

The term *neogarrettismo* was employed by Jacinto Prado Coelho in order to classify all the most important aesthetic and intellectual works that appeared in Portugal starting at the end of the nineteenth century (1976); the author refers to the duration of this widespread ideological current with a neo-Romantic character that lasted throughout the twentieth century. António José Saraiva and Óscar Lopes, for their part, have noted the contours of a late-Romantic revivalism at the end of the nineteenth century. The evolution of these sensibilities gave rise to

---

* "There are truths on this side of the Pyrenees which are falsehoods on the other."

various currents, the authors distinguishing between "neogarrettismo," "nacionalismo," "integralismo," the "renascença portuguesa" and "saudosismo" (1989: 1013; also Lopes 1987: 209–71). José Augusto França corroborates these suggestions in a more ample record, documenting the persistence—which he refers to, in passing, as anachronistic—of expressions of a romantic character in Portugal up to the present (França 1993). Eduardo Lourenço has said that romanticism has introduced a dimension of "interioricity" into the collective reality of the country.

It is important to note—in addition to the possible detailed discriminations among different schools and ideological positions—that the intention to create a national culture was a commitment shared by these various groups of intellectuals. At the time similar dispositions existed across the whole of Europe—we have looked closely at the Galician example—and in different places around the world transforming each of its casuistical manifestations as the situated existence of a hegemonic "international ideology"; as O. Löfgren said, "the international thesaurus is transformed into a specific national lexicon, local forms of cultural expression, which tend to vary from nation to nation" (1989: 22)

Among the pioneering *neogarrettistas,* J. Prado Coelho identifies Leite de Vasconcelos, Alberto Sampaio (1841–1908), Adolfo Coelho, Joaquim de Vasconcelos (1849–1938), Martins Sarmento, and Rocha Peixoto, for example. Among these names, it is Adolfo Coelho and Teófilo Braga who are pioneers in introducing an interest in ethnological questions in Portugal, and who are still acknowledged in the historiographic work of contemporary anthropologists (Branco 1985, 1986; Leal 1993; Pina-Cabral 1991; see also Ramos 1994). But, taking into account the thematic plurality of these authors' studies—and still others of their contemporaries with assured places in the pantheon of the most recognized Portuguese ethnologists—they must really only be considered reluctant practitioners of ethnography, if we are to value "presentist" criteria (Stocking 1968; Di Brizio 1995).[6]

Certain bibliographic references from the mid-twentieth century, in which one finds an inventory of ethnographic interests in Portugal, suggest a definite impression of fluidity in the criteria for judging what is "ethnographic" and who is an "ethnographer" or "ethnologist." In random texts by José Leite de Vasconcelos, António Mendes Correia, Luís Chaves (1888–1975), Fernando Castro Pires de Lima, Jaime Lopes Dias (1890–1977), Flávio Gonçalves (1829–1987), and even Jorge Dias we can find earlier valorizations, which confirm our impression that they are different from the criteria that we employ today.[7] An empathy for "ethnographic attitudes" (Silva 1987) that influenced the more popular books of Almeida Garrett or Júlio Dinis (1839–1871) seem the most significant in those sketches of intellectual genealogies. For example, Fernando C. Pires de Lima (1948) wrote many paragraphs praising the ethnographic contents of the works of Almeida Garrett, Júlio Dinis, and Camilo C. Branco (1825–1890); on the contrary the attention given to the works of Rocha Peixoto or of Consiglieri Pedroso is minimal. These are authors to whom Luís Chaves does not even refer in his meticulous inventory of ambitious titles—*Fases da Cultura Etnográfica* (1947)[8]—where the ethnographic qualities of the works by Bernardim Ribeiro (1482?–1552?), D. Francisco Manuel de Melo (1608–1666), and even the painter, Silva Porto, are enthusiastically referred to.

In 1913, the young Jaime Cortesão gave an account of the motivations that impelled—or should have impelled—ethnographic studies. "So that a national consciousness is finally formed or clarified, giving us an account of a definitive unity, the knowledge of the collection of popular songs is indispensable, as the whole spirit of the people is revealed therein. ... The study of popular songs, a branch of another vaster study—Popular Traditions—has for a long time been of concern in all of the nations of Europe, urged on more by national sentiment, than by scientific curiosity" (n. d.: 9). These judgments, proclaimed on the brink of the "war of nations"—and whose reasoning Almeida Garrett and Alexandre Herculano would have accepted—suggest an interest in conceiving the greater part of ethnographic studies in Portugal during the nineteenth and twentieth centuries as a mere object of study. I believe the same would be the case with the works of Jorge Dias, in spite of his notorious scientific scruples and a greater familiarity with the anthropological concerns that are still of interest today. The same Jaime Cortesão—yet fifty years after the citation above—impressed by a reading of the most famous works of Jorge Dias, would say of it that it was a "living remnant of pre-history, utterly rare in a Europe so evolved, Vilarinho is a flash that comes to us still hot with humanity and pregnant with lessons, from the abyssal cavern of the first ages" (1966: 30). We can read the work by Jorge Dias—or his later and more famous work, *Rio de Onor. Communitarianismo Agro-Pastoril*—secure in the knowledge that the "first ages" that are analyzed therein are those of the Portuguese nation (see also Dias and Oliveira 1962).

At this point we can do away with the parable told by John Davis about the possibility of placing young British "Mediterraneanists" in the field with Tylorean professors, unaware of the new theoretical trends in anthropology, like the old Japanese soldiers lost in the jungle without any idea that World War II had ended (Davis 1977; see also the interesting gloss by Leal 2001). That which for the British social anthropologists from the 1950s to the 1970s would be like finding the "skeletons in the closet" of a different Europe, anachronistic and exotic (Cutileiro 1971b), would have, at the end of the day, little chance of happening, at least in Portugal. Here, there was only a single figure who was influenced by Tylor and by other evolutionist theoreticians: Consiglieri Pedroso. In the Portuguese case we can say that the particularism of ethnographic interests went beyond the imagination of British social anthropologists, like John Davis. This oddity would have reflected their lack of familiarity with the cultural dimensions of the national sphere, certainly relevant for one whom, in this context, would proceed into the "field."[9]

At this stage, I take up the suggestion that there was a very diverse idea of what constituted ethnography, that its practitioners were engaged in a process of apparent "nativization" of the theoretical writings that they employed, which in turn led to a conspicuous use of such ideas in the nationalization of the masses. In connection with this point, it is worth citing at length an important remark by Rui Ramos on Portugal as it moved from the nineteenth into the twentieth century:

> One of the most crass errors the historians have made has been to see these *"reaportuguesadores"* as provincials or simply naïve. The most important of these writers, painters and architects have studied abroad—and what is more: their attempts at *"reportuguesamento"* correspond to what in the same period was happening in England, in France and in Germany, etc. … As such, it would be possible to understand that *"aportuguesamento"* constituted one of the most radically cosmopolitan and modern intellectual movements. Also one of the most "democratic" ones, in the sense that an art for the middle classes was defined, without the obscure Greco-Latin references of the ancien régime. (1994: 570–71)

Portugal, a state spoken of as a nation throughout the last century and a half, owes to its very specific anthropology of nation building many effective possibilities for being imagined that remain active and are manipulated to create new social facts even today. Thus, it would be naïve to think that it is possible to understand well a variety of very contemporary phenomena if we do not take into consideration the particularities of the "Portuguese School" of ethnography, in spite of the fact that we do not recognize pertinent reasons for identifying ourselves with it professionally.

An Argument about Images

Examining the theoretical problems that emerged in his own texts on the history of Portuguese ethnography, João Leal recently described the "weakening" of the theoretical concerns of Portuguese ethnography between the 1910s and the 1930s and 40s (1996: 31). The author questions this, adding that his observations still need further analysis. Leal even suggests that "the non-institutionalization of ethnography and anthropology in Portugal until the 1940s ... [and] a merging marked by a folklorizing nationalism lacking in theoretical ambitions are some of the endogenous factors at the base of my [earlier] observations. But it is also be important to see to what extent the Portuguese situation of this period does not form part of a wider pattern, which extends to a variety of national traditions of European anthropology of the same epoch" (1996: 31). He then remarks that the proximity with the privileged dominion "of this nationalist ethnography with a folklorist orientation—'popular art'"—is most salient in the work of José Leite de Vasconcelos during the 1920s; and that the important magazine *Alma Nova* in its third series "adopted the subtitle, *Revista de Ressurgimento Nacional,* creating a program which aimed to awaken 'the cult of the virtues of the motherland and love of things Portuguese.' It brought in ethnographers like Luís Chaves and Cláudio Basto, in the context of opting for a nationalistic ethnography which would pay special attention to the study of regional dress" (1996: 32–33).

The remarks cited above are geared to the characteristics of the ethnography of the early 1920s: we can note a "theoretical weakening" and a lack of ambition, as well as an inflated attention being paid to folklore, "popular art," dress, and images in general. It is even suggested that this pattern would be replicated at an international level, a pertinent opinion that is conferred by consulting some of the comparative literature that is available. I believe that these kinds of concerns date to an even earlier period, with clear expressions already coming out of the end of the nineteenth century, also at an international level, and that these tendencies were intensified from the 1910s to the 1920s.

The consolidation of the knowledge of nations was dependent upon a scientific discourse that developed in new academic disciplines—or in reformulated ones—in the last decades of the nineteenth century. Jacques Le Goff has said that a "new civilization of inscription" arose in mid-nineteenth-century Europe; he would refer to this as an epoch in which "the academic movement aimed at furnishing the monuments of remembrance to the collective memory of nations accelerated" (1984: 38).[10]

If we take the example of what happened in Portugal—or in Spain and Galicia—it would be risky to view academic studies as central, or even as particularly important, to the definition of countries and their internal diversity. These studies were dependent upon previous proposals that, while not very rigorous, were nevertheless quite efficacious. The total sum of available resources for describing a country's overall characteristics, and the distinctions between its different parts, reads like a palimpsest of literary, iconographic, and academic representations that are inextricably superimposed.

Michel Roncayolo has said the following about geographic readings of the French countryside at the end of the nineteenth century: "The wise reader is no stranger to the aesthetic, the stereotype of the journey and the discovery of the exotic, to the description of the countryside as a performance or an object of consumption" (1986: 488).

Roncayolo's characterization suggests important analogies for the intersection of references that marked the influential ways of speaking about Portugal and its inhabitants in the nineteenth century, ways that also survived into the next century. Recognition of the fecundity of these mixed processes of classification was accepted by the scholars of the day, such as Sampaio Bruno (1857–1915), when he refers to the efficaciousness of knowledge previously obtained through the "the suggestive intensity in literary works" (Bruno 1987: 181), or even by José Leite Vasconcelos, who said with great solemnity at the end of his career: "Artists often anticipate what researchers of history discover at the cost of tiring mental labor" (1980a: 246). In the imaginative theory of Oliveira Martins—the "historian-artist"—we would find a good example of what Vasconcelos had in mind (or in the laudatory pages he wrote on Almeida Garrett and on Alexandre Herculano's *O Pároco de Aldeia*).[11] If we return to the Galician examples, to the purposefully cultivated memory of Rosalía de Castro or Castelao—which contrasts with a relative neglect of the "hard-working" "historical researcher," Manuel Murguía—we will recognize one more illustration of the unequalled efficacy of poetic and aesthetic metaphors in the establishment of knowledge about nations (see chapters 2 and 3).

The definition of ethnography as "the art of painting the customs of nations" was contemporaneous with Almeida Garrett.[12] Between 1870 and 1880 a new meaning was consolidated, summarized as the "description of traditions" or, stronger in its insinuations, the "description of tradition," which does not contradict the earlier definition; on the contrary, it strongly depends on it.[13] In the second sense, that which will be retained by the Romantic vision, the *hic et nunc* of the daily life of the subaltern classes of the rural world, re-created in physical images and allegorical texts—set forth in painting, in novels, in the first collections of traditional songs (even the "affected" ones)—might now seem subject to being saved in the group of traditions, as part of the "tradition." Soon there would be a multiplication of possibilities for increasing these assets, which increasingly included registers such as photographs, photo-gravures, and postcards, as techniques of mechanical reproduction that expanded greatly during the last half of the nineteenth century. Vasconcelos and certain of his contemporaries remained surprisingly attentive to these many different types of documents produced in the most diverse circumstances.

As part of the great circuit of "sources of ethnographic investigation" proposed by José Leite de Vasconcelos at the end of his career in 1933, he brought an array of definitively eclectic authors to our attention. Vasconcelos recalls sources as disparate as the *Promptuario Augustiniano das Indulgencias da Correa,* a work of the seventeenth century, or the lit-

Figure 9. Photmaton, young girl dressed in Minho style, ca. 1940.

erary works of Almeida Garrett, Alexandre Herculano, Camilo Castelo
Branco, and Júlio Dinis. But he also draws his sources from—even more
unpredictably—the caricatures of Rafael Bordalo Pinheiro (1846–1905),
or news items from the important daily newspaper, *O Século*. It is worth
citing a suggestive passage from volume I of *Etnografia Portuguesa:*

> For this overflowing of a tendency toward ethnographic studies to have
> occurred, no one would deny the practices of specialized periodicals; and
> some will attribute it to the museums, ergological-industrial exhibitions,
> regionalist congresses and to the artists, due to the execution of works
> inspired by acts and objects of traditional life that are truly inspiring.
> Newspapers and magazines of various kinds compete to develop that
> which is being spoken about: they publish articles on ethnography and
> folklore; others sponsor, for example, song, proverb, or guessing "com-
> petitions" and report on festivities, superstitions and customs. We owe as
> much equally to the illustrated magazines which create, graphically, an
> analogous species; the same could be said of postcards, so much in style
> today everywhere, and where we can see, for example, drawings of dress,
> of the instruments of transport, the "types" of streets, the street peddlers,
> shepherds, entertainers, markets, houses, palaces and castles, a thousand
> things in the end, from the various areas of Portugal. (1980a: 323–24)

In 1933, the author could have also referred to the movie industry, its
sets and costumes, the tradition of carnival processions in the large cities, the first attempts at ethnographic processions, at least one opera, an
operetta, and the theater magazines. Each of these visual and performative registers contained descriptions of the people. Each of them could
be suggestive, could contain preliminary possibilities of verisimilitude
and, thus, possibilities of being used as a "source" for the establishment
of national traditions. I believe that nearly everything said by Vasconcelos in the passage cited above should be highlighted. I also believe that it
suggests our thin knowledge of the ethnographic sensibilities predominant in the age of nationalisms.

As a matter of fact, Vasconcelos pointedly resented the ambiguities
generated through the tremendous efforts the mainstream press spent
in creating images of the country and the people of his period. For example, in volume III of *Etnografia Portuguese,* the scholar lamented the
contamination of his academic arguments by the contingencies generated through the strong market for the *aportuguesamento* of culture. At
issue were the images of the Minho that he used to illustrate the pages
of this part of his magnum opus:

> Fig. II: 42—Minhotan from previous times. The same source as figs.
> 5–10.—Already after the printing of these figures, in the present work

I found out that some of them had come out in *Lusa* and Dr. Cláudio Basto told me that part, or all, of them were being sold as postcards; and the illustrious researcher informed me as well that, according to Figueiredo da Guerra, not all of it is accurate. If I had known this would happen before the printing of the book, perhaps I would have abstained from its reproduction. (1980b: 757)

As a key passage in the citations of Vasconcelos, it points to the existence at the time of an "overflowing of the taste for ethnographic studies," which was susceptible to being expressed by such a great variety of means (Bertho-Lavenir 1988). By following the trail of images, we will understand the importance the polymaths of the "Portuguese school of anthropology" attribute to it (Dias 1952). In an undated and less well-known text, yet one that Flávio Gonçalves tells us was destined for the important magazine, *Portugália,* entitled "The Archeology and Ethnography of Postcards," Rocha Peixoto has the following to say about these mainstays of very widespread images:

It is then an iconic document that rises up and triumphs, thanks to the accessible price, for their novelty and even that they are in style. Many of them are graphically excellent, especially the monochromes. We should distinguish, however, between those dealing with ethnographic subjects that faithfully reproduce scenes, customs and architecture from those that sacrifice reality in the name of some affected and puerile aesthetic. ...

With the preoccupation for all that is new, the concurrence and the usefulness of the photograph and the engraving, the truth is that illustrative subjects are now sought out in remote places that were until now inaccessible even to the most zealous investigators. It is correct to presume that, some years from now, rare will be the monument or regional type that is not registered in this curious and inexpensive gallery of postcards. (1975: 401–2)

It is clear that the great haste to know the country registered above and the massive spread of these images produced serially could only have multiplied the "overflow" referred to by Leite de Vasconcelos. Rocha Peixoto, considered the most rigorous of the ethnographers of the "Portuguese school," also confirms this. In this process of the imagination of the parts of the country and its inhabitants, the selective choice of icons susceptible to being manipulated to serve projects of collective identification also remains a possibility (Chamboredon 1994).

Peixoto's commentary is curious for yet another reason. We know that the author covered the mountains of the north of the country, firmly placing himself—as Flávio Gonçalves said—in the first group of interpreters of one of the most typical aspects of Portuguese *ethnosociologia* (1968: xi).[14] This author resented, as Leite de Vasconcelos did, the competition of other specialists, who were also the makers of images, namely, of "remote places" in the space of the nation-state. The possibilities for conceptualizing such places are enclosed in a space and a time of their own,[15] due to the diversity of contributors: historians, archeologists, and ethnologists, but also thanks to the dynamics of a robust market of images and texts that were anything but serious.

A consultation of the illustrated magazines of the last half of the nineteenth century would suggest that the trails over the northern mountains of the country began to serve those who made images of remote places, a movement that would intensify as the new century approached. Some of the ethnographers that we praise most are of this group. We will also see that a part of the symbols of the "primitive" chosen during this period have lasted until today. Manuel Monteiro (1879–1952)—an art historian and also an important figure in the task of the *aportuguesamento* of the country—had the following to say: "*Sr.* Rocha Peixoto, a gifted man of science, who adds, to his singular erudition, the excellencies of an unmistakable plasticity, in a lucid précis, *kodaquisou* [photographed] the *vivenda barrosã* [Barroso house], which he personally examined and thoroughly scrutinized" (in Biel 1902–1908, vol. VII, sp.).

It is clear that there is much to think about with respect to those places or objects that become iconic. (Herzfeld 1997). Rocha Peixoto did not photograph *any* "vivenda barrosã, but rather *the* "vivenda barrosã," as Monteiro suggests.[16] This tendency toward typification was apparent in Rocha Peixoto's earlier preoccupations, for example, in a 1904 text originally entitled "A Casa Portugueza (a propósito do novo prédio da Rua do Conde)" and later published under a more restrictive title, "A Casa Portuguesa."[17] This curious text—collected by Flavio Gonçalves in *Estudos de Etnografia e Arqueologia* in the complete works of Peixoto— was published in *Serões,* a widely distributed illustrated magazine from the beginning of the century.

An article from another more lasting and influential illustrated magazine of the turn of the century, *A Illustração Portuguesa,* documented the pedagogic potential of postcards and the intensity of their use, preceding Rocha Peixoto's reflection noted above:

> They say that in Portugal nearly a million cards of this type are employed in illustrating our streets, our squares, portraits of our celebrated men, picturesque corners of our hamlets, the lovely customs of our provinces, the ruins of our centuries-old towers, our ancient churches and our grand houses where so many beautiful things have happened.

He also refers to one of the possibilities for collective identification that postcards can provide:

> … the most picturesque corners of our land, the most beautiful streets of our cities, the most singular aspects of our life, the faces of our peasants will show foreigners that we have beautiful places and beautiful faces,[18] Negroes do not live on this side of the Pyrenees as some imagine. (*A Illustração Portuguesa*, no. 38, 1906)

This last question was not a minor one at the time. It worried Rocha Peixoto, leading him to write a newspaper article some years earlier, in which he also dealt with the manipulation of images and the possibility of their use in circulating depressing stereotypes of the nation among European academics. In the text entitled "O sangue do preto no povo português" [The Black Blood in the Portuguese People], Rocha Peixoto discusses the fact that one of his countrymen had sent certain photographs to the "antropologista Zaborowski" (Sigismond Zaborowski-Moindron 1851–1928) and the hurried conclusions that this allowed:

> This singular thoughtlessness even explains the exhibition of seven representatives of the Portuguese people in the book already alluded to and entitled "Le Portugal." They are: haberdashers, traveling merchants, a languid elegant clerk and, as an example of the Portuguese woman, a girl just released from an asylum!

> The book, *Le Portugal*, which certainly must have had great success on the market, and now this presentation to the Anthropology Society of France, will do us that deplorable service. (1975: 268–70)

It was this circulation of faces representing the Portuguese nationality on the international market of the images of nations (Thiesse 2000) that made Peixoto indignant. We can correctly deduce from his phrases the suggestion of a grave lack of confidence—the breaking of tacit principles of concealing that which belongs to the sphere of the "intimate." We have the unveiling—"puerile," it should be noted—of what happens behind the doors of the nation, which, in the end, includes haberdashers in the gallery of types normally recognized.[19] I am following Michael Herzfeld's argument in these commentaries, who has the following to say with respect to contemporary Greece: "Hence cultural intimacy. It is no accident that the pat Greek phrase for the defense of that intimacy, often heard as a reason for not discussing admitted weaknesses of the nationalist argument before a foreign audience, should be: *ta en iko mi en dhimo* (matters of house [classical Greek *oikos*] [should] not [be exposed] in the public sphere)" (1997: 95).

None of the many photographs taken by Rocha Peixoto survive as identifying icons of the areas that he traveled through, such as the Minho, the Trás-os-Montes, the north of the country, or even Portugal as a whole. In the context of what we understand ethnography to be today, with its origins in the nineteenth century, the documentary photographs taken by Rocha Peixoto are not, paradoxically, "ethnographic." The images of the mountain dwellers—of Gralheira, Arga, Montemuro, among others—miserable and ungainly, captured by the naturalist sensibility of Rocha Peixoto, were not used in the production of a nationalized culture of the masses, which took place in the decades of the twentieth century that followed. On the contrary, more fortunate were the representations of "popular art" or "typical dress" gathered around the *Terra Portuguesa* and other even older products, texts, and images, dating back to the time in which ethnography was defined in the dictionary as the "art of painting the customs of nations." Thus, we can argue that anthropology, "weakened theoretically" during the last years of the nineteenth century, was mainly capable of producing images and did so profusely; through making them, it was able to demonstrate its modernity and also contribute to the production of the nation-state and its monuments (Appadurai 1986; Le Goff 1984; Herzfeld 1992).

Here, by way of the various references suggested—emphasizing first the recognized place of paintings, postcards, and photographs in the margins of the works of the great ethnographers, then the illustrators and illustrations between the lines of João Leal's text (1996), or, more detailed yet, Rui Ramos's calling our attention to the importance of a market of images and objects that symbolized the country and the dis-

Figure 10. Young women dressed in Minho style. Postcard, ca. 1910.

tinguished parts of it, produced by "naturalists," "neo-romantics," and "modernists" since the beginning of the twentieth century (cf. Medeiros 1995, 1996)—we can introduce a suggestion by James Fernandez: "Not only do the subtleties of consensus pose a challenge to the notion of 'generalized belief,' there is also the problem of the process of collective mentation—the kind of information processing that goes on in the crowd. It is my view, and here I am in agreement with Le Bon, that the crowd's thinking mainly takes place through an argument 'of images'" (1989).

The circulation of images of the Minho beginning at the end of the nineteenth century was a mass phenomenon that affected the growing middle classes, which were able to learn their nationhood in many different ways. The vehicles of this process were graphic representations and texts produced in series, tourism, parodic mimeses of the people in processions, Carnival dances, parties, student celebrations, and so on. This learning process occurred with apparent freedom under the democratic regimes consisting of a constitutional monarchy and the First Republic. But there were also dimensions of the process that were starkly imposed—along with certain strains of totalitarianism—under the Estado Novo, when the prominence of the Minho as the chosen province of the nationalizing discourse began to decline and images of the other provinces became abundant, as we have already learned from Oliveira Martins's descriptions of 1879. It is worth citing a later formulation by another author:

> If the importance of ethnography and of Folklore is demonstrated and cannot be contested, it is urgent that its constitutive elements, which are many, be spread by all forms possible: by textbooks, literature, by public talks, by exhibitions, by processions, by the cinema and by the radio, especially the latter, which reaches all houses and all ears but without adulterations and obeying the highest principles of morality, composure and patriotism. (Dias 1956: 22)

This sentence was written by Jaime Lopes Dias (1890–1977)—one of the most prolific ethnographers of the midcentury period—and what he has to say is surprisingly modern and completely conscious of the available technical resources and their capacity to create a totalitarian production of mass culture. But these types of preoccupations can be found in two very different European personalities from previous decades. There is Antonio Gramsci, who said: "Folklore must not be considered an eccentricity, an oddity, or a picturesque element, but as something which is very serious and to be taken seriously. Only in this way will the teaching of folklore be more efficient and really bring about a new culture among the broad popular masses"(1985: 191). On the other hand we have António Ferro (1895–1956), in charge of propaganda for the Portuguese authoritarian regime from 1933 to 1949, whose action can be understood in the context of complete political involvement with similar concerns to those that are suggested in the extract from Gramsci above. Ferro said, for his part, appropriating the words of a French critic upon the premiere of the famous ballet *Verde Gaio,* the choreography and costumes of which were clearly nationalized, full of ethnographic citations: "Today we are entranced by the hastened rhythm of modern life and trained in the school of the rapid ideograms of the cinema, that make us used to thinking in images. … the 'screen' and the choreographic lyricism blend elegantly in a civilization that has forgotten the luxurious cost of empty hours in favor of the problem of a collective and accelerated culture" (1950: 102). Ferro exercised an enormous power in the spread of a new culture, one that is nationalized, from the beginnings of the 1930s; however, we can already find similar metaphors in the texts of his younger years, when he was a young "modernist" during the 1910s (Ramos 1994), texts contemporaneous with the moments in which ethnography had become "exclusively descriptive" (Oliveira 1968) or, formulated differently, had begun to experience a theoretical "weakness."

Notes

1. I found this same phrase applied to Galicia—origin unidentified—in a much later text by Castelao. It could hardly have been one of J. A. Vieira's original formulations, keeping in mind the cosmopolitan circulation of Celtic stereotypes from the beginning in of the nineteenth century (Chapman 1992; see chapter 10).

2. This passage seems hardly adequate to the task of characterizing the production being criticized. It contained the people—the country's undifferentiated group of the lower classes—which was the object of ethnographic interpretation, and there were ample spaces that referenced the classification of their results: municipalities, provinces, and even the whole country. The lines referred to here would be more characteristic of what implicitly justifies Jorge Dias's community studies. These monographs were eminent examples of the construction of localities in the sense of Appadurai, cited above, and they were referenced theoretically by precepts of the *Volkskunde* (a very specific anthropology of nation building) (Stocking 1982; Bendix 1997; Bausinger 1990).

3. Vasconcelos is, however, in my opinion a little-known figure, and his place in the construction of a genealogy of ethnographic interests in Portugal is ambiguously rendered in the literature. The recognition of his importance has begun to establish itself in a clearer fashion as he has been mentioned in recent works by Branco (1994 and 1995) and Leal (1996).

4. Compare affinities and particularisms in the European context in studies by Bendix (1997), Herzfeld (1986), and Aguilar Criado (1990), for example.

5. Mendes Correia was mainly involved in physical anthropology and archeology, having been an institutionally influential figure with important international contacts (he was the key figure in terms of having contacts with Galician intellectuals during the 1930s and 1940s, as we already mentioned above).

6. As to one of the personalities of reference, Teófilo Braga, a colleague told me with a good bit of wit: "He was even President of the Republic. ..." The observation obviates the need for any further commentary, yet we might add, in the same tone, that Braga was one of the most influential ideologues of republicanism and even an organizer of public celebrations geared toward nationalizing on the occasion of the 1880 commemorations of Camões. This was an important moment in the pedagogical use of civic corteges as an instrument for the nationalization of the Portuguese masses.

7. It is important to note that the authors referred to now—with the exception of Flávio Gonçalves—were influential figures in the institutional contexts that fostered the authorized reproduction of "Portuguese ethnography."

8. The texts cited by Fernando C. Pires de Lima and Luís Chaves appeared in *Mensário das Casas do Povo,* a widely circulated magazine that was present in many Portuguese parishes. These intentions to popularize are very similar to the articles included by Risco in *A Nosa Terra* under the epigraph, "What all Galicians must know." These are discussed above.

9. J. Davis recognized anthropologists' intimidation in the face of the overabundance of historical documents in these contexts that social anthropologists had begun to look at.

10. In Portugal, academic practices geared toward the creation of "monuments of memory" intensified beginning in the 1870s. Local practitioners of disciplines like geography, physical anthropology, ethnology, archeology, and musicology began to appear; the writing of history was once again taken up and popularized (Ribeiro 1977; Vasconcelos 1980; Catroga 1993).

11. See Vasconcelos 1980a.

12. This is the definition given in the 1831 edition of the *Dicionário de Morais* (Vasconcelos 1980a: 18).

13. The apologetic definitions of this term in Vasconcelos's first important text from 1882 are suggestive. It is nationalized Portuguese "tradition" that he is trying to define (cf. Vasconcelos 1986; Guerreiro 1986).

14. The reference to Gonçalves is suggestive: we know how this aspect remained typical in Portuguese ethnography, running through the works of Jorge Dias and even being echoed in the much later works of Brian O'Neill (1984) and of Joaquim Pais de Brito (1996).

15. Compare, for example, Ardener 1989; Herzfeld 1986, 1987; Anderson 1991; Smiles 1994.

16. Around 1900 "remote places" like Soajo, Caldas de Gerês, Castro Laboreiro, and Barroso would have been easily recognized by the readers of illustrated magazines. The iconic figuration of these places had already begun to be spread through the lithography used in the pioneering magazines, like *O Panorama* and the *Revista Universal Lisbonense,* which were being published beginning in the mid-1800s. Barroso—with its thatched houses and *a barrosã de capucha* [a typical local woman dressed on harsh woolen cap] that Peixoto *kodaquisou*—was already one of the "national landscapes" (Medeiros 1995; cf. Belgum 1998).

17. Nationalizing preoccupations analogous to those that Rocha Peixoto expresses in the cited article can be found in Galician newspapers and magazines of the 1910s through the 1930s, for example in *A Nosa Terra,* but as well in the now forgotten *Vida Gallega.* In these publications, one could find announcements for prizes for monographs on *A Casa Galega,* the airing of the plan to nationalize the *Casa de Rosalía,* and discussions of how Galician the recent work of the most important contemporary architects was. At the beginning of the 1920s, Goméz Román, a Galicianist architect, introduced a model for the Galician house—a project that he wanted to create for Castelao's residence, in the form of a present to the famous leader on behalf of the newspaper, *Galicia a Castelao.* The "Galician house" would become an important object of reflection in the context of Galician ethnography, for example, in the work of Xaquín Lorenzo, but also for contemporary anthropologists, and principally J. A. Fernández de Rota, who all attempted to create typologies.

18. A good part of the covers of that famous magazine comprised the faces of "female peasants," many of them quite "beautiful," nearly always dressed "à moda do Minho," embellished with all the turn-of-the-century trappings and unequivocally considered through antonomasia to be the *traje nacional* [the national dress] (Basto 1924, 1930; Medeiros 1995).

19. I came to understand that in the locales of the rural Minho where I did my fieldwork, people were very careful to systematically keep hidden the internal dissension within *casas* [households]. Children were understood to be the weak link, and were taught the arts of dissemblance early on. In the Minho even specific localities, parishes, and municipalities are seen as being easily embarrassed or insulted, that is, capable of losing face in certain kinds of confrontations that involve homologous entities. (This doesn't, as far as I could tell, happen at the provincial level.) Citizens of a country or members of a nation can also lose face, as some of my notes relating to Galicia would suggest.

Chapter 8

The First Portuguese Colonial Exposition and the Ethnographic Representation of the Provinces

The Portuguese Colonial Exposition was held in Oporto between 15 June and the end of September in 1934. In its epoch, this was an important event, even if today it is practically forgotten. Around a million and half people visited the central grounds of the "Palácio das Colónias" [Palace of the Colonies], the name, at the time, of the "Palácio de Cristal [Crystal Palace], in the summer of 1934, when it was transformed temporarily by a façade created along modernist lines.[1] This quantitative data will easily suggest the exposition's importance and social impact on the northern districts of the country since it was one of the first large-scale propagandistic initiatives of the *Estado Novo* and aimed at the masses. The regime was, at the time, still very recent. The Colonial Act [*Acto Colonial*] dated back to 1930 and the new political constitution, the Estado Novo's principal legal reference, was promulgated in 1933 (see the respective "entries" in Rosas and Brito 1996). Recent bibliographies about the first years of the *Estado Novo*—which was marked by ideological effervescence and by intense propaganda—have paid little attention to this early event of 1934. The Portuguese World Exposition, held in 1940 in Lisbon, attracted much more interest. The latter was an initiative that could count on better material support, attracted more visitors, and left more ostentatious monuments (see, for example, Acciaiuoli 1998; França 1974).

In addition to exhibiting the "colonies" [*colónias*], their products, and inhabitants, new ways of creating an ethnographic representation of the metropole's provinces were experimented with at the Colonial

Figure 11. Palácio da Colónias First Colonial Exhibition, Oporto. Photograph by Alvão, 1934.

Exhibition. This occurred primarily in the context of two large processions held at the time, the "Parada Regional de Entre Douro e Minho" and the "Cortejo Colonial," which were highpoints in the itinerary of events.

It is important to note that historic or ethnographic processions became, in the 1930s, recurring forms of promulgating ideology that were mostly strictly controlled by the authorities of the new regime. The greatest interest of the 1934 Exposition resided in the fact that it provided a context for experiments with previously untried ways of representing Portugal that were accessible to the masses; this, despite the fact that the pretext for this pedagogic exercise was the presentation of the different "colonies." In light of the ideology that was being officially consolidated at the time, it was an ample and inclusive community that was being imagined: no less than the "Portuguese empire." Its demonstration would include representations of the metropole and its internal diversity, because the empire, according to the doctrine contained in the Colonial Act of 1931, was configured as an indivisible unity. From then on the colonies began to be thought of as "overseas provinces"—as much of the literature published on the occasion of the Colonial Exposition would suggest—in spite of the fact that this designation would only be consecrated as a legal term in 1951.

We saw in the last chapter how discourse about the nation created at the turn of the nineteenth century became a decisive reference in the consolidation of different ways of describing the Minho province. These were taken up in texts and images and appropriated through leisure activities that were mainly exercised by those members of the top social strata at the national level. In this composition of motifs, a rich and highly determined representation of a provincial culture was sketched out and, as a matter of fact, emulated when clear images of the rest of the provinces were brought together. This happened gradually, mainly beginning in the second decade of the twentieth century. In the 1934 event, the experimental dimension of the new formulas used to link knowledge of the country and its diversity was patent; for this reason, I believe in the particular pertinence of recalling this event.

In this case, what is once again suggested is the influence of the appropriations of ideological, cosmopolitan references in the construction of representations of vernacular cultures. I would like to underline anew the importance that the authority of the state retained as the locus of respective legitimacy. At the Colonial Exposition a popular culture, modern and nationalized, composed of synthetic forms and assessable by the masses, was brought to bear by the hand of the Portuguese state—and the public at which this knowledge was directed was expanding. This included images that represented the regional variety of the metropole and its various provinces, making the exposition a privileged moment for the invention of traditions, some of which were a real success. In fact, some of the forms of ethnographic representation tested in 1934 are still today viewed as legitimate and repeatable, in spite of more than half a century having passed, and many political changes having occurred in Portugal (see the suggestion of Branco 1999).

Traces of a New Culture

The majority of my informants in Oporto knew practically nothing about the Colonial Exposition. However, their childhood memories—of weekend trips to the gardens of the Crystal Palace—accounted for their encounters with certain marks that had been left over from that initiative. Examples would have been the towering monument of white limestone that evoked "the Portuguese colonial spirit," a "colony of monkeys" (on the small lake on which sat the "Aldeia Lacustre Biajoz"), a lion that had survived in a miserable state for some decades afterwards, and an aviary that stank, where exotic birds were maintained for many years. In June of 1934, a journalist had noted without an iota of guilty conscience: "The exoticism of the Colonial Exposition is mostly the result of the presence of indigenous people and the zoological specimens, that provided the public with a motive of exceptional curiosity" (*O Co-*

Figure 12. "Bijagoz island" at the First Colonial Exhibition, Oporto. Photograph by Alvão, 1934.

mércio do Porto Colonial, 16/6/1934). Today practically all traces of the pedagogic initiative that the state promoted in 1934 have disappeared from the gardens of the Crystal Palace.

It is difficult to dramatize the course that my research on memories of the Colonial Exposition of 1934 took in Oporto. The object itself was already remote and had become insignificant for various reasons. These would have to do especially with the vicissitudes of colonial policy in subsequent decades and the decolonization of the 1970s, not to mention a variety of developments that occurred in more recent decades. These would include, namely, integration into the European Union and the production of new forms of objectifying Portuguese culture that contrasted significantly with the attempt in 1934 to educate the masses in an "imperial mentality." In Oporto, during the period of my field research in October of 1999, preparations for the "European Capital of Culture" events that the city would host two years later in 2001 were already in full swing.

Going into the field in Oporto could hardly be seen as an analogue to attending Balinese cockfights, where a fortuitous event would allow a stranger to become involved in the "web of meanings" from a culture different from his own, according to the story told by Clifford Geertz (1983). My work was done in libraries and in a photographic archive, and also through conversations with those who still recalled the changes in the gardens of the Crystal Palace during the decades after the Colonial Exposition. Encountering surviving visitors to the 1934 event—I eventually came across them in a variety of places in the Minho—made it possible mainly to create anecdotal registers of the discrepancies between the intentions to teach an "imperial mentality" supported by the promoters and what people had actually learned.

The clearest articulations of "culture" and the "colonial mentality" that were intended to be linked together in 1934 could be found in texts or photographic registers that documented the different displays that the "Palace of the Colonies" hosted or the variety of parallel initiatives promoted at the time. Of the great exhibitions, Burton Benedict tells us with some irony: "They were presenting an ordered world. Many of these ideas could be seen in concrete (or at least plaster) form at the expositions" (1983: 2).[2] Retrospectively, we get a sense of order and clarity from the written, graphic, and photographic documentation that the exposition produced. All mention of the conflicts that marked Portuguese society of the period are extinguished, along with the a posteriori failures of this pedagogic exercise in creating "an imperial mentality."

Yet, in addition to the artificial consciousness that the written exhortations, guides, and promotional photographs of the exposition suggest, we should also take note—while weighing the different and random failures that show up in contemporaneous reports—of the relative success over the long term of these new intentions to order ethnographic representations. The exhibition in Oporto in 1934 was an attempt to make people knowledgeable about the "Portuguese empire"—the idea was to create a new and synthesized understanding about an "imagined community" of immeasurable dimension and variety. It now seems justified to use Benedict Anderson's famous notion (1991), if we take into account that Fernando Rosas defines the Colonial Act of 1930 as a "*nationalizing* and centralizing development" (1994: 202, italics mine). This idea to synthetically represent the "empire" manifested itself through articulated ethnographic representations of each of its parts; each one of these arose as an integral component in a vast allegorical composition furnished to the imagination of the masses of visitors. As has already been said, in this context of the articulation of an "imperial" discourse, new ways of creating an ethnographic representation of the "metropolitan" provinces were experimented with. These proved more durable after having overwhelmed the image of an imperial "whole" articulated during the 1930s.

In addition to the commercial interests that gave it substance, the Colonial Exposition was above all an authoritarian exercise in imperial and nationalistic pedagogy conducted under the aegis of the state with the intention of legitimizing the recently established regime, as I will explain below. As such, the target public was the Portuguese people as a whole, even though the relative modesty of the means available would, in practice, restrict its impact mainly to the northern provinces. At the end of the day, for example, the news coverage in Lisbon was spotty at best, and there were not many visitors from the capital and the southern provinces. On the other hand, there were no exhibitors from abroad and very few foreign visitors. For these reasons it ended up being an atypical "great exhibition," given its limited projection across borders.

In spite of the fact that the propaganda was directed at a domestic audience, the organizers still wanted to boast their international success. These attempts were somewhat inflated as far as I can tell, but they would be understandable because the attempt to project the image of nations is one of the strongest characteristics of these kinds of events (Benedict 1983; Greenhalg 1988). This can be found in the *Report and Accounts* produced after the exposition closed.

> The crowds which came to the exposition arrived from all points of the country; some arrived in interminable retinues of trucks, others in special trains, many in automobiles and carts of all kinds—some came by air. The reach of this center of propaganda was enormous and didn't leave a single part of this land uncovered.

> The influence of the Exposition was also felt in foreign lands—much more extensively than was supposed. The whole of the European press, or at least that which is of interest to us, and without this having cost the Management of the exposition very much, made extensive and dignified references, not only to the Exposition itself—which would be expected, but to the pretext of the Exposition, to the work of the *ressurgimento português* [the Portuguese resurgence] and our colonizing efforts. (41)

In fact, the only really numerous groups that came from abroad were those from Galicia, most precisely from Vigo, a city in which certain efforts were made to advertise, which resulted in excursions organized by the local Press Association [Asociación de Prensa]. It is interesting to look at some of the news that resulted from visits by Spaniards because it repeats interesting ambiguities that speak to the lack of knowledge about the regional diversities of the neighboring country and of the persistence with which the *flamenquista* vision (Fernández 1988; see as well chapter 1 of this book) monopolized the possibilities of imagining it.

> Posters from the Oporto *Associação dos Comerciantes* were distributed widely by the establishments located on the principal streets of this city greeting the Galician excursionists who arrive in Oporto today.

> The pretty and artistic posters which represent the Cathedral of Santiago de Compostela have a beautiful figure of an Andalusian woman

in traditional dress which fills the whole poster. (*O Comercio do Porto*, 8/8/1934)

Other initiatives of this friendly welcoming of "Galician" visitors included printing 5,000 broadsheets of the poetry of the "*poetisa* Amélia Vilar." One of the quatrains "in Spanish" is worth quoting: "A carnation of wonder / You are my Lusitanian kiss / Give me a shawl from Manila / I want to seduce you, Gitano."

Modern Representation of an Imagined Community

We should emphasize the point that people at the time, including politicians, journalists, and the majority of the public, accepted the high praise of and the instruction in empire in 1934 as incontestable and legitimate facts. With respect to France and the Parisian Exposition coloniale internationale in 1931—and taking as a point of reference the nearly consensual condemnation of colonialism that we share today—Charles- Robert Ageron comments: "After that, it must have been difficult to imagine those relatively recent times when colonial imperialism triumphed with a clean conscience" (1986: 561). With respect to Portugal, Fernando Rosas also has the following to say of similar purport: "Even the Portuguese Communist Party, despite its adherence to the 3rd International, maintained until 1956 and their 5th Congress, and clearly during the 1930s, a position which actively defended the integrity of the Portuguese colonial heritage" (1994: 412). In 1934, apparently, voices contesting the merits of the initiative were not noticed, beyond a few backbiting *reviralhistas* [those against the *Estado Novo*] with their weak attempts at protest or remote allusions to the badly treated "blacks." These rumors of protest are difficult to reconstruct today; but we know that they were in circulation, given the frequency of accusations of weakness and denunciations of "demoralizing" or "subversive" conspiracies reported in the press. These denunciations—accumulating in the form of asides uncovered in the bibliography that I consulted—point mainly to the somewhat neurotic sensibilities of the men of the new authoritarian regime, still not securely in place.

The "colonial culture" that the regime wanted to transmit in 1934 was founded on allegorical figurations of the uses and customs of the colonized lands; at the same time, the respective economic possibilities were demonstrated with great attention to detail, as can be conferred in the accompanying guide.[3] Taking into account these two most important facets and the general propositions of the intended indoctrination, in 1933 Henrique Galvão had the following to say:

Thus, we will have, in addition to a dazzling representation of the economic activities of the Empire, the most complete ethnographic section ever exhibited in Portugal.

All of the colonies will send indigenous families that will be installed in settings as close as possible to their own and the exhibition will constitute for all Portuguese that lesson in colonialism which is so important. (*Portugal Colonial*, no. 32, 21)

In the following issue of the same publication, in November 1933, Galvão specified the ideological intentions of the exposition and the pedagogical procedures that he wanted to implement when it was held:

Via the exposition as a whole, we will mainly be attempting to give the people instruction: with simplicity, with emotional and picturesque power, using at times naïve elements that will impress and teach them, since for the people it is, and it should be, the First Portuguese Colonial Exhibition.

And if those who visit the Exposition come to substitute their possible prejudices for an exact idea, or illuminate their ignorance with new knowledge, or gain new faith in our future colonial power—the Exposition will certainly have reached the noblest of its goals. (*Portugal Colonial*, no. 33, 11)

In Oporto, in 1934, staged representations—guided displays, dioramas, and processions—were conceived to be visually consumed by the masses. This is the mode of cognitive appropriation that is most characteristic of modernity; Susan Buck-Morss (1990) notes a comment by Sigfried Giedonn—picked up by Walter Benjamin—that compared exhibitions to complete works of art (*Gesamtkunstwerke*), suggesting that they are synthetic visual experiences that work to great pedagogic effect. Yet later, still commenting on Benjamin, the author takes note of the changes brought about by the twentieth century and the exercise of the arts of propaganda directed to the masses: "Whereas, for example, Wagner in the late Romantic era had envisioned individual artistic genius as fabricating a totalizing mythical world through art, the producers of the modern 'collective' imagination were, as the Passagen-Werk exposé emphasizes, photographers, graphic artists, industrial designers, and engineers—and those artists and architects who learn from them" (1990: 255–56). The list proposed by Buck-Morss leaves out one very important type of protagonist, as the example we seem to have before us suggests: modern political commissioners like Henrique Galvão (see the first note in this chapter).

The technical director's emphasis on "simplicity," "emotional power," and the "picturesque" are solid indications of discursive modernization. These were the characteristics that the exposition appropriated and the ideological contents that it used in its aim of ensuring that the event would have some impact on the masses of visitors. However, it is important to underline that the available resources for the Colonial Exposition were ostensively modest, at least when we compare them with similar initiatives that took place at the time in other European countries, namely, the model most directly emulated: the Exposition of 1931 in Paris.[4] The modes of exhibiting colonial populations were well established in 1934, already set by the large exhibitions in the previous century.

In Oporto, the organization employed the same means—though on a very modest scale, as those responsible recognized—to stage the exotic environments that had featured some very exuberant moments at the Exposition coloniale inernationale de Paris in 1931 (Greenhalg 1988; Lebovics 1992; Golan 1995). Henrique Galvão began to direct a new illustrated magazine in 1931 called *Portugal Colonial. Revista Mensal de Propaganda do Império Português,*[5] which contained constant illustrated

Figure 13. A room at the First Colonial Exhibition; note the painted allegory at the bottom. Unknown photographer, n.d.

news of the great exposition being held in France and in whose pages we can say that the idea of a similar initiative in Portugal came to fruition.

In 1934 it was mainly the improvisation and audacious use of certain simple scenographic artifices that succeeded, making up for the very weak material basis of this underfunded endeavor. Special care was taken with the lighting work, some of the technology used for the sets at the Crystal Palace having been ordered from Germany.

In Portugal it was only later, in 1940, that a similar initiative (the "Exposição do Mundo Português" [Portuguese World Exhibition], which was principally a state-sponsored exercise in propaganda) could count on more advantageous material possibilities and the full collaboration of the most avant-garde visual artists of the day. Yet, despite the general modesty of the collaborations of visual artists at the Oporto event, the very contemporary styling of certain of the decorative motifs of the sets created in the "Palace of the Colonies" and even in some of the floats in the Colonial Procession was "notable."[6] Notable, as well, was the influence of the then brand new Art Deco style, used to represent more or less distant, exotic cultures, the parts of the empire as an imagined whole, which the exposition was designed to address.

The dioramas—also modern resources, products of the era of mechanical reproduction—served to elucidate the regional diversity of the metropole. The authors of the guide, *Roteiro—Elucidativo do Visitante,* gave special emphasis to these images of the provinces, aware of the novelty of the syntheses the dioramas proposed. In the end, these were judged to be more in need of explanation than the ethnographic representations of the colonies, which were easily seen as well-defined marks in a narrative of progress. The *Roteiro-Guia* had the following to say about the National Council of Tourism: "Understandably, there was a concern with bringing the public into contact with the regions, with the diverse regions of Portugal, from the Minho to the Algarve, to Madeira and the Azores in synthetic, yet expressive, dioramas of customs and landscape, full of color and life. It is curious to observe, in this animated representation, how different, one from the other, are the various Portuguese provinces" (412–13).

To See "the Blacks" and "Something More"

In the colonial expositions,[7] the expeditious representations proposed—created by using ample plaster scenarios representing distant places and exhibiting the people who came from them—were a reflection of political domination and economic exploitation by the great centers of imperial power. These events served to demonstrate the power to mobilize the material means of modernized societies with their huge technical capacities for convincingly exhibiting possessions or commercial prowess exercised on a global scale.

In order to recuperate the illustrative virtues of Ferdinand Tönnies's distinction, the mass of visitors to such events can be considered—and consider themselves—as the sum of subjects integrated into a "society," consumers of representations of exotic "communities" that would represent previous steps on a path of constant progress that the expositions bring up to date (Tönnies 2001). This effect is achieved by emphasizing the ethnic characteristics of the people brought from the most distant spots in order to be exhibited, a constant presence in the history of the great expositions. In Oporto this rhetoric was also exercised: it was used in the "ethnographic section" to tell a story of progress that culminated in the successes achieved by the modern colonial economy.

But in the Portugal of 1934 there were notable deficits in the registers of modernization that I referred to in the paragraph above. On the one hand, political and economic control in the colonies was still weak—a control that was needed to strengthen the consequences anticipated by this initiative. As well, the material resources and the technical possibilities available for staging such representations were insufficient. On the other hand, the social structure that existed in the country at the time was hardly favorable to drawing a mass of voluntary visitors from the middle classes, the type that would normally attend the great international exhibitions (Benedict 1983).

Interpreting the news reports of the day, the inability of the majority of visitors to the gardens of the Crystal Palace in 1934 to engage in a well-codified consumption of exotic images (visual, ethnographically informed, and distancing) is made clear. The comments of the director of the organization were not very favorable in this sense, even though he would talk about the initial efficacy of the "lesson of colonialism" that he intended to transmit. The majority of the visitors, Henrique Galvão tells us,

> came to celebrate, with the same happy spirit and sense of amusement with which they go to the beach or to the theatre, to the bullfights or the soccer match. Some say: let's go see the blacks. ... Those that came with an air of celebration, just to see the blacks and run around in the grass of the *Luna Parque,* also saw something else. (Henrique Galvão, in *Ultramar,* no. 18)

In other contexts, more modern in terms of their social structure, this type of aesthetically elaborated visual consumption used to valorize the "tribal" and "primitive" in a fragmented form was common and even seen as being cosmopolitan and prestigious. For this reason, it could be thought of as being about "community." This was a widespread sensibility that left a vast trail, and is particularly apparent in ethnographic bibliographies (Clifford 1988; Manganaro 1990; Cantwell 1993).

In Portugal, during these years, individuals able to engage in this type of appropriation would have been very much in the minority. As a good example of these discrepancies, we have the fact that the commission for the poster distributed in France to publicize the exposition was given to a French artist who produced a stylized image of a the head of a black man by appropriating the design of an African sculpture, one with strong lines and a very refined "primitivism." This was a more sophisticated approach to publicizing the event, geared towards a public seen to be more select and prepared for the aesthetic appreciation of exotic motifs than the Portuguese public. One example of these difficulties in the consumption of exotic images can be found in the reasoning of a contemporary journalist who attempts to see a moral lesson in the ethnographic representations of the colonies: "I can't imagine that the idea of exhibiting, in a European city, the *savage* life of our colonies' indigenous people with the goal of presenting, to our *civilized* people, examples which are dignified and merit imitation. ... No, rather the grandiosity of the Nation and its dominions beyond the tiny metropole should be demonstrated" (*Gazeta das Aldeias*, no. 1804, italics in the original).

This judgment appears in an article entitled "The Renaissance of Rural Life," a title that is in a certain way characteristic of the period marked by great transformations and during which feelings of there being a crisis of values affected all. This led to a range of proposals for redemption that emanated from the most diverse political quadrants and were founded upon the local appropriation of internationally circulating ideologies. "The hunger for wholeness," which Peter Gay identified, was very pronounced in the "modern" generation contemporaneous with the Great War—perhaps better articulated among the intellectuals of the right[8]—and was a direct consequence of the anguish caused by the imposition of the most hostile aspects of modernity (Gay 1968).

In the citation in the *Gazeta das Aldeias* what is above all resented is a lack of the patina of the "old" bourgeois and cosmopolitan openness to the consumption of the exotic. Lacking as well is the willingness to understand that to speak of the "empire" is no longer at odds with the new ways of imagining the rural world of continental Portugal. The empire and the rural world were parts of a *whole,* made ideologically coherent by the ideologues of the regime. Below we will see how the identification of the *sauvage de l'interieur* was strengthened via the exhibition of the peasants of provincial Portugal, whose life would be seen to be equal to those inhabitants of the colonies brought to the exposition. As I said at the beginning of this chapter, the Colonial Exposition of 1934 was also important because it established and put into circulation on a national scale ethnographic images of the rural populations of the metropole. The representations of the exotic cultures of the colonies and the elements used to portray the Portuguese provinces intermingled and became mutually fixed in the course of certain heightened moments during the exposition.

Afonso do Paço—an archeologist and important ethnographer of the epoch—reflected on the opportunity for establishing new museographical policies out of the opportunity propitiated by the exhibition of the "empire" in Oporto: "It is an occasion to deal with the valorization of our Empire ... and one of matters with which this problem should be faced is that of the organization of an ethnographic museum which takes in continental and overseas Portugal, as it would be unfortunate to have a museum of the ethnography of the colonies while forgetting about one for the continent" (Paço 1934). In the same text, Paço cites the work of remodeling that Paul Rivet conducted starting in 1928 in the Trocadero museum in Paris, transformations that had been justified by the expectations raised by the Exposition coloniale of 1931 (see the French policies pertaining to ethnographic exhibitions during the 1930s in Lebovics 1992).

The accounts of the events of 1934 suggest that "metropolitan" ethnographic motifs had accrued new conventions because they were obliged to coexist and, in some ways, to mimic the more well-established forms used for creating representations of the colonies. This perception is apparent in a journalistic commentary on the large procession that formed part of the closing of the Exposition—the "Colonial Procession"—which was held on 30 September:

> All of those who attended the procession will recall the very interesting and well organized representation of agriculture. The folk dancers and the regional groups constituted a flagrant moment of national folklore, colorful and picturesque, which in itself would provide for a curious parade.

> Brought together were motifs and representatives of the provinces of the Minho, Trás-os-Montes, the region demarcated as the Douro, the Beira Alta and the Beira Baixa, the Ribatejo, Alentejo, Estremadura and the Algarve, which balanced out the demonstrations of the overseas colonies. (*Ultramar;* no. 18, 2)

The Beginning of the End of Parody

It becomes evident in a variety of passages from the news of the period that the majority of those responsible for the organization of the exposition, the journalists, and, certainly, the great majority of the public still did not understand the precepts that we can identify as a modernist grammar for the exhibition of regional cultures. To judge by the documents of the epoch, only Henrique Galvão held clear ideas about the new discursive methods that he intended to implement, conscious of the possibilities of, on this occasion, a new kind of popular culture, served by the modern resources of propaganda.

Beyond Galvãos's always clear and ideologically well-informed statements, we are surprised at the incongruities in the interpretations of the Colonial Exposition by some of its organizers, journalists, and the greater part of the public. The documentation of the period suggests that there were many differences in what was expected, as well as parodic appropriations and weak readings that were ill informed about the importance of the discursive transformations that the political commissioner wanted to implement through this act of propaganda.

I understand these discrepancies as indicating a lack of references and of readiness by the majority of contemporaries to understand the rapidity and radical nature of the changes that were occurring during those years. At the time certain of the elites of the state apparatus rapidly modified the modes of creating a representation of the state, proposing new historical and ethnographic syntheses, foundations of a new culture grounded in the use of images. One image, quite Baudelairean—employed in 1931 by António Ferro, another of the key names in the propaganda machine of the new regime, equal to Galvão—suggests a very radical consciousness of the transformations that the work of propaganda could imply. Ferro says: "In truth Salazar saved the country. … he almost completely remade the façade of the Nation" (*Journal das Colónios,* no. 1, 13/4/1933).[9]

Beyond the work of very few relatively specialized ethnographers, the ethnographic representation of the country had become fixed in a mode that was open and playful, in which parodic imitations of rural customs took on real importance in the leisure activities and literary interests of the various strata of the bourgeoisie. This had occurred in the context of a long process through which these groups had nationalized their cultural references starting in the middle of the nineteenth century. Let's look at an example of the persistence of these free-flowing and humorous ways of portraying popular culture, wherein, not to anyone's surprise, proposals for the mimesis of rural customs in the form of a celebration for summer visitors, who were looking for diversion in a "national" mode, are centered on ethnographic motifs that are vaguely Minhotan.[10]

The following is excerpted from a report in a newspaper called *O Comércio do Porto* about a celebration held in August of 1934 at the Caldas de Vizela Spa, while the Colonial Exposition was already in progress:

> As was expected the purely national celebration sponsored by the owners of the Cruzeiro do Sul Hotel for their guests was of a grandiosity never before seen. ... unexpectedly a large group of ladies and gentlemen dressed in the traditional costumes of the Minho and of the Marias de Portugal created a mood of happiness and good cheer. ... Around two in the morning a Portuguese supper began to be served, which started with the traditional *caldo verde*. ... The tables were set with thick plates, three branched candelabra, candles, small saucers of *tremoços*, iron forks and corn bread creating the impression of a farmer's table. (14/8/1934)

During the same month, another newspaper *O Primeiro de Janeiro* spoke of a similar event that was held on one of the most popular beaches in the suburbs of Oporto:

> The "Baile de Costumes Regionais" [Regional Costumes Dance], held in the Salão Nobre Grande Casino [Noble Grand Casino Salon] in Espinho was a real social success. ...

> The large group present was notable for its elegance and the great numbers of ladies beautifully dressed in different costumes from the Minho, Tras-os-Montes, Beirã and Vareira. (*O Primeiro de Janeiro*, 26/8/1934)

At the beginning of the 1930s, when the regime's intention was to officially put into place an ideology with certain characteristics of totalitarianism, the teaching of a new national culture also created the need for clearer forms of representing the cultures of the provinces. In this sense, the disposition for parodic mimesis of the people could be dispensed with as a practice that had been relatively common among certain strata of the bourgeoisie under the anterior democratic regimes (and, as we have seen, still apparent in 1934 in the "purely national" celebration organized in the "Hotel Cruzeiro do Sul"). Under the new political conditions it became possible to compel the rural working classes to create a representation of themselves as regional subjects, dressed up in traditional garb that the work of objectification exercised by ethnographers in previous decades had authenticated as traditional.

As we will see below, at the exposition the attempt was made to get the members of the popular classes who were present to interpret the ethnographic representation of the metropole themselves (having been compelled to participate by the new authorities, much as were the "indigenous" people brought from the various colonies to be exhibited in the gardens of the Crystal Palace). But it is true that, at the margins of the official initiatives, the exposition was marked by curious and mutually mimetic dispositions, openings for novel encounters and forms of learning, none of them programmed.

The editor of *O Comércio do Porto Colonial*—a supplement of this important newspaper published during the course of the exhibition—said the following: "I myself saw a black drumming to the most characteristic regional dance of the North" (16/7/1934). Also, there is frequent mention in the documentation of expressions of desire, for example, and momentary notes of eroticism on the part of a reporter who enthusiastically describes the bodies of the dancers—"strange profiles of naked and sweating bodies"—who had come from Guinea. Journalists witnessed the desire of the bourgeoisie and the proletariat of Oporto, whom they described as lurking around, staring at the naked breasts of the African women from the "indigenous villages" set up on the patio of the Palace, wooing "Inez, svelte, beautiful and lovely" or a "*preta Rosinha*" [black Rose]—momentarily famous while the exposition lasted—who appears to be nationalized in a bizarre manner in the prose of the journalist: "If you take off her skin—the blackness of her skin, rather—and make her into a white woman, you would see in her figure a delicate girl from the Minho. For the way she moved. Because of a certain *exquisite* air which she had while walking" (*O Comércio do Porto Colonial,* 1/7/1934).

The following is yet another of the chance encounters that the exposition has afforded us, particularly surprising for the intensity of the impulse for mutual mimesis:

> The famous traditional *rancho* [folk dance] of the "Zés P'reiras" from Marco de Canavezes ... visited the pavilion of *O Comércio do Porto Colonial* and, for a few moments, put on a spectacle of color and noise.
>
> A black man from the lacustrine village of Guinea, by chance watching this spectacle of a regional visit, improvised an agitated and violent dance in the middle of the group of "Zés P'reiras."
>
> For a few moments there was a coming together of the Douro and Guinea. ... the strange dance of the Negro who wiggled and grunted in the barbarous fashion of his African bush in the middle of the scarlet, green, black exuberantly colored traditional dress. The sound of the bass

drums made the girls and the men of the Douro go crazy. (*O Comércio do Porto*, 17/7/1934)

There is still an ambiguous note in the writing of the Count d'Aurora (1896–1969), marked by the unprofessional practice of ethnography of the beginning of the twentieth century.[11] In April of 1934, in an article entitled "O Minho província do império" [The Minho Province of the Empire], he delineates certain aspects of what he imagined must be the "Parada Regional." The text is curious because it prefigures the purifying dispositions that would characterize ethnographic representation under the new regime at the same time that it retains a kind of outdated—and likeable—sensibility in its description of popular customs. The author tells us the following: "The pilgrimage only has a picturesque, rural scope, spiritual in its representation. ... Folklorists of my land, why don't you collect museum recordings of the characteristic shout of the ox driver, which you can hear across the whole plain of fertile riverbanks?" He does indulge in an emotive evocation of the naive syncretism belonging to the popular practices that he himself regularly observes: "Oh! Curious rivalries between the pilgrimage songs—playing passages of Wagnerian opera, forgetful of 'Regadinho,' of 'Cana Verde,' of Malhão,' which no one ever orchestrated" (*A Aurora do Lima*, 27/4/1934).

It is easy to think that the hybrid characteristics and the constant mimesis of urban customs and the well-to-do classes would be, at the end of the day, an ever-present note in the customary practices of the lower classes. We can find evidence of these "contaminations" throughout the whole of the nineteenth century, from that point when the observation of the popular classes became a frequent practice. However, the bonhomie with which the popular /folk customs were appreciated varied over time. For example, Alberto Sampaio sympathetically described the taste for philharmonic music of peasants living on the outskirts of Guimarães in a suggestive text from 1888 entitled *A Propriedade e a Cultura no Minho*. Some decades later, on the other hand, ethnographers closer to Salazar's autocratic regime will demonstrate a special ferocity in denouncing this syncretism and the corruption of older customs that it mirrored. In this context, initiatives to reinstate the older customs were abundant. At this point it would be pertinent to mention Michael Taussig's suggestion, referring to Horkheimer and Adorno, which outlines the following characterization:

Fascism ... is an accentuated form of modern civilization which is itself to be read as the history of repression of mimesis. ... But above all, fas-

cism is more than outright repression of the mimetic; it is a return of the
repressed, based on the "organized control of mimesis." (1993: 68)

One of Michael Herzfeld's suggestions can be seen as being concomitant with Taussig's line of argumentation, allowing us to understand
the dynamic behind the authoritarian censorship of many of the popular customs that became especially pronounced during the 1930s and
1940s in Portugal. Taking into account the nationalist discourse of the
Greek state, Herzfeld tells us how consolidating icons is a way of articulating discourses of power, a procedure that forces the narrowing or
selection from among the variety of already existing cultural forms. The
iconizing of provincial cultures, which saw its pioneering experiment
in the Colonial Exposition, can be understood as an unfolding of these
processes of censorship and delimitation. Herzfeld tells us: "The very
heterogeneity of iconicity is what recommends it to reductionist needs
of ideology: it simplifies the awkward, complicated, messy truths about
ethnic and other kinds of internal diversity that undergird its bland assertions of homogeneity" (1997: 73).

One of the aspects of the Colonial Exposition that is today most surprising can be found in the nonspontaneous dimensions that a visit to
the exposition implied for the majority of individuals; there are a variety
of examples we could call upon. For example, the parish priests were
very active in directing their parishioners, following the recommenda-
tions of their superiors. Also the local political bosses actively mobilized
their fellow residents, pressed on by those higher up in the hierarchies at

Figure 14. Dressing up the nation, tentatively … Unknown photographer,
n.d.

the level of the municipality or district of the recently organized União Nacional [National Union]. Business owners distributed tickets at lower prices to their employees. But the latter sometimes resold them, a fact denounced as embezzlement by the management of the exposition, which threatened those who bought these tickets with public humiliations (*O Comércio do Porto,* 14/8/1934).

On the other hand, as the documentation of the period suggests, the more modest rural visitor appeared, simultaneously, as the *sauvage de l'intérieur,* and, because of this, became one of the components of the exposition. Some months after its opening, in February, an article compiled some very curious syncretic references where this overlapping of habits was clearly stated:

> During the Colonial Exposition various visits to the Palace of the Colonies were made by rural workers from the different municipalities of the Entre Douro e Minho, and possibly other districts of the country.
>
> In Braga, Oporto, and Viana do Castelo much labor went into the organization of these visits. The groups marched through the city of Oporto from the Praça de República to the grounds of the Exposition, dressed in their traditional garb, clutching their work tools and singing their regional songs … the verses of the Count of Villas Boas which we will publish later and which the various groups sang during the procession. These verses would get their music from the chorus of shepherds from the opera, *A Serrana,* by Alfred Keil. (*Ultramar,* no. 1, 1/2/1934)

A Serrana, an opera by Alfredo Keil (1850–1907) that debuted in 1901, offers an excellent example of the ways that the nationalization of bourgeois culture in Portugal at the turn of the century had been accomplished. In the opera, the "Minhotan" costumes of the choruses appear as a characteristic note of syncretism, since it was in the *serra da Estrela* [a mountain range in central Portugal] that the action was situated. The "verses" referred to—unbearable and obsequious—by Villas Boas came to be identified as "popular" in some articles, in a curious game of discordant attributions, in the end reflecting the most surprising ways that the new regime could be legitimized. These "verses" are an example: "I eat the tangerines / one fruit with so many segments / Our Provinces across the ocean / Are Portuguese like us."

What is important to emphasize once again is that a great part of those who visited the exposition were also objects of exposition and simultaneously participants—hardly voluntary ones!—in a continuous demonstration of support for the new regime. This occurred mainly in the context of the processions, which were the high points of the whole event: the Parada Regional de Entre Douro e Minho on 15 July and the

Cortejo Colonial that closed the exposition, on 30 September. These were the dates when greater quantities of people converged on the city of Oporto, adding to the spectators and to the multitudinous parades organized at the time.

In the end, for many of the groups of people brought to Oporto for the occasion, it becomes difficult to distinguish between their status as users and consumers of the exposition and their participation as objects of the exposition or performers obliged to create an allegorical portrait. Taking up the terms of Michael Herzfeld (1997), we can understand them as subjects that because of the compulsion of others created an iconographic figuration of themselves. This can be observed more clearly in the first of the large processions, the Parada Regional de Entre Douro e Minho, where the quantity of "extras" mobilized to play a part in its composition was impressive, more than 15,000 according to the news of the period.

A notice in the local news of the daily newspaper *O Primeiro de Janeiro* of 7 July seems to further clarify the political intentions of the initiative. Taking up the Parada Regional de Entre Douro e Minho, it has the following to say: "The enthusiasm for this grandiose celebration in the municipality of Vila Nova de Gaia continues. The rural class knows that this is not just a Parade of customs, dances and regional 'folklore,' but also a civic procession of the people of the villages who have come to patriotically manifest their contentment and admiration for the glorious deeds of their betters" (cited in *Ultramar,* no. 1, 1/2/1934).

When we consider the extensive participation in the *parada* of 15 July, we should take into account the powers that were indeed exercised in the localities of the Minho and of the coastal area of the Douro by members of the elite classes and those occupying political positions in the new regime. Yet, in addition to these special moments, like the processions, the whole of the recruitment of the masses of visitors to the exposition had aspects of compulsion that were more or less out in the open. As becomes evident when we read between the lines in the texts, the desire to make this initiative a success predominated, activating the collaboration of the town governments and elites, and, as the *Comércio do Porto* would say, "the people most representative of each municipality" (18/5/1934), as a way to bring the maximum number of visitors to Oporto.

However, on various occasions it becomes obvious that even some of the most important collaborators in this initiative had an insufficient understanding of what was at stake—beyond the most immediate political gains—in this latest art of convoking and of manipulating the masses. The words of the old count of Villas Boas (the organizer

of the Parada Regional de Entre Douro e Minho and then, later, of
the representation of the metropole in the Cortejo Colonial that closed
the exposition) reveal the relative naïveté of the Galvão's collaborators:
"Many people think ... that 'Parada' has a panoramic and picturesque
character, and is limited to a kind of ambulatory exposition of regional
customs, costumes and folklore. ... It is mainly about a manifestation
of the affection for our Province and Portugal's other Provinces which
are brought together with their brother Provinces overseas" (*Notícias de
Viana*, 5/5/1934).

Only Henrique Galvão, as his texts suggest, dominated, with an un-
heard-of alacrity, the new precepts of propaganda and the possibilities
that it could be used to articulate synthetic representations of a new
culture. It is worth citing passages from one of his texts, certain in its
clarification of specific ideas. It was written about a later exposition and
cortège, but reiterates precepts already experimented with in Oporto
in 1934. Galvão has the following to say about the Cortejo do Mundo
Português, which took place in Lisbon during the famous Exposition
of 1940.

> It posits itself as one of the events that is best able to correspond to the
> intentions of the Government ... : a grandiose parade about the glories
> of the Past, about the imperial goals of the Present and also of the beauty,
> the charm and the colorful picturesqueness of the Portuguese people of
> the twenty-one provinces of the Empire. ...
>
> A cortège is essentially ephemeral.
>
> A cortège goes by—but an image remains that sometimes is hardly re-
> membered—it is fleeting—but other times becomes fixed in the heart
> and stays with us of the rest of our lives.
>
> It was an image of this latter type which we tried to create. (1940: 27–31)

The Parada Regional de Entre Douro e Minho was the first large-
scale ethnographic staging by the Estado Novo. The difficulties of organizing the event were formidable, characteristic of a hurried initiative
and one in which the lack of the promoter's experience became patent.
We have seen that the greater part of the emphasis was on the need to
assure the presence of the masses in order to legitimize the new regime;
on the contrary, any kind of rigor in ethnographically representing the
different parts of the metropole was notoriously neglected. Certain specialists close to the regime and especially preoccupied with questions of
authenticity of ethnographic representations—like Abel Viana or Luís
Chaves—would mention The Parada Regional de Entre Douro e Minho
on various occasions as an example of what an ethnographic proces-

sion should not be. In the parade, the mass of members of the popular classes that participated did so in a disorderly fashion without observing, except in the rarest cases, any kind of rigor in the use of traditional dress or in the representation of customs. Rather—to use the terms of Abel Viana in a later text written to create a set of general norms—what prevailed were "imitations of the foreign," "insipid and ridiculous little inventions" and a notable lack of "dignity" (Viana 2000: 149–50).

In that attempt at the representation of an "historical province"—now revived in the context of an initiative conceived of as "modern"—many parodic and carnivalesque aspects persisted. These were characteristic of the mimesis of the people enacted by the bourgeois classes in the process of Portuguesifying the culture, a process that we saw intensify at the end of the nineteenth century. If we take into account the channels that worked to ensure the convocation of the crowd of 15,000 participants we will understand the difficulties faced by the organizers in obtaining any kind of verisimilitude in the staging of the tradition. We have already said that there were priests, presidents of administrative councils, mayors, heads of industry, and landowners connected to the regime who were the most important recruiters of the participants for the parade of 15 July.

During this epoch there were very few localities where—through the initiative of the educated and the famous—advances in the objectivity of the modes of representation of local culture had occurred. Moreover even in these cases, these processes were weak and quite recent, dating from the end of the 1920s (Viana 2000). For this reason, the multitudinous procession of 15 July was filled with fire departments, tourist groups, choral societies, student singing groups, *Zés Pereiras,* and local elites, "*vianesas*" and the capuchins of the Cabeceiras de Basto. But there were more; for example, the Grupo Ervidense os Estoiras and innumerable groups of excursionists with equally improbable names, all of them in a festive mood. In fact, the *parada* seemed more a mixture of traditional civic processions held on important dates and a typical carnival procession. The reception of some of these "bizarre" groups—as the report in *O Comércio do Porto* would say—was festive in the streets of the city. But this was the death knell for parodic ethnographic representations that had prevailed over the previous decades.[12]

Even in the Cortejo Colonial, which closed the exposition in the month of September, the representation of provincial cultures was more soberly presented. With Henrique Galvão himself in charge of the staging of the event, it was brought off with more "composure," more "gravity," "vibration," and "feeling." In addition to industrial and commercial interests, this extremely long allegorical procession included

"Mandinkan chiefs" and "Bijagoz and Balantas, naked backs, tall and handsome," a "Quipungo virgin" and "marimba players," and "savage-looking blacks, primitive Vátuas." There were also "herdsmen," "boys with Arab faces from the Algarve," "peasant women," "corn threshers," and more. He wanted to represent the "21 provinces of the empire." About the representation of the homeland it was said: "A busy, stereo-typical flux of a humble people, resigned and healthy, who struggle and dream, who sing and suffer from the flower gardens of the Alto-Minho to the immense golden coast of the Algarve" (*Ultramar,* no. 17).

It was in the 1930s in Portugal that the first ethnographic processions took shape in a form that has been maintained until this day. Now they have become very frequent and are especially esteemed for their representation of local cultures in many different parts of the country. In general, processions, cortèges, marches, and parades—ancient forms of military, religious, or civic display—multiplied during the 1930s, most of them sponsored by the state, city governments, or associations of corporate interests. This revitalization of the employment of cortèges contained clear authoritarian proposals for the kind of indoctrination that its promoters wanted to enact. They were especially efficacious means to ideologically influence the masses (Connerton 1993; Mosse 1996). A good example of these intentions could be seen firsthand at the First Portuguese Colonial Exposition.

Even so, in Oporto in 1934, this attempt at the modernist refinement of an ethnographic discourse was badly implemented. This discourse was clarified rapidly and effectively by the "Portuguese World Exhibition" of 1940 (see, for example, Melo 2001; Acciaiuoli 1998). But in addition to these staged *collages,* the state hindered any attempt at educating the people about the provinces for their own sake. The appropriation of emblematic motifs identifying the provinces—as established by the ethnographic sensibilities of the mid-twentieth century—was segmentary, conducted at the local or municipal level. In the Minho today ethnographic processions are held even in the parishes most distant from the seats of municipal power. These very closely replicate the model that matured under state supervision between 1933 and 1940.

Notes

1. That is, if we accept the optimistic calculations of Henrique Galvão (1895–1970); he was the "technical director" of the Colonial Exposition and also responsible for the various commemorative events and the propaganda promoted by the *Estado Novo* from 1930 to 1940. Along with António Ferro (1895–1956) and José Leitão de Barros (1896–1967), Galvão was one of the most capable and well-informed

propagandists on whom the authoritarian regime counted. His career during the 1930s was meteoric; he was the first director of the Emissora Nacional (Portuguese national radio), established in 1935. His rupture with the regime—he became one of its most fearless and famous critics—occurred during the mid-1940s. Fernando Rosas (1994) notes how in the 1930s various sympathizers with fascism—as with various vanguard aesthetic currents that were characteristically fascinated with recent technical possibilities—were able to accommodate themselves to the Salazar regime, becoming its first, and very much needed, propagandists.

Let me transcribe a portrait of Galvão's circumstances: "Henrique Galvão put ... his astute, vibrant and impartial intelligence in the service of this undertaking, an intelligence that we could classify as *modern* [italics in the original] ... Henrique Galvão—like us—belonged to a generation shattered by the hecatomb that ended in 1918" (in *Portugal Colonial*, no. 35: 2). Here we find familiar references to the First World War as an "opening" and a matrix of twentieth-century sensibilities. Modernism was characterized by its "vibrancy," its "velocity," its "fragmentation of experience," but also by the synthesis of new modes of art and political ideology (see, as examples, Buck-Morss 1990; Eksteins 1990; Hobsbawm 1994; Schnapp 1992; Gay 1968; Herf 1998; Nochlin 1994).

2. See some of the most suggestive ideas written about the expositions by authors like Kracauer (1995), Kirshenblatt-Gimblett (1991), Buck-Morss (1990), Harvey (1996) and Simmel (1991).

3. See *Roteiro. Resumo Elucidativo do Visitante da Primeira Exposição Colonial Portuguesa*.

4. See Lebovics (1992) and Golan (1995). The terms Golan uses to describe the Paris Exposition Coloniale Internationale are curious: "the most spectacular extravaganza ever staged in the West" (1995: 115).

5. Galvão was also the Portuguese representative at the Colonial Congress, which was held in Paris along with the 1931 Exposition Coloniale.

6. Contrary to what was the case in Lisbon in 1940, today the visual artists and architects that worked on the stage sets of the Colonial Exposition are practically unknown. On the other hand, Galvão was capable of rallying the participation of nearly all the great actors of his day to participate in various parts of the 1934 program, namely, in the Cortejo Colonial, which closed the event. Linda Nochlin suggests that it is worth considering, by analogy, the totalizing potential of expositions' discourses that is implicit in the processions, an important part of these initiatives, and in the collaboration of the artists who invariably became involved. "We can now begin to see that it is by no means possible to assert that modernity may only be associated with, or suggested by, a metaphoric or actual fragmentation. On the contrary, paradoxically, or dialectically, modern artists have moved towards its opposite, with a will to totalization embodied in the notion of the *Gesamtkunstwerk*, the struggle to overcome the disintegrative effects—social, psychic, political—inscribed in modern, particularly modern urban, experience, by hypostatizing them within a higher unity. One might, from this point of view, maintain that modernity is indeed marked by the will toward totalization as much as it is metaphorized by the fragment" (1994: 58).

7. In fact, the whole tradition of large expositions was imperial, as a rule, and remained so up until World War II. The exposition was a tradition consolidated in the nineteenth century, and it is significant that its invention happened during the French Revolution, an opening moment of our age (Benjamin 1999). One moment of reference was the Great Exhibition of London in 1851. After 1937 and the Exposition Internationale de Paris the promotion of such events began to wane, a decline that

was already much in evidence at the 1939 New York World's Fair (Benedict 1983; Greenhalg 1988).

8. See the references to the special prestige and influence that intellectuals of the right gained in Portuguese society from the 1910s to the 1920s in Ramos (1994).

9. Well known is Baudelaire's aphorism, "The street is the school of modern man." An understanding of the virtues of the use of synthetic images, of façades, of cortèges— in the "street" and in propaganda—as a means to inculcate a new popular culture for the modern masses is very well represented in all of Henrique Galvão's writings (see, for example, his *Album Comemorativo da Exposição do Mundo Português. Secção Colonial;* see as well comparative references suggested by Eksteins 1990 and Schnapp 1992, in relation to the uses of propaganda in Germany and Italy during the same period).

10. Hermann Bausinger notes, "The dominant influence of the idea of the national on the folk culture of the nineteenth and earlier twentieth centuries can hardly be over-estimated" (1990: 44).

11. The author was an "integralist" monarchist, a polymath and, sporadically, an ethnographer who was close to the Salazar regime.

12. Curiously, the censorship of carnival-like festivities and their excesses is a topic that Portuguese newspapers of the 1930s and 1940s often took up; in many cases the use of regional dress was censored.

Chapter 9

A Place in the Mountains or the (Mis)encounters of Soajo

The strongest images that I retain from my many visits to the village of Soajo are superimposed upon a common and well-known iconography. First, the small oxen with their black muzzles and lyre-shaped horns crossing in front of the cars on the mountain road. Then, in the village, old women dressed in black sitting on their doorsteps wishing visitors a "good afternoon." There is the "communitarian" threshing floor and its famous *espigueiros* [tall, wooden-framed or granite constructions that resemble small narrow huts on stilts] for storing dried corn and a familiar granite pillar in the main square. These images circulate on various material platforms—postcards, stamps, fabrics, engravings, craftworks, match boxes, photographs—and are easily identifiable by many Portuguese.

When they visit Soajo, as a rule, tourists normally lament the modern constructions that have popped up, which they feel degrade the place's "archaic" profile; others may say "typical" or "characteristic," "vernacular" or "traditional." Then they visit the threshing floor and the famous cluster of *espigueiros* constructed out of granite. Here, rather vaguely, the communitarian habits that would be typical of this village are alluded to. Next, some of the small streets that run through the middle of the village are quickly taken in, passing the square where the pillory is located; perhaps comments are made on the morality of the story about the "judge of Soajo." Most of the visits to this old town and capital of an old district, which was abolished in 1852, tend to be short ones.

In the Spring of 1993 I found myself doing fieldwork in a coastal parish in the Minho. During the time I was there, my hosts decided to take a family outing to Soajo and invited me to come along. We left early one morning in five automobiles carrying around twenty people, a part of the extended family of the man and the woman, small farmers, who were hosting me. I was the only one of the group who had already visited the famous village of Soajo. It was a very agreeable day. There were two different picnics, and we visited the dams at Lindoso and Soajo and put a foot over the border into Spain (see chapter 1). Everything was recorded on video by one of the sons-in-law of my hosts.

In Soajo, I thought I should say something about the village, the *espigueiros,* and the famous communal, or "communitarian," threshing floor, which in the local designation was referred to as *eira do Penedo* and where, at the moment, we were sitting. If my companions saw in me a certain professional specialization, it would have been only that of having a good understanding or a kind of special interest for the particularities of places like the one we were now visiting. As a matter of fact, at various points since I had arrived they had asked about the reasons that had brought me to their coastal parish. They saw it as modernized and therefore quite ordinary, since the old customs had already been corrupted, customs that, in some way, they imagined were preserved in the village we were now visiting.

Some of the suggestions implied here could suggest various paths of analysis. The very rapid processes of change that the rural parishes of the Minho have witnessed in recent decades could be seen as subjects for study. For example, there is the fact that small farmers drive automobiles and take trips that can be vaguely described as ethnographic, habits that were exclusive to the bourgeoisie until quite recently. Then there is

Figure 15. Soajo's *espigueiros,* a partial view. Photo by the author.

the use of the new media to produce family memories or resources for regional and national identity. The roles attributed to anthropologists by the people among whom they are conducting their research offers them new possibilities for analysis, or even—as the expanding literature demonstrates—of becoming important actors in the production of local traditions. Here I would simply like to introduce certain notes on this shared experience: a visit to Soajo with neophytes to this very peculiar excursion, a peculiarity that results in complex attributions whose significance we will understand if we take into account the bibliography and the images that this mountain village has given rise to for more than a century now.

I should emphasize that the oldest couple, my friends and hosts, held rather vague expectations about this visit to Soajo. The excursion came about as an opportunity to bring the extended family together and for a trip to a distant area described as beautiful and of different and "typical" customs. Distant places like this had only become accessible in the past few years, given the fact that all of their children owned automobiles. It had been these younger members of the "household" who had proposed the trip to the mountains, because they had expectations of encountering a way of life already out of date, a place that was "traditional" or "typical," the reasons they gave for the choice of this particular destination.

However, in my opinion, this new generation also felt rather insecure about the meanings that could be given to the excursion. I followed this process of decision, which lasted for two weeks, listening to a range of enthusiastic speculations around the fireplace. The fact that Soajo was chosen as the final destination of this little trip depended quite a bit on the fact that its promoters were able to put to use their formal education, more complete than that of their parents. For this reason, they had a different frame of reference available to them that gave meaning, if only in relatively vague fashion, to the excursion. In truth, and I believe this to be significant, they would not consider the possibility of visiting one of the famous religious sanctuaries in this part of the country, a choice that their parents had suggested. On the contrary, we can now see that these types of excursions, designed to enjoy the countryside and to observe the local customs, have for some time now become part of the leisure activities of the better-off social classes in Portugal.

A Very Imagined Place

This chapter is justified primarily for providing a commentary on the images and texts referring to Soajo. As has been said, there is a great

quantity of these documents, a fact that, in itself, constitutes a phenomenon that is worthy of our interest and is a legitimate object for
the attention of anthropologists. I must note that this is not an original
proposal, since a variety of the available texts were already the object
of previous studies, one of which was undertaken by Colette Caillier-
Boisvert, in a 1987 text entitled *O Soajo Visto de Fora* [Soajo Seen from
the Outside]. The intensity of attention paid to Soajo has also been recognized by António do Paço, journalist and polymath from Viana do
Castelo, the capital of the district in which the village is located: "Soajo
is, of all the localities of Portugal, the one which has drawn the most
attention of scholars, journalists and ethnographers; they bring us their
views in delicious articles and detailed monographs, many of which
come with elucidating illustrations. The granite pillar, or *pelourinho,* and
the village threshing floor and the numerous *espigueiros* constitute the
representative themes of the tourist posters of Soajo" (1975: 66).

Beginning at the end of the nineteenth century and continuing over
the decades, the regularity with which a variety of ethnographers and
anthropologists, musicologists, historians, geographers, and archeologists, not to mention writers, film makers, and artists, visit or allude to
or were attracted to work in Soajo is, indeed, notable. This mountain
community became the unprecedented focus of erudite attention un-
paralleled in Portugal, a very conspicuous "locality," in the words of
Arjun Appadurai (1995). One suggestive term of comparison can be
found in the municipality in which Soajo is located: in numerical terms
the bibliography dedicated to this particular village is more extensive
than all of the rest of the fifty parishes of Arcos de Valdevez put together,
as is the prestige of the authors of these references.[1]

In the terms proposed by Edwin Ardener, Soajo is a "remote area"
(Ardener 1989). As such, one of the first interpretations suggested by
the author is that it is the type of place that "anthropologists have considered to be 'fit' for their study." If we take into account the most recent
anthropological sojourns to Soajo, we can consider Ardener's slightly
ironic characterization correct. In the most recent decades there have
been at least three professional, academic anthropologists who did some
sort of fieldwork there and produced texts that took various aspects of
the social life of the village for their subjects: Collette Callier-Boisvert,
Alice Geraldes, and Luís Polanah. It is the first author who stands out
for her long involvement with this "terrain," which gave birth to a number of her texts that have appeared over the last three decades. As such,
we can consider C. Callier-Boisvert to be the greatest expert on the ethnography of contemporary Soajo.

Contrary to what the António do Paço's citation suggests, Soajo had not been described in any "detailed monograph" by the time of his visit. This kind of attention has only arisen recently as a result of Callier-Boisvert's long involvement with the terrain. Recognizing that dearth might help to explain how Soajo gained its very particular place in the ethnological interests in Portugal that have been prevalent now for over a century.

In some way, the lack of a monograph of recognized authority has left the terrain open to a divergence of opinions about the relative ethnological importance that has been attributed to Soajo by a succession of visiting specialists. Curiously, for this same reason the imagination of those less specialized visitors, who are not as interested in the minute details of ethnography, has been given freer reign. It could be argued that the dispersal of references, the vague character of the erudite legend of difference that surrounds the village, prevent in some way the local adoption of a coherent and legitimate way of representing the locality to the outside world. The existence of exhaustive and prestigious ethnographic work would have replaced that necessity with a pedagogic reference.

There are a variety of texts—some of them by important authors, as I have indicated above—that since the 1880s have denied that there is anything original about Soajo. However, we can see in certain contemporary uses of this place the effects of an aura of difference that has crystallized around it. So, it is evident that since the last century there has been an efficacious process of the production of this village and its surroundings as a "remote area" or as a "locality," if we accept Appadurai's formulation cited above. This might partially justify the excessive presence of anthropologists during recent decades, or even the occasional refusals to conduct fieldwork there, or in villages with similar reputations in the mountainous region of the Minho (Pina-Cabral 1989, 1992). Trips to Soajo and the comments that are made about them are one of the more curious aspects of Portuguese ethnography since the last three decades of the nineteenth century. Because of this, and in spite of the fact that many of the said allusions, news items, and commentaries are fragmented and underdeveloped, this can be considered an important part of the debate on the identity of the country that gained prominence and took on new features during the period being examined.

Soajo gained fame and a very particular place in the gathering of images considered representative of the remote past of the Portuguese nation and its boundaries. Because of this, tourists who visit the village normally arrived with already-formed expectations. These could have been created by a television report, book, painting, photograph, or article in the newspaper, or by consulting a tourist guide or pamphlet about the village, or, in the most extreme case, through a familiarity with an eclectic group of these references. On the visit that I spoke about in the first paragraphs of this chapter, the participants' expectations were focused mainly on the *espigueiros* and on the "communitarian" threshing floor, certainly for the Portuguese today one of the most recognizable icons of rural Portugal. Certain other episodes that occurred during this excursion to Soajo in the spring of 1993 will illustrate the various differences of opinion that the visit to this mountainous area provoked.

In Lindoso visiting the new dam, my friend told me about running across a woman, also older, who was loaded down with some small agricultural tools. These had seemed antiquated to him, "just like the ones we used to use in former times." He even added that the woman had an "enslaved air about her" and that "these people around here must be really behind the times." Paradoxically, this conversation took place next to one of the most sophisticated industrial projects in Portugal, the huge gallery of underground machines that controlled the new dam. Already close to Soajo, we stopped once more, this time next to the old hydroelectric station, whose construction began in 1910. This was the first undertaking of its kind in Portugal, at the time constituting a daring capitalist venture that had an obvious impact on the local life that is still remembered today.

After the visit to the community threshing floor and having passed by some old women dressed in black, an example of the "backwardness" and the typicality that we obviously expected to see, we arrived at our destination of a restaurant with its adjoining bar, which surprised my friends for its modernity and good taste. They commented on these characteristics, the large patio as well as the regional "motifs" that decorated the interior. Following this they were a bit shocked at having to pay 120$00 [escudos, the pre-Euro currency of Portugal] for a bottle of water, an unimaginable price in any of the more modest cafés of the coastal parish where they had come from.

For the couple from the coast of the Minho, who are, as I have said, farmers, already a bit advanced in age, the suggestion of "backwardness" that they recognized in these fortuitous encounters with the local inhabitants had as a reference a rather shallow chronology. As such, they recognized the types of farming tools that they themselves had used up until the 1960s and 1970s. These tools remained in use in Soajo because of its topography—which to my hosts, as specialists, seemed difficult and lamentable—being unsuitable for mechanization. The same kind of judgment was implicit in comments made about the presence of women dressed in black, since this type of feminine attire has gone out of fashion in their parish in recent years.

There are other chronologies of reference—radically deeper—that have molded the imagination of visitors to Soajo who are of urban origin and more educated. From their perspective, the aspects of daily life that they come across can be imbued with a very important monumental value. What they are perceiving acts like a catalyst to suddenly and dramatically extend their awareness of history and their own chronological references. This phenomenon frequently occurs in the context of a diffuse system that I designate as "ethnographic disposition," for lack of a more precise expression.

A general and easily recognizable example will clarify this notion: spontaneous verses from the mouth of a "villager" might document, ad hoc, prehistoric or timeless truths. The impromptu artist as much as the performance itself will be taken as evidence of these timeless judgments, due to the fact that the visitor has been rendered so receptive. Visits to Soajo easily provoke this type of construction of timeless documents, in spite of the fact that they are provoked by objects—actions or individuals—able to be situated in chronological and social contexts with relative facility and, to this extent, open to more cohesive and integrated explication.

I think a good example of these types of attitudes can seen in the comments made about the communitarian threshing floor. There visitors are easily predisposed to imagine a very remote period, a period that fully expresses a "communitarianism" of timeless origin, precedents of the process of Romanization experienced by people of Celtic origin, or of even more obscure origins that cannot be referenced. However, that very important group of constructions in this breezy place can only be explained by the relatively recent introduction of maize. This is an exotic plant whose appearance would have imposed very important transformations on the local society and economy (Ribeiro 1963). The oldest *espigueiro* built near the threshing floor in Penedo dates back to the middle of the eighteenth century.

For a good part of the visitors to Soajo, the most significant impressions are crystallized as the sum of visual experiences that confirm and reinforce their already-existing expectations. Concomitantly, other images omitted or ignored are easily eligible as alternatives. Let me explain: to fulfill the most common expectations of the visit means loading the group of *espigueiros*, the "communitarian" threshing floor, and the presence of old women dressed in black with metaphorical meaning. Contrary to this, the allegorical pertinence of a modern truck that distributes Panrico products a few dozen meters away, or the ATM inside a bank, will be ignored. To photograph an old woman dressed in black with blue eyes close to the *pelourinho*—of the "Celtic" or "Suevian" type, as more well-read visitors frequently suggest—runs against the possibility of including the darker-complected grandson raised in New England and wearing a Chicago Bulls jersey.

Edwin Ardener said with a degree of humor: "The native of such an area sometimes feels strangely invisible—the visitors seem to blunder past, even through him" (1989: 214). For this reason, the young Portuguese-American boy's jersey or the ATM might provoke the visitor into a jeremiad on what he imagines to be the irreversible corruption of Soajoan tradition.

The professional producers of images and the tourists will spend a great deal of energy framing their photographs of the community threshing floor in order to leave a rotting camper that has been rusting away in an adjacent field out of the picture. They will hardly ever photograph a curiously designed and well-cared-for house—inspired by the types of regional houses of Raúl Lino (1879–1974, one of the most influential Portuguese architects), the property of an old primary school teacher— which is set near a group of *espigueiros*. It would be absurd to register the image of an old pillow of synthetic satin covered with images of Canada's most important cities, which a mongrel dog sleeps on under one of the *espigueiros* spread around the village, or the "art deco" motifs of the house of an "American." But the shepherd wrapped up in an old jacket on the mountain slope can represent the timeless Soajoan—"a Celt" or an "old Lusitanian," for example—a nearly perfect image of a very old mode of life that today has irremediably disappeared. However, there is a small story that they once told me in Soajo: that shepherd could very well be a "man who has 100,000 *contos* in the bank, money earned in America." (Today this would be worth 500,000 euros, or close to $650,000.)

We should also consider the visitor who takes note of such coexistences—even one who notes them ironically. There is a preponderant perception in play during these visits: this place allows for the contemplation of extremely pertinent evidence of a remote past, even if its integrity is spoiled by eruptions of the banal signs of modern life. To this extent, the focal points of attention most reiterated will be understood as ruins, as documents/monuments that still remain from times long past and that are in imminent risk of being lost. Included in this perception are not only the remains of the material culture that marked the past of this mountain village. We also have certain of the inhabitants themselves, who are the target of questions—or merely taken as a given, or as the object of speculations— about the preservation of older and different customs, or the vivacity of their respective memory. For this reason, as was suggested, the prototypical visit to Soajo has been, for the majority of visitors who have gone there during the last 120 years, an ethnographic excursion.

There is reason to emphasize the final passage in António do Paço's citation, which was transcribed above. The "basic motifs of the Soajo tourist poster," which the author identifies in the "granite pillory" [the *pelourinho*] and in the "public threshing floor with the numerous *espigueiros*," are simultaneously the central and incontestable motifs of the representation of the culture of Soajo. It is this culture—objectified in a basic series of motifs—that the Soajoans themselves also make claims to, a fact that can be proven through a detailed analysis of *O Juiz do Soajo. História da Vila de Soajo em banda desenhada* [The Judge of Soajo. A Comic-strip History of the Town of Soajo]. This album represents an effort to create a representation of the culture of Soajo out of the place itself. A local cultural organization took responsibility for and created the plot, contracting with one of the country's most famous cartoonists. The idea was to create a great impact, since large editions in Portuguese, French, and English were printed so that the book might be accessible to tourists and the children and descendants of Portuguese emigrants.

In this way, we see how the registers of visits to the village—marked by ethnographic curiosity and a deepening, more or less, of ethnological interrogations—directly influence the process of establishing representations of local culture that take place there contemporarily. I would say that there is a parallel here. We can think of Soajo—or of the Minho or Galicia—in the same way that James Boon said we could think of Bali: "What has come to be called the culture of Bali is a multiply authored invention, a historical formation, an enactment, a political construct, a shifting paradox, an ongoing translation, an emblem, a trademark, a non-consensual negotiation of contrastive identity and more" (1990: ix). I believe that many of the passages that we have commented upon throughout this text suggest the aptness of this definition as a general comparative reference.

Diverging Citations

The majority of visits that are made to Soajo these days are rapid. We can predict that almost all of the written narratives that create the image of a "remote area" were produced on the basis of this characteristic celerity. It could suggest that the choice of Soajo as a place of significantly unique possibilities comes from the fact that tourists began to frequent the province in which it is situated relatively early on.

Tourism, an essentially modern phenomenon—initially a nineteenth-century perquisite available to the bourgeoisie to expand their possibilities of experiencing the world—arrived relatively late to Portugal. Its first significant developments coincided with the age of nationalisms. This temporal and ideological contextualization is worth looking at, given that nationalist sensibilities greatly conform to the vivid expressions of the touristic experience, as can be noted in a whole gamut of accounts from the period. They make explicit the fact that it was during those years that there was a convergence between tourist destinations and the possibilities for observing the peasant classes. These practices were often loaded with transcendent significations, with respect to the possibilities of imagining the national community in terms of its physical space, history, character, and oldest origins.

Tourism in the Minho, very much facilitated by the appearance of the automobile and by the improvement of roads during the nineteenth century, increased notably during the 1870s and 1880s as a consequence of the expansion of road and rail networks, which were constructed under *Fontismo* [a period of relative stability (1868–1889) following the political instability of the constitutional monarchy]. From that point onwards, this province became a preferred place for middle- and upper-class vacationing. Their destinations included farms, spas, beaches, and other pleasant places. The intensity of this activity is documented in a varied literature, including memoirs, the social columns in newspapers and magazines, various types of reporting and fictional texts, as well as photographs, engravings, paintings, and postcards.

It was also at the end of the nineteenth century that Soajo became a destination for short excursions—these were more one-offs and exclusive—narrated as effortful adventures whose protagonists were more well-known intellectuals with more or less specific ethnographic interests. However, we can also detect a presence in the available references of mere allusions based on the accounts of others by people who never actually visited. One distinctive criterion for the authenticity of one's knowledge of this place would be the ability to designate the inhabitants of Soajo as *Soajeiros* and not *Soajeneses*. The latter designation would be used by "someone who never went to Soajo" a phrase oft repeated in various texts, proof of the intense circulation of references to this location.

A visit to Soajo would have been relatively difficult until the second decade of the twentieth century, when the hydroelectric plant was built at Lindoso, a construction project that benefited the whole area by creating new means of access. Nevertheless, the village only became completely accessible by automobile when the inhabitants of Soajo undertook the construction of a stretch of road four kilometers long (about two and a half miles) in the early 1950s. This road connected the plant at Lindoso with the village. As such, it is only in the last four decades that it has become much easier to visit Soajo. This has turned the village into a leading consumption experience, from its mountainous landscape to the customs that its inhabitants are presumed to maintain. These motives for enjoyment had by then already been constructed through a longstanding process.

Soajo's relative inaccessibility until a short time ago could partially explain the multiplication of references to the village from that period in which tourism in the Minho began to intensify. It is from the end of the nineteenth century that, to employ Edwin Ardener's terms, the "topological" distancing of the village is increasingly noteworthy, and its effects felt. Notwithstanding, the relative "topographical" distancing that had separated Soajo from some of the more important urban centers, like Oporto, Braga, and Ourense, had been mitigated to a large extent (Ardener 1989). In truth, Soajo's isolation is certainly relative, situated, as it is, within a few dozen kilometers from the coast and quite close to the two other towns that any traveler around the year 1900 would have been disposed to consider "civilized." The general improvement in terms of access, making it possible to travel from Braga to Viana by train, and by public stagecoach—and quite soon after that by automobile—along improved roads towards towns located deeper in the countryside would have been a contributing factor to an imaginary distancing.

What I would like to say can be illustrated by a bit of irony. For King Don Dinis (1261–1325), who visited Soajo, or for any functionary of the crown employed during the seventeenth or the eighteenth centuries, this village would have certainly seemed hardly inaccessible, like any other village equally distant from the court. A reading of Leite de Vasconcelos or, to give a recent and quite obvious example, the televised comments of the *presidências abertas* promoted by Mário Soares (b. 1924) in the final years of the 1980s, suggest other ways of seeing things.* Apparently, a conceptual distancing is imposed on places that are less accessible to modern transport.

I imagine that the impossibility of reaching Soajo by road until quite recently, when the use of private, motorized transport had already increased, would have been a very prosaic factor in exciting imaginations and helping to establish an aura of the primitive around the locality.

---

* Mário Soares, 1924, one of Portugal's best known politicians, held the office of president of the Portuguese Republic from 1986 to 1996; his famous "open presidencies" brought him to some "remote places" in Portugal accompanied by high levels of media coverage.

Obviously, the inhabitants themselves had a different perspective during this century and half in which this topological distancing of their village was emphasized. A long and intense history of migration to Brazil, Lisbon, and, in the twentieth century, to the United States, Europe, Canada, Australia, and even to New Caledonia accounts for the way that the people of Soajo have felt a "permanent contact with the world." Edwin Ardener suggests that is what invariably happens with the inhabitants of "remote areas."(1989).

The idea that the inhabitants of mountainous areas are particularly primitive must be understood as a part of the discourse about the countryside produced from within cities which dates back a considerable period of time (Williams 1993). These views can be seen as the result of the historical exercise of political and symbolic power to which dominated peripheries have been subject.[2] In addition to general considerations about the genealogies of this discourse and its accompanying ramifications, it is important to keep in mind that in Portugal at the end of the nineteenth century, new attributions directed at the interpretation of the mountainous areas and their inhabitants suddenly began to appear. In Portugal, a Romantic fascination for the dramatization of mountainous landscapes and for the different ways in which their memory was preserved persisted until quite late. Nevertheless, certainties and new speculations fed by evolutionist notions and also by ethnogenealogical preoccupations whose expressions gradually became more popular eventually meshed with the numerous statements about these landscapes and their inhabitants. It is in this intersection of ideological references that we can better explain the multiplication of references and new qualities attributed to Soajo from the 1870s onwards.

The documentary references related to the village date back to the first centuries of the existence of the Portuguese state. Because this is a border area and rich in big-game hunting, it was the object of continual legislation (Pereira 1914). Afterwards, as Colette Callier-Boisvert remarks, more detailed information about the village, even before the end of the nineteenth century, begins to take on a certain form. A descriptive canon began to take shape in the chorographic dictionaries of the day, especially in terms of two principal references:

> The "difference" attributed to the people of Soajo is based, then, in sources like the Inquisition records, that furnish the material of two anecdotes that appear in various Portuguese chorographic dictionaries, starting with the *Corografia Portuguesa* by P. António Carvalho da Costa (1706), which served as a model for many works of the same genre. These anecdotes illustrate the fame of the "dignity" and bravery of the *Soajeiros*: on the one hand, the reclamations that they made against the nobility

proves that they do not accept insults or affronts; on the other hand, we have the noble attitude attributed to the judge from Soajo in Oporto, referred to succinctly by José Leite de Vasconcelos.

The parish-level inquiries that began to be administered in 1758 were also utilized for successive chorographic dictionaries. (Pereira 1914: 7–8)

It was in the last decades of the nineteenth century that visitors' accounts or allusions to the locality became frequent, directed now to an expanded public of readers. Each one of these accounts underlines other aspects of heritage, from the village's physical aspect to the daily life of its inhabitants. It is patent that a new sensibility guided these expanded ways of discussing its significance. Soajo was evolving into one of the localities specially favored for thinking about the remote past of the country. In this way, the village took on the qualities of a living document—even though it was always perceived as being in a state of relative ruins—and so was subject to varying interpretations of visitors, or of those who were merely alluding to it literarily.

It is worth comparing some of the descriptions and expectations that Soajo gave rise to with the idea of illuminating the mutation of perspectives to which I have been referring. This will be possible by comparing two authors who were working just a few years apart from each other. Gathering data from the old chorographies and news items, in 1880, Pinho Leal (1816–1884), the great compiler of the discredited *Portugal Antigo e Moderno,* describes Soajo and its inhabitants in the following way:

> This parish is situated in extraordinarily wild countryside, in the *Gabirarra* or *Gavieira* mountains, also known as the *Soajo Range,* near Castro-Laboreiro. ...
>
> The population here dresses in a coarse woolen cloth, made right there, from the wool of their sheep; they walk barefoot, and, if civilization has still not penetrated their mountains, disbelief or religious indifference has, as well, not arrived; for this reason they are true Catholics, even though somewhat superstitious. ...
>
> In this parish they also make a lot of charcoal, which is exported. ...
>
> When it was a game preserve it had a regular judge, two councilors, an attorney, two scribes and a company of messengers, of which the judge was the captain. (1880: 406)

It is worth emphasizing some of the presuppositions that are behind the above-cited extracts. Pinho Leal never visited Soajo. The methodology behind the creation of his magnum opus consisted above all in the gathering together of old bits of news and charters. For this reason,

Portugal Antigo e Moderno mirrors a compilation of geographical and sociological sensibilities that were already anachronistic at the time of publication. However, what is important to note is that various sugges-tions about this locality's "normality" are expressed in the description, following a standard successively reiterated in many other entries in this curious dictionary. In my interpretation, Pinho Leal—even if he points to the harshness of the climate, the relative lack of "civilization" of the *Soajeiros,* the poverty that led them to walk about barefoot[3]—leaves us with the strong suggestion that this is hardly an exotic locality. Soajo possesses its industries (livestock, rough woolen fabric, charcoal), is completely inserted into the history of the country, shares the same reli-gious beliefs, and exists under the same bureaucratic framework as other places.

The expectations raised by J. Leite de Vasconcelos in 1882 and re-corded in a text entitled *Uma Excursão ao Soajo, Notas numa Carteira* [An Excursion to Soajo. Notes in a Wallet], were very different indeed:

> Just as in the study of a vegetal or animal organism, when it reaches a certain point of development, we can at times recognize organs that have atrophied. In the history of humanity, some peoples are also spoken about that, through circumstances that impede their progress, or cause them to regress, represent civilization's archaic phases: these peoples are savages. Some authors even call them *primitive peoples, people that live by the law of nature.* In a refined nation the villagers mirror, in a certain fashion, that archaic phase that I refer to; and this is mainly true of the villagers from the mountains.

> Among the great number of mountain ranges that exist in Portugal, we often hear Soajo spoken about as a central site of primitive people, who preserve a kind of social organization particular to themselves, a dialect and a variety of truly curious and extraordinary customs. (1882: 3–4)

In truth, Leite de Vasconcelos soon lost his illusions when he visited the village, which, to his surprise, contained some "large houses" and even a parish church with whitewashed walls. Using his talents as a stu-dent of epigraphs, he revealed in an inscription on a fountain "which to someone less informed could have appeared to be Egyptian," the prosaic statement of a modest commemoration: "Manuel Cruz, name of the craftsman." Vasconcelos is one of the most famous protagonists of that discrepancy between reality and expectations that actually visiting Soajo has created for certain travelers. It is worthwhile to look at a another quotation in order to understand the intensity of his illusions and, con-sequently, the extent of his self-deception: "In proportion, however, to our coming to see and study the indigenous of Soajo, my utopic idea of finding there a specific dialect and a primitive civilization disappeared little by little: the *Soajeiros* can hardly be distinguished from the rest of the inhabitants of the Alto-Minho" (1882: 4).

If we take into account these utopian expectations, we might ask ourselves where Vasconcelos's conviction that he would find a "primitive civilization" in Soajo originated. Colette Callier-Boisvert suggests that Leite de Vasconcelos would have undertaken the journey to Soajo because of the "fame" of this village, a fame that would have been founded on old historical documents and parochial inquiries, as has already been noted in the citation above (Callier-Boisvert 1987). It is true that in his writings, Leite de Vasconcelos demonstrates a very detailed knowledge of historical Portuguese bibliography. However, this knowledge, rather than justifying, fails to reconcile beliefs in the presence of "primitivisms" in Soajo, as I have suggested already.

In addition to the "anecdotes" to which Callier-Boisvert refers—doubtlessly interesting and which even today are a justification for local pride among the people of Soajo—it must be agreed upon that nothing extraordinary about the village is said in the old documents, as I noted above when I examined *Portugal Antigo e Moderno*. It seems to me that the process of primitivizing Soajo and its inhabitants—and the peasantry in general, as the first citation of Vasconcelos suggests—spread rapidly between the years 1870–1880. It became a cliché in the mouths of the erudite already influenced by the theory of evolution. The fact that this was a recent phenomenon meant that Pinho Leal was unaware of it, leading him to a description that was closer to that of the eighteenth-century chorographers.

In the first years of the twentieth century, another author, José Cândido Gomes (1870–1936), published several volumes on Arcos de Valdevez entitled *As Terras de Valdovês* (1903), which made no special mention of Soajo. In truth, these are historical and descriptive memoirs written at the end of the nineteenth century, whose interest focuses on the "antiquities" of the parishes that constitute the municipality of Arcos de Valdevez before the administrative reform of 1852. For this reason Soajo would be left out because of the municipal autonomy that it enjoyed until that date. However, the author also includes in his work an account of an excursion to the famous sanctuary of the Senhora da Peneda, a place that was then on the boundary of the municipality of Soajo. Passing over the Alto do Mezio peak, and imagining the village of Soajo in the distance, Gomes had observed:

> Near to the road I had the occasion to observe the incomplete *Dolmen* of which José Augusto Vieira printed an image in his very interesting *Minho*

Pittoresco [Picturesque Minho] *ben como diversas mamôas* [as well as a variety of Paleolithic tumuli] that some archeologists claim to be Celtic graves. But, none of these prehistoric monuments hold out much interest for the traveler because they are rough and imperfect. (1903: 11)

The indifference with which the author comments on these remains of a remote past and the speculations that the archeologists had provoked is, indeed, noteworthy—these stones are merely "rough." What is important to note in this passage is that the lack of interest in the dolmen and the tumuli demonstrated by Gomes is ideologically loaded, as it is linked to a purposeful deemphasis on confirming or denying the "primitiveness" of the people of Soajo, already at the time a topic of discussion. Like Leal, Gomes writes from the perspective of the antiquarian, with little interest in the ethnological speculations that were already widespread in his time. On the contrary, he pays close attention to the sanctuary of the Senhora de Peneda, a late and impoverished replica of the Bom Jesus de Braga, and to the flow of many thousands of pilgrims traveling from distant places in the Minho and Galicia on feast days. There, in Peneda, the author indifferently registers the fact that "in those areas nearby to Gavieira and Peneda, according to some authors, still at the beginnings of the last century, semi-savage people lived, not being obedient to any authorities and paying an annual tax of five dogs" (1903: 27).

The bookish citation appears without any additional commentary or fascination expressed for the "semi-savage" people referred to in the passage. We find a similar indifference in the few antiquated references in which the same subject is mentioned. The author did not feel that he was in a "remote area" and, for this reason, this account by an "antiquarian" is particularly interesting. It tells of the presence at the Viana do Castelo workers' celebration of Galicians from various places, including a doctor of medicine, and even speaks of "Doctor José Maria Rodrigues, a professor from the University of Coimbra," as being among the many thousands of pilgrims.

Abel Viana (1896–1964)—a disciple of Leite de Vasconcelos who became one of Portugal's most important archeologists—wrote in the following way about the *Soajeiros* and the megalithic monuments in 1932:

From the photograph, taken without the intention of reconstructing the past, but rather to give a faithful reproduction of the present ... these two *soajeiros,* though their style of dress shows one more step taken in the path to modernization, form, with their hovel of rough stone, a typical ethnographic example among many that the mountainous Alto-Minho can still provide excursionists and scholars.

This is nothing more than a reminiscence of a vague yet significant trace of an older style of life which emerges from the prehistoric mists, surviving like this megalithic construction which greets us like an extemporaneous nucleus—a stage lost in the evolutionary path—the genesis from which sprung the ancestral *castreja* dwelling. (1932: 130)

When Abel Viana wrote this passage, the figure of a "*soajeiro*" had already been on display in the Museu Etnológico de Belém for quite some time, according to a reference made by Félix Alves Pereira (1868–1931) in 1914 (see also Vasconcelos 1922). As such, this type of "mountain dweller" par excellence was already monumentalized as at the symbolic center of the representation of the Portuguese people that Leite de Vasconcelos had instituted (Branco 1975). There was also, on the other hand, already an important bibliography of references out of which arose more statements disagreeing with the more daring speculations about the "documentary" value represented by the inhabitants of Soajo. The figure and the respective clothing had been a gift of Félix Alves Pereira, the curator of said museum, archeologist, and ethnographer from Arcos de Valdevez.

Pereira wrote about Soajo with great sensitivity and in minute detail employing very precise historical information. At the beginning of his text he casually mentions "Soajo, this species of Andorra of the Alto Minho, whose originalities travelers and chorographers have delighted in unscrupulously forging," remarking in a footnote, "I exclude the living from this appreciation; to do otherwise would be unjust" (1914: 25). However, in spite of the graciousness of this remark, it is notable that the "originalities" of Soajo would have their most remarkable success in the texts of the twentieth century, namely in the chorographies and other works of general reference that ended up registering these very originalities.

Curiously, Abel Viana bows to Alves Pereira when he cites Pereira's description of a traditional local costume: "This is the way in which the honest investigator and eminent teacher, Dr. Félix Alves Pereira describes it in 'Notícia sumária ácerca de Soajo'" (1932: 25). If we put to the side the hypothesis that Viana had not attentively read Alves Pereira's text—which seems hardly probable, since he was the editor of the periodical in which it was republished—some curious questions are raised. In the first place, we can speculate that it had been the regionalist passion and the intention to establish icons of the district's culture that impelled him to write in such anachronistic and grandiloquent prose. This is a strong probability that could be corroborated by any number of contemporary examples produced in the district and that primarily deal with Soajo, manipulating its representation along the same ideological lines. But we should also raise the suggestion that these lines express the degree of freedom felt in the register of ethnographic writing with respect to the elision of chronological considerations. Such freedom corresponds as well to the perceptive disposition of a good part of contemporary visitors to Soajo, as I have already suggested.

Another citation about the people of Soajo—more recent and especially curious in terms of the presuppositions on which it is based—will allow us to introduce questions developed in the passages that follow. Eugénio Castro Caldas, author of *Terra de Valdevez e Montaria do Soajo*, narrates a relatively recent episode in this monograph. It occurred following 25 April 1974 (the date on which the authoritarian regime in Portugal fell), and took place in Portela do Mezio, a high pass on the border of the parish of Soajo. The incident in question involves an altercation arising out of claims to the right of free pasturage in the mountains that at the time targeted installations of the Peneda-Gerês National Park. Sometime later, having become aware of the disturbances and vandalism that followed, the author went to see the area for himself:

> Right at the entrance, we came upon a shepherd who reminded us of a ancient Celt, paused against a stone dolmen of monolithic proportions, his hands and chin supported by his crook, like a vigilant sentinel, watching closely as we approached. ... We paused a bit to meditate over the scene, contemplating the Celt who seemed to us to have been brought back from the dead, someone we dared not communicate with, knowing that our words would say nothing to him because they were not his, but were of those who had made him into "a lackey." And we left with the certainty that this disrespect, that came to him by way of unforgiving history, would never be able to represent a progressive conquest on the way to a world which one day must be. (Caldas 1994: 260)

The assumptions that are contained in this slightly obscure passage are very interesting (suggesting an adjustment, perhaps unconsciously, to a very particular style established for speaking of the "Celts"; see Chapman 1982). In fact, it is the influence of 25 April that is at work here, and some of the consequences of the revolution are in play in the district, particularly in Soajo. Caldas continues with the following: "It was very easy for outside agitators to raise the flag that demanded the 'return of the uncultivated land to the people,' which in the minds of the remaining shepherds who still worked the mountain slopes corresponded to the utopian reestablishment of the traditional pasturage where the practice of burning the forests got in the way of re-forestation" (1994: 260).

I spoke with some of the inhabitants of Soajo who had been present during the unfolding of those episodes. Ironically enough, some of those very "Celts" had already read *Terra de Valdevez e Montaria do Soajo*. They were indignant at the suggestion that it had been "outside agitators" that had promoted those claims; they identified people who had been involved and their respective political affiliations. They guaranteed that all of those who took part in the events, even the principal "agitators," were from Soajo. What became plain to see was the fact that this area lived in synchrony with the course of events that the rest of the country was experiencing. There as well, collaborators with the deposed regime lost their prominence; sympathy for and affiliations with the parties of the Left and the extreme Left were on the rise, and the spirit of reclamation was growing.

Recalling the mind-set underlying the evaluations of Eugénio de Castro Caldas will allow us to clarify certain of the more characteristic uses of the citations about this famous mountain locality. It becomes clear in many texts that they have been used to speak about other things, beyond the locale itself and its inhabitants. They have served, quite ostentatiously, to speak of origins, of the present and of the destiny of the national community; in these uses, the references to the timeless character of this locality, thus placed on the margins of history, stand out. A passage from Jorge Dias's *Abrigos Pastoris na Serra do Soajo* will help to clarify this nearly omnipresent characteristic:

> The massifs of the Northeast of the country are a precious reliquary of living and dead archaisms. ...
>
> It is indeed difficult, at times, to say whether these or those stone mounds, which were dragged there by the hands of men, are pre-historic or just a few generations old. For this it would be necessary to sharpen the concepts of time and History. Of special interest to Ethnography is the fact that the life of man sometimes occurs in historical sub-stages, on vague and imprecise boundaries for those who study the historic and pre-historic sciences, that are by nature essentially temporal. (1950: 1)

A Continuous Composition of Metaphors

No Minho, a book by Don António da Costa (1824–1892) published in 1874, delves into the elements that combined to form the legend of primitiveness that still shrouds Soajo to this day. The book is an account of a trip to a variety of localities in the province, a lovely description of episodes and picturesque places. Its narrative technique emulates that of Laurence Sterne's *A Sentimental Journey,* or Almeida Garrett's *Viagens na Minha Terra.* Don António describes places, meetings, and various occurrences during the course of his travels with a certain attention to detail, namely, of two of the towns that are closest to Soajo, Ponte de Barca, and Arcos de Valdevez. Upon meeting an acquaintance in Ponte da Barca, as a curious example of the observance of rules of etiquette even on the border of what had been described as primitive wilderness, he feels the necessity to wear gloves to go that same night to the local theater.

It seems that his stopover in Arcos de Valdevez, the next town on the way north, was more fleeting. The details of the landscape that Don António includes in his book in order to describe the road, however, guarantee that he had "been there." On the other hand, the description of the customs of the inhabitants of Soajo and of another relatively nearby parish, São Miguel de Entre-Ambos-os-Rios (in the municipality of Ponte de Barca), called for a separate chapter entitled "The Barbarians of the North and the Commune." But when he describes the habits of these localities, his narration does not include even the smallest indication of having been in either of these places and hardly refers to the sources upon which he bases his considerations.

It is important to say that Don António da Costa's description is fundamentally kind. This is the case, for example, when he gives us a complimentary description of the integrity of mountain customs, of communal solidarity, and of their will for independence from the bureaucratic determinations of the state. In this sense, we can imagine that it could end up being adopted as a reference for the politics of local representation, an important question today for some of the inhabitants of Soajo that I know. On the other hand, his imaginary account is very explicit about his subject's lack of contemporaneity. Here Don António takes the *Soajeiros* and their coevals as direct representatives of the Germanic tribes that invaded the Iberian Peninsula in the first centuries of the Common Era:

> This barbarian inhabited our ancient territory and left his bloodlines. The blood transmitted itself, and is still curiously represented in the remote village of Suajo, ten kilometers from Arcos de Valle de Vez.

> They make up an authentic tribe, our people from Suajo, forgotten there for hundreds of years; and, as such, a notable canvas of customs. (Costa 1874: 194)

The origin of this very imaginative text is intriguing, coming apparently out of nowhere, since previous written records that contain descriptions of Soajo with these characteristics do not seem to exist. Alexandre Herculano had alluded succinctly to an ostensible primitivism of the inhabitants of the Soajo Range in the context of a description of the Minho that was run in numbers 27, 29, and 54 (1837–1838) of the famous periodical, *O Panorama.* We also find the following remark in the *Diccionario Geographico de Portugal e Suas Possessões Ultramarinas* [The Geographical Dictionary of Portugal and Its Overseas Possessions] (1852): "It is said that the inhabitants of Soajo still retain certain savage customs." However, these references are sparse and very much predate the articulation of the "primitive" portrait of customs drawn up by Don António da Costa. Rocha Peixoto suggests that this notion of the primitive had arisen from the constant reiteration of fictional descriptions that had led the author to speak of the survival of the "good men" of Soajo, with their clothes still fashioned from the "skins of animals" (Peixoto 1975: 574). The suggestion, which is curious, fails to clarify some of the research into the origin and the way this fiction circulated in times past. Nevertheless, in the context of the focus of this book, it is important to note that *No Minho* is one of the key texts from which the citations about Soajo and the habit of visiting the village spread during the last 125 years.

As had been stated above, Don António entitled his description of the mountain customs "The Barbarians of the North and the Commune." The choice of this title and a number of rhetorical details beg certain questions. The author had learned of communitarian practices and of other idiosyncrasies that marked the daily life of Soajo and of Entre-Ambos-os-Rios (things that were similar to much that existed in other parts of the country, according to the mappings made much later by Rocha Peixoto, Tude de Sousa (1874–1951), Orlando Ribeiro, and Jorge Dias). However, his fairly fantastical description—which would attract, after only a few years, a series of visits by prominent individuals—is a weak attempt to probe the ethnological antecedents of the nation. This is an aspect that would impel the curiosity of future studies by ethnologists of greater renown, all of whom basically debunk the pertinence of early ethnographic descriptions. And yet, Don António's intentions were never ethnographic; at no time did he present himself as an ethnologist or even demonstrate having a special interest in the ethnological discourse. He takes the inhabitants of the locality to be "barbarians," dresses them in animal skins, intensifies the colors of his account, and so satisfies the rules of picturesque description—it is a "sketch of customs" that the author offers.

Nevertheless, through these invented descriptions, he does want to mirror the "Republic" in Soajo and the "commune" in Entre-Ambos-os-

Rios. The author of *No Minho* was a republican and at that time, in 1874, the echoes of the Paris Commune cast a shadow over the whole of Europe. What I would like to say, quite simply, is that with Don António da Costa's proposal the possibilities for representing these two localities are qualitatively altered. It is really just a minor detail that a great part of these descriptions were imagined; we can argue with assurance that the same thing occurred with the older chorographies. The difference is in the much stronger emphasis on alterity that is attributed to these two localities, subverting their apparent "normality" suggested by earlier chorographic accounts. What is important is that the belief that there were "primitives" or "primitivisms" anywhere in the country—and not only merely poor people or those who lacked "civilization"—underwent a qualitative change in the context of the old descriptions of Soajo.

Pinho Leal and Tude de Sousa cite references to a curious "philosophical journey" described in a 1782 manuscript entitled *Diario Philosophico da Viagem ao Gerez,* at the time undertaken by the orders of the Archbishop of Braga. It is worth transcribing certain passages from this text, since they are similar to Don António da Costa's descriptions of Soajo and Entre-Ambos-os-Rios: "The village of Caldas belongs to the parish of Vilar da Veiga ... constituting a small republic, similar to that of our forefathers before they fell under the Roman, the Gothic and the Arabic yoke. ... The government is democratic, decision-making is confided to the village council and the sages' prudence is considered sacred" (Sousa 1927: 5 and ff.).

We see how this hand-written account of these "*ilustrados*" ["enlightened" individuals] diverges from the more accessible tone present in the chorographic reports, which were the most frequently employed means for learning about the country until the end of the nineteenth century. Having remained unpublished, its interest lies in the possibility of being considered as a marker for the beginnings of the history of the ethnological discourse in Portugal, which in its more refined expressions looked with great insistence at how the populations of Portugal's northern mountains lived. As Jorge Freitas Branco has suggested, we can identify the initial and decisive period of ethnography's gestation in the eighteenth century (1985). It is in this period of the "enlightenment," when the end of the ancien régime was already anticipated, that we find a remote antecedent—yet, nevertheless, a very direct one—in the famous monographs of Jorge Dias written in the mid-twentieth century. With this example, it is possible to think about an earlier starting point for the discursive construction of representations of difference, of "exoticisms of the countryside" as modes of representing the most unfathomable origins of the nation.

With Don António da Costa's description, Soajo and Entre-Ambos-os-Rios were now to be used for representing things other than themselves. The referential intentionality that animated the old chorographic reports was replaced. Now metaphorical strategies are valued—both localities were now to be used as available allegories for the appreciation of a wider reading public. To a certain extent, it is still for these same allegorical reasons that at least a part of the interest in visiting Soajo is sustained even today.

In fact, over the decades, some of the visitors who have left accounts of their visit saw quite surprising things. This suggests that something different affected, or had affected this place and its social life. These are differences that are freighted with an exemplary tone. As I have suggested above, these embody a mode of imagining the most remote origins of the nation. Along with this came commentaries about contemporary Portugal and suggestions for its future. In this way, Soajo became equipped to provide moral readings that transcended its mere existence, its actual history, and the daily life of its inhabitants.

Jaime Cortesão (1966) helps us to better understand the allegorical destiny of Soajo and other mountain villages that share the same kind of semantic notoriety in the context of imagining the country and the national community. *Portugal. A Terra e o Homem* does not directly allude to Soajo, but I think that the arguments raised in this chapter find common ground with this author's research.

Cortesão dwells on some of the most important works of the mid-twentieth century, and he deduces several lessons from these books; they are, respectively, *Villages et communautés rurales au Portugal,* by Orlando Ribeiro (1940), *A Cultura Castreja. Sua Interpretação Sociológica,* by Joaquim de Carvalho (1946), and the very well-known monographs by Jorge Dias (1948 and 1953). These are texts that, according to the author, show a "profound knowledge of the relationships between certain contemporary human groups and their deepest historical roots in the national soil" (1966: 63). These are ideas that were inspired by and received direct contributions from Francisco Martins Sarmento (1833–1899), from Rocha Peixoto, and from his editorial board at *Portugália,* as Cortesão confirms. He poses certain questions:

When we recall that the *castrejo* [fortified] organization of villages … dominated the northern and most populated part of the country, it is legitimate to inquire as to whether this fact, whose profound roots are still a part of many localities in the Minho, in the Tras-os-Montes and the Beira, is reflected in the formation of nationality or in the special kind of Portuguese patriotism.

He adds yet another significant observation a bit later:

> We believe as well that political sociology can, from these vestiges of an
> archaic and long-lasting social organization, uncover eloquent examples
> of the solution of the old problem of the relation between the individ-
> ual and the community, between morality and the strength of the state.
> (1966: 63–64)

We might also note some similar suggestions made over time about
Soajo, especially after having seen it promoted as a prototype of the
"Republic" in Don António da Costa's interpretation of its customs in
1872. In a book edited in 1902, we find Soajo singled out as an example
of an improvement in the democratic institutions of the constitutional
monarchy: "Conservative and independent, they have for many years
maintained their ancient traditions, among which their rural democratic
assemblies stand out. These are inheritances from the ancient Lusitanians, so simple, practical and beneficial" (Vilarinho de São Romão 1902:
59). During the years of the First Republic, Alfredo Guimarães declared
that Soajo was the "holy ark of native traditions," commenting on a
painting by the well-known artist Silva Porto (1850–1893)—*A Barca de
Serreleis*—where one of the most conspicuous icons of the nationalizing
discourse, the "Minhotan woman, peasant filled the foreground against
the backdrop of the Soajo range" (Guimarães 1916: 158). Later, in the
1930s, the Count d'Aurora would suggest that an exemplary precedent
of the realizations and the harmony promised by the ideological program of the *Estado Novo* could be found in the famous mountain village:
"Good people, those of Soajo. They are already experiencing the New
State. They meet in a General Assembly of Good Men—and there de-
cide upon the common good in a social sense, when the harvest should
begin, when it is right to gather firewood, who should go to look after
everyone's livestock" (1936: 138).[4] From the other end of the ideological
spectrum, in a more recent period, I recall that it was common to hear
people closer to the parties of the Left comment on how the habits maintained in Soajo exemplified, in a certain fashion, the possibilities promised
by "socialism." These ideas circulated in Viana do Castelo, the principal
city of the district where Soajo is located, in the years following 25 April.
But this is a widespread and persistent idea for which more-or-less explicit
illustrations are to be found in the reports of a variety of newspapers and
magazines that have appeared during the last three decades.

The occasional disappointments provoked by people's visits to
Soajo—"the (mis) encounters of Soajo"—are part of the same system of
interpretation. As has already been suggested, only some of the visitors,
once they have arrived there, testify to the fact that certain exemplary

anachronisms have already disappeared. A variety of reasons are invoked, like the fact that these days the place has been rendered mundane due to the intensity of the tourism that the village attracts and the corruption of customs caused by the return of natives to the village after having spent decades as emigrants.

The negation of the more imaginative originalities attributed to Soajo is practically as old as the pages of Don António da Costa. We can see how Leite de Vasconcelos had denied them already by 1882, after having made a trip to the mountains suggested by the enthusiastic description put forth in *No Minho.* A few years later, José Augusto Vieira, in *O Minho Pittoresco,* would also refute the more suggestive particularities of Soajo in a well-informed way and with plenty of humor:[5]

> It was nearly two o'clock when we entered the village. ... on the threshing floor of Penedo we made a sketch of the old and legendary mountain parish. ...
>
> It was the right thing to do to visit the abbot, and we did not want to deprive ourselves of this pleasure, especially since he more than anyone could open the treasures of the traditions we were seeking. ...
>
> He was a good type, venerable, from the Rocha Peixoto family, who cleaned the webs of illusion that Don António's book had placed in our soul. There they speak, for example, about respectable men who resolved arguments. Individuality does not exist in Soajo. Everything runs according to ordinary laws of this bureaucratic system that rules us. ...

J. A. Vieira tells the story of the "judge of Soajo" as an example of what "these still living traditions" consist of, as they "are little by little being absorbed in the great bath of sociability, and that much more promptly, as the people of Soajo emigrate today in great numbers to our principal cities and to Brazil" (1886: 336–40).

If we take into account that attentive observers, such as the more specialized ones like Rocha Peixoto and Leite de Vasconcelos, considered the existence of "primitivisms" in the social life of Soajo of little significance, we can ask why clichés about this village continue to persist. I believe that a small argument that occurred between these two famous ethnologists will shed some light on this question.

Lands of Traditions—Encounters

At the beginning of the century, a short and harsh polemic pitted José Leite de Vasconcelos and Rocha Peixoto against each other. This bit-

ter friction between the two scholars was concerned namely with the
Minho and where this province fit in the mapping of the ethnological
monuments of the country. A hardly favorable critical review of "Ensaios Ethnographicos" written by Rocha Peixoto in *Portugália* started
the controversy. Vasconcelos responded in the pages of O Archeologo
Português. The dispute came to a close, as far as I know, with Rocha
Pereira's counterresponse, once again in his famous magazine.

One of the phrases employed by Leite Vasconcelos in the *Ensaios* is
one of the topics subjected to harsh criticism: "in the Minho, classic
land of our traditions and ancient customs." Rocha Peixoto wanted to
refute this affirmation and did so with the following words:

> With the authority that he enjoys it surprises us that he locates in the
> Minho that which belongs by right to the Trás-os-Montes and the Beira.
> Mr. Leite de Vasconcelos knows the Eastern *transmontana* zone, includ-
> ing the town of Miranda, and certainly the multiple forms of supersti-
> tion, unparalleled in the Minho, have not escaped him. And as to the old
> customs, in Arga, in Castro Laboreiro, in Soajo, in Cabreira and in the
> Gerês [other mountain localities in Minho], only vestiges of what is now
> extinct exist —when they have lasted—of what is still the lively pastoral
> regime of some of the localities of the *barrosão* plateau and the lower
> slopes of Larouco. (1975: 573)

Rocha Peixoto would have been very familiar with the areas that he
refers to in the passage just cited. He had covered all of the mountain
byways of Northern Portugal, photographing individuals and the material culture of many of these "remote places." As well, with respect to
Soajo, his relatives were well-known and politically influential in the
whole of the surrounding region. However, I believe that his excellent
knowledge of the locality—and of the Minho in general—do not provide sufficient reasons to confirm or definitively negate the patrimonial
value of the customs of this province.[6]

We can observe that the dynamic underlying these preferences for
"primitivisms" is, as a rule, very subtle and should be perceived as assertions emerging from specific contexts. Localities or social groups can
be conceptualized as "remote," "primitive," or, more benignly, as "traditional" or "conservative," singularly close to the elites that bestow such
classifications because they feel authorized to produce representations of
local, regional, and national culture. One example taken from Viana do
Castelo, capital of the district in which Soajo is located, will allow us to
clarify the dynamics of the reproduction of the clichés of ethnographic
description.

In texts and in images referring to the city that have an ethnographic character, allusions to the fishermen of Ribeira or to the "old" wagoners or the journeymen of Abelheira always come up. These were the most emblematic inhabitants of the "traditional" neighborhoods of the urban perimeter. But when the focus of the ethnographic discourse widens to the level of the municipality, references to the customs of the fishermen from Castelo do Neiva and of the mountain parish of São Lourenço da Montaria become unavoidable topics. Both of these are located on the borders of the municipality, one situated in the mountains, the other on the coast. Ultimately, when the space of reference takes into account the whole district, then the mountain villages of Castro Laboreiro and Soajo, occasionally along with Castelo do Neiva, are mentioned.

This way of choosing ethnographic objects derives from the perceptions that were already supported by Leite de Vasconcelos and by his contemporaries. They implicitly regarded social-spatial borders as a type of monument that served to document the nation's past. On the other hand, I believe that these texts must be understood as being part of a traffic in erudite citations, always motivated by an allegorical intentionality, in which the referential material is the least important part, and even negated by its prosaic nature when these kinds of topical descriptions are proffered. I did fieldwork in Castelo do Neiva, for example, and all of the people with whom I met in that "remote place" felt in "permanent contact with the world," in spite of what the ethnographers have to say about the village.

The conflict of opinions between Rocha Peixoto and Leite de Vasconcelos must be understood as a dispute about classificatory precedents between two nationally influential scholars involved in a very specialized discussion. Both of the authors were perfectly situated to dispute specific classifications of the whole of the national territory. They agree between them in considering the mountainous areas to be contexts that are more archaic than the lower territories. But from this point on, they disagree about how to acknowledge and analyze things enduring from remote times, according to the knowledge they each gained from respective excursions to the mountains. It should be recognized that it is Rocha Peixoto who brings into the discussion a reference to "documents" of relative, yet incontestable, primitiveness in light of the criteria of the period: the presence of communitarian practices. According to his point of view, these practices remained alive in the mountainous areas of the Trás-os-Montes, while nearly dying out in the Minho.

The meaning of this dispute between these two learned men would be made redundant, in the narrower terms of academic debate, by the

Figure 16. Leite de Vasconcelos doing fieldwork in another "remote" Portuguese locality.

influential theses proposed by Orlando Ribeiro in his important article "Villages et communautés rurales au Portugal" and later in his famous book *Portugal. O Mediterrâneo e o Atlântico* (Ribeiro 1940, 1945). These texts defined a Portugal that was mountainous, "archaic," a sociological characterization divorced from an appreciation of the borders of "historical provinces" that had been a reference for the most important discussions at the end of the nineteenth century and the beginning of the twentieth. The ideas developed by Ribeiro in the 1945 text—which are present in an incipient form in some of the writings of Rocha Peixoto—

would become of central importance for the elaboration of the better-known works of Jorge Dias—an author who had already constructed a representation of the localities of the northern mountainous fringe of the national border without bothering to privilege the provincial mosaic as a reference.

Let us take up once again the ethnological polemic referred to above. Leite de Vasconcelos's response to the apparently more solid arguments of Rocha Peixoto is surprising and very interesting.

Figure 17. Rocha Peixoto (on the right) at the Pelourinho de Rebordãos.

Here is the meaning in which I employed the term *Classic* in the passage alluded to; *terra clássica,* that is, those areas that everyone (reasonably, or not—this is a different problem) whenever they speak or write
about them always consider them to be full of typical traditions and the
usual ancestral things. ... In other countries similar things occur. Ancient
Greece emphasized Arcadia; France emphasizes Brittany. (1907: 46)

In spite of all of the (mis)encounters that have occurred here, in spite
of the daily life and the diverse life stories of its inhabitants,[7] Leite de
Vasconcelos's citation provides us with a comparative thesis about Soajo's destiny. This has been, for its innumerable visitors, a classic site of
the imagination of the limits of the nation, a "remote area" instituted
through a peculiar history that this chapter has described. It is worth
presenting once again Edwin Ardener's rhetorical question: "A lifetime
of being treated as a princess turns you into a ordinary-princess; a lifetime as an untouchable makes you just an unexceptional-untouchable.
A lifetime of being in a remote area, turns you into an ordinary? What?"
(Ardener 1989: 218).

On various occasions I have traveled to Soajo to gather notes for
this chapter. These trips were attempts to reiterate the pattern characterizing common visits there, fleeting ones, as I have said. One Sunday,
in April 1998, for example, I traveled from Vigo to Soajo. There were
many other visitors at the "community threshing-floor," and lunch in
a restaurant in the village was "regional." Later, walking up and down
the narrow old streets there was time to greet the old women sitting in
the sun like photographs. It was possible, at each corner—inscribed in
buildings, in the window displays, or in each of the sporadic encounters
with the inhabitants—to document paradoxical expressions that touch
upon the daily life of "remote places." With respect to the activities of
the present-day "innovators," the most evident and systematic concern
the recuperation of many different houses and ruins. These are being
undertaken by ADERE-Peneda-Gerês in accordance with apparently
very purist criteria for the interpretation of the oldest local architecture.
Thanks to political will and the availability of more abundant budgets
these days, the Soajo of the next decades—in particular the character of
the village center—will better justify visitors' expectations.[8]

At the end of a tour through the texts on Soajo it seems important to
allude to one of the more recent references, a report entitled *Programa de
Recuperação de Centros Rurais, Plano Global de Intervenção, Centro Rural
Soajo-Lindoso* [Program for the Recuperation of Rural Centers, General
Plan for Intervention, Soajo-Lindoso Rural Center]. Here, in the very
objective language of the anonymous technicians of ADERE-Peneda-

Gerês, we are told of how the representations of Soajo are closely linked to the possibilities for its future. The mountain range, "environmental tourism," crafts and "mountain" products, classified monuments, and "traditions" are the principal resources for development in this zone. It is suggested that they be used and this use be gradually put into place by the actions of entities authorized for this purpose by the state. As is emphasized in their report, "It is necessary to reinvent the rationale for the mountainous regions, now integrated into a protected area." This report can be read to our advantage alongside the comic strip, *The Judge of Soajo*. There the "judge," brought back to life in this story, renders his "sentence" for the new generations of locals: "Unite and defend the ancestral culture of Soajo! Create activities that combat the human exodus, guaranteeing places of work in the region."

I believe that the positions of the state on the destinies of this "remote place" could come into conflict with the lives of the local inhabitants, as is indicated by a long story of frictions that has not been taken up here. But there are also various suggestions of encounters that are occurring that take into consideration the interests of both parties, in light of visitors' expectations. Through these adjustments the possibilities for representing the culture of Soajo will be secured.

Notes

1. This village was also sketched, painted, filmed, and, mainly, heavily photographed. For example, near the *largo do pelourinho,* a plaque marks the place where José Brito, "the painter of Soajo," spent long periods of time. Many were the drawings and paintings that over time were to be found in private homes, exhibited in various places, reproduced in magazines, and even printed on fabrics. At least three films were made in the village: *Lobos da Serra* in 1942, *Serra Brava* in 1948, and *Emigrantes* in 1975. There were others that never got off the ground for budgetary reasons. One of the soap operas (*Os Lobos*) recently broadcasted on the Portuguese television channel RTP began in Soajo.
2. See, generally, Williams (1993), Chapman (1992), and also François Walter (1991); the latter deals with the social construction of representations of the Swiss Alps starting in the eighteenth century. The case that Walter studies is important since this country's Alpine landscapes became a paradigmatic referent for the literary discourse on mountain ranges throughout Europe, including in Portugal and Galicia.
3. Something that, as a matter of fact, occurred in various parts of the country until fairly recently.
4. The citation from the Count d'Aurora is much more curious than one of the references we find in his very interesting *Roteiro de Ribeira Lima,* 1929, which is somewhat less mystifying: "The people from Soajo are in the habit of emigrating to Lisbon as bakers and those that return are called *Lisboanos.*" This note is echoed by what Leite de Vasconcelos, Rocha Peixoto, and A. José Vieira had already observed.

We should note that the ideological climate of the country was different in 1936 when *Pelo Grei, Exortações* was published—a suggestive title that is the origin of this citation.

5. In Soajo it was the priest who served as José Augusto Vieira's informant. He was a member of the influential Rocha Peixoto family from Ponte da Barca. The relatives of the famous ethnographer and publisher of *Portugália* controlled local politics for a number of decades, a fact that can be understood by curious references dispersed throughout his writings. The place of local mediators—from the council or the district—in the representation of the culture of Soajo is interesting and is worth specific treatment, for which there is not room in this context.

6. Rocha Peixoto knew Soajo well: there are scattered references in his works, he took photographs, and a relative of his was the local priest. In his article "O traje serrano (Norte de Portugual)" he notes, "The *Soajeiro*, who has emigrated to the capital in numbers, truly adapts, contrasting with the usual types, with their bell-bottomed trousers like those worn by the *fado* singers in the Lisbon dives."

7. In Soajo I met people with extraordinary experiences of emigration. For example, there was one person who had sold vacuum cleaners in the deserts of Australia, which reminded me of the stories of Raymond Carver; then there were two old men who had spent decades in the baking industry of New Caledonia. In fact, most of the people there have had a more cosmopolitan life experiences than majority of their middle-class visitors.

8. See what Edwin Ardener has said about the "paradoxes" that mark life in remote localities. The author lists nine suggestive points, which are accompanied by humorous illustrations. Points two and three pertain precisely to this paragraph and are entitled: "Remote areas are full of innovators"/ "remote areas are full of ruins of the past" (1989: 218–19).

Chapter 10

Trail of the Celts and the Lusitanians

In Santiago de Compostela in the Spring of 1999 I participated in the *Simposio de Antropoloxía "Etnicidade e Nacionalismo* in memoriam *Manuel Murguía"* [Anthropology Symposium "Ethnicity and Nationalism in memoriam to Manuel Murguía"], an event organized by the Ponencia de Antropoloxía of the Consello da Cultura Galega. The Late-Romantic historian, a pioneer of the nationalist discourse who also systematically outlined an argument defending the thesis about the Celtic origins of the Galician nation, was evoked. I recalled at the time an episode that I had witnessed in the summer 1997 on the stairway that divides the Praza da Quintana; I was there doing fieldwork in the "city of the Apostle." The stairway is a special place that serves, for example, as tiers of seats for the huge nationalist rallies on the 25 July national holiday and provides a place for the crowd on the Dia da Patria Galega, or during the nighttime concerts that the city government promotes. But, in addition to the tourists, it is a group of varied young people who have a reserved place there on any sunny day.

Often you can see someone in the group dressed vaguely in the "Celtic" style, or like a "medieval pilgrim," more or less ragged figures that always seem to me to have been inspired by the French comic books of the 1970s and 1980s.[1] They consume light drugs, drink a lot of poor-quality wine out of cartons, and there is always someone ready to play some kind of instrument. But as the day wears on, in addition to the moments of fun and calm, there are arguments and annoyances, and police intervention is frequent. One day when I was sitting in the sun close by, a characteristic argument broke out among the members of the group. In the middle of the racket, I was only able to clearly hear the shouting of one of the disputants: "You Basques don't even know where you come from ... the mother that you were born from ... where your language comes from. ... us the Galicians we're Celts ... Celts ... Ceeeeelts!"

The ethnogenealogical claim heard in Quintana made relatively rigorous use of the "myths of ethnic descent" (Smith 1999) that have been cultivated for such a long time now in the Basque and Galician nationalist discourses. "The Basque Mystery" is well known, as Joseba Zulaika tells us: "Humbolt and other renowned linguists have shown that *euskera* is an autonomous and distinct idiom in the world context. Its words and Basque grammar are *non*-Indo-European. This poetics of 'no' and of 'separation' is the first act for converting that which is Basque into a pristine ethnographic object. It establishes an intentionally irreducible differentiability" (1996: 21, author's italics). On the contrary, the defense of Galician Celticism was a component of particularist claims supported by various scholars even in the nineteenth century, registers that, as we have seen, predate the institutionalized political mobilizations of the beginnings of the twentieth century; this inheritance has been preserved in the Galician nationalist discourse up to the present.

Unlike Galicia, the trail of the Celts in Portugal, which we can follow up to the present, has been more discreet. This is due to the fact that other ethnogenealogical choices were stressed when nationalism began to emerge more intensely at the end of the nineteenth and the beginning of the twentieth centuries as an international ideology. At the time in Portugal it was the memory of the "Lusitanians" that was valued more. These were one of the populations of Iberia in the distant past that was mentioned in Greek and Latin sources. The Lusitanians had lived mainly on swathes of land that today constitute territory of the Portuguese state. The favoring of this interpretation stifled the mentions of the Celts that could still be found as part of the ethnogenetic speculations of some of the most notable Portuguese scholars of the late nineteenth century. This was due to the direct influence of discussions spreading throughout Europe in which Celtic themes periodically came to the fore (Chapman 1992; Juaristi 2000; Poian 1997; Poliakov 1971).

In recent years, however, one once again sees references to the Celts in Portugal. This follows an eclipse, the beginning of which is roughly datable to the transition from the late nineteenth century to the twentieth century. On the contrary, today it can be said that there is less mention of the Lusitanians and they have a lesser, or at least less exclusive, presence in the market of images about the past. Such references were, in contrast, unavoidable at the end of the nineteenth century and were popularized mainly in the decades following World War I, once they had begun to appear in literary descriptions, were put to rhetorical and commercial use, and employed in a variety of ways.

Apparently, it is in the north of Portugal that these new evocations of the Celts have multiplied the most, even though their mapping is still uncertain and it is also vague as to how they are consumed. What is especially curious is that this implies a set of emerging proposals for individual or communitarian identification until now unheard of in the Portuguese context. Here we will recognize one of the consequences of the growing fluidity in the traffic of ideas, of people, and of goods that the construction of the new European political and economic space has intensified, part of a more all-encompassing process that John Borneman and Nick Fowler referred to as "Europeanization" (1997).

Much of the "politics of difference" (Gupta and Ferguson 1992) that invocations of the Celts give rise to today in Portugal—or in Galicia, in more defined ways—seem to be independent from the immediate attempt to "produce localities" (Appadurai 1995). But it is true that since the end of the nineteenth century nationalist ideologues have used invocations of a Celtic past for their arguments. Today suggestive replicas of this strategy are still used in the transborder context that I am considering here. As such, the market phenomena that Celtophilia induces reveal themselves to be surprisingly dependent on limits imposed by the government formulas used in each of the Iberian states and on the specific histories of the construction of cultures that occurred in the two countries. These political-administrative and ideological boundaries significantly condition the rhetoric of appropriation of the past that the Portuguese and the Galicians can exercise with great prospects. Following U. Hannerz's suggestions, it could be said, from a broader perspective, that this example allows us to refer to how "cultural flows" in contemporary Europe are conditioned in various ways (Hannerz 1992).

In Galicia, "Like in Ireland, Like in Ireland..."

In more recent decades those theses about the Celtic origins of the nation that impassioned successive generations of native scholars are no longer defended in Galician academic circles. I was able to confirm this by consulting certain specialized university publications. The impression was then corroborated by informants who had done historical or archeological studies (see a recent specialized and critical account in Pereira González 1998, which can be compared to, for example, Otero Pedrayo 1980). However, for these informants my questions were in some way uncomfortable, or brought up dilemmas because those consulted were highly conscious of the lasting prominence of Celticism in Galicianist rhetoric and the way in which these ethnogenealogical claims are favored even today. For this reason, it was the measure of their sympathy for Galicianism that influenced the degree of cynicism in their comments on the inevitability of the "invention of traditions."

Nevertheless, those old scholarly theses endure as a general reference—at least the most easily articulated ones—of the ethnogenealogical beliefs maintained by the greater part of the people that I met when doing my fieldwork in Galicia. As I would like to emphasize below, there are various possibilities for finding ideological affinities between the hazy convictions of the more or less marginalized young people—like those who habitually sit on the stairway of the Praza da Quintana—and the foundations of institutional initiatives that are very frequent in today's Galicia. Both, in the end, refer to the same myths of origin that since the nineteenth century have allowed for the portrayal of the Galician nation through history.

In the mid-1960s, the famous Galician writer Alvaro Cunqueiro (1911–1981) gave a lecture in Lisbon where he spoke with real grace and complete poetic license about the Celts and their influence on Galicia.[2] Cunqueiro combined his knowledge as a chronicler of the daily life of his country with an enormous familiarity with legends of the Arthurian cycle, incorporating as well tantalizing considerations of Galician historians' discussions about the lineage of the nation. He evoked the taverns of Vigo and football clubs, brands of cigarettes and a large number of topics, or even industrial products in order to illustrate the lasting memory of the Celts in Galicia during recent decades.

At one point, Cunqueiro commented ironically about the forgetting of another *pobo nobre e valeroso* [noble and brave people] whose memory, he said, would have been worth perpetuating with equal exuberance in his Galicia: the Suebi. But only the name of some of Vigo's innumerable taverns and the title of a hardly relevant magazine published in Buenos Aires in the beginning of the twentieth century (*Suevia*, 1916) served as examples of recent appeals to the memory of that ancient people. Since it is impossible to articulate from where all the twists and turns of Cunqueiro's imaginative lecture derived, I would like to simply note that manifestations of Celticism have multiplied in Galicia and that even today the *valerosos* Suebi remain forgotten.[3]

Celticism owed its introduction to Galicia to the contributions of some of the most important Romantic historians, scholars like Verea y Aguiar (1775–1849), Benedito Vicetto (1824–1878), and Manuel Murguía, all of them inspired by the European circulation of these ideas, which had become more intense since the end of the eighteenth century

(Chapman 1978, 1992; Dietler 1994; Pomian 1997; Thom 1995). Galician intellectuals depended mainly on French sources, but also benefited from the circulation of these ethnogenealogical theories that had already begun to take place in Spain (Barreiro Fernández 1988; Juaristi 2000).

Barreiro Fernández gives the best account of the paths that Celticism followed in Galicia during the nineteenth century, noting at the same time the possibilities revealed in its later political deployment as a predominant reference for the articulation of particularist definitions of the Galician nation: "The discovery of Celticism and its later mythification allowed for the pseudo-historical argumentative axis which completed a double function: to coherently articulate the historical process experienced by Galicia in the double dimension of internal and state history and make claims through history for the singularity of Galicia, the first step to making further claims" (1988: 77).

In fact, Manuel Murguía was the bright light in consolidating Celticist speculations and their use. In one of his most famous works he has the following to say:

> The day on which the Celtic tribes got their first foothold in Galicia and took over the extensive territory comprised by the Galician province, to which they would give a name, a language, a religion and customs, in one word, a whole life, this day ended the power of the inferior peoples of our country. Whether or not they were more refined or more humble people, yellow in complexion, monosyllabic language and a rudimentary intellectual life, they had to simply move aside and disappear. Neither in their race, nor in their customs and superstitions, not even in the names of the locality did they leave marks of their passing. (Murguía 1985: 21–22)

Celtophilia would continue to occupy a very relevant place in the theoretical establishment of Galicia's national particularities, which the so-called *xeración Nós* began presenting by the end of the 1910s. In the first issues of the periodical, which gave its name to this famous group of Galicianist intellectuals, some of the more substantial articles laid the ground for these kinds of interpretations with older and revised arguments, arguments proffered, namely, by the imaginative and well-informed Vicente Risco, the decisive theoretician of Galician nationalism during the years in which it became consolidated as a political movement.

In a 1919 text entitled "O druidismo no século XX" [Druidism in the Twentieth Century], Risco clearly demonstrates that he would take on the role of "archdruída" [archdruid] of Galicia, expressing his fascination with the white robes, the crowns of "follas de carballo feitas de cobre" [oak-leaf clusters made of copper], and the "torques d'ouro" [torcs of gold] glittering in the *Gorsedd* [a meeting of bards] as he reported in the *Cambria* or in the *Armórica* (that is, in Wales and Brittany). The text concludes with the following:

> If these customs were to be adopted in our land, they would not only gain the help of brother peoples, they would also advance our artistic and patriotic education and raise up all the virtues of our race. Galicia is the only Celtic nation that does not link up with the others in order to maintain the spirit of its race. And whatever fails in the spiritual confederation of kimvs and Gaels, it is time for Arthur's horn to respond to the horn of Breogán. Long live the Celtic countries. (*A Nosa Terra*, no. 93, 1919)

Prior to Risco's neodruidic fantasies and the erudite arguments that circulated among his co-religionists, Celticism had earlier infused the culture of the Galician masses in more prosaic ways. One of the common vehicles for it was the "American" periodicals of the last decades of the nineteenth century, which heavily influenced the worldview and imaginations of the many thousands of emigrants of the large Galician communities of Havana and Buenos Aires, for example. Its influence in Galicia was linked to the return of emigrants and their money, which stimulated new expressions of capitalism in the major Galician cities at the beginning of the twentieth century. It was in Vigo and in La Coruña—and through the advertising of new industrial products or sports for the masses—that Celticism flourished conspicuously, beyond poetic and scholarly circles where it had been cultivated since the beginning of the nineteenth century. In this way, viewing the subject as Álvaro Cunqueiro does, we can note that the soccer club, Real Celta de Vigo, is as old as the Celtophile texts published the magazine *Nós*.

References to Brittany and to Ireland were very frequent in Galicianist rhetoric from the beginning, and these locations were increasingly emphasized once politically nationalist claims began to emerge in 1916–1918. Ethnic affinities among these distant places were stressed, as were cultural similarities; the parallels in these respective particularist movements and declarations of solidarity were resounding. However, I believe that direct contact was rare or practically nonexistent and that the circulation of information between Galicia and the other "Celtic nations" was likewise limited; this is evidenced by the type of references found in the Galician press over the decades. For example, references to the Irish movement in support of Home Rule were literary and distanced, like those maintained by the exceptionally well-informed "regionalist" intellectual, Alfredo Brañas, author of the influential poem/slogan still repeated today in Galicia: "Ergue, labrego! Erguete e anda! Coma en Irlanda! Coma en Irlanda!" [Rise up peasant! Rise and go forth! Like in Ireland! Like in Ireland!] (see, generally, Brañas 1990). It was notably through the large information agencies that Galician nationalists received their knowledge about the course of the war for the independence of Ireland towards the end of 1910. Those of the *xeración Nós* sung with emotion of the martyrs of Irish independence, or wrote articles about the demands of the regionalists of Brittany. However, there are no explicit pieces of news about direct contact with politicians or intellectuals of any of the movements active at the time in the "Celtic fringe."

For a variety of reasons, references to Ireland had an exemplary character. Some were founded on old myths, given that, supposedly, it was Celts coming from Galicia who conquered Ireland in remote times. According to the *Leabhar Gabhala (Book of the Conquests of Ireland)*, this expedition had occurred under the mandate of King Breógan.[4] This is a mythical person who is alluded to in the Galician Anthem—which dates back to the end of the nineteenth century and was interpreted for the first time in Havana in 1907. Today it is official. Various versions allude to the Galicians as *fillos* [sons and daughters] of *Breógan*, or to *The Nation of Breógan*. I witnessed the emotional performance of this hymn by thousands of Galicians on variety of occasions. On the other hand, from the middle of the nineteenth century onwards, under the influx of the Celtic Revival, the intellectual and artistic circles of Ireland and the Irish diaspora in North America provided especially prestigious representations of what was "Celtic": these constituted ideas and elements of material culture that were widely circulated in cosmopolitan contexts, as T. J. Eldstein (1992) suggests. Other noteworthy aspects were more practical in political terms. They were expressed through examples of radicalism and the conquests achieved in the context of the Irish nationalist movement, which culminated in the establishment of the Republic of Ireland in 1921, when the political organization of Galician nationalism was still in its very early stages.

The neo-Latin origins of Galician should have been one of the more noticeable weaknesses in the argument for attempting to include Galicia among the "Celtic nations." We have seen how Murguía also saw his presumed Celtic ancestors in their bestowal of the language, an important question at the time, given the prestige of philology as the model discipline for securely speculating upon ethnic origins (Poliakov 1971). The mysterious vanishing of the linguistic inheritance of the Celts in Galician lands remained a compartmentalized theme in much of Murguía's work as in those of his successors, save, as a rule, those philological speculations about certain toponyms thought to be the most promising.

Still today, this absence is one of the most important reasons for why the Galician culture is hardly recognized in the context of "Celtic Europe." Its more comprehensive linkage to the circuits of exchanges and solidarities that exist among the ethnolinguistic nationalist movements that function in France and the United Kingdom is hindered (see the suggestive illustrations of McDonald 1989).

What the Archeologists Say and Lessons in a Head of Beer

Recently, an archeologist from one of the most important Spanish universities raised the delicate subject of the possibilities for determining the past presence of Celts in Galicia. Ruiz Zapatero narrates the fluctuations of interest in the Celts and the Iberians on the part of Spanish intellectuals from the beginning of the nineteenth century, relating these interests to the succession at the state level of ideologies and regimes. He suggests, in passing, that these fluctuations were especially curious in the first decades of Franco's authoritarian regime, when the pan-Celticism of the protohistorical interpretation of Iberia was an advantageous stance to take in official archeological circles, reflecting to a great degree the political sympathies that ruled in the new regime, dovetailing with the Germanic training of some of the then prominent archeologists. Speaking of more recent years, from the beginning of the 1980s onwards, Ruiz has the following to say: "For example, Celtic mythologizations appear to awaken a response in the North of Spain, in regions such as Galicia and Cantabria, precisely where the rigorous examination of the archeological evidence makes it very difficult to 'see' any Celts in the traditional sense" (Ruiz Zapatero 1996: 190).

I would note in passing that, in this illustration of recent appropriations, we can perhaps recognize an instance of irony in the dynamics of the peripheralization of customs—and of the localization of the Celts—thoroughly discussed by M. Chapman (1982). The truth is that Ruiz Zapatero does not even cite the Galician archeologists of the twentieth century who spent their lives looking for scientific proof of those ethnogenetic claims, and who are today celebrated through the most diverse initiatives in the Comunidade Autónoma de Galicia. However, it is also true that in the most unsuspected reference works of the second half of the twentieth century—like in the monumental *Historia de España,* which was written under the direction of Menéndez Pidal, or in *Los Pueblos de España,* by Julio Caro Baroja—references to Galicia as a bastion of the Celtic presence on the peninsula are still reaffirmed.

I believe, however, the most fascinating question suggested here—beyond the quality of the scientific information that the great Galician nationalist archeologists have at their disposal, like Florentino Cuevillas or his disciple Fermín Bouza Brey (1901–1973)—is to be found in the expressions of Celticism in contemporary Galicia. In this register preferred by anthropologists the conditions of scientific proof from the work of archeologists are irrelevant, but the fascination with the possibilities of analysis that the reproduction of a national culture offers is all engrossing.

In more recent years, with the end of the dictatorship in Spain, the possibilities for contact between Galicia and other areas of Europe have become increasingly possible, privileging the so-called *orla céltica* of Europe, which includes Ireland, Brittany, Scotland, Wales, Cornwall, and the Isle of Man—considered for a long time now by the more enlightened Galicianists as the only remaining "Celtic Nations." Today these kinds of recognitions are becoming more widespread and popularized through different individual and institutional initiatives or by way of various habits of consumption, to which a flourishing market in contemporary Galicia responds.

In Portugal, for example, I have heard the Celticism of the Galicians confirmed by reference to widely differing—and debatable—factors, such as the quantity of people with light complexions, or the existence of megalithic monuments, but also by the variety of Celtic music heard in the bars, or the importance given to having Irish beers on offer, and the designs used in the jewelry sold by street sellers in Santiago or in Vigo. Also for many foreign visitors to Galicia whom I've met in Compostela, the recent abundance of images and the merchandise on offer confirm their expectations that they have come to a "Celtic country." I do not think that these apparently superficial associations should be neglected, since today the quantity of theoretical references that allow us to relate the circulation of stereotypes to patterns of consumption and claims for social identities is considerable.[5]

If we highlight the matrix-like character of the pre-1936 arguments that go into the description of Galician culture and its supposed proto-historical roots, and which today have spread rapidly among the population, we will be able to account for the reflexivity of many of the current expressions of Celtophilia in Galicia. Thus, the conviction that there are pan-Celtic affinities has led various Galicians that I know to travel to Scotland and Ireland for holidays. A variety of others have sought out partners for theater projects in Brittany, organized excursions for livestock farmers to go to Wales, begun to play music originating in

the "Celtic nations," fraternized with the Irish when working season-
ally in London, passionately translated Irish authors, participated in the
organization of "Celtic" music festivals in Galicia, and learned how to
engrave Celtic motifs in *talleres* [workshops] sponsored by the Xunta de
Galicia.

I have now summarized the many stories I've been told over time,
whether related to specific consumption, or biographical peripeteias
that are familiarizing contemporary Galicians with the Celtic world. All
of them, in some way, can be related to the currency of a group of references that are being reproduced in a cumulative fashion and are favored
by both the new political conditions existing today in the Spanish state
and through the parallel process of European integration.

In a recent text, Jon Juaristi parodies the kind of cosmopolitan images that more generally represent what is categorized as Celtic:

> When we hear the Celt spoken about we immediately think of Ireland,
> Scotland, Wales and Brittany. Perhaps also in Galicia. The better in-
> formed contemplate this group together with Cornwall and the Isle of
> Man. We will also think of bagpipes and harps, in misty landscapes at
> the sea's edge, whiskey, woods populated with fairies and little dwarves,
> phantom armies, banshees, companies of saints, jigs, Merlin the magi-
> cian, sad ballads, kilts and plaids, tuna pastries and films by John Ford.
> You must be clear that this vision happened yesterday afternoon. (Juaristi
> 2000: 229)

In recent years, in Galicia, in addition to the habitual *empanadas*
[savory pastries]—and the beliefs in the *Santa Compaña,* which, as was
noted in chapter 2, has so attracted ethnographers since the nineteenth
century—there has been a multiplication of images of gnomes, translations of stories and fairytales, the native production of this kind of children's literature, performances of witches and magicians in the streets of
cities and towns, and so on. The Comunidade Autónoma has become
the *terra meiga*—that is, a land of witchery—in the official tourist pub-
licity, and the scenographic effect of mists in the images of cliffs and
forests has been emphasized in its propaganda. Dyck whiskey, which
was consumed in the Spartan period of the Franco regime, has been
substituted in the bars by 100 Pipers, bottled in Scotland, the brand that
is commonly referred to in Galicia as *cen jaiteiros.* Musicians who play
electric guitar, *rockeros* from the late 1970s, have switched to bagpipes,
harps, and accordions, some of them gaining fame for their Celtic music
on world music circuits. Already a promising younger generation, players of Galician music—which is nearly always described as Celtic—are
graduating directly from the bagpipe schools, which, in recent years,

have multiplied infinitely and produced "regimental" bands mimicking the Scotch.[6] There are also visionary columnists who editorialize in the newspapers that Galicia has optimal conditions to compete against Wales as the setting for large-scale American films with a "Celtic ambiance."

In the end, the examples of what we can gather from Galician daily life are infinite, where each day the signs of a new material culture multiply. This culture replicates or appropriates traditions already invented long ago in Scotland or in Ireland. Yet, in addition to the objects, there are also people who circulate with increasingly greater freedom in the ambit of the Celtic fringe and through these experiences decidedly transform the course their lives are taking.

In Santiago, one of my informants was a Scottish man, Shawn, a long-time resident in Galicia, who had met his present wife—a Galician-speaking teacher with nationalist leanings—when she was traveling in Scotland. After their marriage, he found work in an Irish bar in Santiago, very typical establishments that can be found in all of the world's major cities. Even if Santiago is not a large city—nor are Vigo or La Coruña—there are various Irish bars there, or others where you can get drinks imported from Ireland. When I was doing my fieldwork in 1997–1998, these were numerous and older than those that could be found in Portuguese cities. In fact, there was such a variety on offer that it could be considered an indication as to how the Celtiphilia that infuses national culture has precociously turned Galicia into a market especially interesting for promoters of this kind of global business.

In the first job that he was able to get in Galicia, Shawn had learned to make a small and perfect clover—one of the symbols of Ireland—in the foam of the pints of Guinness. This trick charmed the customers at the new bar where he worked while I was living in the city. My informant never learned how to speak Spanish, so that he expressed himself exclusively in Galician, giving rise in this way to a rare case of monolingualism in a context vigorously marked by diglossia, as in Santiago (and Galicia as a whole). In our conversations he showed himself to be quite convinced about the Celtic character of many of the monuments, music, and traditions of Galicia. He told me that he wanted to learn Gaelic shortly, a desire he clearly linked to a return to his ancestral roots, something that his experience of living in a rural locality near to his parents-in-law has inspired in him.

In Scotland, where he had spent most of his life, Shawn had lived in one of the major cities of the south where English was spoken. On his visits to the village in the Highlands where his parents were from, he had never felt the need to learn Gaelic (see MacDonald 1997). As I was able to verify over time, it was not detailed bookish references that had formed Shawn's recognition of what could be considered to be "Celtic," and that this seemed shared between Galicia, Scotland, and Ireland.[7] It was, above all, a group of quite fluid beliefs, transmitted orally, that he had come to mainly since his arrival in Galicia. The expansion of references was due to the fact that the people he came to know after leaving Scotland were more highly educated—and sympathetic to the nationalist cause—than the people of the working-class environment in which he had been raised. For this reason, it does not surprise me that Shawn should valorize his experiences of the rural context and speak about what he imagined to be "Celtic" in Galicia and common to other nations. Even if these conversations occur more often in urban centers, it is as a discourse about the rural world and about its alleged mysteries that it could be more legitimately analyzed.

The Somewhat Well-known Stories of Nicolas Thomas and the Gossip of Primitivo

The Simposio Etnicidade e Nacionalismo was an international meeting at which scholars of these phenomena—historians, anthropologists, and political scientists for the most part—of various "peripheral nationalities" of Europe, like the Basque Country, Catalonia, Ireland, Scotland, Brittany, and Flanders, were present. The content of their lectures varied, but mostly they were very up to date in relation to the critical bibliography that the themes under debate had given rise to in recent decades.

One of the guest speakers was an academic from the University of Rennes, in Brittany, Nicolas Thomas. I had plenty of opportunities during the three days of the conference to speak with this professor of political science. His presence had been arranged through an institutional contact arranged by the Consello da Cultura Galega together with the University of Rennes, there having been interest expressed by the organization in having a representative of Brittany present, as the coordinator of the event explained to me. I understand that institutional contacts with Brittany had not been frequent, at least on the part of the Consello da Cultura. But, on the other hand, in Santiago, institutionally sponsored events that can count on the presence of academics from Brittany, Scotland, Wales, and Ireland are now frequent, mainly taking place at the University of Santiago, an institution that has been Galicianized in recent decades under the auspices the Estatuto de Autonomía. This is also the case in areas connected with commerce and industry, if we take into account the news reports on the Galician television station TVG or in Galician newspapers at the time. It seems that there was a noteworthy desire to favor these contacts that fall within the ambit of the Celtic fringe, suggesting an intertwining of prosaic desires to emulate the erst-while economic successes of the "Celtic Tiger"—Ireland—with the de-sire to use old metaphors that supposedly describe cultural affinities.

In one of the sessions of the symposium, Nicolas Thomas presented a lecture entitled "Mouvement Breton: la culture au coeur du politique" (see Thomas 2001). In it he related the more salient phases of the na-tionalist movement in Brittany throughout the twentieth century, em-phasizing the importance of claims made in terms of the language and the autochthonous culture, in contrast to claims for political autonomy. In our earlier conversations, I was surprised by the quantity of auto-biographical references and descriptions of the culture of Brittany that he introduced that I would have thought stereotypical. They seemed like parts of the descriptive discourse—at moments sardonic and hardly common in ethnographic texts—as described by Maryon McDonald in her work on the Breton movement.

For example, Thomas told me about the harshness of the repression imposed in the past—indeterminably long ago, in fact—on those chil-dren in the schools who spoke Breton instead of French. He also spoke of the classist humiliations that the use of Breton could presumably give rise to in the more modest social classes or for the inhabitants of small rural or fishing communities. In his case, his middle-class parents did not speak Breton. Only his paternal grandparents did, which meant that he did not have the opportunity to learn the language as a child.[8] He lamented his ignorance of Breton and had made some attempt later to learn this difficult language (McDonald 1989), but failed for lack of time. Another characteristic in McDonald's description seemed to be the epic dimension superimposed on the narration of the constancy of the Bretons' resistance to the French and their culture. At certain mo-ments in our conversation, Thomas even suggested to me that there was a dual opposition between two irreducible worlds in which one of them seemed condemned to disappear for being weaker and dominated (see also Chapman 1978, 1992).

In truth, our ongoing conversation allowed Thomas to speak less dramatically about suggestions of oppression and the imminent disap-pearance of the defenseless, autochthonous language and culture. There was, as a matter of fact, some good news. He'd talked in his lecture about progress being made in the recuperation of the use of Breton, of the current strength of the nationalist movement and of the legal guarantees that it had received. On one of the mornings, however, news from France stopped Thomas in his tracks: a bomb had exploded in a McDonald's restaurant in a small town in Brittany, leaving one man dead. The radicalism of the antiglobalization movement was discussed and later, inevitably, because we were in Spain, the demands for independence of many in the Basque Country.

Yet, in addition to the disastrous news that each morning can bring, and taking Edward Bruner's suggestions as a reference, we can affirm that in this case a "new narrative" or "dominant story" was emerging about Breton culture (Bruner 1986). The darker threats of assimilation, which in the past seemed ineluctable, have been exorcized, and the account of affronts has been ascribed to an indefinite past and to distant and badly defined victims. The persistence of cultural militancy has clearly contributed to the "resurgence" of Breton culture (Bruner 1986).

These same generally positive perspectives are also thriving in Galicia. Even if alarmist references to the threats that could lead to the loss of "identity" and "the language" are still active, I believe that the current time can be characterized by celebration and hope for the future of the autochthonous culture. This had been defined in a way that up to the present has been very influential, by Murguía and by the Galicianist intellectuals of the 1920s and 1930s, in whose contributions the Europeanist vocation of the Galicians and their supposed affinities with the countries of the "Celtic Fringe" of Europe are invoked. They have arisen as a clear counterpoint to the Berber origins of the Iberians, whose descendants were supposed to have been responsible for the centuries of oppression of the *Terra* in the context of a centralized Spanish state (see for example, Castelao 1976).

On one of those April afternoons—the conference was still underway—I ran into Primitivo, an informant and a friend who was always up on the latest intrigues connected with the cultural world of the Comunidade Autónoma. As I have already noted, this is a terrain of intense political disputes that mainly center on prioritizing the attribution of important resources available for the promotion of Galician culture by the Xunta, which, as a rule, the nationalist opposition considers either insufficient or badly managed. He told me that he had recently heard that the Festival Internacional do Mundo Celta at Ortigueira would be financed by the Xunta de Galicia.

Primitivo was a bit confused and indicated that he had ambiguous feelings about this news that was being whispered about at the time. His connection to that pioneering event in Galicia was an old one and very emotional, as I had already come to know from past conversations. Primitivo had come from one of the coastal villages in the north of Galicia, near Ortigueira, and he had been connected to the management of the Festival do Mundo Celta from the beginning, in 1978. For example, he had already described the police charges, frequent in those tumultuous years of the democratic transition following the death of Francisco Franco. He had also explained to me the reason behind the interruption of the festival for several years: the growing attendance of heroin addicts had made producing the event impossible. It has only recently been re-initiated. Primitivo told me, humorously: "Non sei porquem, os yonkies a musica celta cae-les bén" [I don't know why, Celtic music goes down well with junkies].

The truth is that some time later, when I returned to Lisbon, this privileged information received from my friend was confirmed: the website of the Consello da Cultura Galega announced, in very suggestive, self-congratulating terms, that the Xunta had become the sponsor of the International Festival of the Celtic World.

Other *Lições de Cousas** on This Side of the Minho River

In *Ricos e Pobres no Alentejo* [The Rich and the Poor in the Alentejo], José Cutileiro takes note of the opinion of one of his informants who had described genealogy as a "marvelous science" because it obliged us to lie only once (Cutileiro 1977). I believe the possibility for broadening the use of this strong image is contained in certain recent literature that links this expression to nationalist phenomena (see, for example, Smith 1999 and de Heush 1997). If we accept that which Rui Zapateiro suggests—and if we consider Cutileiros's suggestion—we can say that "one" ethnogenealogical "lie" was told long ago in Galicia that gained an enduring efficacy. As we have seen, Celticism has remained notoriously impermeable to the prosaic results of bringing our knowledge of the protohistorical past up to date; today it feeds many of the expressions that most mark the new Galician national culture. This is the case with the music, in design themes, in new consumption practices, and in a diversity of initiatives by "resurrectionists" (Samuel 1994). These tendencies have already spread to small rural localities where, for example, Celtic festivities are becoming increasingly frequent and children read fairytales about elves written in Galician.

On the contrary, in Portugal, the adherence to a well-defined (nation-constituting) ethnic ascendancy was less linear. This was a process that began to be disputed in the 1870s with the comparison of different theses that today would surprise us for their speculative fantasy. The major role in the gallery of ancestors of the Portuguese nation was given to the Lusitanians, although in an "unwilling" way, as João Leal suggests

---

* "Lessons of things," literally; "things" is spelled in the antiquated form.

in a text in which he links these claims to a small group of academics and writers—mainly Martins Sarmento, Leite de Vasconcelos, and Jorge Dias—all of whom, in his opinion, did not come to feel completely assured in their defense. Leal himself views their theses as "unbalanced and incomplete, perhaps even failed" (Leal 2000).

The choice of the Lusitanians as the most important ancestors for the programs to nationalize the masses presumes the exclusion of Celticism, or at least a diminution of its stature. This is a process that was carried out at the turn of the century, but one that was already being delineated in earlier contributions by authors such as Martins Sarmento and Leite de Vasconcelos during the 1880s. But it is important to note that Celtomania had noteworthy echoes in Portugal, following the enduring and influential European vogue, the expressions of which, as I have already indicated, had such an impact on nineteenth-century Galicia. Its varied references punctuated chorographies and novels that emulated those of Walter Scott, etymological speculation and propagandistic texts illuminated by beliefs that prospered in the "Aryan era" (Poliakov 1971), enforced by scientist and positivist convictions of the time (Catroga 1993).

Names as important as Oliveira Martins, Adolfo Coelho, Francisco Martins Sarmento, and Teófilo Braga were prominent in the interrogation of the "progeny of the nation," even defending Celtic theses with variable conviction and constancy. But, at the end of the day, in the final phase of the nineteenth century, the memory of the Lusitanians gained more notoriety than that of the Celts. The works of Sarmento were fundamental in this process (Leal 2000; Fabião 1996, 2002). To use one of José Leite de Vasconcelos's expressions, it seems that the "lições de cousas" [teaching based on material things] were an indispensable resource for this noteworthiness to be consolidated (Vasconcelos 1915).

The excavations of the fortified towns of Briteiros and of Sabroso undertaken by Martins Sarmento allowed for the monumentalization of the Ligurian theses that the author came to defend after an attraction to Celticism, which he maintained only until the end of the 1870s. In the following years the author became a champion of the Ligurian origins, even more remote, than the Lusitanians, with the idea of attributing "one of the purest genealogical trees of the ancient peoples" to the Portuguese population, a phrase that various Portuguese intellectuals would delight in citing with pride throughout the twentieth century. His posture made it possible to add new proofs of Portugal's special antiquity to prestigious genealogical claims that were already historical and had been used vaguely by Luís de Camões and later by historians and chorographers of the sixteenth and seventeenth centuries.[9] So it could now be said that the presence of the Lusitanians predated the Celtic invasions of the peninsula. We know that the possibility of going back as far as possible in terms of the genealogy of the nation was not a question of trivial importance in these times in which nationalist discourses were exacerbated.

In 1900, Rocha Peixoto had the following to say about the beginnings and the patriotic "ends" of Martins Sarmento's excavations:

> In those times, everything that was pre-Roman was exclusively Celtic. But the study of all the hugely rich objects excavated together the interpretations of famous texts, such as the Phoenician periplus that served as a basis for the poem by Avieno, and even the poem of Apollonius of Rhodes, as far as ancient Lusitania is concerned, revealed that a similar civilization was pre-Celtic, that is, rooted in more distant Aryan genealogy of an even more distant antiquity.
>
> Through his works, his opuscules and numerous articles scattered through magazines and newspapers, the reconstitution of *Lusitano,* until then imagined and vague, constitutes a memorable work of eminent critical value, of knowledge, of precision, or rigor, and, in a model way, of subtle and exceptional penetration. (Peixoto 1975: 415)

The work of the "reconstitution of *Lusitano*" could have proceeded in various ways and served, under the influence of multiple material expressions, for the imagining of a culture of the nationalized masses, as happened mainly from the 1890s onward, when the material means that helped to spread an imagined world that could be called Lusitanian had become sufficiently diverse.

In the fortified town excavated in Briteiros, Rocha Peixoto uncovered "one of the most famous pieces of evidence for the investigation of our ancient life and implicit knowledge of the ethnic lineage as a people" (1975: 414). I could have written a long article, or perhaps a book, about the data gathered on visits to the fortified town of Briteiros beginning in the 1880s, mainly about those specific moments of scientific and patriotic celebration that took place there. But I prefer to evoke my own visits to Briteiros as a high school student, when our excursion would intersect with others from different cities and the teachers would tell us about the Lusitanians. At the time, it was easy for us boys to distinguish their shadows on the front of the city walls or in the narrow paths between the round houses of the village, some of them reconstructed and furnished, which, in turn, furnished our imaginations.[10] I know that if I had grown up in Galicia and, as a high school student, visited another famous pre-Roman fortification, of the Monte de Santa Tecla, which rises over the Minho river, I would have come across an ostensible sign upon arriving saying "Poblado Celta," also some reconstructed houses and *colmadas* [thatched cottages]. But the teacher's lessons would have been quite different, and thus, consequently, the possibilities for imagining.

Lusitanian origins were taught in Portuguese schools throughout the twentieth century and were popularized in a variety of ways, until they became common knowledge among more educated citizens. This happened in addition to the feeble arguments that attempted to scientifically prove the said origins and even in spite of references to the Celts, which continued to appear in the texts of influential specialists. Were we to make an overview of the significant publications in the field, we would come across countless remarks on the excesses of *Lusitanista* enthusiasm in Sarmento's theses, alongside unavoidable praise for the patriotism underlying his proposals. These are, in the end, implicit recognitions of the necessary violence that the disclosure of ethnogenealogical "lies" presupposes (see, for example, Severo 1924; Correia 1933; Cardoso 1933, 1959). Yet it was not articles by academic specialists that taught the majority of the Portuguese to see the antecedent presence of Lusitanians in any enclosure where the stones were "constructed," or caused them to forget the folkloric "Moors" who had delighted the imagination of their mostly illiterate parents and grandparents, but rather the increasingly popularized practice of going on excursions, widely published texts and images, and industrial products whose circulation multiplied throughout the twentieth century.

Evocations of the Lusitanians were used in the names of a variety of academic journals and politico-cultural movements; we can cite, for example, the *Revista Lusitana* and *Lusitânia,* or "neogarrettismo lusitanista" and "integralismo lusitano." In 1923 "the first and only attempt to create a fascist movement within the ambit of the liberal parliamentarian republic occurred: the so called 'Nacionalismo Lusitano'" (Pinto 1989). These same evocations even inspired certain public sculptures and peopled the imagination of those who visited *castros* (fortified hilltop towns) throughout the twentieth century; they were used in the names of soccer clubs and gymnasiums, youth groups and insurance companies, automobile dealerships and pharmacies, the Portuguese news agency, an association of yogis, and even a recent gated community on the outskirts of Lisbon. These are just some of the many examples that can be cited. There were also boys baptized with the names Lusitano or Viriato; *viriatos* was the designation of those armed men sent from Portugal to support the Francoist *alzamiento* [the military uprising that overturned the Spanish Second Republic] in 1936–1939;

the most prized horses bred in Portugal are called "Lusitanos." Since the end of the nineteenth century, many industrial enterprises that fabricate porcelain, kitchen stoves, and fabrics, printing products, hardware, and an unlimited array of products, many of which are still on the market today, were all designated "Lusa" or "Lusitana." *Lusitano*—or *luso*—are references by which we continue to identify Portuguese institutional initiatives and university programs that promote study abroad, providing encounters with "Magyars," "Anglo-Saxons," "Franks," "Gauls," and "Goths," among others. This is a register that accounts for how speculations about the nineteenth-century genealogy of nations penetrated, leaving open the possibility of dividing Europe today along the lines of the denominations of ancient barbaric populations.

The evocations of the Celts that circulated in Portugal were confined until not long ago to two very peculiar registers from different periods. On the one hand, there were the monographs written from the perspective of specific municipalities by local intellectuals, where it is common to find philological interpretations of the "Celtic" origins of the names of many Portuguese villages. These are enduring propositions, as a rule, gathered from the conclusions of nineteenth-century chorographers, which until a short time ago were rarely read by the public because of the paucity of resources at the municipal level for making local history available. Another register is found in the translations of books dealing with the esoteric, where, as a rule, there were no analyses associated directly with the Portuguese context; this was a phenomenon mainly of the 1980s, but one that is still growing and that today has undergone curious local adaptations.

In Portugal, contrary to what occurred in Spain, during the nineteenth and twentieth centuries there were no well-defined regionalist demands. Therefore, the results of research into ethnogenealogies that were consequential and thus subject to popularization were projected in the context of the country as a whole. In these cases the practically exclusive role of the Lusitanians was particularly stressed, as we have seen, in a multiplicity of ways. And if we also introduce the pertinent perspective of Álvaro Cunqueiro, we will see that, in terms of the market, the names of businesses or brands of products intended for regional consumers that evoked the Turduli or Civets, Phoenicians or the Vvetoes, the Mozarabic or the Turdetani, did not prosper in Portugal. Not to mention the Suebi and the Celts. But some things are changing, and new expressions of Celticism, to a great extent similar to those that we saw flourish in Galicia, are multiplying in Portugal, mainly in the north, close to the border with the Comunidade Autónoma.

Trails Taken by the Celts in the Northwest

Whoever travels from Ponte de Lima in Portugal in the direction of the Galician province of Ourense will come across the logotype of a brand of coffee on the awnings of many of the roadside establishments on both sides of the border. The name of this small factory for roasting coffee—which was established only a few years ago in one of the inland towns of the Minho—is suggestive: "Bricelta." I wasn't able to contact its owners in order to learn the reason for this choice of name. Yet, each time I passed over the roads of rural Galicia, I could see that their market was expanding. The coffee from "Bricelta" is not very agreeable in my opinion, but Portuguese coffees have a certain notoriety in Spain. They are referred to, curiously enough, as "lusos," a term that is also used in the Comunidade to refer to those who come from Portugal.

In a recent pamphlet promoting an international brand of domestic pottery, a line by a Galician designer famous for one of his new collections is promoted among the Portuguese public in a curious way: "The influx of Celtic wisdom. The Urban series pays homage to the world of the ancient Celts. ... To revive this legacy for our own times, Roberto Verino e Saloni have created a selection of pottery that is urban, elegant, stripped of superficial details, simple in its lines, yet rich in practical spirit." These days as well, "inter-Celtic" festivals have begun to multiply in the north of Portugal, the kind of event that became common in Galicia during the 1980s and 1990s.[11] The perception of a Portuguese reporter who, on a recent Internet site, notes the differences between Portugal and Galicia with respect to "Celtic" music is curious:

> We can say that in Galicia the vast territory of folk music, mainly that with Celtic roots, is not confined to a small elite group of "amigos da terra" [friends of the earth]. Rather, it is an expression that reaches the masses. And if here in Portugal the countless village festivals that invade the country during the summer, like *nossas senhoras dos Remédios, da Agonia, do São Matias,* etc., are musically drenched by groups doing cover versions from Oliveira do Hospital or Arcozelo who play the latest *"pimba"* hit [a form of popular Portuguese music] in Galicia such events call for the accompaniment of groups playing traditional music, whether local or from abroad. (http//antigo.etc.pt/xfm/tp-galiza.htm)[12]

An ethnography of the promotion of this kind of event would allow us, in the end, to illustrate that, as a rule, intervention by the urban "elites," groups of "friends of the earth," was decisive in the initial promotion of these musical events with "Celtic roots," or of a variety of related products, in Portugal just as in Galicia. A group of disconnected stories that I heard on both sides of the border—impossible at the moment to relate—allows me to confirm this conclusion about recent diffusions of the expression of Celticism. In the end, we are looking at a complex transference of references, of goods, of possibilities for consumption that are taking place between centers and peripheries—geographical and social. We can compare and contrast different instances of this process, even in light of the general theses with which Malcolm Chapman characterized the dynamics of categorizing what is Celtic (1982, 1992).

Reasons of geographical adjacency and of occasional cross-border emulation are insufficient explanations for why it is that "traces of Celticism" have multiplied recently mainly in the north of Portugal and not in the south, in the Alentejo, for example, the only area for which there seems to be conclusive archeological proof of their presence in the past (Fabião 1992). These are specific dimensions of the process of "Europeanization" that allow us to understand, on the scale of a new cultural and political space, the existence of a "Celtic fringe" stretching beyond the limits set by the ethnographic imagination of the peripheries created in France or the United Kingdom of the nineteenth century (Chapman 1992). The possibilities for the popularization of Celticism in Portugal and Galicia in recent years originated out of different situations in each case because of historical and politico-administrative realities that I have already noted. The scale of this phenomenon is local and recent in the Portuguese case; it finds expression in new patterns of consumption or in the diffuse claims of identity founded on them. In the case of Galicia, Celticism has emerged on a national scale, a fact that propitiously secures justifications for expressions of individual and collective identity, frequently brought up to date and now widely spread among the population of the Comunidade Autónoma de Galicia.

Notes

1. These young people of a variety of origins are part of Santiago's urban landscape. In the end, they are peaceful, and the most tolerant among us take them as one of the supplementary attractions the city has to offer to its visitors. They can be understood as interpreters of an alternative style of life, and it is possible to draw suggestive comparisons with ethnography about other contexts of the so-called Celtic fringe (see, for example, MacDonald 1997; McDonald 1989; Chapman 1978). These similarities could be further drawn if one considers certain Galician rural contexts, where in recent years abandoned villages have sheltered groups of young people from different countries of Europe for whom Galicia has become a "Celtic" place.
2. The lecture referred to that took place in Lisbon is available as a sound document published by the Consello da Cultura Galega. I would note the existence of commen-

taries from various audiences of this hilarious torrent of a monologue that the writer delivered at the premises of the Juventud de Galicia [Galician Youth Association].

3. Likewise, historiographic references and popularized images of the Swabians are rare in Portugal. Their important dominion created a political entity based within the old borders of Galicia during the fifth and sixth centuries. A curious appraisal of the Suebi inheritance in the North of Portugal and Galicia was written by Jorge Dias and Ernesto Veiga de Oliveira (1963).

4. See the proposal to translate this work into Galician made in the 1931 issue, no. 86, of the periodical *Nós*. Curiously, a 1993 book intended for the high school classroom was entitled *Fogar de Breogán: Ciencias Sociais* [Home of Breógan: Social Sciences]. Another imaginative title of an essay on economy and political behavior in contemporary Galicia is *El Talante del Sr. Breogán* [The Will of Mr. Breogán].

5. See Herzfeld (1992), Miller (1987), and Appadurai (1986) and finally the more in depth argument about consumption proposed by Campbell (1994). There are curious references to an already shrinking transatlantic circulation of elements of material culture inspired by the Celtic revival in the collection organized by Eldstein (1992).

6. Galician Folk, or Galician music with Celtic roots, has, in the last twenty years, become one of the most successful products of local exportation through the circuits of consumption of so-called world music (or "roots" music). Names such as the bagpipers Xosé Manuel Budiño or Carlos Nuñez—both of them trained in the recently established bagpipe schools—and groups like Milladoiro, the Cempés, etc., are among "Celtic" music's most famous interpreters.

7. The music, the objects, and the alcoholic drinks—the principal references in the consumption of goods with a Celtic origin—come from Ireland and also Scotland. Contrastingly, citations from Brittany are more narrowly confined to design, less commercial music, and literary references. References to Cornwall or to the Isle of Man are normally succinct, comprising merely the enumeration of the members of the group of Celtic nations, or, in recent years, justifying invitations to musicians of more modest cachet to participate in Celtic musical festivals.

8. In Galicia—contrary to the case of the native languages of Brittany, the Basque Country, and Scotland—it is easier to learn Galician. There are still a great number of people whose mother tongue is Galician, a fact that can be read, in this particular case, as a lateral consequence of the weak indices of the modernization of the Galician economy and society (until recently only the political, economic, and professional elites spoke Castilian). Even though they are dated and relatively frequent, the stories of repression of the use of the vernacular language of Galicia seem to be less frequent and intense in comparison with the cases of Brittany or Scotland. In my opinion, this is true because the majority of the members of the new Galician middle classes—a fringe of the electorate that is sympathetic to nationalist positions—still have recent peasant origins. In many cases they are the first generation to speak Castilian and see bilingualism as valuable and difficult to acquire, though it is thanks to the efforts of their parents that they do. Many of the denunciations of repression that could be found in the more radical nationalist periodicals were notoriously stereotyped; frequently, they were inspired by citations of examples originating in other nations of the Celtic fringe (well covered by the critical readings of Malcolm Chapman, Maryon McDonald, and Sharon MacDonald, already cited above.)

9. The first significant articulation of these ethnogenealogical claims was made in 1594 by André de Resende (1996).

10. Since they were the remains of urban settings, the ruins of pre-Roman castles and fortified villages in the north of the county gave material meaning to imagining the way of life of the Lusitanians. These were places where "things" could propose objective lessons, "furnishing" the ethnogenetic imagination of visitors in a way unequalled in other regional contexts of Portugal (in spite of the fact that the province of the Beira, especially the Serra da Estrela, was said to be the center of the Lusitanian occupation and the imagined wanderings of Viriathus, their famous military leader). We find the strongest reasons for the success of Sarmento's ideas in the equation of these propitious scenarios that his excavations unearthed with the ennobling "Ligurian" theses.

11. The oldest—and until 2000, the only—of this kind of event in Portugal has been held in Oporto since 1986, the result of an initiative of the French Institute, following Lorient's famous Interceltique model (also emulated in the pioneering initiative in Galicia, the Festival do Mundo Celta, at Ortigueira, which dates back to 1978, as was noted above). In Oporto there is now a "Café Celta." Irish bars are establishing themselves, and sometimes we can see flags with Celtic crosses being waved by football fans in the cities' large stadiums. This is all new since the end of the 1980s when I lived there.

12. Yet, in truth, these kinds of events have already begun to be promoted in localities in the Portuguese hinterlands; in 2001 the first Festival Intercéltico de Sendim was held, and then its homonymic version was held in Vizela (in 2003 they were held for the second and third times, respectively).

Bibliography

1940. Álbum Comemorativo. 1940. Porto: Litografia Nacional.

Abu-Lughod, Lila. 1991. "Writing Against Culture," in Richard G. Fox (ed.), *Recapturing Anthropology: Working in the Present.* Santa Fe: School of American Research Press, 137–62.

———. 1997. "The Interpretation of Culture(s) After Television," *Representations* 59: 109–33.

Acciaiuoli, Margarida. 1998. *Exposições do Estado Novo.* Lisbon: Livros Horizonte.

Ageron, Charles R. 1986. "L'Exposition Coloniale: Mythe Républicain ou Mythe Impérial," in Pierre Nora (ed.), *Les Lieux de Mémoire I. La République.* Paris: Gallimard, 561–91.

Aguilar Criado, Encarnación. 1990. *Cultura Popular y Folklore en Andalucía. Los Orígenes de la Antropología.* Seville: Deputación Provincial.

Aguirre Baztan, Ángel, et. al. 1986. *La Antropología Cultural en España. Un Siglo de Antropología.* Barcelona: PPU.

Agulhon, Maurice. 1988. "Conscience Nationale et Conscience Régionale en France de 1815 à nos Jours," in *Histoire Vagabonde. Idéologie et Politique dans la France du XXe Siècle.* Paris: Presses du C.N.R.S.: 109–19.

———. 1992. "Le Centre et la Péripherie," in Pierre Nora (ed.), *Les Lieux de Mémoire III. Les Frances.1. Conflits et Partages.* Paris: Gallimard, 824–49.

———. 1992. "Combats d'Images. La République au Temps de Vichy," *Ethnologie Française* 24(2): 209–15.

Album Fotográfico da 1ª Exposição Colonial Portuguesa. n.d. Porto: Litografia Nacional.

Almeida, Carlos Alberto Ferreira de. 1987. *Alto Minho.* Lisbon: Presença.

Álvarez, Eloísa, and Isaac Alonso Estraviz. 1999. *Os Intelectuais Galegos e Teixeira de Pascoaes. Epistolário.* Sada-Corruna: Ediciós do Castro.

Álvarez Junco, José. 1996. "The Nation-Building Process in Nineteenth-Century Spain," in Clare Mar-Molinero and Angel Smith (eds), *Nationalism and the Nation in the Iberian Peninsula.* Oxford/Washington, DC: Berg, 89–106.

Álvarez Junco, José. 2001. *Mater Dolorosa. La Idea de España en el Siglo XIX.* Madrid: Taurus.

Anderson, Benedict. 1991 (1983). *Imagined Communities: Reflections on the Origin and Spread of Nationalism.* London/New York: Verso.

Andrade, Luís Oliveira. 2001. *História e Memória. A Restauração de 1640: Do Liberalismo às Comemorações Centenárias de 1940.* Coimbra: Minerva.

Antunes, Manuel de Azevedo. 1993. *As Nossas Raízes Comunitárias—Para uma Compreensão do Comunitarismo na Peneda-Gerês.* Lisbon: Casa do Concelho de Arcos de Valdevez.

Appadurai, Arjun. 1988. "How to Make a National Cuisine: Cookbooks in Contemporary India," *Comparative Studies in Society and History* 30: 3–24.

———. 1995. "The Production of Locality," in Richard Fardon (ed.), *Counterworks: Managing the Diversity of Knowledge.* London/New York: Routledge, 204–25.

———. 1997. *Modernity at Large: Cultural Dimensions of Globalization.* Minneapolis/London: University of Minnesota Press.

Aranzadi, Juan. 2000 (1981). *Milenarismo Vasco. Edad de Oro, Etnia y Nativismo.* Madrid: Taurus.

Araújo, José Rosa. 1957. "A Serra de Arga," *Arquivo do Alto-Minho* 7(1–2): 89–110.

———. 1982–1989. *Serão,* 3 vols., Caminha: Edições Camínia.

Ardener, Edwin. 1989 (1985). "Remote Areas—Some Theoretical Considerations," in Malcolm Chapman (ed.), *Edwin Ardener. The Voice of Prophecy and Other Essays.* Oxford/New York: Basil Blackwell.

Assayag, Jackie. 1997. "The Body of India: Geography, Ritual, Nation," *Etnográfica* 1(1): 33–56.

Austin, J. L. 1970 (1962). *Quand Dire c'est Faire (How to do Things With Words).* Paris: Éditions du Seuil.

Azcona, Jesús. 1984. *Etnia y Nacionalismo Vasco: Una Aproximación desde la Antropología.* Barcelona: Anthropos.

Baliñas, Carlos. 1987. "Marco para un Cadro. A Recuperación da Consciencia Galega nos Anos 50," *Grial* 96: 15–24.

Baptista, António Marinho. 1980. "O Pelourinho do Soajo," *Terra de Valdevez* 1.

Barnard, Alan, and Jonathan Spencer (eds). 1996. *Encyclopedia of Social and Cultural Anthropology.* London/New York: Routledge.

Barreiro, Xosé Luís (ed.). 1992. *O Pensamento Galego na História.* Santiago de Compostela: Universidad de Santiago.

Barreiro Fernández, Xosé Ramón et al. 1979. *Los Gallegos.* Madrid: Istmo.

———. 1988. "A Historia da Historia. Aproximación a unha Historiografía Galega (Seculos XVI–XIX)," in Xavier Castro and Jesús de Juana (eds), *Historiografía Galega. XIV Jornadas da Historia de Galicia.* Ourense: Deputacion Provincial, 17–78.

———. Xosé Ramón. 1991a. *Galicia. Tomo VII. História Contemporánea Política (Siglo XIX).* A Corruna: Hércules de Ediciones.

———. 1991b. *Galicia. Tomo VIII. História Contemporánea Política (Siglo XX).* A Corunna: Hércules de Ediciones.

Barros, Carlos. 1994. "Mitos de la Historiografía Galleguista," *Manuscrits* 12: 245–66.

Barth, Fredrik. 1992. "Towards Greater Naturalism in Conceptualizing Societies," in Adam Kuper (ed.), *Conceptualizing Society.* London/New York: Routledge, 17–33.

———. 1998 (1969). "Introduction," in Fredrik Barth (ed.), *Ethnic Groups and Boundaries. The Social Organization of Cultural Difference.* Prospect Heights, IL: Waveland Press.

Basto, Cláudio. 1922. *O Chamado "Instituto Histórico do Minho."* Viana do Castelo: Edição Revista Lusa.

———. 1924. *A Mulher do Minho.* Famalicão.

———. 1930. *Traje à Vianesa.* Vila Nova de Gaia: Apolino.

Baudrillard, Jean. 1968. *Le Systéme des Objects.* Paris: Gallimard.

Bausinger, Hermann. 1990 (1961). *Folk Culture in a World of Technology.* Bloomington/Indianapolis: Indiana University Press.

Belgum, Kirsten. 1998. *Popularizing the Nation. Audience, Representation, and the Production of Identity in the Die Gatenlaube. 1853–1900.* Lincoln: University of Nebraska Press.

Bello, Luis. 1973. *Viaje por las Escuelas de Galicia.* Madrid: Akal.

Beiras, Xosé Manuel. 1968. "Vicente Risco e Nós. Notas pra unha Leria," *Grial* 20: 162–83.

———. 1997 (1972). *O Atraso Económico da Galiza.* Santiago de Compostela: Laiovento

Benda, Julien. 1969 (1928). *The Treason of the Intellectuals (La Trahison des Clercs).* New York/London: Norton.

Bendix, Regina. 1992. "National Sentiment in the Enactment and Discourse of Swiss Political Ritual," *American Ethnologist* 19(4): 768–90.

Benedict, Burton. 1983. *The Anthropology of World's Fairs. San Francisco's Panama Pacific International Exposition of 1915.* London/Berkeley: Lowie Museum of Anthropology/Scholar Press.

Benjamin, Walter. 1991. *Écrits Français.* Paris: Gallimard.

———. 1992 (1973). *Illuminations.* London: Fontana.

Beramendi, Xusto. 1981. *Vicente Risco no Nacionalismo Galego,* 2 vols. Santiago de Compostela: Ed. do Cerne.

———. 1995. "Risco Teórico do Nacionalismo," in *Congreso Vicente Risco.* Santiago de Compostela: Xunta de Galicia: 175–86.

Beramendi, Xusto, and Xosé M. Nuñez Seixas. 1995. *O Nacionalismo Galego.* Vigo: A Nosa Terra.

Bermejo Barrera, José Carlos. 2000. *Pensar la Historia. Ensaios de História Teórica.* Vigo: Ir Indo.

Bertho, Catherine. 1980. "L'Invention de la Bretagne: Génese Sociale d'un Stéréotype," *Actes de la Recherche en Sciences Sociales* 35: 45–62.

Bertho-Lavenir, Catherine. 1988. "La Géographie Symbolique des Provinces. De la Monarchie de Juillet à l'Entre-deux-guerres," *Ethnologie Française* 18(3): 276–82.

Biel, Emílio. 1902–8. *A Arte e a Natureza em Portugal,* 8 vols. Porto: Emílio Biel e Cª.

Billig, Michael. 1986. *Banal Nationalism.* London: Sage.

Bobillo, Francisco J. 1981. "Limiar á 'Teoría Nacionalista,'" in Vicente Risco (ed.), *Obra Completa. I. Teoria Nacionalista.* Madrid: Akal, 5–27.

Boon, James. 1982. *Other Tribes, Other Scribes. Symbolic Anthropology in the Comparative Study of Cultures, Histories, Religions, and Texts.* Cambridge: Cambridge University Press.

———. 1990. *Affinities and Extremes.* Chicago: University of Chicago Press.

Borneman, John, and Nick Fowler. 1997. "Europeanization," *Annual Review of Anthropology* 26: 487–514.

Borofsky, Robert, Fredrik Barth, Richard A. Shweder, Lars Rodseth, and Nomi M. Stolzenberg. 2001. "When: A Conversation about Culture," *American Anthropologist* 103(2): 432–46.

Bourdieu, Pierre. 1962. "Célibat et Condition Paysanne," *Études Rurales* 5–6: 32–135.

———. 1989. *O Poder Simbólico.* Lisbon: Difel.

Bouza Brey, Fermín. 1982. *Etnografía y Folkore de Galicia,* 2 vols. Vigo: Edicións Xerais de Galicia.

Bóveda, Alejandre. 1935. "Envío as Mocedades. Temos que crear o noso Baile Nacional," *A Nosa Terra* 296: 3.

Boyd, Carolyn P. 1997. *Historia Patria: Politics, History and National Identity in Spain, 1875–1975.* Princeton, NJ: Princeton University Press.

Bradbury, Malcolm, and James McFarlane. 1991 (1976). *Modernism 1890–1930.* Harmondsworth, UK: Penguin.

Brañas, Alfredo. 1990. *Obras Selectas.* A Corunna: Xuntanza.

Branco, Jorge Freitas. 1985. "A Propósito da Presente Reedição," Preface to Teófilo Braga, *O Povo Português nos Seus Costumes, Crenças e Tradições.* Lisbon: Publicações Dom Quixote: 15–25.

———. 1986. "Cultura como ciência? Da consolidação do discurso antropológico à institucionalização da disciplina," *Ler História* 8: 75-101.

———. 1994. "Portugal e as Suas Etnografias: Para uma Análise da Herança Leitiana (Compilação Bibliográfica)," *Revista Lusitana* 12: 95–110.

———. 1995. "Lugares do Povo: Uma Periodização da Cultura Popular em Portugal," *Revista Lusitana* 13–14: 145–77.

———. 1999. "Autoritarismo Político e Folclorização em Portugal: *O Mensário das Casas do Povo,*" in António Medeiros, A. Barrera, and C. Feixa (eds), *Mesas de Trabajo I. Recreaciones Etnograficas: Textos, Emblemas y Escenarios.* Santiago de Compostela: Federación de Asociaciones de Antropología del Estado Español, 29–45.

Brandes, Stanley. 1990. "The Sardana. Catalan Dance and Catalan National Identity," *Journal of American Folklore* 103: 24–41.

Brettell, Caroline. 1986. *Men Who Migrate, Women Who Wait.* Princeton, NJ: Princeton University Press. (*Homens que Partem, Mulheres que Esperam. Consequências da Emigração numa Freguesia Minhota.* Lisbon: Publicações D. Quixote, 1991).

Breuilly, John. 1996. "Approaches to Nationalism," in Gopal Balakrishnam (ed.), *Mapping the Nation.* London/New York: Verso.

Breully, John. 2001 (1993). *Nationalism and the State.* Manchester: Manchester University Press.

Brito, Joaquim Pais de. 1996. *Retrato de Aldeia com Espelho. Ensaio sobre Rio de Onor.* Lisbon: Publicações D. Quixote.

Brito, Raquel Soeiro. 1953. *Uma Aldeia de Montanha: O Soajo. Estudo de Geografia Humana* [offprint from *Revista da Faculdade de Letras* 18(1, 3)]. Lisbon.

Bruner, Edward. 1986. "Ethnography as Narrative," in Victor Turner and Edward Bruner, *The Anthropology of Experience.* Urbana/Chicago: University of Illinois Press, 139–55.

Bruno, Sampaio. 1987. *Os Modernos Publicistas Portugueses.* Porto: Lello & Irmão.

Buck-Morss, Susan. 1990. *The Dialectics of Seeing. Walter Benjamin and the Arcades Project.* Cambridge, MA: MIT Press.

Bunzl, Matti. 1996. "Franz Boas and the Humboldtian Tradition. From *Volkgeist* and *Nationalcharacter* to an Anthropological Concept of Culture," in George W. Stocking, Jr. (ed.), *Wolkgeist as Method and Ethic: Essays on Boasian Ethnography and the German Anthropological Tradition.* Madison: University of Wisconsin Press, 17–78.

Cabo Villaverde. Miguel. 1998. *O Agrarismo.* Vigo: A Nosa Terra.

Cabrera Varela, Julio. 1996. "Cambio Cultural e Identidade Colectiva en Galicia," *Grial* 130: 227–43.

———. 1992. *La Nación Como Discurso. La estructura del Sistema Ideológico Nacionalista: El Caso Gallego.* Madrid: CIS.

Cachin, Françoise. 1997. "Le Paysage du Peintre," in Pierre Nora (ed.), *Les Lieux de Mémoire 1.* Paris: Gallimard, 957–96.

Cacho Viu, Vicente. 1997. "Francia 1870-España 1898," in *Repensar el Noventa y Ocho.* Madrid: Biblioteca Nueva, 77–97.

Caldas, Eugénio de Castro. 1994. *Terra de Valdevez e Montaria do Soajo. Memória Monográfica do Concelho de Arcos de Valdevez.* Porto: Verbo.

Callier-Boisvert, Colette. 1987. *Soajo Visto de Fora* (offprint from *Terras de Valdevez* 10). Arcos de Valdevez.

———. 1990. "Femmes et Mères Célibataires dans le Nord-Ouest du Portugal (1860–1986), *Ethnologie Française* 20(2): 189–202.

Calo Lourido, Francisco. 1996. "Comentario. II. Pensamentos ó fío dunha análise sobre a construción dun texto etnográfico," in X. M. González Reboredo (ed.), *La Construcción del Texto Etnográfico a Través de dos Autores. Aportación a una Historia de la Etnografía en Galicia* [comentarios de Xosé Ramón Mariño Ferro y de Francisco Calo Lourido]. Santiago de Compostela: CSIC/IPSEG, 71–73.

Campbell, Colin. 1994 (1987). *The Romantic Ethic and the Spirit of Modern Consumerism.* Oxford/Cambridge: Blackwell.

Campbell, John K. 1964. *Honour, Family and Patronage: A Study of Institutions and Moral Values in a Greek Mountain Community.* Oxford: Clarendon.

Canetti, Elias. 1999. *The Memoirs of Elias Canetti.* New York: Farrar, Straus, and Giroux.

Cantwell, Robert. 1993. *Ethnomimesis. Folklife and the Representation of Culture.* Chapel Hill: University of North Carolina Press.

Carballo Calero, Ricardo. 1981 (1976). *Historia da Literatura Gallega Contemporánea.* Vigo: Galaxia.

Cardoso, Mário. 1933. *Dr. Francisco Martins Sarmento (esboço bio-bibliográfico).* Guimarães.

———. 1959. *Alberto Sampaio. Breve notícia da sua Vida e Obra.* Guimarães: Sociedade Martins Sarmento.

Carey, John. 1992. *The Intellectuals and the Masses. Pride and Prejudice Among the Literary Intelligentsia, 1880–1939.* London/Boston: Faber and Faber.

Carmona Badía, Joán. 1990. *El Atraso Industrial de Galicia. Auge y Liquidación de las Manufacturas Textiles (1750–1900).* Barcelona: Ariel.

Carr, Raymond. 1982. *Spain. 1808–1975.* Oxford: Clarendon.

Carvalho, Joaquim de. 1946. *A Cultura Castreja. Sua interpretação Sociológica.* Lisbon: Tip. Editorial Império.

Carvalho Calero, Ricardo. 1990. *Do Galego e da Galiza.* Santiago de Compostela: Sotelo Blanco.

Casares, Carlos, Artur Lezcano, and Antón Risco. 1997. *Para Ler a Vicente Risco.* Vigo: Galaxia.

Castañeda, Maria Isabel. *Fogar de Breógan. Ciencias Sociais.* A Coruña: Adormideiras.

Castelao, Alfonso R. 1976. *Obra Completa II. Sempre en Galiza.* Madrid: Akal.

———. 1982a. *Cousas da Vida. 1.* Madrid: Akal.

———. 1982b. *Obra Completa II. Diarios de Arte.* Madrid: Akal.

Castro, D. João de. 1907. "Arcos de Valdevez" in Emílio Biel, *A Arte e A Natureza em Portugal,* vol. 7. Porto: Emílio Biel & Cª.

———. 1909. *Jornadas no Minho. Impressões, Aventuras e Travessuras de dois Excursionistas Meridionaes.* Lisbon: Ferreira & Oliveira.

Cátedra, María. 1991. "'Desde una Fresca Distancia': Por Qué no Estudiamos a los Norteamericanos?" in María Cátedra (ed.), *Los Españoles Vistos por los Antrópologos.* Madrid: Jucar, 252–68.

Catroga, Fernando. 1993a. "Os Caminhos Polémicos da Geração Nova," in José Mattoso (ed.), *História de Portugal. Vol. V. O Liberalismo.* Lisbon: Círculo de Leitores, 569–81.

———. 1993b. "Cientismo, Política e Anticlericalismo," in José Mattoso (ed.), *História de Portugal. Vol. V. O Liberalismo.* Lisbon: Círculo de Leitores, 569–81.

Certeau, Michell, Dominique Julia y Jacques Revel. 1993. "La Beauté du Mort," in Michel Certeau, *La Culture au Pluriel.* Paris: Seuil, 44–72.

Chamboredon, Jean-Claude. 1994. "L'Édification de la Nation. Naissance, Diffusion, Circulation de Quelques Motifs Iconographiques," *Ethnologie Française* 24(2): 187–97.

Chapman, Malcolm. 1978. *The Gaelic Vision in Scottish Culture.* London: Croom Helm.

———. 1982. "Semantics and the Celts," in David Parkin (ed.), *Semantic Anthropology.* London: Academic Press, 123–44.

————. 1992. *The Celts. The Construction of a Myth.* London: St. Martin's Press.

————. 1993. "Copeland: Cumbria's Best Kept Secret," in Marion McDonald (ed.), *Inside European Identities. Ethnography in Western Europe.* Providence/Oxford: Berg, 194–218.

Christian, William Jr. 1992. *Moving Crucifixes in Modern Spain,* Princeton, Princeton University Press.

————. 1996. *Visionaries: The Spanish Republic and the Reign of Chris.* Berkeley/London: University of California Press.

Chun, Allen. 2001. "From Text to Context. How Anthropology Makes its Subject," *Cultural Anthropology* 15(4): 570–595.

Cintra, Luís Lindley. 1983. *Estudos de Dialectologia Portuguesa.* Lisbon: Sá da Costa.

Cláudio, Mário. 1996. "Endovélico: Continuidade Cultural de uma Mística Reprimida na Periferia Atlântica," in Margarita Ledo Andión (ed.), *Comunicación na Periferia Atlántica. Actas do I Congreso Internacional.* Santiago de Compostela: Universidade de Santiago de Compostela, 379–82.

Clifford, James. 1986. "On Ethnographic Allegory," in James Clifford and George Marcus (eds), *Writing Culture. The Poetics and Politics of Anthropology.* Berkeley: University of California Press, 98–121.

————. 1988. *The Predicament of Culture. Twentieth-Century Ethnography, Literature, and Art.* Cambridge, MA: Harvard University Press.

————. 1997. *Routes: Travel and Translation in the Late 20th Century.* Cambridge, MA: Harvard University Press.

Clifford, James, and George Marcus (eds). 1986. *Writing Culture: The Poetics and Politics of Ethnography.* Berkeley: University of California Press.

Cocchiara, Giuseppe. 1981. *The History of Folklore in Europe.* Filadélfia: Institute for the Study of Human Issues.

Coelho, Adolfo. 1993. *Obra Etnográfica. Vol II. Cultura Popular e Educação* (organização e prefácio de João Leal). Lisbon: Publicações D. Quixote.

Coelho, Jacinto do Prado. 1976 (1960). *Dicionário das Literaturas Portuguesa, Galega e Brasileira.* Porto: Figueirinhas.

Cohen, Anthony P. 1996. "Personal Nationalism: A Scottish View of Some Rites, Rights, and Wrongs," *American Ethnologist* 23(4): 802–15.

Cohn, Bernard S. 2000 (1987). *An Anthropologist Among the Historians and Other Essays.* New Delhi: Oxford University Press.

Cole, Sally. 1991. *Women of the Praia.* Princeton, NJ: Princeton University Press.

Connerton, Paul. 1989. *How Societies Remember.* Cambridge, Cambridge University Press (*Como as Sociedades Recordam.* Lisbon: Celta, 1993).

Conversi, Daniel. 1997. *The Basques, the Catalans and Spain: Alternative Routes to Nationalist Mobilization.* Reno/Las Vegas: University of Nevada Press.

Corbin, Alain. 1997. "Paris-Province," in Pierre Nora (ed.), *Les Lieux de Mémoire* 2. Paris: Quarto/Gallimard, 2891–905.

Cores Trasmonte, Baldomero. n.d. *De la América Real a la Galicia Inventada.* Santiago de Compostela: El Correo Gallego.

————. 1983. *Ramón Suárez Picallo. Socialismo, Galleguismo y Acción de Masas en Galicia.* Sada-Corruna: Ediciós do Castro.

————. 1986. *Los Símbolos Gallegos.* Santiago: Velograf.

Correia, António Mendes. 1933. *Martins Sarmento e a Consciência Nacional.* Guimarães: Minerva Vimaranense.

Cortesão, Jaime. 1942. *O Que o Povo Canta em Portugal.* Rio de Janeiro: Livros de Portugal.

————. 1966. *Portugal. A Terra e o Homem.* Lisbon: Artis.

Costa, Américo. 1948. *Dicionário Corográfico de Portugal Continental e Insular,* vol. 11. Porto: Civilização.

Costa, D. António. 1874. *No Minho.* Lisbon: Imprensa Nacional.

Crépon, Marc. 1996. *Géographies de l'Esprit. Enquête sur la Caractérisation des Peuples de Leibniz à Hegel.* Paris: Payot.

Cutileiro, José. 1971a. *A Portuguese Rural Society.* Oxford: Clarendon.

————. 1971b. "Prefácio à Edição Portuguesa. Honra, Vergonha e Amigos" in J. G. Peristiany (ed.), *Honra e Vergonha. Valores das Sociedades Mediterrânicas.* Lisbon: Fundação Calouste Gulbenkian, pp. ix–xxiii.

————. 1977. *Ricos e Pobres no Alentejo.* Lisbon: Sá da Costa.

D' Aurora, Conde. 1929. *Roteiro da Ribeira Lima.* Ponte de Lima: author's edition.

————. 1936. *Pela Grei—Exortações.* Porto: Canedo & Cª.

Dabelmireau. 1882. "Pelo Minho. Da Barca à Peneda" (2 textos) and "Historia. Revolta dos Suajenses," *Pero Gallego. Folha Literaria, Scientifica, etc.,* no. 5, 6, and 31.

Davis, John. 1977. *People of Mediterranean: An Essay in Comparative Social Anthropology.* London: RKP.

Dias, Jaime Lopes. 1956. *Problemas de Folclore.* Lisbon: Ferin.

Dias, A. Jorge. 1949. *Minho, Trás- os-Montes, Haut Douro.* Lisbon: Congrés International de Géographie.

————. 1950. *Abrigos Pastoris na Serra do Soajo,* extrato do *Trabalhos de Antropologia e Etnologia* 12(3–4).

————. 1952. *Bosquejo Analítico de Etnografia Portuguesa.* Coimbra: Casa do Castelo.

————. 1953. *Rio de Onor. Comunitarismo Agro-pastoril.* Porto: Instituto de Alta Cultura/ Centro de Estudos de Etnologia Peninsular.

————. 1964. *Museu Nacional e Museus Regionais de Etnografia.* Barcelos: Museu Regional de Cerâmica.

————. 1970. *Da Música e da Dança como Formas de Expressão Expontâneas aos Ranchos Folclóricos.* Lisbon: APPPC.

————. 1981 (1948). *Vilarinho da Furna. Uma Aldeia Comunitária.* Lisbon: Imprensa Nacional/Casa da Moeda.

Dias, A. Jorge, and Ernesto Veiga de Oliveira. 1962. *A Cultura Castreja e a Sua Herança Social na Área Galaico-Portuguesa.* Porto: Centro de Estudos de Etnologia Peninsular.

Dias, Jorge, Fernando Galhano, and Ernesto Veiga de Oliveira. 1963. *Sistemas Primitivos de Secagem e Armazenamento de Produtos Agrícolas. Os Espigueiros Portugueses.* Porto: Centro de Estudos de Etnologia Peninsular.

Díaz Andreu, M. y T. Champion.1996. *Nationalism and Archaeology in Europe.* London/ San Francisco: University of California Press.

Díaz Pardo, Isaac. 1990 (1987). *Galicia Hoy y el Resto del Mundo.* Sada: Ediciós do Castro.

Di Brizio, Maria Beatrice. 1995. "«Présentisme» et «Historicisme» dans l'Historiographie de G. W. Stocking," *Gradhiva* 18: 77–89.

Dietler, Michael. 1994. "'Our Ancestors the Gauls': Archeology, Ethnic Nationalism, and the Manipulation of Celtic Identity in Modern Europe," *American Anthropologist* 96(3): 584–605.

Dorman, Robert L. 1993. *Revolt of the Provinces: The Regionalist Movement in América.* Chapel Hill, N.C.: University of North Carolina Press.

Durães, Margarida. 1994. "O Minho no Pensamento Geo-Histórico do Portugal Moderno e Contemporâneo," *Cadernos do Noroeste* 7(2): 93–113.

Durán, J. A. 1972. *El Primer Castelao. Antología y Biografía Rotas.* Madrid: Siglo Veintiuno.

———. 1976. *Historia de Caciques, Bandos y Ideologías en Galicia no Urbana (Rianxo 1910–1914).* Madrid: Siglo Veintiuno.

———. 1981. *Crónicas—3. Entre la Mano Negra y el Nacionalismo Galleguista.* Madrid: Akal.

———. 1986. *Crónicas—4. Conflictos de Hoy, Historias Románticas y Diarios Modernos.* Madrid: Akal.

———. 1990. *Camilo Díaz Baliño. Crónica de Otro Olvido Inexplicable.* Sada-Corunna: Ediciós do Castro.

———, (ed.). 1984. *Aldeas, Aldeanos Y Labriegos en L Galicia Tradicional. Alfredo Vicenti. Prudencio Rovira. Nicolás Tenorio.* Madrid: Imprenta del Servicio de Publicaciones Agrarias.

Eagleton, Terry. 1999. *Scholars and Rebels in Nineteenth-Century Ireland.* Oxford: Blackwell.

Eagleton, Terry. 2000. *The Idea of Culture.* Oxford: Blackwell.

Edwards, Elizabeth (ed.). 1992. *Anthropology and Photography.* New Haven, CT: Yale University Press.

Eksteins, Modris. 1990 (1989). *Rites of Spring.* New York: Anchor Books.

———. 1999. *Walking Since Daybreak: A Story of Eastern Europe, World War II, and the Heart of Our Century.* Boston/New York: Houghton Mifflin Company.

Eldstein, T. J (ed.). 1992. *Imagining an Irish Past in the Celtic Revival 1840–1940.* Chicago: David and Alfred Smart Museum of Art/ University of Chicago.

Eliot, T. S. 1996 (1945). *Notas para a Definição de Cultura.* Lisbon: Século XXI.

Evans-Pritchard, E. E. (1940). *The Nuer. A Description of the Modes of Livelihood and Political Institutions of a Nilotic People.* New York/Oxford: Oxford University Press.

Fabian, Johannes. 1983. *Time and the Other. How Anthropology Makes its Object.* New York: Columbia University Press.

————. 1990. "Culture, Time and the Object of Anthropology," in Johannes Fabian, *Time and the Work of Anthropology. Critical Essays 1971–1991.* Chur: Harwood Academic Publishers.

Fabião, Carlos. 1996. "Archaelogy and Nationalism: The Portuguese Case," in M. Díaz Andreu e Timothy Champion (eds), *Nationalism and Archaeology in Europe.* London: UCL Press, 90–107.

———— . 2002. "Leite de Vasconcelos e a Génese de *Religiões da Lusitânia,*" in Luís Raposo (coord) *Religiões da Lusitânia. Loquuntura Saxa.* Lisbon: Museu Nacional de Arqueologia, 341–346.

Fabre, Daniel. 1992. "Le Manuel de Folklore Français de Arnold Van Gennep," in Pierre Nora (ed.), *Les Lieux de Mémoire III. Les Frances. 2. Traditions.* Paris: Gallimard, 640–75.

Fardon, Richard (ed.). 1990. *Localizing Strategies: Regional Traditions of Ethnographic Writing.* Washington, DC: Smithsonian Institution Press.

Faubion, James D. 1993. *Modern Greek Lessons. A Primer in Historical Construtivism.* Princeton, NJ: Princeton University Press.

Faure, Christian. 1989. *Le Project Culturel de Vichy. Folklore et Révolution Nationale (1940–1944).* Lyon: Presses Universitaires de France.

Felgueiras, Guilherme. 1932. *Espadeladas e Esfolhadas.* Porto: Pátria Gaia Portuguesa.

Fernandez, James. 1985. "Folklorists as Agents of Nationalism: Legends Asturian Mountain Villages Tell Themselves (and Others) about Themselves and the Problem of Local, Regional and National Identity," *New York Folklore* 11(1–4): 135–47.

————. 1986. *Persuasions and Performances: The Play of Tropes in Culture.* Bloomington: University of Indiana Press.

————. 1988. "Andalusia on Our Minds: Two Contrasting Places in Spain as Seen in a Vernacular Poetic Duel of the Late 19th Century," *Cultural Anthropology* 3(1): 21–35.

————. 1994. "The Dilemmas of Provincial Culture and the Framing of Anthropological Inquiry," in San Martin, Ricardo (ed.), *Antropología sin Fronteras. Ensayos en Honor a Carmelo Lisón.* Madrid: Centro de Investigaciones Sociológicas, 71–91.

————. 1997. "The North-South Axis in European Popular Cosmologies and the Dynamic of the Categorical," *American Anthropologist* 99: 725–28.

Fernández Prieto, Lourenzo. 1992. *Labregos con Ciencia. Estado, Sociedade e Innovación Tecnolóxica na Agricultura Galega 1850–1930.* Vigo: Xerais.

Fernández del Riego, Francisco. 1954. *Galicia no Espello.* Buenos Aires: Ediciones Galicia.

————. 1981. *Vicente Risco. Escolma de Textos.* Corunna: Publicacións da Real Academia Gallega.

————. 1983a. *Pensamiento Galeguista no Século XIX.* Vigo: Galaxia.

————. 1983b. *Pensamiento Galeguista no Século XX.* Vigo: Galaxia.

————. 1984. *Historia da Literatura.* Vigo: Galaxia.

————. 1996. "Risco na Lembranza," *in Congreso Vicente Risco.* Santiago de Compostela: Xunta de Galicia, 423–26.

Fernández de Rota, Jose Antonio. 1984. *Antropología de un Viejo Paisage Gallego.* Madrid: CIS/SigloXXI.

———. 1988. "Releyendo 'Una Parroquia Galega' de Vicente Risco," *Cuadernos de Estudios Gallegos* 100: 585–93.

———, (ed.). 1994. *Las Diferentes Caras de España.* Corunna: Universidade de A Coruña.

Ferro, António. 1950. *Verde Gaio.* Lisbon: SNI.

Filgueira Valverde, Xosé. 1978. "Limiar" da Segunda Edición in VVAA, *Terra de Melide* (Ed.facsímil.). Sada-A Coruña: Ediciós do Castro.

Forgacs, David (ed.). 2000. *The Antonio Gramsci Reader. Selected Writings 1916–1935.* New York: New York University Press.

Foster, George. 1991. "Making National Cultures in the Global Ecumene," *Annual Review of Anthropology* 20: 253–60.

Fraguas, Antonio. 1973. *La Galicia Insólita.* Corunna: Librigal.

———. 1988. *Romarías e Santuarios.* Vigo: Galaxia.

———. 1985. *El Traje Gallego.* Corunna: Fundación Pedro Barrié de La Maza.

———. 1994. *Do Entroido.* Santiago de Compostela: Museo do Pobo Galego.

———. 1996. *A Festa Popular en Galicia.* Corunna: Ediciós do Castro.

Fraguas, Antonio, and Xosé A. Fidalgo Santamariña (eds). 1996. *Tecnoloxía Tradicional. Dimensión Patrimonial. Valoración Antropolóxica. Actas do Simposio Internacional Xaquín Lorenzo.* Santiago de Compostela: Consello da Cultura Galega.

França, José A. 1974. *A Arte em Portugal no Século XX.* Lisbon: Bertrand.

———. 1993. *O Romantismo em Portugal.* Lisbon: Livros Horizonte.

Frazer, James G. 1894. *The Golden Bough. A Study in Comparative Religion.* New York and London: Macmillan.

Frykman, Jonas, and Orvar Löfgren. 1996. *Culture Builders. A Historical Anthropology of Middle Class Life.* New Brunswick, NJ: Rutgers University Press.

Fusi, Juan P. 1999. *Un Siglo de España. La Cultura.* Madrid-Barcelona: Marcial Pons.

———. 2000. *España. La Evolución de la Identidad Nacional.* Madrid: Temas de Hoy.

Fusi, Juan P., and Antonio Niño (eds). 1997. *Vísperas del 98. Orígenes y Antecedentes de la Crisis del 98.* Madrid: Biblioteca Nueva.

Fussel, Paul. 2000 (1975). *The Great War and Modern Memory.* Oxford/New York: Oxford University Press.

Gable, Eric, and Richard Handler. 1996. "After Authenticity at an American Heritage Site," *American Anthropologist* 98(3): 568–78.

Galvão, Henrique. 1935. *Primeira Exposição Colonial. Relatório e Contas.* Lisbon: Agência Geral das Colonias.

Galvão, Henrique. 1940. *Exposição do Mundo Português: Secção Colonial.* Lisbon: Neogravura.

Garcia Iglesias, José Manuel. 1974. "Santiago.VII. Iconografía Jacobea," *Gran Enciclopedia Gallega* 28: 50–58.

Garrett, Almeida. 1954 (1846). *Viagens na Minha Terra.* Lisbon: Sá da Costa.

Gaspar, Jorge. 1993. *As Regiões Portuguesas.* Lisbon: Ministério do Planeamento e da Administração do Território/Secretaria de Estado do Planeamento e Desenvolvimento Regional.

Gaspar, Silvia. 1996. *A Xeración Nós e o Camiño de Santiago.* Santiago de Compostela: Xunta de Galicia.

Gay, Peter. 1968. *Weimar Culture: The Outsider as Insider.* New York: Harper and Row.

Geertz, Clifford. 1973. *The Interpretation of Cultures.* New York: Basic Books.

———. 1983. *Local Knowledge: Further Essays in Interpretive Anthropology.* New York: Basic Books.

———. 1988. *Works and Lives: The Anthropologist as Author.* Stanford, CA: Stanford University Press.

Gellner, Ernest. 1964. *Thought and Change.* London: Weinfeld & Nicolson.

———. 1993 (1983). *Nações e Nacionalismo.* Lisbon: Gradiva.

———. 1996. "The Coming of Nationalism and Its Interpretation: The Myths of Nation and Class," in Gopal Balakrishnan (ed.), *Mapping The Nation.* London/New York: Verso, 98–145.

———. 1998 (1997). *Nationalism.* London: Phoenix.

Geraldes, Alice. 1979. *Castro Laboreiro e Soajo. Habitação, Vestuário e Trabalho da Muzher.* Lisbon: ICN (Colecção Parques Naturais nº 4).

Geuss, Raymond. 1996. "Kultur, Bildung, Geist," *History and Theory* 35(2): 152–64.

Giddens, Anthony. 1985. *The Nation State and Violence. A Contemporary Critique of Historical Materialism.* Cambridge, MA: Polity Press.

Gillis, John R. (ed.). 1994. *Commemorations. The Politics of National Identity.* Princeton, NJ: Princeton University Press.

Girão, Aristides de Amorim. 1933 (2nd ed.). *Esbôço de uma Carta Regional Portuguesa.* Coimbra: Imprensa da Universidade.

Goddard, Victoria, Joseph Llobera, and Chris Shore. 1994. *The Anthropology of Europe. Identities and Boundaries in Conflict.* Oxford/Providence: Berg.

Golan, Remy. 1995. *Modernity and Nostalgia: Art and Politics in France Between the Wars.* New Haven, CT: Yale University Press.

Goldsworthy, Vesna. 1998. *Inventing Ruritania. The Imperialism of Imagination.* New Haven, CT: Yale University Press.

Gomes, José Cândido. 1903. *As Terras de Valdovês. Memórias Históricas e Descritivas do Concelho dos Arcos de Val de Vez,* vol. 3. Guimarães: Minerva Vimaranense.

Gonçalves, Flávio. 1967. "Prefácio," in A. Rocha Peixoto, *Obras. I.* Póvoa de Varzim: Câmara Muncipal da Póvoa de Varzim, ix–lii.

Gondar Portasany, Marcial. 1989. *Romeiros do Alén. Antropoloxía da Morte en Galicia.* Vigo: Xerais.

González Pérez, Clodio. 1998. *Antonio Fraguas: Profesor, Xeógrafo, Historiador, Antropólogo—Galego de Ben.* Vigo: Ir Indo.

González Cuevas, Pedro C. 2000. "La Recepción del Pensamiento Conservador-Radical en España (1913–1930)," *Ayer* 38: 211–31.

González Reboredo, X. Manuel. 1995. "Vicente Risco e a Antropoloxía Galega," *Actas do I Congreso Vicente Risco.* Santiago de Compostela: Xunta de Galicia, 235–54.

———. 1996. *La Construcción del Texto Etnográfico a Través de dos Autores. Aportación a una Historia de la Etnografía en Galicia.* Santiago de Compostela: CSIC/IPSEG.

———. 2001a. *La Invención del Estado Nación.* Barcelona: Ronsel.

———. 2001b. "A Construcción de Referentes de Identidade Etno-Nacional. Algunhas Mostras sobre Galicia," in X. Manuel González Reboredo (ed.), *Etnicidade e Nacionalismo. Simposio Internacional de Antropoloxía.* Santiago de Compostela: Consello da Cultura Galega: 201–48.

———, (ed.). 1997. *Galicia. Antropoloxía.* Corunna: Hércules de Ediciones.

Goodman, Nelson. 1995. *Modos de Fazer Mundos.* Porto: Asa.

Gramsci, Antonio. 1985. *Selections from Cultural Writings.* London: Lawrence and Wishart.

Greenhalg, Paul. 1988. *Ephemeral Vistas. The Exposition Universelles, Great Exhibitions and World's Fairs, 1851–1939.* Manchester: Manchester University Press.

Guerreiro, Manuel Viegas. 1986. "Tradições Populares de Portugal. Génese de uma Obra," in José Leite de Vasconcelos (ed.), *Tradições Populares de Portugal.* Lisbon: Imprensa Nacional-Casa da Moeda, 7–28.

Guia de Portugal—4º volume. Minho. n.d. Lisbon: Fundação Calouste Gulbenkian.

Guimarães, Alfredo. 1916. *Livro de Saudades.* Lisbon: Typografia Annuario Comercial.

Gupta, Akhil e James Ferguson. 1997. "Beyond 'Culture': Space, Identity and Politics of Difference," in Akhil Gupta and James Ferguson, *Culture, Power, Place: Explorations in Critical Anthropology.* Durham, NC: Duke University Press.

Hagen, James M. 1997. "'Read All About It': The Press and the Rise of National Consciousness in Early Twentieth-Century Dutch East Indies Society," *Anthropological Quarterly* 70(3): 107–26.

Handler, Richard. 1985a. "On Dialogues and Destructive Analysis: Problems in Narrating Nationalism and Ethnicity," *Journal of Anthropological Research* 41(2): 171–92.

———. 1985b. "On Having Culture. Nationalism and the Preservation of Quebec Patrimoine," in George Stocking Jr. (ed.), *Objects and Others: Essays on Museums and Material Culture.* Madison: University of Wisconsin Press, 192–217.

———. 1988. *Nationalism and the Politics of Culture in Quebec.* Madison: University of Wisconsin Press.

———. 1994. "Is 'Identity' a Useful Cross-Cultural Concept?" in John Gillis (ed.), *Commemorations: The Politics of National Identity.* Princeton, NJ: Princeton University Press.

———, (ed.). 2000. *Excluded Ancestors, Inventible Traditions. Essays Toward a More Inclusive History of Anthropology.* Madison: University of Wisconsin Press.

Hannerz, Ulf. 1992. *Cultural Complexity. Studies in the Social Organization of Meaning.* New York: Columbia University Press.

Harvey, Patricia. 1996. *Hybrids of Modernity. Anthropology, the Nation State and the Universal Exhibition.* London/New York: Routledge.

Heiberg, Marianne. 1989. *The Making of the Basque Nation.* Cambridge: Cambridge University Press.

Henderson, Tracy. 1986. "Language and Identity in Galicia: The Current Orthographic Debate," in Clare Mar-Molinero and Angel Smith (eds), *Nationalism and the Nation in the Iberian Peninsula.* Oxford/Washington, DC: Berg, 237–54.

Herculano, Alexandre. 1934. *Cenas de um Ano da Minha Vida.* Lisbon: Bertrand.

———. 1981 (1825). *O Pároco de Aldeia.* Porto: Lello Editores.

Herf, Jeffrey. 1998 (1984). *Reactionary Modernism. Technology, Culture, and Politics in Weimar and the Third Reich.* Cambridge: Cambridge University Press.

Hermida Garcia, Modesto. 1987. *As Revistas Literárias en Galicia na Segunda República.* Corunna: Ediciós do Castro.

Hermida, Marcelo, and Emilio Martínez. 1996. "As Industrias Audiovisuais en Galicia," in Margarita Ledo Andión (ed.), *Comunicación na Periferia Atlántica. Actas do I Congreso Internacional.* Santiago de Compostela: Universidade de Santiago de Compostela, 115–24.

Herzfeld, Michael. 1985. *Poetics of Manhood: Contest and Identity in a Cretan Mountain Village.* Princeton, N.J.: Princeton University Press.

———. 1986. *Ours Once More: Folklore, Ideology and the Making of Modern Greece.* New York: Pella Publishing Company.

———. 1987. *Anthropology Through the Looking Glass. Critical Ethnography in the Margins of Europe.* Cambridge: Cambridge University Press.

———. 1991. *A Place in History: Social and Monumental Time in a Cretan Town.* Princeton, NJ: Princeton University Press.

———. 1992a. "Segmentation and Politics in the European Nation-State: Making Sense of Political Events," in Kirsten Hastrup (ed.), *Other Histories.* London/New York: Routledge, 62–81.

———. 1992b. "La Pratique des Stéréotypes," *L'Homme* 32(121): 67–77.

———. 1997a. *Cultural Intimacy.* London/New York: Routledge.

———. 1997b. "Filología Política: Consequencias Cotidianas de las Gramáticas Grandiosas," in Xaquín Rodríguez Campos (ed.), *As Linguas e as Identidades. Ensaios de Etnografía e de Interpretación Antropolóxica.* Santiago de Compostela: Universidade de Santiago de Compostela.

———. 1997c. *Portrait of a Greek Imagination: A Ethnographic Biography of Andreas Nenedakis.* Chicago: University of Chicago Press.

———. 2001. *Anthropology. Theoretical Practice in Culture and Society.* Malden, MA: Blackwell.

Heush, Luc de. 1997. *Postures et Imposture. Nations, Nationalism, etc.* Bruxelles: Éditions Labor.

Hobsbawm, Eric. 1985 (1983). "Mass-Producing Tradition: Europe, 1870–1914," in Eric Hobsbawm, and Terence Ranger (eds), *The Invention of Tradition.* Cambridge: Cambridge University Press: 263–307.

———. 1992 (1990). *Nations and Nationalisms since 1780. Programme, Myth, Reality.* Cambridge: Cambridge University Press.

———. 1994. *Age of Extremes. The Short Twentieth Century. 1914–1991.* London: Michael Joseph.

———. 1996. "Ethnicity and Nationalism in Europe Today," in Gopal Balakrishnan (ed.), *Mapping The Nation.* London/New York: Verso, 255–66.

Hobsbawn, Eric, and Terence Ranger (eds). 1985 (1983). *The Invention of Tradition.* Cambridge: Cambridge University Press.

Hoyos Sancho, Nieves de. 1961. *La Representación de Galicia en el Museo del Pueblo Español.* Madrid: G. Bermejo.

Hroch, Miroslav. 2000 (1985). *Social Preconditions of National Revival in Europe: A Comparative Analysis of the Social Composition of Patriotic Groups among the Smaller European Nations.* New York: Columbia University Press.

Hutcheon, Linda. 1989 (1985). *Uma Teoria da Paródia.* Lisbon: Edições 70.

Hutchinson, John. 1987. *The Dynamics of Cultural Nationalism. The Gaelic Revival and the Creation of the Irish Nation State.* London: Allen & Unwin.

Império Português na Iª Exposição Colonial Portuguesa. Albúm-Catálogo Oficial. n.d. Porto: Mário Antunes Leitão.

Iturra, Raúl. 1988. *Antropología Economica de la Galicia Rural.* Santiago de Compostela: Xunta de Galicia.

Jackson, Anthony. 1987. *Anthropology at Home.* London/New York: Tavistock.

Juaristi, Jon. 1998 (1987). *El linaje de Aitor. La Invención de la Tradición Vasca.* Madrid: Taurus.

———. 1999. *El Chimbo Expiatorio (La Invención de la Tradición Bilbaina, 1876–1939).* Madrid: Espasa.

———. 2000. *El Bosque Originario. Genealogias Míticas de los Pueblos de Europa.* Madrid: Taurus.

Karp, Ivan, and Steve Lavine. 1991. *Exhibiting Cultures.* Washington, DC: Smithsonian Institution.

Kavanagh, William. 1991. "Fronteras Simbólicas y Fronteras Reales," in X. M. González Reboredo and X. A. Fernández de Rota (eds), *Actas do Simposio de Antropoloxia "Lindeiros da Galeguidade I."* Santiago de Compostela: Consello da Cultura Galega: 67–72.

Kelley, Heidi. 1991. "Unwed Mothers and Household Reputation in a Spanish Galician Community," *American Anthropologist* 18: 565–80.

Kracauer, Siegfried. 1995. *The Mass Ornament: Weimar Essays.* Cambridge, MA: Harvard University Press.

Kiberd, Declan. 1996. *Inventing Ireland. The Literature of the Modern Nation.* London: Vintage.

Kuper, Adam. 1999. *Culture: The Anthropologist Account.* Cambridge, MA: Harvard University Press.

Löfgren, Orvar. 1989. "The Nationalization of Culture," *Ethnologia Europaea* 20: 5–24.

Lamas, Maria. 1948. *As Mulheres do Meu País.* Lisbon: Actuális Lda.

Le Goff, Jacques. 1984. "Memória" and "Documento/Monumento," in *Enciclopédia Einaudi,* vol. 1. Lisbon: Imprensa Nacional-Casa da Moeda: 95–106.

Leal, João. 1987. "Prefácio," in Teófilo Braga (ed.), *Contos Tradicionais do Povo Português, I.* Lisbon: Publicações Dom Quixote: 13–19.

———. 1988. "Prefácio," in Consiglieri Pedroso (ed.), *Contribuições Para Uma Mitologia Popular Portuguesa e Outros Escritos Etnográficos.* Lisbon: Publicações Dom Quixote, 13–40.

———. 1993. "Prefácio," in Adolfo Coelho (ed.), *Obra Etnográfica. Volume I. Festas, Costumes e Outros Materiais para uma Etnologia de Portugal.* Lisbon: Publicações Dom Quixote, 13–36.

———. 1995. "Imagens Contrastadas do Povo: Cultura Popular e Identidade Nacional na Antropologia Portuguesa Oitocentista," *Revista Lusitana* 13–14: 125–44.

———. 1996. "Prefácio," in José Leite de Vasconcelos, *Signum Salomonis. A Figa. A barba em Portugal. Estudos de Etnografia Comparativa.* Lisbon: Publicações D. Quixote, 15–43.

———. 1999. *"Saudade,* la Construction d'un Symbole. 'Caractère National' et Identité National," *Ethnologie Française* 30(2): 177–89.

———. 2000. *Etnografias Portuguesas (1870–1970): Cultura Popular e Identidade Nacional.* Lisbon: Publicações D. Quixote.

———. 2001. "'Tylorian Professors' and 'Japanese Corporals': Anthropological Theory and National Identity in Portuguese Ethnography," in D. Albera, A. Blok, and C. Bromberger (eds), *Anthropology of the Mediterranean.* Paris: Maisonneuve et Larose, 645–658.

Lebovics, Herman. 1992. *True France: The Wars over Cultural Identity.1900–1945.* Ithaca, NY: Cornell University Press.

Ledo Andión, Margarita. 1982. *Prensa e Galeguismo.* Sada: Ediciós do Castro.

———. 1996. *Comunicación na Periferia Atlántica. Actas do I Congreso Internacional.* Santiago de Compostela: Universidade de Santiago de Compostela.

Lema Bendaña, Xosé. 1990–1991. "Apuntes en Aportación a Unha Bibliografía de Tema Etnográfico," *Boletín Auriense* 20–21: 429–97.

Lembranza de Ramón Piñeiro. Catro Discursos. 1994. Santiago de Compostela: Xunta de Galicia.

Lemos, Álvaro. 1926. *O Minho Alegre e Cantador.* Coimbra: Minerva.

Lévi-Strauss, Claude *e alter,* 1977, *L'Identité. Seminaire Dirigé par Claude Lévi-Strauss,* Paris, Quadrige/PUF.

Lima, Augusto C. Pires de. 1947–1951. *Estudos Etnográficos, Filológicos e Históricos,* 5 vols. Porto: Junta da Província do Douro Litoral.

Lima, Joaquim Pires de, and Fernando Castro Pires de Lima. 1938. *Tradições Populares de Entre-Douro e Minho.* Barcelos: Companhia Editora do Minho.

Lisón Tolosana, Carmelo. 1966. *Belmonte de los Caballeros: A Sociological Study of a Spanish Town.* Oxford: Clarendon.

————. 1971. *Antropología Cultural de Galicia.* Madrid: Siglo XXI.

————. 1974a. *Perfiles Simbólico-Morales de la Cultura Gallega.* Madrid: Akal.

————. 1974b. *Brujería, Estrutura Social y Simbolismo en Galicia.* Madrid: Akal.

————. 1977. *Invitación a la Antropología Cultural de España.* Coruña: Adara.

————. 1998. *A Santa Compaña: Fantasías reales, realidades fantásticas,* Madrid, Akal.

Liss, Julia E. 1996. "German Culture and German Science in the *Bildung* of Franz Boas," in George W. Stocking, Jr. (ed.), *Wolkgeist as Method and Ethic: Essays on Boasian Ethnography and the German Anthropological Tradition.* Madison: University of Wisconsin Press, 155–84.

Livro de Honra da Exposição Nacional de Trajos Regionais, 2nd ed. n.d. Lisbon: Comissão Executiva da Exposição Nacional de Trajos Regionais.

Llobera, Josep R. 1994. *The God of Modernity. The Development of Nationalism in Western Europe.* Oxford/Washington, DC: Berg.

————. 1998. "The Role of Historical Memory in Catalan National Identity," *Social Anthropology* 6: 331–42.

Löfgren, Orvar. 1989. "The Nationalization of Culture," *Ethnologia Europaea* 20: 5–24.

Lomnitz-Adler, Claudio. 1991. "Concepts for the Study of Regional Culture," *American Ethnologist* 18(2): 195–214.

————. 1992. *Exits from the Labyrinth. Culture and Ideology in the Mexican National Space.* Berkeley: University of California Press.

————. 2001. *Deep Mexico. Silent Mexico. An Anthropology of Nationalism.* Minneapolis/London: University of Minnesota Press.

Lopes, Óscar. 1987. *Entre Fialho e Nemésio. Estudos de Literatura Portugues Contemporânea.* Lisbon: Imprensa Nacional/Casa da Moeda (2 vols).

López Mira, Álvaro X. 1998. *A Galicia Irredenta.* Vigo: Xerais.

Lorenzana, Salvador. 1979. "O Galeguismo Ideolóxico de Vicente Risco," *Grial* 63: 56–66.

Lorenzo, Xaquín. 1957. "Cuevillas etnógrafo," in VVAA, *Homaxe dos Amigos e discipulos do Petrucio da Prehistoria Galega Florentino L.A. Cuevillas no LXX Aniversario do seu Nacimento.* Vigo: Editorial Galáxia.

————. 1962. "Etnografia: Cultura Material" in Ramón Otero Pedrayo (ed.), *Historia de Galicia.* Buenos Aires: Edit. Nós, 3: 7–739.

————. 1982. *A Casa.* Vigo: Galaxia.

Lourenço, Eduardo. 1978. *O Labirinto da Saudade: Psicanálise do destino português.* Lisbon: D. Quixote.

Lowenthal, David. 1994. "European and English Landscapes as National Symbols," in David Hooson (ed.), *Geography and National Identity.* Oxford/Cambridge: Blackwell, 15–38.

Lugrís, Ramón. 1963. *Vicente Risco na Cultura Galega. Ensaio* ("Prólogo" de Ramón Piñeiro). Vigo: Galaxia.

Luque Baena, Enrique. 1991. "La invención del otro y la alienación del antropólogo en la etnografía hispana," en María Cátedra (ed.), *Los Españoles Vistos por los Antropólogos.* Madrid/Gijón: Júcar.

MacDonald, Sharon. 1997. *Reimagining Culture. Histories, Identities and the Gaelic Renaissance.* Oxford/New York: Berg.

Máiz, Ramón. 1984. *O Rexionalismo Galego. Organización e Ideoloxia.* A Coruña: Ed. do Castro.

————. 1997. *A Idea de Nación.* Vigo: Edicións Xerais de Galicia.

Mandianes, Manuel. 1999. "Las Serpientes Contra Santiago. Identidad Galega," in Christiane Stallaert (ed.), *Hechos Diferenciales y Convivencias Interétnicas en España (Foro Hispânico* 16). Amsterdam/Atlanta: Rodopi.

Manganaro, Marc. 1990. "Introduction. Textual Play, Power, and Cultural Critique: An Orientation to Modernist Anthropology," in Marc Manganaro (ed.), *Modernist Anthropology. From Fieldwork to Text.* Princeton, NJ: Princeton University Press, 3–47.

Marçal, 1954. "O Significado do Vocábulo 'Galego' e a sua Extensão na Etnografia e no Folclore," *Douro Litoral* 6(1–2): 3–16.

Marcus, George. 1986. "Contemporary Problems of Ethnography in the Modern World System," in James Clifford and George Marcus (eds), *Writing Culture: The Poetics and Politics of Ethnography.* Berkeley: University of California Press, 165–93.

————. 1998. *Ethnography Through Thick & Thin.* Princeton, NJ: Princeton University Press.

Marfany, Joan-Lluís. 1996 (1995). *La Culture del Catalanisme.* Barcelona: Empúries.

Mariño Ferro, Xosé Ramón. n.d. *Bibliografía Etnográfica e Antropolóxica de Galicia.* Photocopy.

————. 1996. "Comentario. I," in X. M. González Reboredo (ed.), *La Construcción del Texto Etnográfico a Través de dos Autores. Aportación a una Historia de la Etnografía en Galicia [comentarios de Xosé Ramón Mariño Ferro y de Francisco Calo Lourido].* Santiago de Compostela: CSIC/IPSEG, 67–69.

Mark, Vera. 1987. "In Search of the Occitan Village: Regionalist Ideologies and the Ethnography of Southern France," *Anthropological Quarterly* 60(2): 64–70.

Mar-Molinero, Clare, and Angel Smith (eds). 1996. *Nationalism and the Nation in the Iberian Peninsula.* Oxford/Washington, DC: Berg.

Martí, Josep. 1996. *El Folklorismo. Uso e Abuso de la Tradición.* Barcelona: Ronsel.

Marx, Karl. 1984 (1852). *O 18 de Brumário de Louis Bonaparte.* Lisbon/Moscow: Editorial "Avante."

Mathur, Saloni. 2001. "Living Colonial Exhibits: The Case of 1886," *Cultural Anthropology* 15(4): 492–524.

Mattoso, José. 1985. *Identificação de um País. Ensaio Sobre as Origens de Portugal. 1096–1325,* 2 vols. Lisbon: Editorial Estampa.

Mazower, Marc. 1998. *Dark Continent. Europe's Twentieth Century.* Harmondsworth, UK: Penguin.

McCrone, David, Angela Morris, and Richard Kelly. 1995. *Scotland—The Brand. The Making of Scottish Heritage.* Edinburgh: Edinburgh University Press.

McDonald, Maryon. 1989. *We Are Not French!. Language, Culture and Identity in Brittany.* Oxford: Oxford University Press.

Medeiros, António. 1994. *À Nossa Moda: Contextos e Discursos de Identidade Minhota,* Trabalho de Síntese para Provas de Aptidão Pedagógica e Capacidade Científica. Lisbon: Lisbon, I.S.C.T.E.

———. 1995. "Minho: Retrato Oitocentista de uma Paisagem de Eleição," *Revista Lusitana* (Nova Série) 13–14: 97–123.

———. 1996. *Ruínas/Notícias da Arcádia Atlântica,* offprint from *Trabalhos de Antropologia e Etnologia* 36.

———. 1997. "Returning to the Whole em Edimburgo. Entrevista com James Fernandez," *Etnográfica* 1(1): 135–43.

———. 1998. "Pintura dos Costumes da Nação: Alguns Argumentos," *Trabalhos de Antropologia e Etnologia* 38: 131–69.

———. 1999. "Na Serra; Os Desencontros do Soajo," *Ler História* 36: 177–220.

Medeiros, Isabel. 1984a. "Acerca do Povoamento na Serra da Peneda," *Terra de Valdevez* 7: 35–56.

———. 1984b. *Estruturas Pastoris e Povoamento na Serra da Peneda.* Lisbon: INIC.

Melo, Daniel, 2001, *Salazarismo e Cultura Popular (1933–1958),* Lisbon: Imprensa de Ciências Sociais.

Méndez Ferrín, Xosé Luís. 1999. *No Ventre do Silencio.* Vigo: Xerais.

Messerschmidt, Donald A. 1981. *Anthropologists at Home in North America. Methods and Issues in the Study of One's Own Society.* Cambridge: Cambridge University Press.

Miguélez Díaz, Xosé A. 1999. "O Xacobeo e a Religiosidade Popular. Poder Mediático," *Terra e Tempo* 11.

Miller, Daniel. 1987. *Material Culture and Mass Consumption.* Oxford and Cambridge: Blackwell.

———, (ed.). 1998. *Material Cultures. Why Some Things Matter.* London: UCL Press.

Mitchell, W.J.T. 1986. *Iconology. Image, Text, Ideology.* Chicago/London: Chicago University Press.

Molina, Cesar Antonio. 1987. *Prensa Literaria en Galicia,* 2 vols. Vigo: Edicións Xerais de Galicia.

Monteagudo, Henrique (ed.). 2000. *Para Ler Castelao. 2. Estudios Sobre a Obra Escrita.* Vigo: Galaxia.

Morais Silva, António. 1831. *Diccionario da Lingua Portugueza.* Lisbon: Impressão Regia.

———. 1999. Novo Dicionário Compacto da Língua Portuguesa. Lisbon: Horizonte (5 vols).

Morales Moya, Antonio. 2000. "Estado y Nación en la España Contemporánea," *Ayer* 37: 234–69.

Mosse, George L. 1982. *Nationalism and Sexuality. Respectability and Abnormal Sexuality in Modern Europe.* New York: Howard Fertig.

————. 1988 (1961). *The Culture of Western Europe*. Boulder, CO: Westview Press.

————. 1996 (1975). *The Nationalization of the Masses: Political Symbolism and Mass Movements in Germany from the Napoleonic Wars Through the Third Reich*. Ithaca, NY: Cornell University Press.

Murguía, Manuel. 1985. *Galicia* (Prólogo e Bibliografía por Justo G. Beramendi), 2 vols. Santiago de Compostela: Sálvora.

Nadel-Klein, Jane. 1991. "Reweaving the Fringe: Localism, Tradition, and Representation in British Ethnography," *American Ethnologist* 18: 500–517.

————. 1995. "Occidentalism as a Cottage Industry: Representing the Autochthonous 'Other' in British and Irish Rural Studies," in James Carrier (ed.), *Occidentalism. Images of the West*. Oxford: Clarendon Press, 109–34.

Narotzky, Susana. 2001. *La Antropología de los Pueblos de España. Historia, Cultura y Lugar*. Barcelona: Icaria.

Nicholas, Michel. 2001. "Le Mouvement Breton: La Culture au Coeur du Politique," in Xosé Manual González Reboredo (ed.), *Etnicidade e nacionalismo: actas do simposio internacional de antropoloxía*. Santiago de Compostela: Consello da Cultura Galega, 453–73.

Nochlin, Linda. 1994. *The Body in Pieces. The Fragment as Metaphor of Modernity*. London: Thames and Hudson.

Nora, Pierre (ed.). 1986–1992. *Les Lieux de Mémoire*, vol. 1–7. Paris: Gallimard.

————. 1997. *Les Lieux de Mémoire*, vol. 1–3. Paris: Quarto/Gallimard.

Nuñez Seixas, Xosé M. 1990. "Eduardo Blanco Amor no Nacionalismo Galego (1919–1939). Liderado Étnico e Galeguismo," *Grial* 28(1): 448–66.

————. 1991. "Portugal e o Galeguismo ata 1936. Algunhas consideracións históricas," *Grial* 113: 61–77.

————. 1992. *O Galeguismo en América 1879-1936*. Sada - A Coruña: Ediciós do Castro.

————. 1995. "Historia e Actualidade dos Nacionalismos na España Contemporánea: Unha Perspectiva de Conxunto," *Grial* 128: 496–540.

————. 1998. *Emigrantes, Caciques e Indianos. O Influxo Sociopolítico da Emigración Transoceánica en Galicia (1900–1930)*. Vigo: Xerais.

Oliveira, A. Lopes. 1970. *Soajo: Uma Aldeia Diferente. Cabeça de Montaria*. Viana do Castelo: Junta Distrital.

Oliveira, Ernesto Veiga de. 1968. *Vinte Anos de Investigação Etnológica do Centro de Estudos de Etnologia Peninsular. Porto 1947-Lisboa 1967*. Lisbon: IAC.

Oliveira Martins, J. P. 1942 (1879). *História de Portugal*, 2 vols. Lisbon: Parceria A. M. Pereira.

————. n.d. (1881). *Portugal Contemporâneo*. Lisbon: Europa América.

Oliven, Ruben G. 1992. *A Parte e o Todo. A Diversidade Cultural no Brasil-Nação*. Petrópolis: Vozes.

————. 1999. "Brasil, uma Modernidade Tropical," *Etnográfica* 3(2): 409–27.

O'Neill, Brian J. 1984. *Proprietários, Lavradores e Jornaleiras. Desigualdade numa Aldeia Transmontana 1870–1978*. Lisbon: Dom Quixote (*Social Inequality in a Portuguese Hamlet: Land, Late Marriage and Bastardy 1870–1978*. Cambridge: Cambridge University Press, 1987.

———. 1995. "Emular de Longe: O Povo Português de Malaca," *Revista Lusitana* 13–14: 19–67.

Ortega y Gasset, José. 1993 (1937). *La Rebelión de las Masas*. Madrid: Austral.

———. 1999. *La España Invertebrada. Bosquejo de Algunos Pensamientos Históricos*. Madrid: Espasa Calpe.

Ortiz, Carmen, and Luis Sánchez Goméz. 1994. *Diccionario Histórico de Antropología Española*. Madrid: C.S.I.C.

Otero Pedrayo, Ramón. 1922. "Encol da aldeia." *Nós* 14, p 1 e ss.

———. 1933. *Ensayo Sintético sobre la Cultura Gallega*. Santiago de Compostela: Nós.

———. 1980. *Florentino L. Cuevillas*. Vigo: Galaxia.

———. 1991 (1926). *Guia de Galicia*. Vigo: Galaxia.

———. 1993 (1929). *Pelerinaxes I. Itenerario d'Ourense ao San Andrés de Teixido* (prólogo e ilustracións de Vicente Risco. Sada-Corunna: Ediciós do Castro.

———. 1998 (1930). *Arredor de Si. Novela*. Vigo: Galaxia.

———, (ed.). 1979 (1962). *Historia de Galicia,* 3 vols. Madrid: Akal.

Outeiriño, Xosé Manuel Outeiriño. 1990. "Limiar," in Vicente Risco, *Las Tinieblas de Occidente. Ensayo de una Valoración de la Civilizatión Europeia*. Barcelona: Sotelo Blanco, s.p.

———. 1996. "Políticas de Cultura e Comunicación Europeas: Entre a 'Weltliteratur' e a Lama do Empedrado," in Margarita Ledo Andión (ed.), *Comunicación na Periferia Atlántica. Actas do I Congreso Internacional*. Santiago de Compostela: Universidade de Santiago de Compostela, 225–32.

Paço, Afonso do. 1934. *Da Necessidade de Criação de um Museu de Etnografia*. Porto: Edições da 1ª Exposição Colonial Portuguesa.

———. 1994. *Etnografia Vianesa*. Viana do Castelo: Câmara Municipal.

Paço, António do. 1975. *Peneda. Altar de Fé*. Arcos de Valdevez: Irmandade de Nossa Senhora da Peneda.

Pardo Bazán, Emilia. 1984 (1988). *De mi Tierra*. Vigo: Edicións Xerais de Galicia.

Paulo, Heloísa. 1994. *Estado Novo e Propaganda em Portugal e no Brasil. O SPN/SNI e o DIP*. Coimbra: Minerva.

Payne, Stanley G. 1975. *Basque Nationalism*. Reno: University of Nevada Press.

Peer, Shanny. 1998. *Peasants, Provincials, and Folklore in the 1937 Paris World's Fair*. Albany: State University of New York Press.

Peixoto, A. Rocha. 1967–1975. *Obras* (Prefácio, Organização e Notas de Flávio Gonçalves), 3 vols. Póvoa de Varzim: Câmara Municipal da Póvoa de Varzim.

Pena, María del Carmen. 1998 (1982). *Pintura de Paisaje e Ideología. La Generación del 98*. Madrid: Taurus.

Pereira, Benjamim Enes. 1965. *Bibliografia Analítica de Etnografia Portuguesa*. Lisbon: Instituto de Alta Cultura/Centro de Estudos de Etnologia Peninsular.

Pereira, Felix Alves. 1914. *Estudos do Alto-Minho,* vol. 15–16. Lisbon: Manuel Lucas Torres.

Pereira González, Fernando. 1998. "O Mito Celta na História," *Gaellecia* 19: 311–33.

Pereiro Pérez, Xerardo. 1995–1996. *Identidade e Alteridade: Galicia Vista Polos Boaleses (Asturias Occidental),* offprint from the journal *Britonia* no. 2.

———. 1999. "Patrimonialización, Museos y Arquitectura: O Caso de Allariz," in Esther Fernández de Paz and Juan Agudo Torrico (eds), *Patrimonio Cultural Y Museología. Significados y Contenidos.* Santiago de Compostela: FAAEE/AGA, 97–110.

———. 2001. "Reflexão Sobre a Antropologia na Galiza de Hoje," *Etnográfica* 5(1): 175–83.

Pérez, Yolanda, Nuria Serrano, and Manuel Vilar. 1997. "El Desaparecido Museo de Pías en el Balneario de Mondariz," in *Actas do III Congreso de Historia da Antropoloxía e Antropoloxía Aplicada* Tomo II. Santiago de Compostela: Instituto de Estudos Gallegos "Padre Sarmiento" (CSIC), 145–68.

Pick, Daniel. 1996 (1989). *Faces of Degeneration. A European Disorder, c. 1848– c. 1918.* Cambridge: Cambridge University Press.

Pina-Cabral, João. 1989 (1986). *Filhos de Adão, Filhas de Eva. A Visão do Mundo Camponesa do Alto Minho.* Lisbon: Publicações D. Quixote.

———. 1991. *Os Contextos da Antropologia.* Lisbon: Difel.

———. 1992. *Aromas de Urze e de Lama. Viagem de um Antropólogo ao Alto Minho.* Lisbon: Fragmentos.

Piñeiro, Ramón. 1978. "A Importancia Decisiva da Xeneración Nós," *Grial* 59: 8–13.

———. 1995. *Filosofía da Saudade.* Vigo: Galaxia.

Pinto, António Costa. 1989. "o Fascismo e a Crise da Primeira República: Os Nacionalistas Lusitanos (1923-23), *Penélope* nº 3: 44–62.

Pintor, M.A. Bernardo. 1972. *Senhora da Peneda (Senhora do Minho).* Braga: n.p.

———. n.d. *Por Terras de Soajo. São Bento do Cando, na Freguesia da Gavieira.* Braga: n.p.

Pires, Daniel. 1996. *Dicionário da Imprensa Periódica Literária Portuguesa do Século XX (1900–1940).* Lisbon: Grifo.

Polanah, Luís. 1987. *Comunidades Camponesas no Parque Nacional da Peneda-Gerês.* Lisbon: Serviço Nacional de Parques, Reservas e Conservação da Natureza.

Poliakov, Léon.1971. *Le Mythe Aryen: Essai sur les sources du racisme et des nationalismes.* Paris: Calmann-Lévy.

Pomian, Krzytof. 1992. "Francs et Gaulois," en Pierre Nora (ed.) *Les Lieux de Mémoire III. Les France: Conflits et Partages.* Paris: Gallimard: 40-105.

Pousa, Luís. 2001. "Conjurados los demónios," *El Correo Gallego,* 16 February, 3.

Prat, Joan. 1991a. "Historia. Estudio Introductorio," in Joan Prat et al. (eds), *Antropología de los Pueblos de España.* Madrid: Taurus, 13–30.

————. 1991b. "Reflexiones Sobre los Nuevos Objectos de Estudio en la Antropología Social Española," in Maria Cátedra (ed.), *Los Españoles Vistos por los Antropólogos*. Madrid: Júcar, 45–68.

Preston, Paul. 1998. *Las Tres Españas del 36*. Barcelona: Plaza Janés.

Price, Richard, and Sally Price. 1995. *On The Mall: Presenting Marson Tradition—Bearer at the 1992 Festival of American Folklife*. Bloomington: Indiana University Press.

Quental, Antero de. 1970. *Causas da Decadência dos Povos Peninsulares*. Lisbon: Ulmeiro.

Quintana, Xosé Ramón, and Marcos Valcárcel. 1988. *Ramón Otero Pedrayo. Vida Obra e Pensamento*. Vigo: Ir Indo.

Rabinow, Paul. 1989. *French Modern. Norms and Forms of the Social Environment*. Chicago: University of Chicago Press.

Ramos, Rui. 1994. *A Segunda Fundação (1890–1926)*, in José Mattoso (ed.), *História de Portugal*, vol. 6. Lisbon: Círculo de Leitores.

Redfield, Robert. 1973 (1960). *The Little Community and Peasant Society and Culture*. Chicago: University of Chicago Press.

Revel, Jacques. 1989. *A Invenção da Sociedade*. Lisbon: Difel.

————. 1997. "La Région," in Pierre Nora (ed.), *Les Lieux de Mémoire* 2. Paris: Quarto/Gallimard, 2907–36.

Ribeiro, Orlando. 1940. *Villages et Comunnautés Rurales au Portugal*. Coimbra: Coimbra Editora.

————. 1945. *Portugal. O Mediterrâneo e o Atlântico*. Coimbra: Coimbra Editora.

————. 1948. "Prefácio," in Jorge Dias (ed.), *Vilarinho da Furna. Uma Aldeia Comunitária*. Porto: Instituto Para a Alta Cultura/Centro de Estudos de Etnologia Peninsular.

————. 1977. *Introducções Geográficas à História de Portugal*. Lisbon: Imprensa Nacional-Casa da Moeda.

Riegl, Alöis. 1999 (1903). *El Culto Moderno a los Monumentos. Caracteres y Origen*. Madrid, Visor.

Risco, Vicente. 1920. "O Sentimento da Terra na Raza Galega," *Nós* 1:4–9.

————. 1936. *Hipóteses e Probremas do Folklore Galego-Portugués* (extracto do tomo XX dos *Anais da Faculdade de Ciências do Porto*). Porto: Imprensa Portuguesa.

————. 1946. *Creencias Galegas. La Procesión de las Ánimas y las Premoniciones de Muerte*. Madrid: C. Bermejo

————. 1959. "Una parroquia gallega en los años 1920-25," *Revista de Dialectología y Tradiciones Populares*, Tomo XV, 4º: 401–433.

————. 1962. "Etnografía: Cultura Espiritual," in Ramón Otero Pedrayo (ed.), *Historia de Galicia*, Buenos Aires: Ed. Nós, 1: 255–777.

————. 1976 (1933). *Manuel Murguía*. Vigo: Galaxia.

————. 1990. *Las Tinieblas de Occidente. Ensayo de una Valoración de La Civilización Europea* (Edición de Manuel Outeiriño). Santiago de Compostela: Sotelo Blanco.

————. 1993 (1959). *Una Parroquia Galega nos Anos 1920–1935*. Santiago de Compostela: Museo do Pobo Galego.

————. 1994. *Obras Completas*, 7 vols. Vigo: Galaxia.

Rocha, Manuel I. 1984. "Uma Visita à Várzea," *Centro de Estudos Regionais. Boletim Cultural* 1: 74–80.

Roche, Alphonse V. 1970 (1954). *Provençal Regionalism: A Study of the Movement in the Revue Félibréenne, Le Feu and other Reviews of Southern France*. New York: AMS Press.

Rodríguez Campos, Joaquín. 1991. "La Etnografía Clásica de Galicia: Ideas y proyectos," in Joan Prat et al., *Antropología de los Pueblos de España*. Madrid: Taurus: 98–111.

————. 1994a. "La Idea de Cultura Atlántica en el Noroeste Peninsular: Mitos y 'Realidades,' in J. A. Fernández de Rota (ed.), *Las Diferentes Caras de España*. Ferrol: Universidad de la Coruña.

————. 1994b. "Cultura e Experiencia Humana: Antropología Romántica de Galicia," *Actas do Simposio Internacional de Antropoloxía* in Memoriam *Fermín Bouza Brey*. Vigo: Consello da Cultura Galega, 41–48.

————. 1999. "Consequencias Sociolingüísticas de las Políticas de la Identidad. El caso gallego," in A. Medeiros, A. Barrera, and C. Feixa (eds), *Mesas de Trabajo. VIII Congreso de Antropología*, FAAE–AGA, Santiago de Compostela: 119–28.

Rodríguez Campos, Xaquín. 1997. "Lingua, Paisaxe e Identidade: Unha Aproximación entre a Semántica e a Pragmática da Lingua Galega," in Xaquín Rodríguez Campos (ed.), *As Linguas e as Identidades. Ensaios de Etnografía e de Interpretación Antropolóxica*. Santiago de Compostela: Universidade de Santiago de Compostela, 85–104.

Rodríguez-Moniño, Antonio. 1959. "Leite de Vasconcellos en dos Revistas Españolas (1882–1884). Notícias Reunidas," *Actas do Colóquio de Estudos Etnográficos Doutor Leite de Vasconcelos* 1: 79–84.

Rof Carballo, Xoán. 1989 (1957). *Mito e Realidade a Terra Nai*. Vigo: Galaxia.

Rogers, Susan Carol. 1987. "Good to Think: The Peasant in Contemporary France," *Anthropological Quarterly* 60(2): 56–63.

Romero Salvadó, Francisco. 1996. "The Failure of the Liberal Project of the Spanish Nation-State, 1909–1938," in Clare Mar-Molinero and Angel Smith (eds), *Nationalism and the Nation in the Iberian Peninsula*. Oxford/Washington, DC: Berg, 119–32.

Roncayolo, Michel. 1986. "Região," in *Enciclopédia Einaudi*, vol. 8. Lisbon: Imprensa Nacional Casa da Moeda, 161–89.

————. 1997. "Le Paysage du Savant," in Pierre Nora (ed.), *Les Lieux de Mémoire 1*. Paris: Gallimard, 997–1033.

Rosas, Fernando. 1994. *O Estado Novo (1926–1974)*, in José Mattoso (ed.), *História de Portugal*, vol. 7. Lisbon: Círculo de Leitores.

Rosas, Fernando, and J. M. Brandão de Brito (eds). 1996. *Dicionário de História do Estado Novo*, 2 vols. Venda Nova: Bertrand.

Ruiz Zapatero, Gonzalo. 1996. "Celts and Iberians. Ideological Manipulations in Spanish Archaeology," in Paul Graves-Brown, Siân Jones, and Clive

Gamble (eds), *Cultural Identity and Archaeology: The Construction of European Communities*. London: Routledge, 178–95.

Ruy, José. 1996. *O Juiz de Soajo. A História da Vila de Soajo em Banda Desenhada*. Lisbon: Editorial Notícias.

Sahlins, Peter. 1989. *Boundaries: The Making of France and Spain in the Pyrenees*. Berkeley: University of California Press.

Said, Edward W. 1990 (1978). *Orientalismo. O Oriente como Invenção do Ocidente*. São Paulo: Companhia das Letras.

Sampaio, Alberto. 1979. *Estudos Económicos. I. "As Vilas do Norte de Portugal"* (Prefácio de Maria José Trindade). Lisbon: Vega.

Samuel, Raphael. 1994. *Theatres of Memory. Past and Present in Contemporary Culture*. London: Verso.

Sánchez Gómez, Luís A. 1994. "Centro de Estudios de Etnología Peninsular. Sección Madrid (1947–1961), in Carmen Ortiz García and Luís A. Sanchéz Goméz (eds), *Diccionario Histórico de la Antropología Española*. Madrid: CSIC, 204–6.

———. 1997. "Cien Años de Antropologías en España y Portugal," *Etnográfica* 1(2): 297–317.

Sánchez Rey, Maria del Carmen. 1992. "O Eco de Alén Miño na Xeración Nós," *Grial* 30(113): 5–19.

Sanchis, Pierre. 1983. *Arraial: Festa de um Povo. As Romarias Portuguesas*. Lisbon: Publicações D. Quixote.

Santuário de Nossa Sª da Peneda. n.d. Gaveira-Arcos de Valdevez.

Sapir, Edward. 1967. *Anthropologie*. Paris: Minuit.

Saraiva, António José, and Óscar Lopes. 1989. *História da Literatura Portuguesa*. Porto: Porto Editora.

Schlereth, Thomas J. 1992. "The Material Universe of American World Expositions, 1876–1915," in *Cultural History and Material Culture. Everyday Life, Landscapes, Museums*. Charlottesville/London: University of Virginia Press, 165–289.

Schaub, Jean-Frédéric. 2001. *Portugal na Monarquia Hispânica (1580–1640)*. Lisbon: Horizonte.

Scherer, Joanna C. 1988. "The Public Faces of Sarah Winnemucca," *Cultural Anthropology* 3(2): 179–204.

Schnapp, Jeffrey. 1992. "Epic Demonstrations: Fascist Modernity and the 1932 Exhibition of the Fascist Revolution," in Richard Golsan (ed.), *Fascism, Aesthetics, and Culture*. Hanover/London: University Press of New England: 1–37.

Sears, John. 1989. *Sacred Places. American Tourist Attractions in the Nineteenth Century*. New York/Oxford: Oxford University Press.

Sequeiros Tizón, J. 1990. *El Talante del Señor Breógan*. Sada: Ediciós do Castro.

Seoane, Luis. 1969. *Castelao Artista*. Buenos Aires: Alborada.

———. 1994. *Textos Sobre Arte Galega e Deseño*. Vigo: A Nosa Terra.

Severo, Ricardo. 1924. *Origens da Nacionalidade Portuguesa*. Coimbra: Imprensa da Universidade.

Silva, Augusto Santos, 1987. *Formar a Nação: Vias Culturais do Progressso Segundo Intelectuais Portugueses do Século XIX. 1ª Parte.* Porto: Centro de Estudos Humanísticos.

———. 1994. *Tempos Cruzados: Um Estudo Interpretativo da Cultura Popular.* Porto: Edições Afrontamento.

———. 1997. "O Porto em Busca da Renascença," *Penélope* 17: 51–69.

Simmel, Georg. 1991. "The Berlin Trade Exhibition," in *Theory, Culture & Society* 8: 119–23.

Sirinelli, Jean-François (ed.). 1992. *Histoire des Droites en France,* vol. 2 and 3. Paris: Gallimard.

Slaney, Frances M. 2000. "Working for a Canadian Sense of Place(s). The Role of Landscape Painters in Marius Barbeau's Ethnology," in Richard Handler (ed.), *Excluded Ancestors, Inventible Traditions Essays Towards a More Inclusive History of Anthropology.* Madison: University of Wisconsin Press, 81–122.

Smiles, Sam. 1994. *The Image of Antiquity. Ancient Britain and The Romantic Imagination.* New Haven, CT: Yale University Press.

Smith, Anthony D. 1991. *National Identity.* Harmondsworth, UK: Penguin.

———. 1998. *Nationalism and Modernism. A Critical Survey of Recent Theories of Nations and Nationalism.* London/New York: Routledge.

———. 1999. *Myths and Memories of the Nation.* Oxford: Oxford University Press.

Sobral, José Manuel. 1999. "Da Casa à Nação: Passado, Memória, Identidade," *Etnográfica* 3(1): 71–86.

Sobrino Manzanares, Mª Luisa. 1996. *O Cartelismo en Galicia. Desdes as Súas Orixes ata 1936.* Sada: Ediciós do Castro.

Soeiro, João (ed.). 2000. *O Alto Minho na Obra Etnográfica de Abel Viana.* Viana do Castelo: Academia de Música de Viana do Castelo.

Sousa, Tude. 1927. *Gerez.Notas Etnográficas, Arqueológicas e Históricas.* Coimbra: Imprensa da Universidade.

Sprengler, Oswald. 1991 (1922). *The Decline of the West.* Oxford & New York, Oxford University Press.

Sterne, Laurence. 1949 (1768). *A Sentimental Journey through France and Italy.* London: Folio Society.

Stocking Jr., George W. 1968. *Race Culture and Evolution: Essays in the History of Anthropology.* New York: Free Press.

———. 1982. "Afterword: A View from the Center," *Ethnos* 47: 172–86.

———, (ed.). 1989. *Romantic Motives: Essays on Anthropological Sensibility.* Madison: University of Wisconsin Press.

Taboada, Jesus. 1955. "La Descalificacion de Galicia en la Literatura y en el Pueblo," *Douro Litoral* 6(7–8): 105–27.

Taboada Chivite, J. 1972. *Etnografía Gallega. Cultura Espiritual.* Vigo: Galaxia.

Taussig, Michael. 1993. *Mimesis and Alterity: A Particular History of the Senses.* New York/London: Routledge.

———. 1997. *The Magic of the State.* New York/London: Routledge.

Tato Fontaíña, Laura. 1999. *Historia do Teatro Galego (das Orixes a 1936)*. Vigo: A Nosa Terra.

Tenorio, Nicolás. 1982 (1914). *La Aldea Gallega*. Vigo: Edicións Xerais de Galicia.

Thiesse, Anne-Marie. 1991. *Écrire la France. Le Mouvement Littéraire Régionaliste de la Langue Française entre la Belle Époque et la Libération*. Paris: Presses Universitaires de France.

———. 1997. *Ils Apprenaient la France: l'Exaltation des Régions dans le Discours Patriotique*. Paris: Maison des Sciences de l'Homme.

———. 2000. *A Criação das Identidades Nacionais. Europa—Séculos XVIII–XX*. Lisbon: Temas e Debates.

Thom, Martin. 1995. *Republics, Nations and Tribes*. London/New York: Verso.

Thomas, Nicholas. 1992. "The Inversion of Tradition," *American Ethnologist* 19(2): 213–32.

Tobia, Bruno. 1998 (1991). *Una Patria per gli Italiani. Spazi, Itenerari, Monumenti nell'Italia Unita (1870–1900)*. Rome/Bari: Editori Laterza.

Tonkin, Elizabeth, Marion McDonald, and Malcolm Chapman (eds). 1989. *History and Ethnicity*. London: Routledge.

Tönnies, Ferdinand. 2001 (1887). *Community and Civil Society*. Cambridge: Cambridge University Press.

Torgal, Luís Reis. 1993. "A Instrução Pública," in José Mattoso (ed.), *História de Portugal*, vol. 5. Lisbon: Círculo de Leitores, 609–51.

Torgal, Luís Reis, José Amado Mendes, and Fernando Catroga. 1998. *História da História de Portugal. Sécs. XIX e XX*, 2 vols. Lisbon: Temas e Debates.

Torrente Ballester, Gonzalo. 1990 (1948). *Compostela y su Ángel*. Barcelona: Destino Libro.

Torres Feijó, Elias. 1999. "Cultura Portuguesa e Legitimação do Sistema Galeguista: Historiadores e Filólogos (1880–1891)," *Ler História* 36: 273–318.

Trigueiros, Luís Forjaz. 1967. *O Minho*. Lisbon: Livraria Bertrand.

Tuñon de Lara, Manuel. 1992 (1984). *Poder y Sociedad en España, 1900–1931*. Madrid: Espasa Calpe.

Turner, Victor. 1967. *The Forest of Symbols. Aspects of Ndembu Ritual*. Ithaca, NY: Cornell University Press.

———. 1990 (1974). *Dramas, Fields, and Metaphors. Symbolic Action in Human Society*. Ithaca, NY: Cornell University Press.

Turner, Victor, and Edith Turner. 1978. *Image and Pilgrimage in Christian Culture*. New York: Columbia University Press.

Tusell, Javier, 1998. *Historia de España en el Siglo XX. I. Del 98 a la Proclamación de la República*. Madrid: Taurus.

———. 1999a. *Historia de España en el Siglo XX. II. La Crisis de los Años Treinta: República y Guerra Civil*. Madrid: Taurus.

———. 1999b. *Historia de España en el Siglo XX. III. La Dictadura de Franco*. Madrid: Taurus.

———. 1999c. *Historia de España en el Siglo XX. IV. La Transacción Demócratica y el Gobierno Socialista*. Madrid: Taurus.

Un País e Unha Cultura. A Idea de Galicia nos Nosos Escritores. Discurso leído o día 26 de Novembro de 1960 na sua recepción pública por D. Francisco Fernández del Riego e resposta de D. Ricardo Carballo Calero. 1973. Corruna: Real Academia Gallega/Artes Gráficas de Galicia.

Unamuno, Miguel de. 1944 (1941). *Por Tierras de España y de Portugal*. Buenos Aires/Mexico: Espasa-Calpe.

————. 1991 (1943). *En Torno al Casticismo*. Madrid: Espasa Calpe.

Vasconcelos, Carolina Michaëlis. n.d. *Lições de Filologia Portuguesa Segundo as Prelecções Feitas aos Cursos de 1911/12 e de 1912/13 Seguidas das Lições Práticas de Português Arcaico*. Lisbon: Dinalivro.

Vasconcelos, José Leite de. 1882. *Uma Excursão ao Soajo. Notas numa Carteira*. Barcelos: Typographia do Tirocinio.

————. (1883). *Tradições Populares de Portugal* (organização e apresentação de Manuel Viegas Guerreiro). Lisbon: Imprensa Nacional-Casa da Moeda.

————. 1907. *Miuçalhas Ethnologicas. A Propósito dos Seis Primeiros Capítulos da "Portugalia."* Lisbon: Imprensa Nacional.

————. 1915. *História do Museu Etnológico Português 1983*. Lisbon: Imprensa Nacional.

————. 1927. *De Terra em Terra. Excursões Arqueológico—Etnográficas em Portugal (Norte, Centro e Sul)*, 3 vols. Lisbon: Imprensa Nacional/Casa da Moeda.

————. 1980a (1933). *Etnografia Portuguesa—Tentame de Sistematização*, vol. 1. Lisbon: Imprensa Nacional-Casa da Moeda.

————. 1980b (1936). *Etnografia Portuguesa—Tentame de Sistematização*, vol. 2. Lisbon: Imprensa Nacional-Casa da Moeda.

Vásquez Cuesta, Pilar. 1991. "Portugal e Nós," *A Trabe de Ouro* 6: 191–203.

————, (ed.). 1995 and 1996. *Nós. A Literatura Galega* [2 monograph issues of *Colóquio Letras* (no. 137/138 and 139)].

Verdery, Katherine. 2000. *The Political Lives of Dead Bodies*. New York: Columbia University Press.

Viana, Abel. 1932. "Nota Etnográfica. O Soajeiro," *Anuário do Distrito de Viana-do-Castelo* 1.

Viana, Abel .1997. O *Alto Minho na Obra Etnográfica de Abel Viana,* (edited by João Soeiro de Carvalho). Viana do Castelo: Academia de Música de V. do Castelo.

Vieira, José Augusto. 1886–1887. *O Minho Pittoresco*, 2 vols. Lisbon: António Maria Pereira.

Vilarinho de São Romão, Visconde. 1902. *O Minho e as Suas Culturas*. Lisbon: Imprensa Nacional.

Villar Ponte, Antón. 1932. *Historia Sintética de Galicia*. Santiago de Compostela: Nós.

————. 1971. *Pensamento e Sementeira*. Buenos Aires: Ediciones Galicia.

Villares, Ramón, 1983, "As Relacións da Galiza con Portugal na Época Contemporánea," *Grial* 81: 301–26.

————. 1997. *Figuras de Nación*. Vigo: Xerais.

VVAA. 1958. *Homaxe dos Amigos e Discipulos do Petrucio da Prehistoria Galega Florentino L. A. Cuevillas no LXX Aniversario do seu Nacimento.* Vigo: Editorial Galaxia.

———. 1978 (1933). *Terra de Melide.* Santiago de Compostela: Seminario de Estudos Galegos.

———. 1984. *I Coloquio de Antropoloxía de Galicia. Museo do Pobo Galego. 4–6 Febreiro 1982.* Sada-Corunna: Ediciós do Castro.

———. 1990. *Actas do II Coloquio de Antropoloxía Santiago de Compostela, Xuño de 1984.* Santiago de Compostela, Xunta de Galicia/Museo do Pobo Galego, 1989. Simposio Internacional de Antropoloxía Identidade e Territorio. Centenario de Otero Pedrayo. Santiago de Compostela: Consello da Cultura Galega.

———. 1994. *Actas do Simposio Internacional de Antropoloxia. In Memoriam Fermín Bouza Brey. Folklore. Etnografía. Literatura Oral.* Santiago de Compostela: Consello da Cultura Galega.

Wagner, Roy. 1981 (1975). *The Invention of Culture.* Chicago/London: University of Chicago Press.

Walter, François. 1991. "La Montagne des Suisses: Invention et Usage d'une Représentation Paysagère (XVIIIe–XIXe Siécle)," *Études Rurales* 121–24 (Janvier–Décembre): 91–107.

Weber, Eugen. 1983 (1976). *La Fin des Terroirs: La Modernisation de la France Rurale (1870–1914).* Paris: Fayard/Éditions Recherche.

White, Hayden. 1973. *Metahistory.* Baltimore: John Hopkins University Press.

Williams, Raymond. 1981. *Culture.* London: Fontana.

———. 1988 (1976). *Keywords. A Vocabulary of Culture and Society.* London: Fontana.

———. 1993 (1977). *The Country and the City.* London: Hogarth Press.

Wilson, William. 1976. *Folklore and Nationalism in Modern Finland.* Bloomington: Indiana University Press.

Yeats, W. B. *Writings on Irish Folklore, Legend and Myth.* Harmondsworth, UK: Penguin.

Zulaika, Joseba. 1996. *Del Cromañon al Carnaval.* Donostia: Erein.

———. 1997. *Crónica de una Seducción. El Museo Guggenheim Bilbao.* Madrid: Nerea.

Index